VOLUME 464   NOVEMBER 1982

THE ANNALS

of The American Academy *of* Political
and Social Science

RICHARD D. LAMBERT, *Editor*
ALAN W. HESTON, *Associate Editor*
RALPH GINSBERG, *Acting Associate Editor*

MIDDLE AND LATE LIFE TRANSITIONS

Special Editor of this Volume

FELIX M. BERARDO

*Professor
Department of Sociology
University of Florida
Gainesville, Florida*

SAGE PUBLICATIONS · BEVERLY HILLS   LONDON   NEW DELHI

THE ANNALS

© 1982 *by* The American Academy *of* Political *and* Social Science

MARY V. YATES, *Assistant Editor*

Editorial Office: 3937 Chestnut Street, Philadelphia, Pennsylvania 19104.

For information about membership* (individuals only) and subscriptions (institutions), address:

SAGE PUBLICATIONS, INC.
275 South Beverly Drive
Beverly Hills, Calif. 90212 USA

From India and South Asia,
write to:
SAGE PUBLICATIONS INDIA Pvt. Ltd.
P.O. Box 3605
New Delhi 110 024
INDIA

From the UK, Europe, the Middle
East and Africa, write to:
SAGE PUBLICATIONS LTD
28 Banner Street
London EC1Y 8QE
ENGLAND

*Please note that members of The Academy receive THE ANNALS with their membership.

Library of Congress Catalog Card Number 82-061685
International Standard Serial Number ISSN 0002-7162
International Standard Book Number ISBN 0-8039-1933-6 (Vol. 464, 1982, paper)
International Standard Book Number ISBN 0-8039-1932-8 (Vol. 464, 1982, cloth)

Manufactured in the United States of America. First printing November 1982.

The articles appearing in THE ANNALS are indexed in *Book Review Index; Public Affairs Information Service Bulletin; Social Sciences Index; Monthly Periodical Index; Current Contents: Behavioral, Social, Management Sciences;* and *Combined Retrospective Index Sets.* They are also abstracted and indexed in *ABC Pol Sci, Historical Abstracts, Human Resources Abstracts, Social Sciences Citation Index, United States Political Science Documents, Social Work Research & Abstracts, Peace Research Reviews, Sage Urban Studies Abstracts, International Political Science Abstracts,* and/or *America: History and Life.*

Information about membership rates, institutional subscriptions, and back issue prices may be found on the facing page.

Advertising. Current rates and specifications may be obtained by writing to THE ANNALS Advertising and Promotion Manager at the Beverly Hills office (address above).

Claims. Claims for undelivered copies must be made no later than three months following month of publication. The publisher will supply missing copies when losses have been sustained in transit and when the reserve stock will permit.

Change of Address. Six weeks' advance notice must be given when notifying of change of address. Please send old address label along with the new address to insure proper identification. Please specify name of journal. Send change of address to: THE ANNALS, c/o Sage Publications, Inc., 275 South Beverly Drive, Beverly Hills, CA 90212.

Origin and Purpose. The Academy was organized December 14, 1889, to promote the progress of political and social science, especially through publications and meetings. The Academy does not take sides in controverted questions, but seeks to gather and present reliable information to assist the public in forming an intelligent and accurate judgment.

Meetings. The Academy holds an annual meeting in the spring extending over two days.

Publications. THE ANNALS is the bimonthly publication of The Academy. Each issue contains articles on some prominent social or political problem, written at the invitation of the editors. Also, monographs are published from time to time, numbers of which are distributed to pertinent professional organizations. These volumes constitute important reference works on the topics with which they deal, and they are extensively cited by authorities throughout the United States and abroad. The papers presented at the meetings of The Academy are included in THE ANNALS.

Membership. Each member of The Academy receives THE ANNALS and may attend the meetings of The Academy. Membership is open only to individuals. Annual dues: $24.00 for the regular paperbound edition (clothbound, $36.00). Add $6.00 per year for membership outside the U.S.A. Members may also purchase single issues of THE ANNALS for $5.00 each (clothbound, $7.00).

Subscriptions. THE ANNALS is published six times annually—in January, March, May, July, September, and November. Institutions may subscribe to THE ANNALS at the annual rate: $42.00 (clothbound, $54.00). Add $6.00 per year for subscriptions outside the U.S.A. Institutional rates for single issues: $7.00 each (clothbound, $9.00).

Second class postage paid at Beverly Hills, California.

Single issues of THE ANNALS may be obtained by individuals who are not members of The Academy for $6.00 each (clothbound, $7.50). Single issues of THE ANNALS have proven to be excellent supplementary texts for classroom use. Direct inquiries regarding adoptions to THE ANNALS c/o Sage Publications (address below).

All correspondence concerning membership in The Academy, dues renewals, inquiries about membership status, and/or purchase of single issues of THE ANNALS should be sent to THE ANNALS c/o Sage Publications, Inc., 275 South Beverly Drive, Beverly Hills, CA 90212. *Please note that orders under $20 must be prepaid.* Sage affiliates in London and India will assist institutional subscribers abroad with regard to orders, claims, and inquiries for both subscriptions and single issues.

THE ANNALS
of The American Academy *of* Political *and* Social Science

RICHARD D. LAMBERT, *Editor*
ALAN W. HESTON, *Associate Editor*

--- FORTHCOMING ---

See page 3 for information on Academy membership and purchase of single volumes of **The Annals**.

CONTENTS

BOOK DEPARTMENT CONTENTS

INTERNATIONAL RELATIONS AND POLITICS

AFRICA, ASIA, AND LATIN AMERICA

EUROPE

ECONOMICS

PREFACE

The articles in this volume reflect a reorientation in the ways that scientists have viewed human growth and development. This shift in perspective has moved from a focus on early infancy and childhood toward the total life span, with increasing emphasis on the latter half of the life cycle. As Perlman noted well over a decade ago, there was a

dearth of theoretical constructs, studies, or even isolated clinical accounts of the long developmental period between late adolescence and old age that bore the catchall label "adulthood" . . . compared to the close attention to, documentation of, and resultant conceptions about the development of children, and consequent useful notions about how to enhance child life, the scripts by which adulthood might be understood were markedly few and sketchy. It was as if human beings were considered "all done," fixed, upon coming of age. And then, alas, un-made, undone, bit by bit, by the decrements of old age.[1]

Second, there has been a welcome shift from a crisis or problematic orientation to an emphasis on role transitions—or turning points, markers, passages, and seasons—and continual developmental tasks to describe common changes in adulthoood.

In this new perspective transitions are viewed as normal situations that are likely to confront anyone. Whatever the situation, each transition encompasses a bridging period often characterized by feelings of uncertainty and instability. During this interval the person engages in various degrees of social and psychological adaptations to the changing situations in his or her life. While such transitional processes have long been characteristic of the human condition, it is only in recent years that social and behavioral scientists have begun to rectify our limited knowledge concerning how people and families negotiate a wide array of mid- and late-life transitions.

As several of the authors in the volume note, the current preoccupation with the transitions of middle and old age has evolved from several historical, economic, and demographic changes that have combined to shift our population toward the middle of the age structure and have produced new stages in the life cycle. The result is that today most Americans can expect to pass through these new stages including long-term survival, the empty nest period, universal retirement, and an extended term of widowhood in late life characterized by solitary living.

Previous investigators appeared to be strongly influenced by psychological and psychiatric conceptions, whereas the contemporary researchers have given increasing attention to the impact of social and environmental factors. The imprint of psychoanalytic theory in particular can easily be detected in much of the early literature. Many of these initial developmentalists concentrated on the stages of infancy and childhood. A major assumption was that personality was essentially fixed by early experiences. Today, however, the underlying assumption is that one's personality and behavioral patterns continue to change throughout the life cycle in response to a variety of events and conditions.

---

1. Helen H. Perlman, "Forward," in *Passing through Transitions*, Naomi Golan (New York: Free Press, 1981) p. xv-xvi.

A transition can be defined simply as moving from one stage or event in life to another with varying degrees of instability in the adaptive process.[2] These passages can be classified in at least three ways:

—those involving specific time intervals,

—those characterized by role shifts, and

—those with clearly notable marker events.

The transitions that fit neatly into chronological time periods have accompanying psychological, physical, and social indicators. These might include, for example, the time frames from the birth of a baby until that child enters college, or from the beginning of work to the usual age of retirement. Many of these so-called age-stage-linked transitions fit the chronological time intervals encompassed by young, middle, or late adulthood.

Other transitions do not adapt so readily to specific ages or stages in mid-life and might occur at any one of several points in the life span. Divorce, widowhood, remarriage, or occupational changes, for example, are not age- or stage-linked but can be defined as social role changes. Such role shifts may involve adding new roles to those already existing (remarriage), subtracting roles (widowhood), or exchanging one role or role set for another (occupational change).

Another way to describe transitions in adulthood is to classify them in terms of a specific part of one's life that is affected. These might include geographical changes—moving from one region of the country to another through job transfers or retirement—socioeconomic changes—including unemployment or swift upward mobility—and physiological changes—such as loss of health, physical impairment, or regained strengths.

Many of these changes have in common that they involve periods of imbalance, often accompanied by strong emotions. Lives must be restructured, adaptations made, and modifications in both mental and physical behavior must occur. The descriptions of these transitions and the processes by which adaptations to them are made are the subjects of the articles in this issue.

FELIX M. BERARDO

2. Golan, *Passing through Transitions*, pp. 12-15.

ANNALS, *AAPSS*, **464**, November 1982

The Demography of
Mid- and Late-Life Transitions

By JUDITH TREAS and VERN L. BENGTSON

ABSTRACT: The extension of life expectancy has made possible the life cycle transitions we have come to associate with middle and later years. Because more and more Americans now live to see middle age, old age, and even advanced old age, these stages of life have been democratized. They have been made accessible to a broad cross-section of the population, rather than to only a select few. In conjunction with more generational independence of living arrangements, longer lifetimes have given rise to the empty nest followed by a postmarital period of solitary living. Changes in labor force participation patterns have meant that older persons today experience a relatively new life-style and life stage called retirement.

Judith Treas is associate professor of sociology at the University of Southern California where she holds an appointment as research associate at the Andrus Gerontology Center. Since receiving a Ph.D. from the University of California at Los Angeles, she has authored articles on aging, population, and the family. Her present research is concerned with postwar trends in family income inequality.

Vern L. Bengtson is currently professor of sociology at the University of Southern California, as well as director, Research Institute of the Andrus Gerontology Center. He received his Ph.D. from the University of Chicago in 1967, and has published over 60 papers on the social psychology of aging, family sociology, cross-cultural studies in behavior, and the methodology of social research. Author of The Social Psychology of Aging, *he has edited* Youth, Generations and Social Change *as well as the six-volume* Brooks-Cole Series in Social Gerontology.

THE personal changes associated with the second half of life have come to fascinate Americans today. On television the difficulties of the displaced homemaker and the second careerist have appeared on prime time right along with the drama of teenage unemployment. In the newspapers the menopausal male and the institutionalized elderly compete for column space with issues like child abuse. Our newfound preoccupation with the transitions of middle and old age represents a shift in the focus of our life-cycle concerns.

This shift has several sources. First, there is the discovery and popularization of adulthood by professionals who specialize in providing us with frameworks in which to interpret our lives. Second, there are historical changes in society and economy. These make the transitions of middle and later life more remarkable. They mean that older Americans are adapting to a world they could not have anticipated—much less have prepared for—in their youth. Third, there are demographic changes that have brought into being new stages in the life cycle. Such changes have given more Americans the chance to live out their middle and later years.

To some extent the interests of ordinary Americans as reflected in television programming are just catching up to the concerns shown by those who study human development. These scholars argue that there is a heretofore unappreciated flexibility in the mature adult phase of the life cycle.[1] Far from being fixed by early experiences, the personality, capacities, and attitudes of individuals change throughout life in response to the new challenges and opportunities that come their way.

Individuals of a given age face many common challenges and opportunities. Children grow up. Parents grow older. The attainable limits of career aspirations become clear. Retirement looms. A number of scholars have detected enough age-related similarity in these transitions to generalize from age to stage. Whether called transitions or passages or turning points or seasons, these schema point out the common concerns that organize and anchor life at different points in the life cycle. While some find fault with the lockstep determinism implied by the notion of stages in adulthood,[2] such compartmentalization of the life cycle serves to remind us that there are predictable and widely shared changes from cradle to grave.

Some characteristic life changes are products of biological aging. The ending of childbearing years or the onset of chronic illness are examples. Other changes, however, are influenced by the social environment in which we live. The state of the job market may determine when offspring choose to leave home, for example. When we retire may depend on the provisions of our pension plan. The social environment is no more immune to the passage of time than is the human body.

In short, the social context of aging is in constant flux. Ongoing

1. Daniel J. Levinson, *The Seasons of a Man's Life* (New York: Knopf, 1978); Roger L. Gould, *Transformations: Growth and Change in Adulthood* (New York: Simon & Schuster, 1979); Marjorie Fiske Lowenthal et al., *Four Stages of Life* (San Francisco: Jossey-Bass, 1977).

2. Bernice L. Neugarten, "Time, Age, and the Life Cycle," *American Journal of Psychiatry*, 136(7):887, 894 (July 1979).

historical change intersects with the biological aging of individuals. Although some life-cycle changes are predictable, societal change adds new and unanticipated twists. The adaptation of mature adults to broad social change is especially challenging. Their schooling or the examples of their parents may be too far removed in time to furnish useful models of behavior. Late-life transitions hold particular fascination in societies such as ours, which are beset by rapid social change. In inventing new ways of coping with their life-cycle concerns, middle-aged and older persons of today may be true pioneers.

The sheer force of numbers may also account for the contemporary concern with the second half of life. As they age into their middle years, many Americans find that their center of gravity has shifted to their beltline. So too with the aging American population. Demographic changes have shifted population toward the middle of the age structure. The median age of Americans, for instance, has moved from a youthful 22 in 1890 to a mature 30 in 1980.[3] Declines in fertility have resulted in fewer young Americans in the population.[4] Declines in mortality have swollen the ranks of the old.[5] Since mature

adults account for a bigger share of population, it follows that the transitions they face loom as more significant than ever before.

What is the upshot of the graying of the population, the rapid pace of social change, and the professional recognition of stages of later life? These forces have combined to create new stages in the life cycle. These stages are not necessarily without precedent in the lives of those who have lived before us. What is new is that these stages have been democratized. They are no longer characterized as rare and uncertain, but rather as commonplace and predictable. These mid- and late-life transitions have become accessible to and recognized by the overwhelming majority of Americans. In this process the content and circumstances of these stages have changed.

In this article we will consider four instances of transitions into newly democratized stages of life. First, there is the surer survival into the middle years and beyond. Second, there is the historical emergence of the empty nest, an extended period in married life after offspring have left home. Third, there is the relatively new phenomenon of universal retirement. Finally, there is late-life singlehood, especially widowhood, now stretching into advanced old age and newly characterized by solitary living apart from kin.

3. U.S. Bureau of the Census, *Historical Statistics of the United States*, Part 1 (Washington, DC: Government Printing Office, 1975); U.S. Bureau of the Census, "Population Profile of the United States: 1980," *Current Population Reports*, Series P-20, No. 363 (Washington, DC: Government Printing Office, 1981).

4. Judith Treas, "The Great American Fertility Debate: Generational Balance and Support of the Aged," *The Gerontologist*, 21(1):98, 103 (Feb. 1981).

5. Samuel H. Preston, Nathan Keyfitz, and Robert Schoen, *Causes of Death: Life Tables for National Populations* (New York: Academic Press, 1972).

SURVIVAL INTO MIDDLE AND OLD AGE

It is well known that life expectancy of Americans has marched steadily forward in this century. Given the age-specific mortality rates in 1900, the average American could expect to live 47 years

TABLE 1
PERCENTAGE SURVIVING FROM AGE 20 TO GIVEN AGE, 1900-1976

	1900		1940		1976	
AGE	MEN	WOMEN	MEN	WOMEN	MEN	WOMEN
45	79.7	80.8	89.9	92.0	93.9	97.1
65	50.6	53.7	60.5	70.0	70.4	83.8
85	6.3	7.6	8.9	14.3	16.3	35.3

SOURCES: Adapted from S. H. Preston, N. Keyfitz, and R. Schoen, *Causes of Death: Life Tables for National Populations* (New York: Seminar Press, 1972); and National Center for Health Statistics, *Vital Statistics of the United States,* Vol. II, *Mortality:* Part A (Washington, DC: Government Printing Office, 1980).

from birth to death. By 1976 life expectancy had climbed to 73.[6] It should be emphasized that much of this improvement came about because infant and child mortality was cut sharply: infants became more and more likely to slip past the gauntlet of infectious childhood diseases and to live to become adults. Even among adults, however, improvements in mortality occurred. More and more persons reaching adulthood could count on living into middle age and even old age.

Table 1 indicates the percentages of men and women reaching adulthood—say, age 20—in various years who could expect to live on until the thresholds of middle age, old age, and advanced old age. Somewhat arbitrarily, we take age 45 as the lower boundary of middle age because it is associated with the end of childbearing for most women. We point to 65 as the border of old age because it has come to be seen as the normal age of retirement. We choose 85 as the marker for advanced old age because life tables do not usually provide information for older age groups.

The table shows that in 1900 about four out of five young adults lived to be age 45, given the death rates extant at the turn of the century. By 1976, however, virtually all adult women and 94 percent of their male counterparts could expect to survive to their middle years. Middle age, then, has become nearly a universal entitlement in our society.

Similar gains in expectable longevity characterized later benchmarks of the life-cycle. At the turn of the century only a scant majority of young adults could hope to live to age 65. By 1976, 84 percent of the women and 70 percent of the men could count on reaching old age. At least for women, old age has become as accessible as middle age was to their counterparts in 1900. The gains for men, however, have fallen short of those for women—a fact that has sparked scholarly curiosity as to the social and biological causes of this widening sex gap in late-life mortality.[7] In 1900 less than one in twelve adults would live to be 85 years old. By 1976, one-third of women and one-sixth of men were living to this startlingly advanced age.

6. National Center for Health Statistics, *Vital Statistics of the United States, 1976* vol. II, *Mortality,* Part A (Washington, DC: Gov-

7. Robert D. Retherford, *The Changing Sex Differential in Mortality* (Westport, CT: Greenwood Press, 1975).

Mortality trends may be said to have led to a democratization of middle age and old age. Declining death rates have opened up these life-cycle stages to a broad cross-section of Americans, rather than to a smaller group of superior constitutions and remarkable luck.

Today we may be seeing a colonization of the frontier of our biologically ordained life span. Taking the lead have been a few advance scouts—the centenarians who have pressed the maximum life span many scientists believe is allotted to our species. Now a small but growing minority of Americans are living to know what it is like to be very very old. Although the future course of mortality is always a matter for speculation, recent improvements in death rates for the elderly suggest that a mere extension of these trends will mean that survival to an advanced age may become the rule rather than the exception.[8]

Developments in mortality have wide-ranging implications. Children are less apt to be orphaned, and spouses less apt to be widowed in the prime of life. Thus we are spared some of the emotional uncertainty and economic insecurity characterizing family life in earlier eras. Even adults today may have parents, grandparents, and great-grandparents alive. This overlap in the lives of the generations suggests unprecedented opportunities for the young and the old to shape one another's experiences. Of course, shared lifetimes may be a burden as well as a blessing, especially as more and more relatives live into those later stages of the life cycle associated with chronic illness and other decrements. The swelling ranks of the aged may tax the capacities of kin to care for the elderly in need while challenging the fiscal integrity of societal provisions like social security.[9]

THE EMPTY NEST

Because more Americans live to middle age and beyond, more and more couples experience an unprecedented length of time together after their children have left home. Women born in the 1880s, for example, reached a median age of only 57 before their marriage was broken by the death of one spouse. Widowhood came less than two years after the marriage of the last child.

By contrast, women born in the 1920s are estimated to enjoy an 11-year hiatus between child's marrying and spouse's burying. This is partly because these women finished childbearing at younger ages than their 1880 counterparts. Their children also married at younger ages. Mostly, however, the empty nest owed its extension to the fact that the later generation of women was older before death claimed one partner or the other. Because their marriages enjoyed the benefits of falling death rates, the median age of these women at the death of one spouse was 64 years.[10]

The upshot of these developments is that goodly numbers of couples

8. Eileen Crimmins, "Implications of recent mortality trends for size and composition of population over 65" (Paper presented at the Annual Meetings of the Gerontological Society of America, San Diego, 1980).

9. Judith Treas, "Family Support Systems for the Aged: Some Social and Demographic Considerations," *The Gerontologist,* 17(6):486, 491 (Dec. 1977).

10. U.S. Bureau of the Census, "Perspectives on American Fertility," *Current Population Reports,* Series P-25, No. 70 (Washington, DC: Government Printing Office, 1978).

today can look forward to marriages of startling duration. Even though higher divorce rates offset declines in early widowhood, today one in five couples in their first marriages can expect to celebrate a golden wedding anniversary. Even among those who have remarried, one in twenty will someday be able to look back on a union lasting 50 years.[11] The impact on individuals of a half century of mutual socialization and shared experiences is no doubt quite staggering. The influence of lengthy marriages is heightened by the fact that so many of these years will be passed in a postparental period of domestic intimacy not shared with other kin.

Not only is the joint survival of husbands and wives more assured, but also couples past midlife have assumed more and more privacy in their residential arrangements. In 1955 families headed by a husband 65 or older averaged 2.6 members.[12] By 1978 their average size had fallen by about one-third person to 2.3. Most of this decline was due to a drop in the number of other adult family members, but these older families also experienced a decline in members less than 18 years old. A general trend toward greater residential separation between generations has assured that the empty nest is really emptied.

As the postparental period has stretched into old age, many have come to see it as posing unique challenges and offering new chances. The postparental era has been portrayed as both a boon and a bane,

especially to women. For some, grown children serve only as a demoralizing reminder that their mothering role is no longer needed.[13] For many others, however, the empty nest is an elating liberation.[14] It offers the opportunity to get reacquainted with one's spouse, to travel, or to undertake a new career. Without the financial drain of dependents, there is a chance to feather the empty nest, buying special things or setting aside money for retirement.

This upbeat view of midlife marriage has been facilitated not merely by the mortality trends that make it possible. It has also been fostered by an affluence that makes intergenerational living more welcome. Today's parent may breathe a sigh of relief when the last child is launched. In the past, however, parents often lost not a demanding dependent, but rather a valued contributor to the household income. On farms, children were a source of farm labor. In cities, their earnings helped to keep home and hearth together. When all their children had moved out to start their own families, couples faced the problem of replacing their economic contributions. They hired farm laborers. They took in boarders and lodgers.[15]

11. Paul C. Glick and Arthur J. Norton, "Marrying, Divorcing, and Living Together in the U.S. Today," *Population Bulletin*, 32(5):14 (1979).

12. Judith Treas, "Postwar Trends in Family Size," *Demography*, 18(3):321, 334 (Aug. 1981).

13. Pauline Bart, "The Loneliness of the Long-Distance Mother," in *Women: A Feminist Perspective*, ed. J. Freeman (Palo Alto, CA: Mayfield, 1975).

14. Norval Glenn, "Psychological Well-Being in the Postparental Stage: Some Evidence from National Surveys," *Journal of Marriage and the Family*, 37(1):105, 110 (Feb. 1975).

15. John Modell and Tamara K. Haraven, "Urbanization and the Malleable Household: An Examination of Boarding and Lodging in American Families," *Journal of Marriage and the Family*, 35(3):467, 479 (Aug. 1973); John R. Gillis, *Youth and History* (New York: Academic Press, 1974).

In short, the postparental period for couples in the last century often meant less privacy, not more intimacy. No doubt many viewed the empty nest with trepidation and uncertainty, rather than with relief. At the present time, a shortage of affordable housing, high unemployment, and the instability of young marriages may portend a return to multigenerational family living. This doubling-up may be less welcome among a present generation of mature couples, who have come to view these sorts of arrangements as undesirable and unnecessary.

For better or worse, the postparental era today virtually defines middle age for married couples. Indeed, everything from condominiums to cruise ships caters to the comfortable life-style of childless couples in the prime of life. The empty nest, however, ranks as a recent development in the phasing of the life cycle. Improvements in mortality have meant that more couples than ever before will experience a long period of togetherness after the children are grown up. Changing living arrangements of adults have meant that married couples in middle and old age will typically live alone. Prosperity has made this privacy possible.

RETIREMENT

Americans have come to take retirement for granted. We have grown used to a large population of retirees who enjoy good health and decent incomes. They cluster in leisure-oriented retirement villages of the Sunbelt. They travel our highways in campers and mobile homes. They organize for political action. This picture of active retirement has become so commonplace that we tend to forget that retirement as we know it is a fairly recent social institution.

In earlier times most older persons worked until they could no longer hold a job.[16] If, for example, they could no longer keep up the pace of the assembly line, they settled for sweeping the floors. If they could no longer farm by themselves, they took on a hired hand to help with the heavy work. When they could no longer find or keep a job, they fell back on family, on savings, or—as a last resort—on the poorhouse. Few American workers could afford the luxury of voluntarily withdrawing from the labor force.

Several factors conspired to create a broadly based life-cycle stage called retirement. Certainly the elderly's claim to employment was undermined. Farming and self-employment had permitted the old to continue to work, albeit at their own pace, but these pursuits were on the decline in corporate urban America. In industry and government the idea took hold that the old were something less than valued employees. They were feeble, old-fashioned, and unproductive. They held jobs that rightfully belonged to younger workers.

In response to this declining confidence in the aged's abilities, private pensions were born. Pensions represented a charitable response to

16. William A. Graebner, *History of Retirement* (New Haven, CT: Yale University Press, 1980); Carole Haber, "Mandatory Retirement in Nineteenth-Century America: The Conceptual Basis for a New Work Cycle," *Journal of Social History*, 12:77, 96 (Fall 1978); John Demos, "Old Age in Early New England," in *The American Family in Socio-Historical Perspective*, ed. M. Gordon (New York: St. Martin's Press, 1978), pp. 240, 244.

FIGURE 1
LABOR FORCE PARTICIPATION RATES OF MEN 65 AND OLDER, 1890-1980

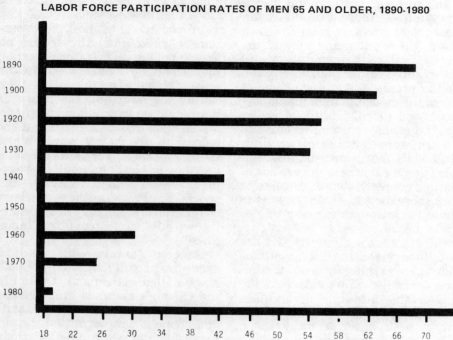

SOURCE: U.S. Bureau of the Census. *Historical Statistics of the United States,* Part 1 (Washington, DC: Government Printing Office, 1975), p. 131; U.S. Bureau of the Census. "Population Profile of the United States, 1980," *Current Population Reports*, Series P-20, No. 363 (Washington, DC: Government Printing Office, 1981).

the serious hardship late-life unemployment inflicted. They also offered employers a means of controlling their workers and setting the tempo of employee turnover. Pensions brought with them the practice of mandatory retirement at a specific, predetermined age. The introduction of social security and the spread of private pension plans meant that more and more workers found that their jobs ran out at age 65. Increasingly, however, a pension took the sting out of retirement.

As Figure 1 shows, labor force participation rates for men 65 and older have been drifting down since the nineteenth century. In 1890 two out of three older men were working. Ninety years later less than one in five older men was in the labor force. On the one hand, they had been squeezed out of the work force by changes in the industrial structure, by mandatory retirement rules, and by age discrimination. On the other hand, they had been lured into retirement by disability and old age benefits that offered an increasingly attractive alternative to work. As a reflection of the greater economic security associated with late-life labor force withdrawal, poverty among families whose heads were 65 or older fell from 35 percent in 1959 to 14 percent in 1978.[17]

These developments meant that more and more Americans could look forward to the life-cycle stage of retirement. Mandatory retirement provisions made this stage predictable. Pensions made it tolerable. An extension of life expectancy made it attainable. Rising labor force participation of women, especially mature married women, meant that they, too, became more and more likely to retire from a job and to draw a pension.

While retirement came to be a nearly universal practice, the timing of the transition into retirement was changing. In a trend traced to the 1950s, American men opted for early retirement. The timing of retirement is known to be quite sensitive to eligibility for retirement income,[18] and such income was increasingly to be had by those in their early sixties and younger. In 1961 social security became available, albeit at a reduced benefit level, to men retiring at age 62. Unions negotiated 20-years-and-out pension provisions for their members. Employers used early retirement incentives to get rid of superfluous workers with high seniority and high salaries.

17. Richard V. Burkhauser, "The Pension Acceptance Decision of Older Men," *Journal of Human Resources* 14:63-75 (Winter 1979); Joseph F. Quinn, "Microeconomic Determinants of Early Retirement," *Journal of Human Resources* 12:329-346 (Summer 1977); Richard E. Barfield and James N. Morgan, *Early Retirement* (Ann Arbor, MI: University of Michigan Institute for Social Research, 1970).

18. U.S. Bureau of the Census, "Money Income and Poverty Status of Families and Persons in the United States: 1980," *Current Population Reports*, Series P-60, No. 127 (Washington, DC: Government Printing Office, 1979).

As retirement spread and trickled down to younger age groups, there was a widely held suspicion that retirement was too good to be true. Researchers went looking for the decline in happiness thought to be associated with the loss of a meaningful work role. They investigated retirement as a possible cause of disease and death. They sought out marital strains assumed to arise in having a newly retired husband underfoot. Interestingly, few of these leads panned out. By and large, retirees in good health and with adequate incomes voiced real satisfaction with retirement. No conclusive link between health and retirement was isolated. Couples demonstrated surprisingly smooth adaptations.

This lack of negative outcomes simply reinforces the conclusion that retirement has attained the status of a genuine social institution. The transition to retirement is smoothed by widely accepted conventions and by exemplars of retirement. One consequence of the democratization of retirement, for example, is that being retired no longer suggests a personal shortcoming. Older Americans who are not in the labor force are not thought to be shirkers; nor is their retirement taken as prima facie evidence of incompetence. The vigor and affluence of a sizable segment of older persons also give the lie to the notion of retirees as down and out. It is small wonder, then, that Americans have been opting to retire at an early age when they still have the resources to enjoy their leisure.

LATE-LIFE SINGLEHOOD

In recent decades increasing numbers of Americans have lived out the last years of their lives in life-cycle circumstances so new that we have yet to develop a catchy term for this life-cycle stage. Whatever one calls it, the distinguishing features of this phase are that one is old, single, and living alone. This is usually typified by the widow who has survived her husband and continues to maintain her own household apart from kin into old age. Given rising divorce rates throughout this century, more and more older divorced persons have come to populate this world as well. To this situation we may add persons who have never married and so-called grass widows whose spouses live apart, possibly in an institution for the aged.

To be sure, there have always been individuals who have faced old age without the companionship of a spouse. If anything, Americans 65 or older are somewhat more likely to be married today than was the case in the last century. Among older men the percentage married has risen from 71 in 1890 to 78 in 1980. For women the comparable percentages are 35 and 40.[19] Declines in widows have more than offset the rise in divorces. Once widowed or divorced, however, longer life expectancies portend a longer life alone.

What is significant about the postmarital period is the fact that it has become a very private phase of the life cycle. In the past this life-cycle stage involved living with other family members. Today it is passed alone. Consider the case of the primary individual, the term used by the U.S. Bureau of the Census for a person who heads a household containing no kin. In 1950 only 28 percent of widowed women 65 or older were classified as primary individuals.[20] Most of the remainder lived in the homes of their grown children or other family members. By 1979 fully 68 percent of elderly widows were household heads living apart from their relations. This increase is most dramatic. If this trend continues, no elderly widows will be living with their relations by the year 2000!

Gerontologists examining survey data have been quick to point out that older people themselves express a preference for private living arrangements.[21] It has also been pointed out that a generational separation of residence does not mean that the aged are bereft of kin. Patterns of contact and exchange of services between the generations are well documented. Nonetheless, the day-to-day solitude of old age in our times must be reckoned with.

On the one hand, the private living of later life suggests that old age may offer the old a freedom and independence unknown to their

19. U.S. Bureau of the Census, *Historical Statistics of the United States*, Part 1 (Washington, DC: Government Printing Office, 1975); U.S. Bureau of the Census, "Marital Status and Living Arrangements: March 1980," *Current Population Reports*, Series P-20, No. 365 (Washington, DC: Government Printing Office, 1981).

20. U.S. Bureau of the Census, *U.S. Census of Population: 1950*, Vol. IV, Special Reports, Part 2, Ch. D, Marital Status (Washington, DC: Government Printing Office, 1964); U.S. Bureau of the Census, "Marital Status and Living Arrangements," *Current Population Reports*, Series P-20, No. 349 (Washington, DC: Government Printing Office, 1980).

21. Ethel Shanas, "The Family as a Social Support System in Old Age," *The Gerontologist*, 19(2):169-74 (Apr. 1979); Vern L. Bengtson and Linda M. Burton, "Familism, Ethnicity, and Support Systems: Patterns of Contrast and Congruence" (Paper presented at the 1980 Gerontological Society of America Meeting, San Diego, Nov. 1981).

forebears. Their life-style—from their choice of bedtimes to their taste in bedmates—remains their own and is not subject to the intimate scrutiny, preferences, and requirements of younger generations of family members. On the other hand, solitary living may cut some older people off from day-to-day contact with others. This privacy in living arrangements poses additional barriers to family help for older parents, since grown offspring find themselves performing housekeeping tasks in two dwellings, carting homecooked meals across town, and generally contending with logistics complicated by distance and duplication between households. A logical extension of the empty nest and lengthening lifetimes, this life-cycle era of solitary singleness has injected a new wrinkle into aging. We have yet to iron out some of the potential problems associated with this stage of old age

CONCLUSION

We have argued that demographic currents have given new defini-

tion to middle and old age. Declining death rates and surer survival have meant that late life has been democratized. Middle and old age have been made accessible as never before to a broad cross-section of Americans. A lengthening life span has also been a prerequisite to the invention and popularization of new life-cycle stages in the late years. Together with changes in living arrangements, mortality trends have given rise to the empty nest and its successor, late-life solitary living.

In conjunction with shifts in labor force participation, longer life expectancies have made possible the life stage and life-stage we know as retirement. While not unknown in earlier times, these new stages in the second half of life did not always constitute the commonplace that they do today. No doubt some of the unique circumstances confronting the very old today will tomorrow be embraced as taken-for-granted transitions in the inevitable process of growth, change, and aging.

Models of Transitions in Middle and Later Life

By LINDA K. GEORGE

ABSTRACT: The topic of change during adulthood is receiving increased attention from social and behavioral scientists, as well as from the general public. This article describes and evaluates the contributions of four types of models designed to further our understanding of the causes and consequences of change during middle and later life: developmental models, life event models, adult socialization models, and integrated models that incorporate elements of multiple perspectives. Special attention is devoted to the recent and appropriate shift from an emphasis upon change as crisis to the more neutral view of change as transition. Two issues are suggested as critical to any useful model of change during middle and later life. First, such models must incorporate recognition of the importance of both individual and social factors for understanding the causes and consequences of change. Second, such models must identify the factors that place individuals at risk for adaptive problems as a result of change.

Linda K. George is associate professor of medical sociology in the Duke University Department of Psychiatry and is senior fellow in the Duke Center for the Study of Aging and Human Development. Dr. George is a fellow of the Gerontological Society of America and is social sciences editor for the Journal of Gerontology. *The author of many books and articles on aging, her recent publications include* Role Transitions in Later Life *(1980),* "Subjective Well-Being: Conceptual and Methodological Issues" in Annual Review of Gerontology and Geriatrics *(1981), and, with Lucille B. Bearon,* Quality of Life in Older Persons: Meaning and Measurement *(1980).*

THE fact that adult life is characterized by substantial amounts of change and associated processes of negotiation and adjustment probably comes as no surprise to most of us—our own lives and the experiences of those we know confirm this assertion. Until recently, however, this conclusion was not compatible with the view of adulthood subscribed to by most social and behavioral scientists—especially developmental psychologists. The belated recognition by developmentalists that change is a normal aspect of adulthood is a testimony to the overarching influence of psychoanalytic theory, especially the work of Freud, which posits that adulthood marks the completion of development. Some sociologists, especially those studying families and work from a socialization perspective, recognized that change occurs during adulthood, but they also typically viewed such changes as less intense and less consequential than those characteristic of childhood.

The changes first examined by social and behavioral scientists were the most dramatic and intense ones, such as widowhood and unemployment—those changes that are most likely to be perceived as stressful or to lead to negative outcomes. Concomitant to the increasing recognition of other types of changes as a normal aspect of adulthood has been the related insight that change need not represent crisis. Consequently, we increasingly hear the more neutral term "transition" used to describe common changes in adulthood.

The recent scramble to set the record straight with regard to change during adulthood has been accompanied by a variety of competing explanations as to the causes and consequences of such change for personal well-being. In a broad sense, these competing explanations comprise models of change during adulthood; and as such they can be examined in terms of a number of characteristics, including the degree to which change is seen as originating in the individual or the environment, the extent to which change is viewed as being age linked, and their ability to specify the conditions under which change is and is not experienced as a crisis. This article briefly describes and assesses the usefulness of the major models of adult change that pervade current literature and guide present research efforts. Four general types of models will be reviewed:

—developmental models,

—life event models,

—adult socialization models, and

—integrated models that include elements of multiple perspectives.

Two notes of caution are prudent before turning to an examination of these generic models. First, the term "model" is used in a broad sense to refer to a general working orientation, rather than to a comprehensive set of interrelated propositions. Although the state of the art certainly permits the development of principles, the topic of change during adulthood is still in relative infancy, precluding the development of completely specified models. Second, because of space limitations, the descriptions and assessments presented here are necessarily brief and focus upon major themes. The purpose is to synthesize and summarize—those readers interested in a richer exposure may wish to consult more detailed sources.

Models of adult development have significance beyond that of general interest and descriptive value. Models guide our interpretation of what we observe and the facets of experience we subject to the rigors of the scientific method. Frequently, models remain implicitly embedded in our perceptions of the world; and when this happens we are unwittingly, rather than purposively, subject to their tenets and assumptions. It is appropriate to render models explicit—to delineate their tenets and assumptions, to assess their strengths and weaknesses, and to identify those issues from which they remove us as well as those issues upon which they focus attention. Most important for the purpose at hand, a comparison of available models can help both to determine how far we have come in our understanding of middle and later life and to provide fruitful directions for further efforts.

DEVELOPMENTAL MODELS

As used here, the term "developmental models" encompasses a variety of perspectives on the nature of change during adulthood. In spite of the breadth of the term, developmental models share several important characteristics. I will begin by identifying the central propositions shared by developmental scholars; subsequently I will discuss some major variations in developmental perspectives in order to illustrate the differences in orientation found among scholars who start from premises that are initially similar.

Developmental models of adulthood typically share four basic premises. First, they focus upon the individual, emphasizing personality, cognition, and other intrapsychic factors. Such models usually acknowledge that social and cultural factors may affect the developmental process to some degree, for example, impeding or facilitating the timing of developmental change, but such factors pale in comparison with the importance attached to intrapsychic characteristics. Second, the impetus for developmental change resides in the individual. Successful development is the effective unfolding of an intrinsic agenda. Third, developmental change will be universally observable because it is an inherent aspect of the human condition. Most developmental scholars acknowledge that developmental changes may differ in form for various groups, but the underlying developmental agenda is characteristic of the species. In this regard it is interesting to note that gender differences are the most frequently anticipated major variations in adult development. Thus major variations in human experience are expected across groups for whom developmental differences can be attributed to biological, rather than or in addition to social, antecedents. Finally, the developmental history is viewed as relevant to subsequent growth. Developmental failure at any life stage is viewed as a significant blow to the prospects of success at future life stages. For developmentalists, success is likely to breed future success and, alternatively, failure is likely to spawn future failure.

Three issues illustrate the major differences among developmental models: the extent to which adult development is viewed as (1) linked to specific chronological ages, (2) involving specific developmental tasks, and (3) characterized by continuity versus discontinuity. There is virtual consensus that child development—including physical and cognitive development—is closely related to chronological age. The relationship between development and chronological age in adulthood remains a matter of debate. Some scholars think that developmental periods are closely tied to age—Levinson, for example, states that developmental periods can be linked to specific four-year intervals.[1] Others explicitly deny that developmental periods are related to specific ages.[2]

Developmentalists also differ in the extent to which psychosocial change during adulthood is believed to involve specific developmental tasks. Erikson, for example, proposes that a sequence of eight psychosocial tasks comprises the agenda of ego development across the life cycle.[3] Levinson, in contrast, assumes a specific sequence of periods of developmental transition and stability across adulthood, but is relatively vague about the particular issues confronted during the transition phases.[4] He suggests that developmental transitions are characterized by general reappraisal and modification of life structure, with the specific content dependent upon the idiosyncrasies of individual personality and biography.

Perhaps most important for our purposes, developmental scholars vary in the degree to which they view adult development as characterized by continuity or discontinuity. Degree of discontinuity is, in turn, related to expectations about the degree to which developmental change will be experienced as a crisis. Some writers view the developmental tasks of adulthood as relatively modest in relation to those that transpire during childhood and adolescence. Haan, for example, concludes that adult development is primarily a process of increased individuation over time, with the pattern of individuation reflecting a refining and strengthening of preexistent personality traits.[5] Such models, which assume that adult development is basically a process of tinkering with a relatively stable personality, suggest that such change is unlikely to be experienced as a crisis. Others suggest that adult development involves rather dramatic discontinuities. This sugges-

1. Daniel J. Levinson with C. N. Darrow, E. B. Klein, M. H. Levinson, and Braxton McKee, *The Seasons of a Man's Life* (New York: Knopf, 1978).

2. Erik H. Erikson, *Childhood and Society* (New York: Norton, 1950).

3. Erik H. Erikson, *Identity: Youth and Crisis* (New York: Norton, 1968).

4. Levinson et al., *The Seasons of a Man's Life*, pp. 40-63.

5. Norma Haan, "Common Dimensions of Personality Development: Early Adolescence to Middle Life," in *Present and Past in Middle Life*, eds. D. H. Eichorn, J. A. Clausen, Norma Haan, M. P. Honzik, and P. H. Mussen (New York: Academic Press, 1981), pp. 117-53.

tion is particularly characteristic of developmentalists who assert that there are major, qualitatively distinct stages of adult development. They readily acknowledge the potential for and frequent experience of crisis and suggest two major ways that crisis can occur. First, if the developmental task represents a major negotiation of self and identity, the process is inherently stressful. It is painful, we are told, to give up the mainstays of identity and to negotiate a new relationship between self and world. The developmental transition ultimately may lead to a more comfortable sense of self, but psychic growing pains are to be expected along the way. Second, developmental failure is possible and, when it occurs, a sense of crisis is likely.

Because the study of change during adulthood is relatively recent, data that would permit a definitive assessment of developmental models remain unavailable. Tentative evaluations of the strengths and weaknesses of these perspectives on adulthood, however, are possible. On the positive side of the ledger, developmental principles appropriately incorporate the role of the individual's personal history, motives, and choices as important considerations in understanding the nature and implications of change during adulthood. The importance of this emphasis upon the active involvement of the individual will perhaps become even more obvious in our discussion of alternative models, some of which neglect this issue. A second source of support for developmental models is an increasing body of studies that document specific changes across the adult life

course. The best documented developmental change is the fact that men become more nurturant and affiliative as they age, while women, conversely, become more dominant and assertive. This pattern has been found in numerous studies, ranging from Jung's clinical observations in the 1930s[6] to Neugarten's studies of American samples[7] and Gutmann's cross-cultural studies.[8] Although it is too early to adopt developmental models in a broad sense, certain specific changes in adulthood appear compatible with the essential elements of this perspective.

Developmental models also have notable limitations. First, the data available strongly suggest that some of the assumptions commonly subscribed to by developmental scholars are untenable. For example, the assumption that developmental failure leads to significant difficulties at subsequent life stages appears to be untrue with sufficient frequency that this assumption could more profitably be transformed into an important and potentially testable research question: under what conditions do developmental difficulties hinder adaptation during adulthood—and, conversely, under

---

6. Carl G. Jung, "The Stages of Life," in *The Portable Jung*, ed. Joseph Campbell (New York: Viking, 1971), pp. 3-22.

7. Bernice L. Neugarten and David L. Gutmann, "Age-Sex Roles and Personality in Middle Age: A Thematic Apperception Study," in *Middle Age and Aging*, ed. Bernice L. Neugarten (Chicago: University of Chicago Press, 1968), pp. 58-74.

8. David L. Gutmann, "The Cross-Cultural Perspective: Notes toward a Comparative Psychology of Aging," in *Handbook of the Psychology of Aging*, eds. J. E. Birren and K. W. Schaie (New York: Van Nostrand Reinhold, 1977), pp. 302-26.

what conditions are individuals able to attain adequate adult adjustment in spite of earlier developmental problems? Most important, developmental perspectives fail to pay sufficient attention to the role of social and cultural factors in the process of personal change during adulthood. As we will see in the context of later discussion, social and cultural factors affect the nature of adult change, the ways change is differentially experienced and negotiated, and the implications of such change for personal well-being. In short, developmental models, by focusing upon the universal and intrinsic aspects of adult change, neglect the social and cultural factors that can explain variations in adult change and its consequences.

LIFE EVENT MODELS

The term "life events" refers to identifiable discrete changes in usual patterns of behavior, changes that can create stress and can pose adaptive challenges to the individual. The types of life events included in previous research include work-related events, such as retirement, starting work, getting fired or laid off; family-based events, such as getting married, separated, or divorced, widowhood, birth of a child, departure of children from the parental home; and changes in finances, friendships, and life-style. The primary emphasis of life event models is understanding the effects of change on personal well-being. It should be noted, however, that life event models are not based upon explicit concepts of or special interest in adulthood in general or particular life stages.

Available literature reveals two broad types of life event models: (1) those that define the significance of life events simply in terms of degree of change, which I will refer to as traditional life event perspectives, and (2) those that emphasize the subjective meaning of life events, which I will call interactionist life event models. The differences between traditional and interactionist life event models are quite dramatic; consequently, it is useful to describe each briefly.

Traditional models emphasize only one aspect of life events: the degree to which they disrupt established patterns of behavior. Life events are assumed to have varying degrees of impact upon personal well-being, depending upon the amount of change that results from occurrence of the event. Perceptions of stress or the meaning that the event has for the individual are viewed as irrelevant to the impact of the life event upon personal well-being. Both events that are presumably positive or pleasant—such as marriage or a promotion at work—and those that are typically thought of as negative—such as widowhood—are viewed as stressful, because both types of events disrupt established patterns of behavior. Traditional life event models also ignore the social and personal circumstances that form the context within which the event occurs. A given event is assumed to have the same impact or generate the same amount of stress for everyone who experiences it. Investigators operating from the traditional life event perspective have devoted most of their efforts to examining the degree to which the experience of life events is associated with adaptive problems—primarily increased risk of physical or mental illness. In general, modest relationships between life events and increased risk of illness have been documented. Additional efforts have focused upon developing alternative methods of quantifying the amount of stress generated by different life events.

Interactionist life event models involve a more complex view of the relationship between life changes and personal well-being. In addition to amount of change in life routines, both the meaning of the event for the individual and the personal and social resources available to the individual are expected to affect the impact of the event. The meaning of a life event refers to the individual's subjective perceptions both of the importance of that event and the degree to which it is evaluated as positive or negative. Retirement, for example, is viewed as relief from drudgery by some people and as loss of a satisfying activity by others. Moreover, regardless of its positive or negative assessment, departure from the labor force will be an important experience for some people and a relatively inconsequential one for others. Interactionist life-event models not only acknowledge these differences in the ways that life events are interpreted by individuals; these differences in meaning also are viewed as essential in understanding the impact of life events. Events perceived as positive and those that are assessed as being inconsequential are expected to have less negative impact on individuals than those that are perceived as negative or important.

Interactionist models also incorporate explicit attention to the personal and social factors that comprise the context within which change occurs. Examples of such factors include individual coping skills and personality traits, the resources provided by social support networks, and financial resources. Personal and social factors are viewed as having potential importance for the likelihood of (1) experiencing a given life event, for example, lower socioeconomic status increases the likelihood of being laid off; (2) perceiving the event as negative or important, for example, having one's car break down can be a tragedy in the absence of financial resources and a mere inconvenience otherwise; and (3) adapting to the event with more or less ease, for example, loss of a friendship can be more easily handled if one has other intimate friends. The interactionist perspective thus acknowledges differences in personal and social resources and hypothesizes that those differences are consequential.

Available evidence is mounting in favor of the more complex models developed by interactionists. As we would expect, both the meaning of life events and the personal or social context within which events occur are important factors that help us to understand the conditions under which life events do and do not have negative impacts upon personal well-being.

Traditional and interactionist life event models also have important implications and expectations about the degree to which changes during adulthood are experienced as crises. Traditional life event models assume that change is stressful and hence have an explicit crisis orientation. Interactionist models, in contrast, transform this assumption into an appropriate and important research question: under what conditions are life events experienced as crises and under what conditions are they experienced as benign—or even enhancing? Indeed, by emphasizing the fact that change need not necessarily be experienced as crisis, interactionist perspectives logically lead to the insight that stability is not always desirable or personally enhancing. We might imagine, by extending this logic, that under certain circumstances not experiencing change may be more stressful than experiencing it. For example, failure to obtain a desired promotion undoubtedly can be more distressing than obtaining it. Thus interactionist life event models provide a neutral perspective from which to explore the implications of change for personal well-being during adulthood.

The impetus for change remains somewhat ambiguous in life event models. Source of change has not been addressed by traditional life event scholars, although change is implicitly viewed as a stress imposed upon the individual. Some interactionists have hypothesized that involuntary life events are more likely than voluntary ones to be perceived as stressful and hence to increase the probability of negative outcomes. The distinction between voluntary and involuntary events indicates that some changes are initiated by the individual and others are imposed on the individual. Again, the interactionist perspective moves away from the assumption that change has an invariant character and toward an understanding of the varying causes and consequences of change.

Interactionist life event models thus have a number of important strengths. The importance of both individual and social factors is explicitly recognized. At an even more basic level, life events research has identified some of the major

arenas of change during adulthood —the contexts of family, work, health, finances, and friendship. Additionally, changes are viewed as differing across individuals in terms of both the likelihood of occurrence and their effects on personal well-being. In short, interactionist life event models take an appropriately complex view of the multiple factors associated with change and its impact.

The major missing component in life event models is an explicit concept of the life cycle in general or of adulthood in particular. Clearly, certain life events are closely linked with age or stage of life cycle. Different family-based events are likely in late life than are typical in early adulthood. Age-related event patterns also are characteristic of work. Further, age or life stage is related to social and personal resources: middle age is generally characterized by greatest financial resources, social support networks tend to shrink in late life, and so forth. Given these relationships, life event models might be enhanced by explicit attention to life cycle issues.

ADULT SOCIALIZATION MODELS

Adult socialization models focus upon the sequence of social roles enacted over the adult life course and the ways in which individuals obtain these roles and are prepared to enact them. Social roles refer to the rights, duties, and expectations associated with defined positions in the social structure. Most adults have multiple roles in the context of their family, work, and community relationships. Some adult roles are obtained by self-selection; others are socially assigned. Socialization is the process by which the individual learns both the rights and responsibilities associated with social roles and the skills and attitudes necessary to successfully perform those roles. Some adult socialization is relatively formal and explicit, occupational training, for example, but much adult socialization occurs in the context of informal social interaction. Regardless of whether role acquisition and socialization experiences are voluntary or not, occupants of social roles are subjected to social evaluation of their role performance, and inadequate performance increases the risk of social sanctions.

From this perspective the major changes of adulthood consist of shifts in the configuration of social roles that the individual enacts during the adult years. There are two primary types of role transitions commonly experienced during adulthood: (1) the relinquishment and acquisition of different roles, which I call role changes; and (2) changing expectations about the rights and responsibilities of the same role as it is enacted over time, which I call career changes. Role changes, in the form of role loss and role gain, are common during adulthood. For example, student roles are relinquished and occupational roles are acquired during early adulthood; similarly, occupational roles are relinquished at retirement. As these examples illustrate, sometimes the loss of one role is complemented by role gain. In other cases, roles are added without a corresponding role loss or, vice versa, roles are lost without a complementary role gain. There is general consensus among scholars of the adult life course that a surplus of role gains is typical of early adulthood, while later life is characterized by a surplus of role losses.[9]

The concept of career is used by social scientists to refer to patterned sequences of duties and rights associated with enactment of a specific role over time. Many adult roles are expected to remain active over a large part of the adult years and to involve changing expectations about role behavior across time. Work roles are the most obvious context in which the concept of career can be applied, but the notion of career also has proven to be useful in other role contexts. The career of parent, for example, includes expectations about changing rights and responsibilities over time; a mother is expected to behave differently toward grown children than she did when her offspring were minors.

One of the important features of adult socialization models is the emphasis upon the degree to which role changes and career changes are socially expected and normatively desirable. Normative expectations prepare us not only for the occurrence of role transitions, but also for their timing or schedule. Effective socialization prepares the individual for role transitions and provides the skills necessary to effectively implement role changes. For example, occupational training prepares individuals to perform adequately as employees. Scholars operating from a socialization perspective often are more interested in the social implications of role change

9. Irving Rosow, "Status and Role Change through the Life Span," in *Handbook of Aging and the Social Sciences*, eds. Robert H. Binstock and Ethel Shanas (New York: Van Nostrand Reinhold, 1976), pp. 457-82.

than they are in the impact of role change upon personal well-being. Thus effective role performance is viewed as socially desirable, regardless of the personal impact of role transitions. Nonetheless, it is clear that the general expectation is that role transitions will not be perceived as crises; effective socialization renders role changes expectable and prepares the individual for successful role performance, thus minimizing the distress generated by new demands on behavior.

Adult socialization perspectives do not negate the possibility that role transitions have the potential for crisis, at both the individual and social level. In some cases socialization is absent or ineffective, in which case the individual may experience a sense of crisis, either because the role transition is unwanted or because the skills necessary for successful role performance are not obtained. Timing issues also may cause problems; if an individual is off-time with regard to a role transition, effective socialization is less likely and the individual may suffer increased discomfort. Widowhood in young adulthood may be more difficult than loss of a spouse at later ages, because it is early. Socialization perspectives view these conditions as being socially undesirable because increased likelihood of inadequate role performance has negative implications for the social system as well as for the individual. Thus adult socialization models incorporate attention to the circumstances under which change during adulthood can be problematic, as well as the conditions under which change is rather easily negotiated.

Adult socialization models provide a number of contributions to our understanding of personal change in adulthood. First, the emphasis upon major social roles directs our attention to the primary contexts of meaningful life experience in adulthood: family, work, and community networks. Second, adult socialization models pay appropriate attention to the influences of social structure and social norms upon change during adulthood. Socialization is a powerful tool. From the viewpoint of the individual, socialization both prepares people for successful role performance and provides them a method of enhancing well-being and social stature in the face of changing behavioral demands. From the perspective of the social structure, socialization increases the likelihood that important social functions are performed in an adequate manner. Finally, adult socialization models help us to understand the conditions under which role transitions are and are not experienced as personal crises.

There are three areas in which adult socialization models are less than comprehensive and would profit from further elaboration. First, adult socialization models devote insufficient attention to the subjective perceptions, motivations, and commitments of individuals. The fact that adult social roles and socialization experiences are likely to be voluntarily selected is commonly acknowledged. Beyond this, however, subjective and intrapsychic factors remain largely unaddressed. Socialization models tend to adopt what Dennis Wrong called an "over-socialized view of man," underestimating the intensity of impact that subjective factors have upon behavior in spite of social norms and socialization experiences.[10] Socialization is a powerful tool, but subjective factors exert a powerful influence on behavior too—and social and personal needs may be at odds more frequently than is recognized in adult socialization models. Second, some important types of change during adulthood probably occur outside the context of formal social roles. It is likely, for example, that the physical changes that accompany the aging process are important for many individuals and that such changes influence behavior. Yet because health behavior typically is not considered a social role, adult socialization models are unlikely to contribute to our understanding of these changes.

Finally, if adult socialization models are to contribute optimally to our understanding of adulthood, increased attention must be devoted to the ways in which multiple roles and role transitions interact across the adult life course. Currently, family life is typically examined exclusive of other social roles, occupational careers are studied without information about the other roles workers enact, and so forth. Hogan[11] and Marini[12] recently examined the timing of multiple role transitions during early adulthood. These works represent important initial

10. Dennis Wrong, "The Oversocialized Conception of Man in Modern Sociology," *American Sociological Review*, 26:183-93 (Apr. 1961).

11. Dennis P. Hogan, "The Transition to Adulthood as a Career Contingency," *American Sociological Review*, 45: 261-76 (Apr. 1980).

12. Margaret Mooney Marini, "The Transition to Adulthood: Sex Differences in Educational Attainment and Age at Marriage," *American Sociological Review*, 43:483-507 (Aug. 1978).

efforts to document the significance of configurations of role transitions in a given life stage, but much more work is needed. The development of explanatory propositions and working tools for examining multiple roles must be a high priority item for adult socialization scholars.

INTEGRATED MODELS

I use the term "integrated models" to refer to models of change during adulthood that are explicitly designed to incorporate more than one of the three types of models previously described: developmental models, life event models, and adult socialization models. As we have seen, each of these three models offers unique contributions to our understanding of change during adulthood. Conversely, each model has limitations that restrict its comprehensiveness or applicability. The strengths of one type of model often are in areas that comprise the limitations of another type of model, for example, one type of model underestimates the importance of social factors while another type of model understates the relevance of subjective factors. This situation is especially true in terms of assumptions: an issue that scholars from one perspective are content to accept as a given will be viewed as a matter of empirical inquiry by proponents of another perspective. Integrated models are designed to incorporate the strengths of two or more models, such that overall improvement in comprehensiveness or applicability is achieved. As we might expect, given the relative recency of scientific interest in change during adulthood, integrated models are relatively rare. In this section I will describe two recent models that incorporate major components of two of the model types previously described: (1) Marjorie Fiske's model of changing hierarchies of commitment, which includes both developmental and interactionist life event orientations;[13] and (2) my model of adjustment to role transitions, which integrates adult socialization and interactionist life event models.[14]

Marjorie Fiske's many contributions to the study of middle and late life span a quarter of a century and have addressed multiple life-cycle issues. Increasingly, however, her evolving concept of change during adulthood integrates interactionist life event and developmental models. Fiske and her colleagues focus upon the self-concept, which is viewed as the "wellsprings of choice and behavior" during adulthood.[15] Their empirical research suggests four important dimensions of adult self-concept:

— an interpersonal dimension, which focuses upon social relationships;

— an altruistic dimension, which incorporates ethical, religious, and philosophical concerns;

— a mastery dimension, which encompasses competence, a sense of efficacy, creativity, and autonomy; and

— self-protectiveness, which includes physical and economic concerns as well as maintenance of a sense of well-being.

People differ with respect to the degree of subjective and behavioral commitment invested in the four dimensions of self-concept, generating different hierarchies of commitment. In addition to differences across individuals, a given person's hierarchy of commitment to these four dimensions of self-concept changes over time—sometimes in dramatic ways over a fairly short interval. Fiske defines changing hierarchies of commitment as central changes of adulthood. She and her colleagues examined changes in commitment hierarchies among four age groups, ranging from late adolescence to old age, experiencing predictable life events. This research documented the extent to which life events trigger changes in individuals' hierarchies of commitment and affect people's ability to behaviorally implement their self-concerns. Of particular relevance to understanding the circumstances under which change is and is not problematic, Fiske and her colleagues found that a sense of well-being was associated with a willingness to reorder one's hierarchy of commitment and/or increased commitment to the self-protectiveness dimension of self-concept.

Fiske explicitly rejects the notion of stages with regard to individuals' changing hierarchies of commitment and, indeed, sees no single developmental pattern emerging with respect to change in the four components of the self over time. Nonetheless, some aspects of her approach and research findings are

13. Marjorie Fiske, "Changing Hierarchies of Commitment in Adulthood," in *Themes of Work and Love in Adulthood,* eds. N. J. Smelser and E. H. Erikson (Cambridge: Harvard University Press, 1980), pp. 238-64.

14. Linda K. George, *Role Transitions in Later Life* (Monterey: Brooks/Cole, 1980).

15. Fiske, "Changing Hierarchies of Commitment in Adulthood," p. 245.

distinctly developmental. At the conceptual level the emphasis upon the self and other subjective or intrapsychic factors, particularly the notion that self-concerns are the impetus for change during adulthood, are highly compatible with developmental orientations. The research findings of certain age-related patterns, for example, increases in self-protectiveness during later life, also offer limited support for a developmental perspective.

Life events also have a place in Fiske's view of change during adulthood. Such events are viewed as external factors that can serve as the impetus for changing hierarchies of commitment or can affect the individual's ability to translate self-priorities into life-style themes. Although Fiske pays attention to social factors as sources of change and as providing the opportunity structures within which self-concerns are actualized, she finds roles per se unhelpful. She points out, for example, that some persons use their occupational roles as contexts for developing mastery while others pursue interpersonal concerns. This reflects her interactionist allegiance—the importance of social roles is found, not in knowing whether the individual has them, but rather in knowing the subjective meaning of those roles for the individual.

In previous work I have attempted to integrate interactionist life event and adult socialization models.[16] The integration of these two perspectives strikes me as a useful and relatively simple one. The primary point of convergence is the fact that most life events examined in previous research are, in fact, role transitions—either role changes, in the form of role gain or role loss, or career changes affecting a given role over time. This interface provides a point of departure for developing a model of the process of adjustment to role transitions/life events that incorporates the major social and individual factors emphasized in both interactionist life event and adult socialization models. This integrated model, which is based on House's model of social stress,[17] is schematically described in Figure 1.

The model presented in Figure 1 includes five basic classes of variables. In essence, the model is anchored by the conditions that generate change during adulthood: role transitions and life events. Second, the meaning of the change to the individual is crucial. Previous studies suggest that the perceived importance and desirability of the change and the amount of behavioral disruption generated by the change will be important components of the meaning of the event as experienced by the individual. Responses refer to relatively short-term reactions to changes that occur. Following interactionist life event perspectives, the model notes the particular relevance of intrapsychic and behavioral coping responses. More long-term consequences are viewed as the outcomes of the change and, as the model indicates, such outcomes need to be assessed relative to the baseline level characteristic of the individual before the change occurred. Life events and role changes can affect multiple aspects of personal well-

16. George, *Role Transitions in Later Life*, pp. 50-54.

17. James S. House, "Occupational Stress and Coronary Heart Disease: A Review and Theoretical Integration," *Journal of Health and Social Behavior*, 15:12-27 (Jan. 1974).

FIGURE 1
MODEL OF ADAPTATION TO ADULT TRANSITIONS

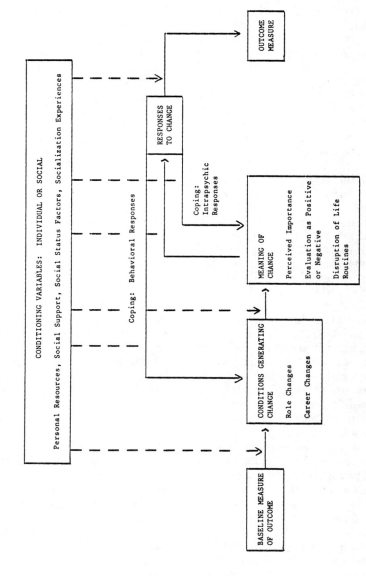

SOURCE: Adaptation from George, *Role Transitions in Later Life* (p. 53).

35

being; previous research suggests that physical and mental health, self-concept, and life satisfaction may be primary indicators of well-being. Finally, the model suggests that the entire process of change and its consequences is affected by a complex configuration of individual and social factors, and that these factors may affect any point of the process. Although there are a myriad of potentially relevant individual and social factors, previous work emphasizes the importance of personal resources, social support, social status factors, and socialization experiences.

The cross-fertilization of adult socialization and interactionist life event models incorporates a number of issues raised by one of the perspectives but ignored or under-represented in the other. Adult socialization models offer two particularly important insights to life event perspectives. First, although life event models typically include both social and individual resources, relatively more emphasis is placed upon individual factors. Moreover, to the extent that social factors are recognized, socialization experiences that can prepare the individual for successful negotiation of a transition have been notably absent in previous life event studies. Second, adult socialization models offer life event scholars a concept of the adult life cycle as a sequence of normatively governed, role-related transitions. Appropriate attention to the normative aspects of life events, including expectations about the timing of events, can help life event students understand the conditions under which changes are and are not experienced as personal crises. Conversely, life event perspectives help to flesh out adult socialization models in two important ways.

First, adult socialization models focus so narrowly upon socialization as the mechanism of interest that the importance of other social factors is understated. We might hypothesize, for example, that a given role transition will be facilitated by the availability of a social support network, regardless of the extent to which the individual also has been exposed to socialization experiences. Second, interactionist life event scholars would suggest that increased attention be paid to the importance of subjective factors in negotiating role transitions. Perceptions of stress, the degree to which the role transition is perceived as positive or negative, and its perceived importance are issues derived from interactionist life event models that are relevant to understanding the impact of role transitions upon personal well-being.

DISCUSSION

The four types of models described are designed to provide a framework for understanding the causes and consequences of change during adulthood, and all four types make contributions toward that goal. Developmental models focus upon maturational processes and continued psychosocial growth across the life course. Life event models identify some of the major arenas of adult change and the individual and social factors that determine the conditions under which such changes do and do not increase the risk of negative personal outcomes. Adult socialization models remind us to pay attention to the normative aspects of adult change and the social mechanisms that prepare individuals to successfully negotiate those changes. It is possible—indeed likely

—that all three of these models are applicable to changes that occur in particular domains of adult experience. Thus some changes characteristic of middle and late life may be understood within a single perspective. Other changes, however, may be better understood by considering the insights and emphases of multiple perspectives. Integrated models that incorporate elements of more than one orientation are designed to serve this purpose.

There are two issues that I view as essential to any useful model of change during adulthood: (1) recognition of both social and individual factors that affect the occurrence and implications of change, and (2) an emphasis upon understanding the circumstances that account for differential outcomes resulting from change. Both these issues were previously mentioned, but they merit reiteration.

First, the most useful models are those that strike an appropriate balance between individual and social factors. Some changes during adulthood represent the culmination of intense individual efforts to bring about that change; other changes occur in spite of avoidance efforts. Even in cases where change is imposed—or at least is not actively sought—individuals can and do respond to change in very different ways. The meaning attributed to transitions varies widely across individuals. Some people cope more effectively than others and, regardless of coping efficacy, preferred coping modes differ across persons. All of these individual factors are essential in understanding the causes and consequences of change during adulthood. Attention to individual factors must be accompanied by awareness of social factors. Social resources affect the likelihood of experiencing a given transition, the meaning attached to the transition, and the impact of the transition on personal well-being. Many of the changes characteristic of adulthood are normatively governed, affecting the meaning and impact of the change. Finally, socialization experiences, when available, prepare individuals to successfully negotiate transitions. In essence, socialization is a mechanism for teaching individuals effective coping behavior. Thus there is no purpose to be gained in debates about the importance of social versus individual factors; both perspectives are crucial, and overly narrow disciplinary allegiances will only limit our understanding of the complex nature of change during adulthood.

Second, although the study of change during adulthood remains in its relative infancy, it already is obvious that attempts to characterize change as positive or negative are overly simplistic. Adult life is too complex for such declarations. There are conditions under which change is beneficial for individuals; conversely, there are conditions under which change is detrimental. An important agenda for the future is identifying the factors that lead to these varying outcomes and eventually, perhaps, developing interventions that can help to decrease the incidence of adaptive problems that result from change.

ANNALS, *AAPSS*, **464**, November 1982

Family Life in Middle and Old Age: The Generation Gap

By LILLIAN E. TROLL

ABSTRACT: Until recently, social scientists have paid more attention to parent-child relations at the early end of the age continuum: young children and their young-adult parents. Many of the same issues and approaches can be applied to the parallel study of parent-child relations at the later end of the age continuum, adults and their parents, and people in early old age and their parents. Generation gaps may be of the same order of magnitude, whether this term refers to value differences or to conflicts. Helping and communication patterns can be examined at both age poles, as can attitudes and feelings. The issue of geographic closeness does not usually apply to minor children who reside in the same place as their parents, but is a salient issue in later years.

Lillian E. Troll is a professor II of psychology at Rutgers—the State University in New Brunswick. Her major research interests are generations in the family and life-span development. She is the author of numerous articles and book chapters on these subjects and of the following books: Early and Middle Adulthood; Looking Ahead: The Problems and Joys of Growing Older *(with Joan Israel and Kenneth Israel);* Perspectives on Counseling Adults *(with Nancy Schlossberg and Zandy Liebowitz);* Families of Later Life *(with Robert Atchley and Sheila Miller); and* Continuations.

IN later life, as in earlier life, family relations are different for men and women. Most older men's family linkages are couple-based. They tend to have married women younger than they, to have had less chance of outliving their first wife because of differential life expectancy, and to have many options for remarrying if they are widowed or divorced. These same factors operate to make most older women's family relations cross-generational, or chains of parent-child linkages. G. Hagestad uses the term the "alpha-omega chain" to designate such a vertical system.[1] Her model shows possible hypothetical consequents of position along the chain. For example, in four-generation families—not uncommon today—members of the middle generations, the grandparents and the parents of the youngest generation, have multiple generational linkages in both directions. They are simultaneously parents and children. Members of the end generations, on the other hand, the great-grandparents and the great-grandchildren, are linked only at one end, downward to children or upward to parents, respectively.

Until recently, it has been the alpha, or beginning-of-life part of the chain that has been of most interest to social scientists, who studied relationships between children and their young-adult parents, or, less frequently, between adolescents and their middle-aged parents. Thinking about older generations, the omega end of the chain, has been from a nonfamily perspective—focusing on individuals rather than on relationships. Occasionally we examine care-giving functions performed upon the omega generation by the next generation down. This is usually not from a relationship perspective, since adult children are seen as acting upon their parents in a unidirectional way.

More and more Americans are entering later-life generational positions and while the appeal of youth remains prepotent, older citizens move toward center stage. There is increasing evidence that relations among parents and their offspring remain important to both generations throughout their lives—and even beyond the life of the oldest generation, if we consider influence and feelings.[2] There is less abundant evidence, but nevertheless a suggestion, that the kind of reciprocal influences between generations that can be seen among alpha-end generations[3] can also be found among omega-end generations. Offspring continue to learn from their parents so long as their parents live, and parents also continue to learn from their offspring.

Parent-child relations in later life have been measured in several ways: geographic closeness, help, communication, and feelings. Data on geographic closeness and help are more ample and substantive than those on communication and feelings, in part because of prevailing perceptions of the old as relatively passive recipients of care.

1. G. Hagestad, "Parent and Child," in *Human Development*, ed. T. Field (New York: John Wiley, 1982).

2. L. E. Troll, S. Miller, and R. Atchley, *Families of Later Life* (Belmont, CA: Wadsworth, 1978); L. E. Troll, *Continuations: Adult Development and Aging* (Belmont, CA: Wadsworth, 1982).

3. L. E. Troll, V. L. Bengtson, and D. McFarland, "Generations in the Family," in *Contemporary Theories about the Family*, eds. W. Burr, R. Hill, Ivan Nye, and I. Reiss (New York: Free Press, 1979), pp. 127-61.

PARENT-CHILD RELATIONS

The generation gap has surfaced historically as an important issue in times of social change, as it did most recently in the late 1960s. There were presumed to be sharp cleavages in values and styles of life, particularly between youth and their elders.[4] The same cleavages are sometimes also seen as applying to the middle-aged and aged. V. L. Bengtson and J. A. Kuypers[5] described three positions on this issue: "great gap," "nothing really new," and "selective continuity." As research accumulates, the last position seems most correct, not only for the alpha-end generations, but also for the omega-end ones.

Three-generational research, such as studies conducted in various parts of the United States and Canada,[6] suggests that there are impor-

tant ties among members of all generations throughout life. The gap may be wider when one family generation—usually at the time of late adolescence—adapts value and life-style components of its "family theme" to create a new "cohort theme."[7] Cohort themes typically include elements that are in tune with current trends in the larger society, and it is in these elements that differences between youth and their parents are most noticeable. Differences between older generations are more likely to reflect societal changes occurring at the time when the younger of such generational pairs was approaching adulthood. For example, generations will differ in values or characteristics that were salient at the time the younger was in late adolescence. In present-day omega-level generations, this contrast may be seen in differential stress upon independence as opposed to familism, as will be noted later. In the Minneapolis study of Hill and his colleagues,[8] the difference in child-

4. Troll, Bengtson, and McFarland, "Generations in the Family," pp. 127-61; L. E. Troll and V. L. Bengtson, "Intergenerational Relations through the Life Span," in *Handbook of Developmental Psychology*, ed. B. Wolman (Englewood Cliffs, NJ: Prentice-Hall, 1982).

5. V. L. Bengtson and J. A. Kuypers, "Generational Difference and the Generational Stake," *Aging and Human Development*, 2:249-60 (1971).

6. A. C. Acock and V. L. Bengtson, "On the Relative Influence of Mothers or Fathers: A Covariance Analysis of Political and Religious Socialization," *Journal of Marriage and the Family*, 40(3):519-30 (Aug. 1978); V. L. Bengtson, and D. Black, "Intergenerational Relations and Continuities in Socialization," in *Life-Span Developmental Psychology, Personality and Socialization*, eds. P. B. Baltes and K. W. Schaie (New York: Academic Press, 1973); V. L. Bengtson, E. Olander, and E. Haddad, "The Generation Gap and Aging Family Members: Toward a Conceptual Model," in *Time, Roles and Self in Old Age*, ed. J. F. Gubrium (New York: Human Science Press, 1976); G. Hagestad, B. B. Cohler and B. L. Neugarten, *The Vertical Bond: Relations among Three Generations in Urban Families* (in preparation); R. Hill, J.

Foote, J. Aldous, R. Carlson, and R. N. Macdonald, *Family Development in Three Generations* (Cambridge, MA: Schenkman, 1970); V. W. Marshall, C. J. Rosenthal, and J. Synge, "The Family as a Health Service Organization for the Elderly." Paper presented at the Annual Meeting of the Society for Study of Social Problems (Toronto, Aug. 1981); L. E. Troll, L. Burdman, and J. Stapley, "The Relation Between Extended Family Connectedness and Health and Happiness of the Oldest Generation" (Paper presented at Workshop, Life-Span and Change in a Gerontological Perspective, Nijmegen, The Netherlands, July 1981); L. E. Troll and J. Smith, "Three-Generation Lineage Changes in Cognitive Style and Value Traits" (Paper presented at the Gerontological Society Meeting, Puerto Rico, 1972).

7. Troll and Bengtson, "Intergenerational Relations through the Life Span."

8. Hill et al., *Family Development in Three Generations*.

rearing values between the oldest and the middle generation of adults was greater than between the middle and young-adult generations. The change in these values had occurred when the now middle-aged generations were young adults. The younger adult generation had focused on other, perhaps more materialistic, values—they came of age in the 1950s—and did not deviate much from their parents in child-rearing beliefs.

Hagestad[9] and Troll and Smith[10] address a different aspect of the generation gap issue. What is interesting is that gaps are in values and approaches to life. Further, gaps do not go together with confrontation and conflict. Rather, family discussions avoid incongruent issues; these issues become a "demilitarized zone," to use Hagestad's term. Bengtson and Kuypers[11] found that even when youth believed there was a generation gap between them and older members of the society, they did not see this gap as existing—at least in terms of conflict—between them and their own parents. Where parents and youth fought over issues, these were usually minor, not major, ones: hair grooming, not cohabitation or politics. We do not, unfortunately, have comparable data about generational conflict at the omega end of the generation chain. There is no reason to believe, however, that the same principle does not apply. For the sake of family integration, touchy issues are avoided.

Bengtson and Kuypers[12] use the term "generational stake" to refer to generational members' estimation of differences that do exist. Youth exaggerates these differences, presumably to enhance its emerging sense of identity. Parents minimize such differences, presumably to preserve their stake in the future. This can apply to old parents and their children as well as to young.[13] Old parents, feeling the end of their own life nearing and wanting to believe that the goals they fought for during their life will endure, tend to minimize the difference in values and characteristics between them and their children. Their offspring, still feeling there is time for them—they have the evidence of another generation living ahead of them—tend to emphasize their uniqueness more than their commonality with those who precede them.

Geographic closeness

Most studies have found that over 80 percent of present-day middle-aged and older people who have ever married—and the overwhelming majority of them have—are parents of living children. It is intriguing to realize that about 10 percent of those over age 65 also have children who are over 65.[14] These parents and children prefer, whenever possible, to live in their own homes but near

9. G. Hagestad, "Problems and Promises in the Social Psychology of Intergenerational Relations," in *Stability and Change in the Family*, eds. R. Fogel, E. Hatfield, S. Kiesler, and T. March (Annapolis, MD: National Research Council, 1979).

10. Troll and Smith, "Three-Generation Lineage Changes in Cognitive Style and Value Traits."

11. Bengtson and Kuypers, "Generational Difference and the Generational Stake."

12. Ibid.

13. Bengtson et al., "The Generation Gap and Aging Family Members."

14. E. Shanas, P. Townsend, D. Wedderburn, H. Friis, P. Milhkoj, and J. Stehouver, *Older People in Three Industrial Societies* (New York: Atherton, 1968); Troll, *Continuations*.

their children, and this is in fact what most of them do. Parents live with their offspring only if one or the other does not have enough money to live alone, if health is so poor that self-care is impossible, or, rarely, if they are widowed or divorced. Where the two oldest generations do live in the same household, the younger is likely to be an unmarried child, and a daughter. Furthermore, the home is likely to be the parent's rather than the child's; unmarried sons or daughters move in with their parents rather than the other way around. These multigeneration households, incidentally, are two- rather than three-generational units; only eight percent of American households are truly three-generational, with grandchildren in them.

Although the two oldest generations do not customarily live under the same roof, they do tend to live near each other, particularly among urban working-class families.[15] More than 80 percent of people over 65 who have children live less than an hour away from at least one of their children. Geographical distance between generations may vary more or less systematically with the periods in the life course of the family members. It may be greatest when offspring are beginning their own households and their parents are involved with jobs and community activities. It may decrease after the youth become parents themselves or the older generations retire from jobs, become more isolated from nonfamily connections, or need help. This pattern may apply more to middle-class families than to those of the working

class who, as noted previously, tend to live near each other.[16]

Help

A number of surveys show that the flow of support between generations in the family is multidirectional rather than primarily from middle-aged to old.[17] In the Minneapolis study referred to earlier, help was specific, not generalized, and all three generations both gave and received (Table 1). Overall, as would be expected, the middle generation usually gave the most and the oldest generation usually received the most, and the eldest also received more than it gave. Care is often a hidden resource rather than obvious and continuous. When old family members—or any others—need a great deal of help, most of such help is provided by family members,[18] most often a wife for a man and a daughter for a woman.

Communication

Living nearby need not mean frequent or meaningful communication; old people who live with children can complain the most about loneliness. Contrariwise, living at a distance need not mean absence of communication; letters, long-distance telephone calls, and longer visits can make up for infrequency of visiting. Most omega-end generational communication,

15. Ibid.

16. Troll et al., *Families of Later Life.*

17. Hill et al., *Family Development in Three Generations;* Shanas et al., *Older People in Three Industrial Societies;* G. Streib, "Intergenerational Relations: Perspectives of the Two Generations on the Older Parent," *Journal of Marriage and the Family,* 27(4):469-76 (Nov. 1965).

18. Troll et al., *Families of Later Life.*

TABLE 1
COMPARISON OF HELP RECEIVED AND HELP GIVEN BY GENERATION FOR CHIEF PROBLEM AREAS, IN PERCENTAGES

	TYPE OF CRISIS											
	ECONOMIC		CHILD CARE		ILLNESS		EMOTIONAL GRATIFICATION		HOUSEHOLD MANAGEMENT	
	GAVE	RECEIVED	GAVE	RECEIVED	GAVE	RECEIVED	GAVE	RECEIVED	GAVE	RECEIVED
Grandparents	26	34	16	0	32	61	23	42	21	52
Parents	41	17	50	23	21	21	47	37	47	23
Married children	34	49	34	78	47	18	31	21	33	25
Total	100	100	100	100	100	100	100	100	100	100

SOURCE: Hill et al., *Family development in Three Generations* (Cambridge, MA.: Schenkman, 1970), Table 21.4.
NOTE: Percentages may not total 100 because of rounding.

43

however, is frequent. In a large-scale study of old people in three industrialized countries: the United States, England, and Denmark,[19] over 80 percent had seen at least one of their children within the previous week and 90 percent within the month. Of course, such visits may only be a brief monitoring or catching up. But they may also include shopping, recreation, and religious activities. Telephone conversations may be constant even when visiting is frequent. The communication linkage, like the residential linkage, is generally stronger along the female line. Many men count on their wives to keep them in touch with their children and parents, and the loss of a wife can almost sever family communication for older men. An exception to this may be the grandfather-son-grandson linkage,[20] which seems to possess more psychological significance than other chains starting with a man. It is still statistically less frequent than the grandmother-daughter-granddaughter chain, because of differential age at birth of children and differential longevity.

Feelings

The previous discussion of the generation gap noted that there was both cross-generational value similarity—family themes—and avoidance of open conflict on important issues. Feelings between parents and children who have been in close communication for 50 or more years are predictably complex. Where love is to be found, so is hate. In some cases duty and obligation may override hate or may substitute for weaker feelings. There is probably an ebb and flow; close feelings

may accompany anniversaries and times when things are going well, but feelings of being overburdened and their accompanying hostility may result from the excessive demands of illness or economic difficulty. B. B. Hess and J. M. Waring say that "[although] years of separate residence and greater self-knowledge may erase some of the minor difficulties and blunt the edge of some of the major ones, struggles for control, patterns of blaming, disappointments about achievement and such, may linger to undermine the possibility of a comfortable relationship between parents and children in the later years."[21]

Times of crisis or transition can reawaken conflict. One might say that there is a continual push and pull of attachment throughout life. Most middle-aged and older parents—and their children—admit that they prefer intimacy at a distance. Their feelings of closeness carry with them a need for some separateness. Both old parents and their middle-aged children report high levels of regard for each other.[22] When adults of all ages were asked to describe a person—any person—the majority, even those in their 70s and 80s whose parents were presumably no longer living, spontaneously referred to their parents.[23] A Boston study[24] found a sig-

21. B. B. Hess and J. M. Waring, "Parent and Child in Later Life: Rethinking the Relationship," in *Child Influences in Marital and Family Interaction*, eds. R. Lerner and G. Spanier (New York: Academic Press, 1978).
22. Bengtson and Black, "Intergenerational Relations and Continuities in Socialization."
23. L. E. Troll, "The Salience of Members of 3-Generation Families for Each Other" (Paper presented at the American Psychological Association Meeting, Honolulu, 1972).
24. E. S. Johnson and B. Bursk, "Relationships between the Elderly and their Adult

19. Shanas et al., *Older People in Three Industrial Societies.*
20. Hagestad, "Parent and Child."

nificant correlation between ratings provided by older parents regarding their relationship and the rating of that relationship by one of their adult children. Both generations felt better about each other when they were in good health and able to be financially independent. Whether the good feelings were engendered by fewer problems or whether they induced better health and well-being, it is not possible to say.

Adult children who had placed their parents in nursing homes felt strained, guilty, and bereaved.[25] Such a decision represents a state of crisis[26] and reawakens many old issues. One of the issues around caregiving in old age, in fact, is the designation of which sibling becomes the one to give such help. It is not uncommon for the one who has been least loved by the parent to emerge as the caretaker, perhaps in a last attempt to try for that love, even at the cost of much sacrifice. Recent studies of caretakers and their parents—mostly women in both cases—show that daughters are more likely to assume that burden and are less upset by doing so than their mothers are by needing to be helped.[27] The values of independence so deeply ingrained in the oldest generations run counter to realistic needs for help. Further, women are socialized to give help, not to receive it. This may be one of the factors in the generally benign attitude toward older men as compared with the generally negative one toward older women.[28] R. Kulys and S. S. Tobin[29] found that while old—over 70—Chicago parents wanted more emotional closeness with their children, their children would rather perform instrumental tasks. The offspring believed that their parents did not understand them, but believed that they understood their parents. There was not very high agreement between generations on such issues as closeness, willingness to sacrifice, and giving help or advice. It is obviously easier to feel close to parents who are not in need. In fact, the very emotional nature of many parent-child relationships may not make children the best caretakers of their parents.

CONCLUSION

In general, parent-child relations are continuations of their relations at younger ages. The strong pull of family feeling induces careful avoidance of difficult issues that might cause conflict. Conflict is not absent, but is restricted to issues that will not sever relations. Most parents who disapprove of important aspects of their children's behavior carp instead about the way they dress or clean their house; they do

Children," *The Gerontologist*, 17(1):90-96 (1977).

25. R. Dobrof and E. Litwak, *Maintenance of Family Ties of Long-Term Care Patients: Theory and Guide to Practice* (Washington, DC: Government Printing Office, 1977).

26. S. Tobin and R. Kulys, "The Family and Services," in *Annual Review of Gerontology and Geriatrics*, ed. C. Eisdorfer (New York: Springer, 1979).

27. L. E. Troll, "Lineage Affect Similarity and Health of Older Family Members" (Paper presented at the Gerontological Society Symposium, Toronto, 1981); Marshall et al., "The Family as a Health Service Organization."

28. L. E. Troll and B. G. Turner, "Sex Differences in Problems of Aging," in *Gender and Disordered Behavior: Sex Differences in Psychpathology* (New York: Brunner/Mazel, 1979).

29. R. Kulys and S. S. Tobin, "The Older Person's Responsible Other: Child vs. Non-Child" (Paper presented at the Gerontological Society Meeting, 1978).

not emphasize errors in marriage or career. Most adult children who are annoyed by values or life-style of their parents criticize them for spoiling the grandchildren or fussing about cleanliness, not about things they hold sacred. Each generation may complain to friends—even to survey interviewers—about their more central angers concerning each other, but ties must not be broken.

Not all parent-child relationships in old age are happy. Most are complex mixtures of anger and love, need for closeness and need for distance. When health deteriorates and money is scarce, however, duty and obligation override other feelings and responsibility for parents falls mostly upon their children. This is true more for old women, of course, who are likely to be without a husband. Old men's care is primarily in the hands of their—younger—wives.

ANNALS, *AAPSS*, **464**, November 1982

Men at Middle Age:
Developmental Transitions

By LOIS M. TAMIR

ABSTRACT: The transition to middle age can simultaneously be a time of peak performance and a time of psychological setbacks in the lives of men. In the process of preparing for the second half of life, the man must deal with health issues, his imminent death, self-assessment, his sex role, and his responsibilities to future generations. The working through of these tasks is reflected in the work, family, and social lives of men at this stage. At the work place the man must either accept his failure to achieve his long-term goals or he must decide if having reached his goals has been worth the effort. Many men, as a result, disengage from the work place as their major source of personal fulfillment. On the other hand, interpersonal relations begin to come to prominence at the middle-age transition. The marital bond and sense of social connectedness felt by the individual become more integrally related to personal well-being at this time. The policy makers and corporate enterprises so entwined in the lives and well-being of men need to take into account these issues of middle age in order to ease the transition and to avoid the necessity of making a painful choice between occupational and interpersonal fulfillment.

Lois M. Tamir received her B.A. (summa cum laude) in sociology from SUNY at Stony Brook in 1974, and her Ph.D. in developmental psychology from the University of Michigan in 1980. She worked from 1978-80 at the University of Michigan's Institute for Social Research as a research fellow. Currently, she is clinical assistant professor of psychiatry at the University of Texas Health Science Center at Dallas, and is adjunct assistant professor of psychology and human development at the University of Texas at Dallas. She has published research in the areas of interpersonal communication, the family life cycle, middle age, and old age from the perspective of life span developmental psychology.

NOTE: The author would like to thank Beverly Bonnheim for her helpful comments on the article.

47

MOST of us, regardless of education or profession, would probably agree that the middle-aged adult is at the apex of life.[1] The middle-aged adult generally operates at his optimum level as he interacts with others, is at his peak earning capacity, and executes projects at his greatest level of efficiency. Why, then, has so much attention been paid to the so-called midlife crisis, a term now well ingrained in our vocabularies? I think an answer lies in the fact that the peak of life often stimulates a period of self-assessment. One cannot remain at a peak forever, but must prepare to face a downhill journey, or perhaps a walk along a plateau. This article examines the tasks confronted by men at middle age by virtue of this psychological state of affairs, tasks that are part of a natural developmental progression. It also takes a look at how these tasks are handled in three central spheres of life: work, family, and social relationships.

TASKS OF TRANSITION

The period in which this developmental dilemma comes to the forefront of the man's life appears to be the time in which he makes his transition to middle-aged status. For most men this transition occurs when they are in their forties.

1. See, for example, J. E. Birren, "Toward an Experimental Psychology of Aging," *American Psychologist*, 25:124-35 (1970); L. B. Bourque and K. W. Back, "The Middle Years Seen through the Life Graph," *Sociological Symposium*, 3:19-29 (Fall 1969); P. Cameron, "The Generation Gap: Which Generation is Believed Powerful versus Generational Members' Self-Appraisals of Power," *Developmental Psychology*, 3:403-4 (May 1970); and B. L. Neugarten, "The Awareness of Middle Age," in *Middle Age and Aging*, ed. B. L. Neugarten (Chicago: University of Chicago Press, 1968). pp. 93-98.

Although scholars of life-span development are often loath to pinpoint even approximate ages for developmental phenomena, the literature suggests that men in their 40s experience significant personal transition, crisis, or simply a heightened awareness of themselves.[2, 3] On a more dramatic level, clinical studies reveal that this population has a significant increase in mental health problems, including depression, alcoholism, and suicide.[4] Whether dramatic or subtle, however, most studies that range over the span of adulthood display something atypical among middle-aged men, whether a blip in a curve, a deviation from the norm, or a qualitative transformation.

The problems a man confronts as he enters middle age are many and

2. See, for example, C. G. Jung, *Modern Man in Search of a Soul* (New York: Harcourt Brace Jovanovich, 1933), who talks about the "afternoon of life" at age 40; B. Fried, *The Middle-Age Crisis* (New York: Harper & Row, 1976), who calls the 40s "middlescence"; and other researchers such as D. J. Levinson, *The Seasons of a Man's Life* (New York: Knopf, 1978); and G. E. Vaillant, *Adaptation to Life* (Boston: Little, Brown, 1977), as well as E. Frenkel-Brunswik, "Adjustments and Reorientation in the Course of the Life Span," in *Middle Age and Aging*, ed. Neugarten, pp. 77-84, who, 50 years ago, talked about personality change among men in their 40s.

3. Note should be taken, however, that the higher the socioeconomic class, the later the onset of middle-age and old-age transitions.

4. See in *Modern Perspectives in the Psychiatry of Middle Age*, ed. J. G. Howells (New York: Brunner/Mazel, 1981); J. H. Boyd and M. M. Wasserman, "The Epidemiology of Psychiatric Disorders of Middle Age: Depression, Alcoholism, and Suicide," pp. 201-21; F. O. Henker, "Male Climacteric," pp. 304-12; and P. M. Mirkin and R. E. Meyer, "Alcoholism in Middle Age," pp. 251-65. Also see R. L. Meile, "Age and Sex Differences in Psychiatric Treatment," *Sociological Symposium*, 3:107-13 (Fall 1969).

varied, overt and covert. Overt changes include his children becoming teenagers and often leaving home soon after, his parents aging and possibly dying, and his job or profession becoming more limited in future options.[5] Covertly, it seems that lack of change may depress the man at middle age.[6] No longer is he the object of attention at momentous events, such as weddings, births, first homes, or outstanding promotions.

This peak of life is also plagued with insults to one's sense of well-being. My own research, which has examined the transition to middle age based on a recent national survey,[7] has documented this slump in a man's sense of well-being during his forties. Of interest is the fact that educational background seems an important criterion as to how a man deals with his move to middle age. College-educated men were more depressed, displayed more symptoms of psychological immobilization, had more drinking problems, and more readily turned to drugs to relieve nervous tension, although,

surprisingly, their self-esteem remained intact. In contrast, men with a high school education or less were more likely to plummet only in the area of self-esteem. It is important to note that all these symptoms were limited to a very small age range, namely, men aged 45-49, a startling result considering that they were compared with men ranging the entire lifespan.

In light of the research to date, it appears that there is an air of discontent seeping into the lives of men at this time, but a discontent that need not be indicative of a full-blown crisis. Instead, it is likely that a period of introspection has begun and has taken a different form in accord with educational background.

This sense of introspection appears to be firmly anchored in the psychological tasks specific to middle age, and in particular to men at this time. These tasks fall under five major headings: health, mortality, self-assessment, sex role, and generativity.

Health

Middle-aged men do not suddenly experience ill health, but the symptoms of physical decline, which had begun perhaps a decade earlier, begin to reveal themselves. The body becomes less reliable and predictable as arteriosclerosis develops, fat deposits appear, arthritis threatens, and testosterone production diminishes, to name just a few physical alterations.[8] Even if these symptoms are minor, it is at this point that men begin to react more emotionally to physical changes.

5. See, for example, D. C. Borland, "Research on Middle Age: An Assessment," *The Gerontologist*, 18:379-86 (Aug. 1978); S. D. Rosenberg and M. P. Farrell, "Identity and Crisis in Middle Aged Men," *International Journal of Aging and Human Development*, 7(2):153-70 (1976).

6. J. M. Bardwick, "Middle Age and a Sense of Future," *Merrill-Palmer Quarterly*, 24(2):129-38 (1978).

7. L. M. Tamir, *Men in Their Forties: The Transition to Middle Age* (New York: Springer, 1982). The total sample from this national survey study included 551 men aged 25-69 years who were married and had children, 133 of whom were in the age range of 40-49 years. For a full report concerning the national survey itself see: J. Veroff, E. Douvan, and R. A. Kulka, *The Inner American*, or J. Veroff, R. A. Kulka, and E. Douvan, *Mental Health in America* (New York: Basic Books, 1981).

8. Henker, "Male Climacteric," pp. 304-12.

Accordingly, their wives are known to monitor their husbands' bodies more closely than their own.[9]

Mortality

Highly related to the issue of health is the issue of mortality, for at middle age the man becomes painfully aware that he has lived perhaps half his lifetime. Bernice Neugarten best describes this phenomenon as a switch in focus from "time since birth" to "time left to live."[10] Elliott Jaques[11] has written most explicitly of the middle-aged man's coming to grips with his mortality, and he believes that this struggle defines middle age. Mortality, however, is not the only issue of middle age—the tasks of self-assessment, sex roles, and generativity are also powerful stimuli to personal change at the midlife transition. Nevertheless, these three tasks are integrally related to the tasks of accepting mortality, since that in itself can force the individual to confront internal psychological issues. The middle-aged man must make peace with himself in order to comfortably survive the remaining future.

Self-assessment

Self-assessment, in contrast to mortality, is possibly the most integral task of middle age. It involves a process of examining one's individual life and one's place in the wider social environment.[12] Self-assessment also involves coming to terms with life's contradictions. During youth and young adulthood the individual, working toward specific life goals, typically relies on principles outlined in black and white. By middle age, however, the wisdom of experience allows the individual to recognize shades of gray and the multiple factors that sway the decision-making process and goal attainment. It is at this point that contradictions are recognized, not with outrage, but with acceptance, and according to the research by Daniel Levinson, life's polarities are reintegrated.[13] The psychologist Klaus Riegel[14] has described this stage as the highest level of cognitive functioning: dialectical thought.

Sex role

One of the great polarities is the masculine/feminine dichotomy. Much research has documented the reintegration of masculine and feminine traits at middle age.[15]

9. B. L. Neugarten and N. Datan, "The Middle Years," in *American Handbook of Psychiatry*, ed. S. Arieti (New York: Basic Books, 1974), pp. 592-608.

10. Neugarten, "The Awareness of Middle Age," pp. 93-98.

11. E. Jaques, "Death and the Mid-Life Crisis," *International Journal of Psychoanalysis*, 46:502-14 (1965).

12. Neugarten, "The Awareness of Middle Age," labels this process "interiority," pp. 93-98.

13. Levinson, in *The Seasons of a Man's Life*, identifies the major polar concepts as young/old, destruction/creation, attachment/separateness, and masculine/feminine.

14. K. F. Riegel, "Dialectic Operations: The Final Period of Cognitive Development," *Human Development*, 16:346-70 (1973).

15. See, for example, D. Gutmann, "Parenthood: A Key to the Comparative Study of the Life Cycle," in *Life-Span Developmental Psychology: Normative Life Crisis*, (New York: Academic Press, 1975); pp. 167-84. Jung, *Modern Man in search of a Soul*; Levinson, *The Seasons of a Man's Life*; B. L. Neugarten and D. L. Gutmann, "Age-Sex Roles and Personality in Middle Age: A Thematic Apperception Study," in *Middle Age and Aging*, pp. 68-71.

While women become more assertive and independent, men become more sensitive and nurturant. There are many possible reasons for this reintegration, in addition to the internal reworking of polarities just discussed. It may be that at this point the man takes stock of all the sacrifices he has had to make in order to maintain a strong masculine image, including enduring the stress of his job, and sacrifices in his interpersonal life and his relationships with his children. He may attempt to remedy the situation by developing a more well-rounded personality. It has been suggested, in fact, that all personality traits either previously submerged or not allowed to develop now begin to make their appearance in the transition to middle age.[16]

Generativity

The final psychological task of middle age involves taking responsibility for future generations, be they one's own offspring or protégés, or a less tangible, more abstract group of younger adults. This means offering guidance and developing a personal legacy that will leave an imprint upon the future cohorts. Erik Erikson[17] writes most cogently of this task, labeling it a crisis of "generativity versus stagnation or self-absorption." If the adult in transition can successfully work through the tasks of middle age, he is free to

contribute to others. If not, he will tend to stagnate, being more absorbed in himself than in what he can do for others.

WORK, FAMILY, AND SOCIAL RELATIONSHIPS

Given these basic psychological tasks faced by men in the transition to middle age, it is useful to examine their repercussions at work, in the family, and with social relationships —three spheres of living upon which personal quality of life is highly contingent.

Work

Perhaps no other role is more integral to the identity of the male than the work role. Not only is work a source of income and sustenance for the man and his family but it is also the clock by which the man assesses life's achievements as to whether they are on time, successfully early, disappointingly late, or woefully not forthcoming. And it is in the work environment that the man becomes most aware when he has reached his peak: most typically at middle age.

Usually by middle age the male worker, be he blue collar, white collar, or professional, has reached a plateau. At best, a lateral shift in occupational position will occur.[18] This tangible work situation in itself may stimulate self-assessment at middle age, for the man must psychologically maneuver himself out of a difficult no-win situation: if he

16. Preliminary research cited in S. Cytrynbaum et al., "Midlife Development: A Personality and Social Systems Perspective," in *Aging in the 1980's*, ed. L. W. Poon (Washington, DC: APA, 1980), pp. 463-74.

17. E. Erikson, *Childhood and Society* (New York: Norton, 1950); also, "Adulthood and World Views" (Unpublished paper prepared for Conference on Love and Work in Adulthood, American Academy of Arts and Sciences, Palo Alto, CA, May 1977).

18. A. J. Jaffe, "The Middle Years: Neither Too Young Nor Too Old," Special Issue of *Industrial Gerontology*, Washington, DC: National Council on Aging, 1971, writes most thoroughly about this process. It should also be noted that blue-collar workers peak earlier than white collar.

has not achieved the success he has worked toward all his life, he will be terribly disappointed; if he has achieved what he has set out to do, he must assess whether it is actually all that wonderful, and where he should go from that point.

Research on how middle-aged men deal with this situation is mixed. While some researchers imply a sense of resignation from the work environment and a distancing from the cutthroat race for promotion,[19] others suggest a period of overinvolvement with work in terms of time and quantity.[20] Part of this overinvolvement may actually be because retirement is nearing and financial security becomes a key to future survival, in particular for the lower-middle- and working-class populations.[21] The national survey research referred to earlier indicates the former pattern of resignation during one's 40s. As in the results described earlier, the patterns differ somewhat for college- and noncollege-educated men. In assessing the relationship between work and well-being, it was found that only during the 40s did work bear no relationship to well-being. Men at this stage could be thriving on the job, yet dissatisfied with life or, on the opposite end, unhappy with the work situation, but generally satisfied with their lives. At all other ages men's work satisfaction was highly and significantly related to their sense of well-being. This surprising result appears to be a key indicator of some sort of disengagement from the work environment by middle-aged men, for work had little bearing upon their psychological well-being at this precarious time in life, especially in comparison with their earlier years.

These survey results are far from isolated. The *Wall Street Journal*[22] recently reported that managers from AT&T who were followed for 20 years displayed a significant drop in desire for advancement when they reached their 40s. No longer was their happiness correlated with work success.

Of interest with regard to the work environment are concerns with interpersonal relationships on the job. For colleged-educated men, the national survey revealed that only at the middle-age transition, the 40s, was the opportunity to talk with others at work highly and significantly related to job satisfaction when compared with older and younger men. If, in fact, there is a degree of job disengagement at this time, the interpersonal aspect of work is considered an important feature of work satisfaction. Perhaps the interpersonal side of work involves the emergence of the mentor-protégé relationship that Daniel Levinson found in his research of men at middle age. Becoming a mentor certainly provides an excellent vehicle for accomplishing the task of generativity so crucial to a successful middle-age transition.

19. See, for example, J. A. Clausen, "Glimpses Into the Social World of Middle Age," *International Journal of Aging and Human Development*, 7:99-106 (1976).

20. See, for example, J. M. Bardwick, "Middle Age and a Sense of Future;" and C. L. Cooper, "Middle-Aged Men and the Pressures of Work," pp. 90-102 in *Modern Perspectives in the Psychiatry of Middle Age*, ed. J. G. Howells (New York: Brunner/Mazel, 1981).

21. M. F. Lowenthal, M. Thurher, and D. Chiriboga, *Four Stages of Life* (San Francisco: Jossey-Bass, 1975).

22. *Wall Street Journal*, Labor Letter section, Mar. 16, 1982.

Family

In light of the difficult psychological work confronted by middle-aged men, there are bound to be repercussions at home and in relationships with wives and children. Other family members, too, are likely to be in transition. Mothers are no longer nurturing small children and possibly are investigating new opportunities outside the home. Children are now teenagers seeking independence and freedom from parents. This situation makes for a complex interplay of interpersonal needs that are fulfilled or suppressed in the multiple relationships of family life.

It appears that during this time of transition, new terms are established for the relationship between husband and wife. Middle-aged spouses must shift their focus from a mutual concern with child care to a mutual concern with their own relationship, from roles of father-mother to roles of husband-wife. This shift of focus, of course, can either arouse interpersonal tension, since members of a strained relationship do not have their children as an outlet to divert attention from themselves, or it can solidify a relationship, allowing husband and wife further time to explore, rediscover, and enjoy one another. Indeed, Marjorie Lowenthal's research has indicated a more intense focus upon the man's role as husband than as father during the middle years.

It is not surprising to read in the clinical literature[23] that marriages that dissolve in middle age often do so as a result of underlying interpersonal problems that have existed from the beginning of the marriage. The presence of children can deflect these problems for quite a while, only to have the problems reemerge when the nest is emptied and husband and wife must face one another as separate persons once again.

The national survey study also reveals a striking pattern of results concerning the family lives of men in their 40s. Only men in their 40s viewed their adequacy as a father and adequacy as a husband as separate. Unlike men younger or older, this middle-aged group felt a psychological split between the two roles, perhaps because men at this age tend more to introspectively assess their lifetime roles. In turn, this split brings with it an emphasis, or rather reemphasis, upon the marital role.

This shift to the ever-increasing prominence of the marital role is displayed in the national study most clearly for men with a college education. Compared with older and younger men, the marital happiness of men in the 40s was most highly and significantly related to their psychological well-being. General happiness, life satisfaction, self-esteem and the presence or absence of depression and alcoholism were more strongly related to marital happiness in the 40s than at any other age. Similarly, the AT&T study revealed that managers began to replace the primacy of work with the primacy of family when they reached their 40s.

The finding that there is a strong interdependence between marital contentment and a sense of well-being is of particular interest in light of the fact that, for men in their

23. See, for example, H. J. Friedman, "The Divorced in Middle Age," in *Modern Perspectives in the Psychiatry of Middle Age*, ed. Howells, pp. 103-15.

40s, a sense of well-being is no longer contingent upon the work place. Apparently, for the middle-aged man, well-being takes an interpersonal turn, and he becomes more firmly embedded in his role as husband than in his occupational role, no matter how prestigious the latter.

Social relationships

The final major sphere likely to have an impact upon the quality of life at middle age is that of social relationships. Little is known about the social relationships of middle-aged men, or even about the social relationships of men at any age. Most psychological researchers simply concede that women maintain more intimate friendships with one another than do men. How men's friendships change through the life span is also unknown. Friendships can be especially important during times of stress. It is an area of living that merits more intensive investigation, especially with regard to transitional periods within the adult life span.

The little work done to date concerning the social relationships of men at middle age is highly contradictory. While some research indicates a renewed interest in friends and community,[24] other research indicates a lull in friendship relations and a shallowness of social ties at this time.[25] Perhaps this mixed set of results is because men at middle age represent a mixed set of individ-uals, some more socially oriented, some more withdrawn. Additionally, it is possible that many of the social relationships of men at this time are highly ambivalent. During a period of self-assessment comparisons of self with others can be discouraging and a blow to self-esteem, thus dampening what could otherwise be cohesive, supportive relationships with others.

A striking pattern of results concerning the social relationships of men in their 40s has emerged from the national survey study. The self-esteem of noncollege-educated men, presumed to be the more working-class segment of the population at large, seemed more highly related to their sense of social connectedness during their forties. Social connectedness includes a sense of feeling cared for, needed, and liked by others. Only at this transitional period in life does social connectedness relate so directly and strongly to self-esteem, a fragile personal characteristic at this time.

The social side of life seems to be a major contributor to a man's sense of well-being when he reaches middle age. Researchers of middle age[26] have shown an enhanced statistical relationship between social fulfillment and stress: those most socially active are least stressed; those most isolated are more subject to stress. Similarly, the men at middle age who feel distant from others are low in self-esteem. Men whose social connections are thriving maintain greater self-esteem.

The trade-off at transition

The findings relayed in this article fit together like puzzle pieces to

---

24. For example, R. L. Gould, "The Phases of Adult Life: A Study in Developmental Psychology," *American Journal of Psychiatry*, 129:521-31 (Nov. 1972); and A. Campbell, P. E. Converse, and W. L. Rodgers, *The Quality of American Life* (New York: Russell Sage, 1976).

25. For example, M. F. Lowenthal et al., *Four Stages of Life.*

26. M. F. Lowenthal and L. Weiss, "Intimacy and Crises in Adulthood," *The Counseling Psychologist*, 6(1):10-15 (1976).

form a clear and integrated pattern of the lives of men in transition to middle age. Foremost is the fact that men at this time are in the midst of reworking their lives. Well-being is altered as lives are evaluated at conscious and subconscious levels.

Work, family, and social relationships appear to be reshuffled in the process of transition. The trade-off is one between occupation and people, between objective accomplishment and interpersonal emotion. The work place is no longer as emotionally central, no matter how hard-working the man in his 40s appears. Instead it is the social side of work that sparks the interest of the middle-aged man, who perhaps is nurturing a protégé, or delegating responsibilities to others in the most efficient yet sensitive manner.

Differences emerge along educational lines in relation to the types of close ties men in their 40s hold with others. The well-educated man appears more reliant upon his wife than are men of more working-class backgrounds, to whom other interpersonal ties become more central. Although these interpersonal ties are not as defined as the marital tie, the marriage may very well be an integral component of a more amorphous sense of social connectedness. Further research is needed to clarify this speculation, for working-class men in particular have difficulty discussing personal issues.[27] The point remains, however, that nonmonetary social security holds the key to happiness at middle age for men of all levels of income and class.

POLICY IMPLICATIONS

The issues pertinent to the middle-age transition of men suggest a

27. L. B. Rubin, *Worlds of Pain* (New York: Basic Books, 1976).

number of recommendations to improve the quality of life for adults of both sexes, for a more well-balanced life for men brings with it a more well-balanced set of options for women as well. Policy makers, businesses, and counseling services would do well to promote a psychological sense of balance for men. This can be achieved by means of an educated awareness of the transitional issues of middle age: namely, the individual's reassessment and reintegration of work, family, and social roles.

Reassessment appears inevitably midway through life, simply because the individual must derive a satisfactory set of plans for the second half of life in light of the successes and failures reviewed from the first half. Just as much time has passed as there is time left to live. The pain of reassessment can be eased, however, if men are encouraged early on, that is, from their childhood years, to live more well-rounded and integrated lives.

The stress upon work, often to the exclusion of sufficient emotional investments in family relationships, needs to be modulated. Work offers the individual a tremendous source of personal accomplishment and financial security. On the other hand, over-investment in work can deplete the individual's life of a sustaining and rewarding series of interpersonal relationships with family and significant friends. It is important that men not allow their work to be all-consuming, lest they find themselves confused and disengaged when reaching the midpoint in life and have little or no emotional and social relationships.

Perhaps the most painful emotion of the middle-age transition is regret. Regrets, however, can be avoided if the individual has taken opportunities to fulfill himself in cognitive, physical, and interpersonal realms. Ideally, he must derive equal enjoyment from work and family, as well as from other enriching activities throughout his adulthood years. Middle age, as a stage in life where polarities and contradictory activities are contrasted, compared, and accepted, can be much more fulfilling if the individual need not sway from one extreme to the other—from labor to love, from macho to maternal, from youthful to aged, and vice versa. A well-modulated life can enable the man in transition to middle age to reap the rewards of his age, his experience, and his insights in beneficial ways.

This is not to say that crisis is bad. Grappling with contradiction, with polarities that pull the individual in opposing ways, is actually the means by which development is promoted. If there were no crises there would be little growing experience; however, crisis out of proportion is painful and often stifling. At all stages in life we must tread the fine line between forces that can bolster and those that can break down our psychological makeup. The man in transition to middle age treads one of the finer lines in this lifelong process. Social supports in work and in family lives can help him better maintain his balance.

ANNALS, *AAPSS*, **464**, November 1982

Women at Middle Age: Developmental Transitions

By ANGELA M. O'RAND and JOHN C. HENRETTA

ABSTRACT: The shapes of women's lives have changed over the twentieth century as a result of declining fertility, extended longevity, new life-styles in marriage and family formation, and increased attachment to the labor force. Midlife role transitions for women are diverse and dependent upon earlier life events related to marriage, child bearing, and work. Trends such as the postponement of marriage and child bearing, divorce and separation, and early career entry have changed the traditional family life cycle. Low fertility among women with patterns of early childbirth has led to an extended empty nest period and to increased labor participation at midlife. All these trends point to the continuities and discontinuities in individual women's lives and in the experiences of different age cohorts of women over time. The future prospects for today's middle-aged women are viewed in terms of both their predictable and variable features.

Angela M. O'Rand is assistant professor of sociology at Duke University. She is currently doing research on cohort variation in women's careers and retirement schedules.

John C. Henretta is associate professor of sociology at the University of Florida. His research focuses on retirement patterns of dual-worker couples and life course homeownership patterns.

AT the beginning of her study of women at midlife, Lillian Rubin contrasts a recently married career woman in her mid-30s about to have her first child with a nonworking wife of the same age whose youngest child is 15.[1] The comparison illustrates the range of family and work situations of women between 35 and 54 years of age. It also points to the distinctive transitions in midlife experienced by women.

The emergence of such studies over the last two decades has shed new light on the middle years of life. Indeed, it can be argued that new approaches to human development have not so much discovered as they have reconstructed middle age, resetting its boundaries and redefining its internal phases for particular groups. Notable in this regard are studies, like Rubin's, that have emphasized the problematic and unique aspects of midlife by referring to the predictable crises and developmental seasons of men and women of a certain age.[2]

These life stage dependent models of midlife role transitions have been appropriately characterized as normative-crisis approaches that tend to highlight age-dependent discontinuities and disjunctive episodes in individuals' lives.[3] Accordingly, Rubin's career-wife-soon-to-be-mother is considered as she faces the new problems of motherhood, joint work, and family responsibilities. Similarly, the woman whose youngest child is approaching adulthood must prepare herself for a new chapter in her family life, including an empty nest and greater freedom from nurturant obligations.

Another perspective on development in the middle years has focused on the continuities among the middle, earlier, and later life phases experienced by different age cohorts of men and women through time. These life course models are distinguished from the life stage dependent approaches by their emphasis on (1) lifetime trajectories of age-related role sequences, particularly in family and work domains; (2) the synchronization of life phases across major role domains; and (3) the birth cohort rather than the individual as the unit of change.[4] In this approach midlife transitions are viewed primarily as they are dependent on lifetime patterns of living and are altered by historical conditions. Accordingly, Rubin's career-wife-mother and her midlife counterpart are of interest as they represent different family and work role sequences that are evident within recent cohorts and whose prevalences vary across successive cohorts of women. As such, life course approaches emphasize the dependence of middle-age patterns on earlier pat-

1. Lillian B. Rubin, *Women of a Certain Age: The Midlife Search for Self* (New York: Harper & Row, 1979), pp. 7-8.

2. Gail Sheehy, *Passages: Predictable Crises of Adult Life* (New York: Dutton, 1976); Daniel J. Levinson, *The Seasons of a Man's Life* (New York: Knopf, 1978); and Rubin, *Women of a Certain Age.*

3. Alice S. Rossi, "Life Span Theories and Women's Lives," *Signs,* 6:4-32 (Autumn 1980).

4. Tamara K. Hareven, ed. *Transitions: The Family and the Life Course in Historical Perspective* (New York: Academic Press, 1978); Peter Uhlenberg, "Cohort Variations in Family Life Cycle Experiences of U.S. Females," *Journal of Marriage and the Family* 34:284-92 (May 1974); and Bernice L. Neugarten and Gunhild Hagestad, "Age and the Life Course," in *The Handbook of Aging and the Social Sciences,* eds. R. S. Binstock and E. Shanas (New York: Van Nostrand Reinhold, 1976), pp. 35-57.

terns and define change as cohort change.[5]

THE MAJOR CONTINGENCIES OF WOMEN'S LIVES

One of the most significant social trends in the twentieth century has been the changing work and family schedules of women across successive cohorts. Recent changes in fertility and in the ties between fertility and role transitions have been large.[6] Low fertility rates have come to be associated with the postponement of marriage, either early or delayed child bearing, patterns of divorce and remarriage, early labor force entry, and lifetime attachment to work among women. These related patterns form the framework that links early and midlife role transitions with the timing of early life events conditioning later opportunities and constraints. Rubin's career woman exemplifies the impact of early career commitment by women on the timing of marriage and childbearing.

Similarly, trends in longevity, in conjunction with low fertility, have reshaped the contours of midlife role sequences. For example, the empty nest period, that is, the period after the last child leaves home, has lengthened since 1900 from 2 to 15 years as a direct result of fertility and longevity changes.[7] Rubin's non-

working wife facing the empty nest period in her mid-30s typifies this trend. Low fertility, early child-bearing, and extended longevity present this woman with distinctive options and role transitions.

In short, changing conditions of fertility and mortality and shifting opportunity structures in family and work contexts have reshaped women's lives and yielded diverse midlife patterns. It is only within this dynamic framework that women in middle age can be understood.

Family transitions: the continuity of family life

Historically, the timing of life events for women has been tied to fertility. This pattern has led to the tendency "to equate the family life cycle with the female life cycle."[8] Since more than nine out of ten women over the age of 35 have been married, and nearly as many have had at least one child, marriage and child bearing have largely defined the schedules of their lives. But the contours of married life and child bearing have changed. Increased technological control of the fertility process and changing marital lifestyles have given rise to a wide range of midlife role constraints and opportunities for women.

First, the median age at first marriage has increased. Today, about one-fifth of all women aged 25 to 29 years are still single.[9] The chances are that these women will marry in the future, but the consequences of this pattern of postpone-

5. Norman B. Ryder, "The Cohort as a Concept in the Study of Social Change," *American Sociological Review*, 30:843-61 (1965); Mathilda W. Riley, Marilyn Johnson and Anne Foner, *Aging and Society*, vol. 3: *A Sociology of Age Stratification* (New York: Russell Sage, 1972).

6. Evelyn M. Kitagawa, "New Life Styles: Marriage Patterns, Living Arrangements, and Fertility Outside of Marrige," *The Annals* of the American Academy of Political and Social Science, 453:1-27 (Jan. 1981).

7. Peter Uhlenberg, "Changing Configurations of the Life Course," in *Transitions: The Family and the Life Course in Historical Perspective*, ed. Hareven.

8. Roxann A. Van Dusen and Eleanor B. Sheldon, "The Changing Status of American Women: A Life Cycle Perspective," *American Psychologist*, 31:107 (Feb. 1976).

9. Kitagawa, "New Life Styles," p. 5.

ment for middle age include increased childlessness, delayed first births, and single parenthood. Women who delay marriage and fertility can find themselves up against the reproductive clock in their mid-30s, forced to schedule child bearing soon after postponed marriage or to undertake the experience without marriage. Thus midlife may come to be crowded by tightly scheduled transitions to marriage and parenthood. Recent increases in first and second births to women between the ages of 25 and 34 are consistent with these patterns.[10] In a few instances the reproductive clock, at least insofar as the late 30s have come to be socially accepted as a reproductive deadline, may encourage the transition to parenthood without marriage. Finally, postponement of child bearing also means the postparental empty nest will be delayed.

A second trend of considerable magnitude in recent years has been the rise of single-parent households, particularly female-headed households. Of all families in 1979 15 percent were headed by single parents, with 90 percent of these headed by women. Female-headed families have grown 10 times faster than two-parent families during the past two decades. One major cause of these changes has been the long-term upward trend of divorce. As such, divorce has replaced widowhood as the basis for single-parent families in general, and female-headed households among younger and middle-aged women in particular.[11]

Of all first marriages that end in divorce, about one-fourth include

women aged 30 to 39 years.[12] Most divorces—about two-thirds—occur for women before the age of 29. Still, the rise in divorce for young and middle-aged women alike alters midlife options with respect to child bearing and subsequent remarriage. Remarriage within a short period following the divorce is the most likely event; however, as the years since divorce increase for older and more highly educated women in particular, the chances of remarriage decrease. Thus for the late-middle-aged woman the transition to single status because of divorce may signal a permanent family situation throughout later life.[13]

The more prevalent divorce and remarriage cycle gives rise to a pattern of serial marriage in the life course. Serial marriage probably influences child bearing in several ways. It can delay the birth of the first child for women who postpone childbirth in their first marriages. Second, for women with children born of their first marriages, the spacing of more children from subsequent marriages may delay the empty nest period. Third, serial marriage may lead to the loss of children through divorce settlements assigning child custody to fathers. The latter trend has significant implications for women of middle age.

Even if women do not postpone marriage and/or experience divorce, the declining size of families has lengthened the so-called empty nest

10. Ibid., p. 7.
11. Heather L. Ross and Isabel V. Sawhill, *Time of Transition: The Growth of Families Headed by Women* (Washington, DC: Urban Institute, 1976).

12. Arthur J. Norton and Paul C. Glick, "Marital Instability in America: Past, Present and Future," in *Single Life: Unmarried Adults in Social Context*, ed. P. J. Stein (New York: St. Martin's, 1981), pp. 57-67.
13. Paul C. Glick and Arthur J. Norton, "New Life Styles Change Family Statistics," *American Demographics*, 2:20 (May 1980).

period. This third trend leaves women, and couples in the majority of cases, with half their lives ahead of them after child rearing has ended. Whether the empty nest represents loss or freedom to middle-aged women and couples is a matter of considerable speculation.[14] Some studies have reported a U-shaped curve of marital satisfaction among couples, indicating that perhaps child rearing itself exerts the greatest stress on marriage and by implication on women, with earlier and later phases of the family life cycle being more satisfying.[15]

Similarly, recent changes in patterns of intergenerational dependency suggest that the empty nest does not mean the discontinuation of economic and social support of offspring. Indeed, recent middle-aged people are confronting intergenerational squeeze, a pattern of increased obligations to support both their parents and their children in various ways.[16] As children delay their own transitions to adulthood and parents confront the economic, health, and social exigencies of old age, the generation in the middle faces new midlife roles.

Work: the diversity of lifetime patterns

The three trends previously reviewed cannot be considered independently of another that has influenced the shape of women's lives. This is the increased labor force participation of successive cohorts of women during this century.[17] Women have increasingly entered the labor force earlier in their lives and have tended either to remain attached to the labor force throughout their lives or else to return to it after competing family-related responsibilities have been met.

Family role transitions have varied in their relationship to women's labor force patterns.[18] At any one time, approximately one-half of all wives are not in the labor force. But succeeding cohorts of women, including wives, increasingly enter and stay in the labor force even during child rearing years. A recent report on the nation's families by George Masnick and Mary Jo Bane graphically depicts this trend as a rising and disappearing M-curve distribution of labor participation across cohorts. The women born early in this century exhibit a clearly interrupted work pattern, with peaks before and after the reproductive ages spanning their 20s and early 30s and a drop in work during these years. Succeeding cohorts, however, are likely to enter the labor force earlier and in greater

14. Norval D. Glenn, "Psychological Well-Being in the Post-Parental Stage: Some Evidence from National Surveys," *Journal of Marriage and the Family*, 37:105-10 (Feb. 1975).

15. Boyd Rollins and Richard Galligan, "The Developing Child and Marital Satisfaction," in *Child Influences on Marital and Family Interaction: A Life Span Perspective*, eds. R. Lerner and G. Spenier (New York: Academic, 1978).

16. Rhona Rapoport, Robert Rapoport, Ziona Strelita and Stephen Kew, *Fathers, Mothers and Society: Towards New Alliances* (New York: Basic Books, 1977); Beth Hess and Joan Waring, "Parent and Child in Later Life: Rethinking the Relationship," in *Child Influences on Marital and Family Interaction*, eds. Lerner and Spenier, pp. 241-73.

17. Valerie K. Oppenheimer, *The Female Labor Force in the United States: Demographic and Economic Factors Governing its Growth and Changing Composition*, Population Monograph Series, no. 5 (Berkeley: University of California Press, 1970).

18. Glen Elder and Richard Rockwell, "Marital Timing in Women's Life Patterns," *Journal of Family History* 1:34-54 (Autumn 1976).

proportions and to remain in the labor force, thus the disappearing M-curve of increased participation.[19]

For mothers of young children much of this labor force activity is part-time and part-year. But whether wives are full-time workers or not, this trend has made two-worker families the norm rather than the exception. And on the heels of the two-worker family is the two-career family. In this regard Masnick and Bane refer to the "three revolutions" in women's work.[20] The first revolution in participation rates by women is completed. Underway is the second revolution that consists of women's increased attachment to careers. Following career attachment should come the revolution in women's contributions to family income.

Women with careers tend to exhibit the same achievement patterns as men, though at lower earnings and status levels.[21] That is, educational attainment, characteristics of first job, and patterns of accumulation of work-related attributes influence the directions of women's careers in the same way as they do those of men. However, the earnings and occupational statuses of women are below those of men. Clearly, the third revolution about which Masnick and Bane speculate is far from complete.

Since women display diverse career patterns, however, midlife transitions in the work context can vary. Women who have started early and maintained job career attachments throughout marriage are the most likely group to have delayed marriage and childbearing. Women who have interrupted their labor participation are less likely to have delayed child bearing or they display shorter delays in child bearing. And women who have never worked are most likely to have had children early. Lillian Rubin's two examples of middle-aged women referred to earlier in this article represent the first and third groups of women.

The middle-aged wife facing an empty nest and perhaps intergenerational squeeze may find herself in the labor market for the first time. Such delayed career entry has both its benefits and its costs. Its benefits include improved family income and the freedom to schedule work independently of the obligations of child rearing. Its costs stem from the fact that delayed career entry is off schedule in the accumulation of work-related attributes, such as experience, skill, tenure, and savings for retirement. Women who are late entrants into the labor force tend to be concentrated in lower-status jobs and in low-wage industries and may find it more difficult to retire early.[22] In short, the timing of career entry in midlife is related to limited occupational opportunities and, ultimately, to reduced retirement options.

Besides the issue of the timing of career events, the synchronization of careers among dual-worker couples can condition midlife choices. Occupational or career mobility is a characteristic of middle age. Career

19. George Masnick and Mary Jo Bane, *The Nation's Families: 1960-1990* (Cambridge, MA: Joint Center for Urban Studies of MIT and Harvard University, 1980).

20. Ibid., pp. 62-109.

21. Rachel Rosenfeld, "Women's Occupational Careers: Individual and Structural Explanations," *Sociology of Work and Occupations*, 6:4-35 (Aug. 1979).

22. Angela M. O'Rand and John C. Henretta, "Delayed Career Entry, Industrial Pension Structure and Retirement in a Cohort of Unmarried Women," *American Sociological Review*, 47 (1982).

ladders in firms and internal labor markets are traveled most heavily by young and middle-aged workers. For the working couple, career turning points or opportunities create special strains and require difficult decisions. The timing of children, of course, becomes an added contingency affecting these decisions.

One kind of midlife career decision can be to change careers. Second careers are increasing as a result of extended longevity and changing economic conditions. Another midlife career decision can be to change geographic location. Still another decision may involve early retirement, especially in later midlife career decisions among dual-decisions, rather than solely individual decisions. The coordination of midlife career decisions among dual worker couples is a family affair, constrained by earlier decisions and opportunities.

The timing of retirement by couples is especially interesting in this regard, since the trend toward early retirement since the 1950s has brought that decision to the boundaries of middle age. Recent studies of the joint retirement patterns of dual-worker couples suggest that couples may prefer to retire simultaneously. Women who are younger than their husbands, however, tend to work beyond their husband's retirement, often because these women are still working for pension eligibility or because of the family's need for her earned income. In all cases the joint retirement decision is contingent on earlier life patterns and decisions as well as on circumstances of economic need, pension vesting, or forced retirement.[23]

23. John C. Henretta and Angela M. O'Rand, "Labor Force Participation Patterns

FUTURE PROSPECTS FOR TODAY'S MIDDLE-AGED WOMEN

It is clear that family and work patterns are interwoven in women's lives. And while women's lives are quite diverse and difficult to force into easy categories, the dominant characteristic of today's middle-aged women can nevertheless be isolated. In this regard it is appropriate to return to the two women described by Rubin with whom we began.

These women exemplify the patterns of low fertility and extended—prospective—longevity of their generation. These patterns suggest that both women can expect to participate in the labor force during the second half of their lives. The career woman has a lifetime pattern of labor participation and commitment to a particular work ladder. She will not face the empty nest for another two decades or so, but she will face the problem of juggling the demands of career and parenthood. She will depend on child-care support systems that will absorb a considerable portion of her earnings. She may find herself supporting both her children and her own parents, either entirely or in part, by the time she reaches her mid-50s. She will probably experience all or part of her retirement years as a single person again, either as a widow or a divorcee. Finally, she will probably retire at the normal time for her cohort since she has had an early

of Older Married Women," *Social Security Bulletin* 43:10-16 (Aug. 1980); John C. Henretta and Angela M. O'Rand, "Joint Retirement in the Dual-Worker Family" (Unpublished manuscript); and Robert L. Clark, Thomas Johnson, and Ann McDermed, "Allocation of Time and Resources by Married Couples Approaching Retirement," *Social Security Bulletin* 43:4-16 (June 1980).

start on her career and has had the capability to maintain it during her period of child rearing.

The normal time of retirement for her will be influenced by her fertility and longevity. Declining fertility will increase the dependency ratio—the ratio of retirees to workers—of the retirement-age to working-age population. Early retirement may become a luxury that modern stationary societies can ill afford. Recent proposals for extensions of the retirement age and the projected fiscal crisis in the Social Security pension system in our society emanate from these trends.

The second woman faces the same prospective economic and life cycle contingencies. Labor participation, possible intergenerational dependence, and change in marital status are all likely prospects. She will, however, experience a less advantaged wage and pension structure that may lead her to work later than her career-oriented counterpart. Age discrimination, lower human capital, sex-segregated occupations and industries, and inflationary trends put her at a serious disadvantage. This career-based disadvantage will be exacerbated by the onset of either widowhood or divorce, since older single women are overrepresented in poverty groups.[24]

In summary, both women reflect the intersection of biography and history, of life course and social change. Each phase of their lives is understood only in relation to the rest of their lives. And their life experiences are understood only in relation to the experience of their cohort. In this context women at middle age are, paradoxically, both predictable and variable. They face turning points and discontinuities, but their individual midlife experiences express more continuity than discontinuity, more synchrony than asynchrony, more transition than crisis.

24. Angela M. O'Rand and John C. Henretta, "Midlife Work History and the Retirement Income of Married and Unmarried Older Women," in *Women's Retirement*, ed. M. Szinovacz (Beverly Hills, CA: Sage, 1982).

ANNALS, *AAPSS*, **464**, November 1982

The Influence of Ethnic Families on Intergenerational Relationships and Later Life Transitions

By CAROL E. WOEHRER

ABSTRACT: Recent studies of American families indicate that pluralism continues to be characteristic of American society. Since a great number of older Americans are either immigrants or the children of immigrants, and many others have spent much of their lives in ethnic communities, understanding the elderly in American society requires insight into ethnic values and family patterns. The foundation for intergenerational relationships is laid early in the family life cycle as children are growing up. Ethnic family structure and socialization of children are closely related to intergenerational interaction in adulthood. Extended family relationships in turn influence social participation outside the family throughout the life cycle and older people's responses to the later life transitions of retirement, widowhood, and decline in health.

Carol E. Woehrer coordinates the licensure and baccalaureate programs in long-term care administration in the School of Public Health at the University of Minnesota. She has published articles on ethnicity and the family, Scandinavian- and German-American women, and family programs in long-term care. She is currently working on a three-generation study of German and Irish families in the Twin Cities.

STUDYING American families is like looking into a kaleidoscope of continually changing forms, colors, and combinations. Because of the multicultural origins of American people, their family structures and values range over a wide spectrum. Traditional family relationships do change when families encounter a new society. In spite of change, however, families of different cultural origins do not become the same. Rather, the pattern and degree of change is mediated by traditional family structures and values. Thus understanding American families requires an appreciation of the rich mosaic of family patterns found in our society.

In families at all stages in the life cycle, ethnic subcultures are quietly expressed through values related to home, family, work, and the community. Insight into ethnic variations in the family is particularly important for understanding older Americans, however, because they are closer to their culture of origin, and because transitions later in the life cycle involve either a change from roles and activities that are more highly prescribed to roles that involve more choice or an increased dependence on other people. When people are employed, for example, a large portion of their daily and weekly activities are determined by the requirements of their jobs. After retirement the individual has a choice of how to spend the time formerly spent on work. The transitions of widowhood or a decline in health frequently involve the need to depend on others for transportation, shopping, assistance with housework, personal care, or emotional support. Whether a person chooses to spend time with family members or friends, on volunteer work, edu-

cation, crafts, or watching TV and whether he turns to family, friends, or institutions when in need of help is influenced by his own values and expectations. These values and expectations are not completely idiosyncratic, but vary to a great extent by cultural background.

As of the 1970s, estimates indicate there were 20 million Italian Americans,[1] 7 million Mexican Americans,[2] 5.5 million Eastern European Jewish Americans,[3] 5 million Polish Americans,[4] 2.5 million Greek Americans,[5] 1.75 million Puerto Rican Americans, 840,000 Central and South Americans, 794,000 Cuban Americans,[6] 591,000 Japanese Americans, 435,000 Chinese Americans, and 343,000 Philippino Americans.[7] In all these ethnic groups older Americans are either immigrants or the children of immigrants. In addition, many older people whose ancestors

1. Richard Gambino, "La Famiglia: Four Generations of Italian-Americans," in *White Ethnics*, ed. Joseph Ryan (Englewood Cliffs, NJ: Prentice-Hall, 1973), p. 44.

2. David Alvirez, Frank Bean, and Dorie Williams, "The Mexican-American Family," in *Ethnic Families in America: Patterns and Variations*, ed. Charles H. Mindel and Robert W. Habenstein (New York: Elsevier North-Holland, 1981), p. 269.

3. Bernard Farber, Charles H. Mindel, and Bernard Lazerwitz, "The Jewish American Family," in *Ethnic Families in America*, pp. 350-351.

4. Helena Z. Lopata, "The Polish American Family," in *Ethnic Families in America* (1976 edition), p. 17.

5. George A. Kourvetaris, "The Greek American Family," in *Ethnic Families in America*, p. 163.

6. Joseph P. Fitzpatrick and Lourdes Travieso Parker, "Hispanic-Americans in the Eastern United States," *The Annals* of the American Academy of Political and Social Science, 454:100 (Mar. 1981).

7. Harry H.L. Kitano, "Asian-Americans: The Chinese, Japanese, Koreans, Philippinos, and Southeast Asians," *The Annals* of the American Academy of Political and Social Science, 454:127 (Mar. 1981).

immigrated during the nineteenth century—Black, Irish, Scandinavian, German, and Anglo Americans—have spent their lifetimes in families, neighborhoods, and churches that were relatively homogeneous in cultural background.

An individual's ethnic background includes the particular values and beliefs that are passed on from one generation to the next within the family, as well as his or her pattern of relationships with family members, friends, and community. Ethnicity can be important to the individual in two ways: as a source of identity and as a source of values, beliefs, and patterns of relationships. Americans vary in their degree of attachment to their culture of origin. People of some ethnic backgrounds tend to have a strong feeling of solidarity with their fellow ethnics while others are barely aware of their ethnic background. The salience of ethnicity as a source of identity, in other words, varies a great deal in American society.

Everyone in American society, however, can be considered to be ethnic in the sense that they have been influenced by cultural patterns in their families that differ from a variety of patterns found in other American families. This article will explain how ethnic values and family relationships established early in the life cycle influence intergenerational relationships and older people's approach to transitions later in the life cycle. It will first show how ethnic family structure and socialization of children is related to older people's interaction with their grown children. It will then relate ethnic family patterns to social participation outside the family and to older people's responses to retirement, widowhood, and decline in health.

THE STRUCTURE OF FAMILY ROLES

A comparison of descriptions of ethnic families shows clear differences among them in the relationships between husbands and wives and between parents and children. In the Japanese-American family, for example, older males provide the family with leadership and authority. When the father reaches a certain age, usually 60 or older, or declines in health, the headship is passed to the eldest son.[8] In contrast, the Black family tends to be more egalitarian with neither husband nor wife dominant.[9]

The structure of roles within a family is determined by the distribution of responsibility and authority among family members and by cultural ideals regarding interpersonal relationships. The responsibility of husbands and wives for earning a living outside the family and for household tasks and child rearing has varied for people of different ethnic backgrounds. While traditionally the father was the authoritarian head of the German family, and children, kitchen, and church were the mother's domain, for example, observers of nineteenth- and twentieth-century Scandinavian families note that Scandinavian women have enjoyed greater freedom and have participated in the labor force to a greater extent than most other European women.[10]

8. S. J. Yanagisako, "Two Processes of Change in Japanese-American Kinship," *Journal of Anthropological Research*, 31:196-224 (Autumn 1975).

9. See Robert Staples, "The Black American Family," in *Ethnic Families in America*, pp. 217-244; Robert Hill, *The Strengths of Black Families* (New York: Emerson-Hall, 1972).

10. See Thomas D. Eliot and Arthur Hillman, *Norway's Families: Trends, Problems,*

For families of Central and Southern European background, the father's responsibility is to provide materially for the family, while the concern of the mother is primarily with homemaking and the private life and emotional well-being of the family.[11] The overriding importance of the husband as provider and the wife as a good homemaker and mother continued to be stressed by studies of Slavic, Italian, and Mexican families in the 1970s.[12]

A second important influence on family structure is the cultural ideal regarding interpersonal relationships. While in some cultures the ideal relationship is a collateral one between equals, in others it is a lineal relationship between a mentor and an apprentice. Richard Gambino makes this contrast in describing Italian-American fatherhood. "The role played by the Italian-American father is in marked contrast to the popular American notion of a father as 'buddy' to his children."[13] Gambino sees the Italian-American family as having a lineal structure, one in which a man guides the younger generation while submitting his own behavior to the scrutiny of older men in his family. In contrast, he views relationships in the American family as collateral, as a relationship between equals, between buddies.

The collateral relationship is probably most characteristic of Irish, Black, and Scandinavian-American families. Andrew Greeley notes, for example, that the sibling relationship is especially important in Irish-American families.[14] An analysis of the father-son relationship in Irish-American literature further suggests that the ideal relationship in Irish culture is one between peers. In Farrell's *Young Lonigan*, Studs's father feels uncomfortable disciplining him and would prefer that Studs were his buddy.[15] Similarly, on returning home from the armed services, both Pete in Hamill's *The Gift* and Timmy in *The Subject Was Roses* decide to get to know their fathers and establish a new comradely relationship with them.[16]

SOCIALIZATION

What gives ethnic families their color and most dramatically differentiates them from each other is

Programs (Philadelphia: University of Pennsylvania Press, 1960), pp. 175-236; H. K. Daniels, *Home Life in Norway* (New York: Macmillan, 1911), pp. 39-40.

11. See Patrick Gallo, *Ethnic Alienation: The Italian-Americans* (Madison: Farleigh Dickinson University Press, 1974), pp. 73-87; Mary Ann Krickus, "The Status of East European Women in the Family," in *Conference on the Educational and Occupational Needs of White Ethnic Women* (National Institute of Education, 1980), pp. 76-101.

12. See Paul Wrobel, *An Ethnographic Study of a Polish American Parish and Neighborhood*, Doctoral dissertation, The Catholic University, 1975, pp. 111-13; Corinne Axen Krause, *Grandmothers, Mothers and Daughters* (New York: The Institute on Pluralism and Group Identity of the American Jewish Committee, 1978), pp. 64, 121, 132-30, 146-63; and Alfredo Mirande and Evangelina Enriquez, *La Chicana, The Mexican-American Woman* (Chicago: University of Chicago Press, 1979).

13. Richard Gambino, *Blood of My Blood* (New York: Anchor, 1975), p. 146.

14. Andrew M. Greeley, *That Most Distressful Nation: The Taming of the American Irish* (Chicago: Quadrangle, 1972), pp. 115-16.

15. James T. Farrell, *Young Lonigan* (New York: Avon, 1972), p. 39.

16. Pete Hamill, *The Gift* (New York: Ballantine, 1973), p. 106; F. D. Gilroy, *The Subject Was Roses*, in *About Those Roses* (New York: Random, 1965), p. 156.

their methods of socializing children. Childhood socialization not only influences the individual's progress through the educational system, choice of occupation, and later marital and family relationships, but it also affects lifelong intergenerational relationships. Methods of socialization could be categorized into four main types: discipline, persuasion, ridicule, and support. The first two methods are related to the source of legitimacy for expected behavior, whereas the last two are related to the emotional affirmation of the child. Families of different ethnic backgrounds vary in the way they combine these four types.

Discipline and persuasion could be considered opposites on a continuum of legitimacy, from blind obedience to authority to rational understanding. Discipline as a method of socialization requires the child to behave according to certain rules on the basis of parental authority, and it administers sanctions when behavior deviates. Persuasion, on the other hand, requires the child to behave in a certain way, not because of the dictates of an authority, but because he understands the reasons why that way of behaving is best for him. Discipline obviously would be more characteristic of a lineal family structure, while persuasion would be more characteristic of an egalitarian family. The ethnic families that most clearly exemplify these methods of socialization are German and Scandinavian families. A comparison by Greeley shows that German families rank highest on the importance of obedience for children whereas Scandinavian families rank lowest.[17] Norwegian children are

taught to guide their conduct more by objective rules than by personal authority.[18] Children are not physically punished, but what is wrong is explained with calmness and reason.[19]

Ridicule and support could also be considered opposites on a continuum from negation to affirmation of the person. Ridicule as a method of socialization makes fun of a person's performance or thought process. In contrast to discipline, which applies a sanction to a particular infringement of a rule, ridicule attacks the person and can undermine the individual's sense of self-worth. It is thus the opposite of support, which includes affection, interest in the pursuits and goals of another, and praise for achievement. Support affirms self-worth.

The use of ridicule is emphasized by scholars writing on the Irish family: "Punishment for disobedience of children was external and expressed by parents, parishioners, and priests. Shame and ridicule, appeals to the embarrassment caused one's parents (especially one's mother), and mocking were used interchangeably by all."[20] Greeley explains that Irish ridicule is intended to hurt and is the matrix for many relationships in Irish-American families.[21] Opposite to ridicule is the affirmation of self expressed in the warmth and affection characteristic of many Italian-

17. Andrew M. Greeley, *That Most Distressful Nation*, p. 159.

18. Erik Gronseth, "Research on Socialization in Norway," *Family Process* 3:302-22 (1964).
19. David Rodnick, *The Norwegians: A Study in National Character* (Washington, DC: Public Affairs Press, 1955), p. 29.
20. Ellen Horgan Biddle, "The American Catholic Irish Family," in *Ethnic Families in America*, p. 101.
21. Andrew M. Greeley, *That Most Distressful Nation*, pp. 106-9.

and Mexican-American families: "Italian parents value love and affection between themselves and their children. Love, enjoyable for its own sake, is also employed to manage and control the behavior of their children."[22]

While most families probably use all these methods of socialization at one time or another, the frequency with which these methods are used and the ways they are combined tend to vary by ethnicity. Italian and Mexican families, for example, use discipline and affection to a high degree. German Catholic families combine discipline with encouragement, but not with the dynamic emotional support of Italian and Mexican families. Scandinavian families emphasize persuasion, but tend to be lacking in support. Norwegians believe that if you give too much praise, a child will become conceited.[23] Jewish families, on the other hand, combine persuasion with encouragement and affection.[24] Family structure and patterns of socialization are directly related to ethnic variations in intergenerational relations.

INTERGENERATIONAL RELATIONS

Studies show that families are the most important source of support for older adults and that family relationships take priority over other social relationships.[25] Intergenerational sharing and exchange of help and resources take place within the context of culturally defined expectations. While the Mexican-American grandmother, for example, may see children daily, freely give advice, and participate in the rearing of her grandchildren, the German or Scandinavian grandmother may perceive carefully defined boundaries around the nuclear families of her children. She may see her children less frequently, and on previously scheduled visits, and not view it as in her place to give advice to her children or to rear her grandchildren. Though dramatically different in their involvement, both grandmothers may view their family relationships as highly satisfactory.

Families lay the foundation for intergenerational relations in adulthood early in the family life cycle as their children are growing up. Families that are lineal in structure and combine discipline and affection as means of socialization have greater intergenerational involvement. Discipline as a method of socialization is perhaps universally used in lineal families. It is in the use of support as a method of socialization that these families differ. The degree of support varies from the dynamic emotional support and affection of Hispanic and Italian families, to the assistance in making life choices and practical material support of Japanese and Polish families, to the encouragement and praise of good work but emphasis on individual

22. Colleen Leahy Johnson, "Family Support Systems of Elderly Italian Americans," *Journal of Minority Aging*, 3-4:34-41 (June-Aug. 1978).

23. Rodnick, *The Norwegians*, p. 29.

24. Andrew M. Greeley, William C. McCready, and Gary Thiesen, *Ethnic Drinking Subcultures* (New York: Praeger, 1980), pp. 21-22.

25. David Gutmann, "Use of Informal and Formal Supports by White Ethnic Aged," in *Ethnicity and Aging: Theory, Research, and Policy*, ed. Donald E. Gelfand and Alfred J. Kutzick (New York: Springer, 1979), pp. 246-62.

decision making and self-reliance in the German family.

As one might expect, Italian and Hispanic families tend to have the greatest frequency of intergenerational interaction, to live in close proximity to family members, and to exchange help. In his research in the 1960s, for example, Greeley found approximately 79 percent of Italian-American respondents visited parents weekly.[26] Italian Americans tend to live close to family members and to be more residentially stable than people of other ethnic backgrounds.[27]

In Italian and Mexican families, members' right to support is acquired at birth and is never threatened, while in the Polish family, members continue to earn their right to cooperative action through their own contributions throughout life.[28] Because of the emphasis on cooperation, Polish families also tend to live in close proximity and to have frequent contact. Of Greeley's Polish-American respondents 65 percent visited parents weekly. Of particular interest, however, is the finding of a study in the 1970s that much visiting of Polish-Americans was service oriented. Younger members often shopped or did heavy cleaning for their elderly parents, while the elderly watched grandchildren or baked treats.[29] While older Polish people are in frequent contact with their children, they tend to feel that no one is available to assist them in problematic situations.[30] In other words, older Polish people feel less secure and seem to expect that their relationship to their children be related to their contribution.

In the German family mutual cooperation is not expected as it is in the Polish family. Children are expected to make their own decisions regarding the choice of an occupation and to be self-supporting once they finish their education. Families do exchange help and favors, but on the whole, each nuclear unit is expected to be independent. Not surprisingly, Germans live much less frequently in the same neighborhood as their parents and visit less frequently than do Italian and Polish families. Forty-eight percent of Greeley's German Catholic respondents and 44 percent of his German Protestant respondents visited parents weekly.

Families that rely on persuasion rather than discipline as a means of socialization tend to be more egalitarian or collateral in structure. Expectations regarding mutual aid between generations are less defined than in lineal families that emphasize support. Similar to the more independent German family, older people in persuasive families tend not to rely on children for aid. Nevertheless, these families vary considerably in their intergenerational relations, and once again intergenerational interaction is directly related to the socialization patterns of support. Jewish children are given emotional support as well

26. Andrew M. Greeley, *Why Can't They Be Like Us?* (New York: Dutton, 1971), p. 77.

27. Frances E. Kobrin and Calvin Goldscheider, *The Ethnic Factor in Family Structure and Mobility* (Cambridge: Ballinger, 1978), pp. 187-90.

28. Helena Znaniecka Lopata, "Polish American Families," in *Ethnic Families in America*, 1981, p. 23.

29. Maria Siemaszko, "Kin Relations of the Aged: Possible Consequences to Social Service Planning," in *Aging in Culture and Society*, ed. Christine L. Fry (New York: Praeger, 1980), pp. 253-71.

30. James E. Trela and Jay H. Sokolovsky, "Culture, Ethnicity, and Policy for the Aged," in *Ethnicity and Aging*, p. 128.

as parental praise and encouragement as they grow up, and in turn they visit parents much more frequently than do Scandinavians, who receive minimal praise and affection. Of Greeley's Jewish respondents 58 percent visited parents weekly, in contrast to 39 percent of his Scandinavian respondents.[31]

The Irish with the socialization pattern of ridicule rank in between on weekly visiting with 49 percent. In the Irish family, ridicule probably ranges from gentle to abusive and from humorous to demoralizing. Thus ridicule could be both supportive or destructive, depending on how it is used. The collateral ideal of the Irish is exemplified by Irish family visiting patterns. In contrast to other ethnic groups, where parental visiting is much higher than sibling visiting, the Irish visit siblings as frequently as they do parents. Both the importance of egalitarianism and the Irish family's lack of support is suggested by a study of residential stability of different ethnic groups. Whereas the usual pattern was for those sons who had lower occupational ranks than their fathers to live close to their parents, the Irish pattern was exceptional. Those Irish sons who had the same occupational rank as their fathers were least likely to move away. Those who were downwardly mobile were most likely to move.[32]

SOCIAL INTERACTION OUTSIDE THE FAMILY

Individuals' participation in society is shaped by family culture.

Some family systems are more closed. In these families, members relate mainly to other family members and do not depend in any significant way on people or groups outside the family for social, emotional, or practical support. Other family systems are more open. Their members participate much more extensively in organizations and friendships outside the family.

The participation of individuals in the wider society throughout the life cycle is related to family structure. People from cultural backgrounds in which the family is lineal with high affective support and intergenerational interdependence tend to interact much less with people and organizations outside the family. In contrast, people from cultural backgrounds in which relationships tend to be collateral or in which independence is emphasized tend to participate in friendships and groups outside the family much more extensively.

Coming from cultures in which family relationships are lineal and the generations highly interdependent, Italian, Mexican, and Polish Americans tend to have fewer friends, to value friends less than kin, and to belong to fewer organizations. Comparing Mexican Americans with Blacks and white Americans, Bengtson found older Mexican Americans to have the least amount of social interaction with nonrelated individuals.[33] According to Greeley's study in the 1960s, about two-thirds of Italian and Polish Americans belonged to no organizations.[34] Describing his

31. Greeley, *Why Can't They Be Like Us?* p. 77.

32. Kobrin and Goldscheider, *The Ethnic Factor in Family Structure and Mobility*, p. 215.

33. Vern L. Bengtson, "Ethnicity and Aging: Problems and Issues in Current Social Science Inquiry," in *Ethnicity and Aging*, p. 23.

34. Greeley, *Why Can't They Be Like Us?*, p. 212.

Polish American family, Wrobel explains that his family did not entertain often, and when it did, guests were usually relatives. Neighbors conversed on the street or over the fence but rarely invited one another into their homes.[35] Writing on the Italian family, Covello notes that a demarcation line was drawn between the home and the community. Allegiance to family was always more imperative than allegiance to groups outside the family.[36]

At the opposite end of the spectrum, Scandinavian Americans, with the lowest frequency of kin visiting, have the highest rate of organizational membership: 60 percent of Scandinavian Americans belong to an organization.[37] Scandinavian Americans lead other ethnic groups in civic mindedness and are second after the Irish in political participation.[38]

For two ethnic groups with a more collateral family structure—Irish and Black Americans—friendship is very important. The meaning of friendship, however, differs for the two groups. Black Americans relate to friends with the idiom of kinship. If two friends exchange mutual help or confidence, they "go for sisters or brothers."[39] Friends and neighbors are classified as kin when they assume the same responsibilities as kin. This flexibility facilitates mutual aid networks that are not bounded by the family. Much more important for one's support network are the close proximity and congeniality of kin and friends.[40]

Rather than conduct friendship in the idiom of kinship, Irish Americans evaluate kin in terms of their capacity to act as friends. A central theme in Irish-American novels is the effort of father and son to establish a friendship, their joy at having succeeded, or their sense of loss at having failed.[41] The significance of friendship is also apparent in the emphasis on enjoyment and common interests in Irish sibling relationships. Irish Americans, in fact, feel a sense of guilt when they are not friends with siblings, when they do not spend enough time and enjoy being with siblings. Although sibling relationships are maintained even when not marked by friendship, the Irish American is intensely loyal to friends. Greeley explains, "Of course you stand by a friend, no matter what he does, and the Irishman is astonished when other ethnic groups seem to disagree."[42] While the ideal Italian relationship is a lineal one in which the father serves as mentor to the son, the ideal Irish relationship is an egalitarian one based on congeniality and common interests. When

35. Paul Wrobel, "Becoming a Polish American: A Personal Point of View," in *White Ethnics*, p. 56.

36. Leonard Covello, *The Social Background of the Italo-American School Child* (Leiden: E. J. Brill, 1967), p. 162.

37. Greeley, *Why Can't They Be Like Us?*, p. 212.

38. Andrew M. Greeley, *Ethnicity in the United States: A Preliminary Reconnaissance* (New York: John Wiley, 1974), pp. 126-29.

39. Joyce Aschenbrenner, "External Families Among Black Americans," *Journal of Comparative Family Studies*, 4:257-68 (Autumn 1973).

40. C. B. Stack, "Black Kindreds: Parenthood and Personal Kindreds among Urban Blacks," *Journal of Comparative Studies*, 3:194-206 (Autumn 1972).

41. See Hamill, *The Gift;* Gilroy, *The Subject Was Roses;* Farrell, *Young Lonigan;* Edwin O'Connor, *The Edge of Sadness* (Boston: Little, Brown, 1961); Eugene O'Neill, *Long Day's Journey into Night* (New Haven: Yale University Press, 1974).

42. Greeley, *That Most Distressful Nation*, p. 116.

friendship is missing from kinship, the Irish American feels sadness, anxiety, loss, and guilt.

TRANSITIONS IN LATER LIFE

Three events that initiate new stages in the life cycle for many older people are retirement, widowhood, and decline in health. Adaptation to these events will be discussed in this section in terms of the influence of ethnic family culture and contemporary changes in the family, including decreasing family size and the greater occupational participation of women.

Retirement

Thorough studies of the adjustment to retirement of older people of different ethnic backgrounds are not available. Nevertheless, one can construct a picture of how people of various ethnic backgrounds approach the stage of life following retirement, on the basis of general studies of retirement, cross-national studies, and studies of the family life of various ethnic groups. Two broad conclusions can be made based on these studies. First, there is a great deal of variation in retirement life styles. Neugarten and associates, for example, delineated several patterns of activity in later life, including participation in a wide variety of activities, focused activity usually devoted to the family, self-directed activity not imbedded in social interaction, dependency on one or two persons, passivity, and disorganization.[43] Second, retirement life is related to personal characteris-

tics, family relationships, and work activities at earlier stages in the life cycle.

Andrew Greeley's research shows that people of different ethnic backgrounds tend to engage in different lines of work. Irish Catholics, for example, are three times more likely than the national average to enter the legal profession, and Jews are three times as likely to be in medicine. Polish Catholics and Germans, whether Protestant or Catholic, are overrepresented in engineering whereas both Jews and the Irish are drastically underrepresented in this discipline.[44]

Given ethnic variation in family life, choice of work, and participation in social activities outside the family, one would expect retirement life-styles to vary considerably by ethnicity. Comparison of findings of a cross-national study of retirement with results of studies of ethnic groups in the United States demonstrates the continuity in cultural patterns. Data on the retirement lifestyles of retired teachers and steel workers parallel the results of studies of Italian Americans. Italian teachers and steel workers show a striking involvement in the roles of parent and grandparent, with very little involvement in formal and informal roles outside the family.[45] Likewise, the importance of the work role and of making a practical contribution is evident in studies of Poles in both Warsaw and the United States. For Poles, the need for self-actualization is expressed by engaging in crafts and hobbies or by

43. Bernice L. Neugarten and Associates, *Personality in Middle and Late Life* (New York: Atherton Press, 1964), pp. 158-68.

44. Greeley, *Ethnicity in the United States*, p. 178.
45. R. J. Havighurst et al. (Eds.), *Adjustment to Retirement* (Assen, The Netherlands: Van Gorcum, 1970), pp. 71-85.

working past normal retirement time.[46]

For people of some ethnic backgrounds, the ethnic community itself is an important source of meaning and social interaction, especially for retirees, widows and widowers, and individuals without family members close by. Gallo notes that the Italian community has a distinctive way of life that marks it off from the broader society. The conscious sharing of language, customs, religion, values, and norms gives the community an awareness of itself and unity.[47] For Polish Catholics the neighborhood Catholic church is the focal point of the Polish community and serves to maintain its cohesion.[48] A major source of support for older Japanese Americans is found among age peers who share the same language and values and allow their traditional basis of self-esteem to guide them through old age.[49] Similarly, Eastern European Jews living in rooming houses and hotels in Los Angeles maintain continuity by sharing a common Jewish heritage, culture, and language.[50]

Widowhood

A second life event that is often more disruptive than retirement is the loss of a spouse. Contact with the late spouse's family often declines, and friends may feel less comfortable with the widowed person and consequently may get together less frequently.[51] In addition, the widow often loses substantial household income when retirement benefits end with her husband's death. Thus leisure and social activities may be curtailed because of inadequate funds. The widow's ability to reconstruct life and regain a sense of meaning and satisfaction depends on her resources—educational background, financial situation, family relationships, health status, social involvement, religious and spiritual beliefs, and community supports.

Which of these resources the widow relies on varies by ethnic background. A comparison of French and Scandinavian Americans, for instance, reveals contrasting social support systems. While over 60 percent of French respondents saw both parents and in-laws every week, only 39 percent of Scandinavian respondents saw parents weekly, and only 31 percent saw their in-laws that frequently. On the other hand, almost four times as many Scandinavians belong to organizations, 60 percent in comparison with 17 percent of the French respondents. While the French-American widow would turn to her children for support, the Scandinavian widow would probably draw on organizations for friends and social support. Greeley's study found that over twice as many Scandinavian (54 percent) as French Americans (26 percent) met new people.[52] Kutner's study of a New

46. Dorota Techniczek, "Retirement Patterns in Warsaw-Area," in *Adjustment to Retirement*, p. 92; Danuta Mostwin, "Emotional Needs of Elderly Americans of Central and Eastern European Background," in *Ethnicity and Aging*, pp. 273-75.

47. Gallo, *Ethnic Alienation*, p. 71.

48. Neil C. Sandberg, *Ethnic Identity and Assimilation: The Polish-American Community* (New York: Praeger, 1974), p. 29.

49. Trela and Sokolovsky, "Culture, Ethnicity, and Policy for the Aged," p. 126.

50. J. B. Kessler, "Aging in Different Ways," *Human Behavior*, 5:56-59 (June 1976).

51. Helena Z. Lopata, *Women as Widows* (New York: Elsevier, 1979), pp. 214-19.

52. Greeley, *Why Can't They Be Like Us?* pp. 77, 212.

York community indicated that Czech, Hungarian, and Italian families included a widowed father or mother much more frequently than British, German, or Irish families.[53]

It is not only the social resources the widow draws on that are important, but also how she conceptualizes relationships. Since the Italian family, for example, operates as a source of nurturance, caring for the dependency needs of both young and old, the onset of dependency of an elderly member is merely an extension of a lifetime pattern. Young Italian families are four times as likely as non-Italians to accept without reservation the idea of an elderly parent living with them.[54] In contrast, in the Polish family, which encourages mutual contribution rather than nurturance, widows prefer to live independently of their children and sometimes express bitterness toward their adult children for failing to help them financially.[55]

It was explained earlier that for Black Americans, friends took the place of kin whereas for Irish Americans the ideal was for kin to be friends. While both Black and Irish Americans rely on social relationships outside the family, the conceptual bases for their relationships are quite different. Black Americans view friends as kin, as people who exchange help. Irish Americans see friends as people who are equal, who have mutual interests and enjoyments. While the older widow who is Black may feel free to call friends for assistance, the older Irish widow

in trouble may be more likely to withdraw. In times of poor health or financial constraint, she may not have the resources to maintain an egalitarian friendship.

Health care

While, for most Americans, norms of independence have governed intergenerational living arrangements, it is more common for single elderly people, especially those in need of health care, to live with kin. Approximately one-third of single people over the age of 65 live with relatives.[56] Approximately 80 percent of home health care is provided by families, primarily by middle-aged daughters.[57] As would be expected from the previous discussion, the source of health care varies for people of different ethnic backgrounds. In families with high levels of interdependence, such as Italian, Mexican, Polish, Japanese, and Chinese families, it is common for older persons who need help to live with their families, while in families that adhere to norms of independence, such as Irish, English, German, and Scandinavian families, it is more usual for the older person to rely on formal or institutional sources of support.

Individuals' use of medical services and their communication regarding pain depend on the values and family relationships of their cultural group. In *People in Pain*, Mark Zborowski reports that Old Americans and Irish-Americans, who value self-reliance and independ-

53. Bernard Kutner, *Five Hundred over Sixty: A Community Survey on Aging* (New York: Russell Sage, 1956), p. 114.

54. Johnson, "Family Support Systems of Elderly Italian Americans," p. 37.

55. Lopata, "The Polish-American Family," pp. 26-27.

56. Charles H. Mindel, "Multigenerational Family Households: Recent Trends and Implications for the Future," *The Gerontologist*, 19(5):456-62 (Oct. 1979).

57. Robert N. Butler and Myrna I. Lewis, *Aging and Mental Health* (St. Louis: Mosby, 1977), p. 214.

ence, prefer to be alone when ill and do not complain because they believe there is no point in burdening others with one's own discomfort. In contrast, withdrawal from people is inconceivable for Jewish and Italian Americans because suffering is with people just as the entire process of living is with people.[58]

While many younger and older people favor traditional norms regarding the care of the elderly, because of the trend toward smaller families, especially during the Depression, many older people do not have an adequate support system to make care at home feasible. Between 1970 and 1976 the population between 40 and 64 years of age increased by two percent, while those aged 65 and over increased by 15 percent, those aged 75 and over by 16 percent, and those aged 85 and over by 40 percent.[59] Employment outside the home also makes it more difficult for women to carry out their traditional care-giving role. As of 1970, half of wives aged 45 to 54 were in the labor force as compared with 11 percent in 1940.[60]

An understanding of cultural variations in reaction to illness and expectations for help from family, friends, and institutional resources should be an important part of the education of health care professionals. The provision of the type of health care for the elderly that best meets their emotional needs requires a careful analysis of family expecta-

tions and resources. The alternative that will provide comfort to the older person without overburdening the family caregivers is often a combination of family assistance and community services tailored to the ethnic values and traditions of the community being served.

THE CHANGING ETHNIC FAMILY

Ethnic families, of course, are influenced by the broader society and culture. While geographic mobility decreases intergenerational contact, marriage outside one's ethnic group and occupational mobility may have an even greater impact on changing the patterns of family relationships. Italian Americans, for example, who have a high degree of residential stability, tend to move outside their community more frequently when they marry outside their ethnic group. The Irish, on the other hand, who tend to be migratory, become more residentially stable when they marry someone who is not Irish.

Occupational mobility varies in its effect depending on family structure and ideals. For lineal and highly interdependent families, the son with a lower occupational rank than his father tends to live closer to his parents.[61] The father can thus maintain his mentor relationship. Polish sons, for example, tend to follow their fathers in the type of job they enter more than do sons of other ethnic groups. This occupational arrangement preserves traditional family relations.[62] This situation

58. Mark Zborowski, *People in Pain* (San Francisco: Jossey-Bass, 1969).

59. U.S. Department of Health, Education and Welfare, *Statistical Notes* (OHDS) 78-20040 (Washington, DC: Government Printing Office, Feb. 1978).

60. Judith Treas, "Intergenerational Families and Social Change," in *Aging Parents*, ed. Pauline K. Ragan (Los Angeles: University of Southern California Press, 1979), p. 61.

61. Kobrin and Goldscheider, *The Ethnic Factor in Family Structure and Mobility*, p. 215.

62. Lopata, "Polish American Families," 1981 edition, p. 34.

dynamically contrasts with the Irish, who tend to move away when they are downwardly mobile. For the Irish, an equal job status tends to best maintain family relationships. When occupational mobility does not complement traditional family ideals, tension and strain may develop between the generations, and parents and children may become alienated.

As in corporate life, much can be learned from the Japanese about transitions in family life. Recent studies of Japanese management explain that, in contrast to Western emphasis on finality and control in decision making, Eastern management lore cautions managers to be wary of mastery and to suspect the notion that at any one time a matter is truly decided. "Whereas Western management beliefs tend to portray a decision as fixed and final, Eastern philosophical tradition emphasizes individual accommodation to a continuously unfolding set of events."[63] This evolutionary approach to new circumstances is apparent in Yanagisako's study of change in the Japanese-American family. Traditionally in the Japanese family, the eldest son and his family lived with his parents, cared for them in old age, and inherited the family business. In the United States, with occupational opportunities available to all siblings and without a family enterprise, it became less feasible for the first son to fulfill all the functions of his traditional role. These functions were, however, still considered the responsibility of the family and began to be shared by all children in the family. The eldest son continued as leader of his siblings and manager of the financial and legal affairs of his elderly parents, but financial support was shared by all sons. Parents generally lived independently of their children, but when this was not feasible because of inadequate financial resources, widowhood, or illness, parents lived with daughters in the family.[64]

The recent study of ethnic family structure and mobility by Kobrin and Goldscheider indicates that ethnic pluralism continues to be characteristic of American society. As this article has indicated, patterns of continuity and change vary for people of different ethnic backgrounds. This variation in older people's values, family patterns, and social participation requires that public policy and services be developed for specific groups of people rather than for older people in general if they are to be effective in enhancing their social lives.

63. Richard T. Pascale and Anthony G. Athos, *The Art of Japanese Management* (New York: Warner, 1981), p. 173.

64. Yanagisako, "Two Processes of Change in Japanese-American Kinship," pp. 201-11.

ANNALS, *AAPSS*, **464**, November 1982

Blacks at Middle and Late Life:
Resources and Coping

By ROSE C. GIBSON

ABSTRACT: An analysis of national data collected in 1957 and 1976 reveals that older black Americans' use of their informal support networks and prayer in times of distress is distinct from that of older white Americans. Black-white disparities in income, education, and widowhood were large and appeared to widen from middle to late life. Blacks, in coping with distress, drew from a more varied pool of informal helpers than whites, both in middle and late life, and were more versatile in substituting these helpers one for another as they approached old age. Whites, in contrast, were more likely to limit help seeking to spouses in middle life and to replace spouses with a single family member as they approached old age. Blacks were much more likely than whites to respond to worries with prayer, but prayer, as a coping reaction among blacks, declined between 1957 and 1976. The role of the special help-seeking model of older blacks in their adaptation to old age is discussed.

Rose C. Gibson is a research scientist at the University of Michigan's Institute of Gerontology. She has been a United States Public Health Service Fellow and has been engaged in extensive research on aging and aged black women.

THERE is a distance between blacks and whites in their middle years. Black Americans are poorer, less educated, more apt to be separated, divorced, or widowed. And the gap widens with age. At midlife, census figures show that 14 percent of blacks have family incomes of less than $5000, compared with 4 percent of whites; 64 percent of blacks have educational attainments of less than high school graduation, compared with 34 percent of whites; and 55 percent of midlife blacks are married with spouse present, compared with 79 percent of whites. For the elderly, census figures show that 27 percent of blacks have family incomes of less than $5000; 80 percent have less than a high school education; and only 38 percent are married and make a home with their spouse. The comparable figures for older whites are 10 percent, 34 percent, and 54 percent, respectively. (See Table 1 and Figure 1.)

Even though they lack financial security, education, and marital harmony—aspects of life assumed to ease one's way—blacks seem to sustain themselves psychologically as they age.[1] Certainly in terms of a gross measure of adjustment—suicide—older blacks fare we National vital statistics indicate suicide rates among the elderly, from lowest to highest, are those of black females, black males, white

females, and white males.[2] This rank ordering corresponds directly to the likelihood of being poor. That is, older black women are most likely to be poor and least likely to end their own lives; older white men are least likely to suffer poverty and most apt to die by their own hand.

So what accounts for the staying power of American blacks? Is it merely a matter of practice, of long experience in meeting adversity? Or have they found resources and strategies that sustain them? This article examines two specific coping practices—prayer and seeking help from family and friends—to which black Americans reportedly resort when times are difficult.[3] Black people in middle and late life turn to prayer more often than do white people of similar years. Blacks use their informal networks differently from whites, and the patterns of prayer and network use are changing. The adaptive values of these two strategies, then, may make blacks' entry into old age more transition than crisis.

METHOD

The data examined here are from the 1957/1976 study, *Americans View Their Mental Health*.[4] This major national study is based on a

1. See Joseph Veroff, Elizabeth Douvan, and Richard Kulka, *The Inner American: A Self-Portrait from 1957 to 1976* (New York: Basic Books, 1981), p. 436; Inabel B. Lindsay, "Coping Capacities of the Black Aged," in *No Longer Young: The Older Woman in America*, Occasional Papers in Gerontology, no. 11 (Ann Arbor: Institute of Gerontology, University of Michigan), pp. 89-94; Rose C. Gibson, "The Survivors: Black Elderly 75 Years Old and Over," (Manuscript in preparation, Institute of Gerontology, University of Michigan, 1982).

2. National Center for Health Statistics, *Vital Statistics of the United States, 1975* (Washington, DC: Government Printing Office).

3. U.S. Senate Special Committee on Aging, "The Multiple Hazards of Age and Race: The Situation of Aged Blacks in the United States" (Washington, DC: Government Printing Office, 1971); see, for example, Joseph Dancy, Jr., "Religiosity and Social-Psychological Adjustment Among the Black Urban Elderly," Ph.D. dissertation, University of Michigan, 1979); James S. Jackson, *Report to Respondents*, The National Survey of Black Americans (Ann Arbor: Institute for Social Research, University of Michigan, 1982).

4. Gerald Gurin, Joseph Veroff, and Sheila Feld, *Americans View Their Mental*

TABLE 1

**TOTAL INCOME, EDUCATIONAL ATTAINMENT, AND MARITAL STATUS
OF BLACKS AND WHITES AT MID- (AGES 45-64) AND LATE-LIFE
(AGES 65 AND OVER)**

	MID-LIFE		LATE-LIFE	
	BLACK	WHITE	BLACK	WHITE
Total income of families by race of Household head, 1979 (in percentages)*				
Less than $5000 a year	14	4	27	10
Total number	1772	17921	789	7911
Educational attainment of persons, 1979 In (in percentages) †				
Less than high school graduate	64	34	80	34
Total number	4054	38737	1677	23505
Marital status of persons, 1978 (in percentages) ‡				
Single	8	5	5	6
Married, spouse present	55	79	38	54
Married, spouse absent	13	2	8	2
Widowed	12	7	43	36
Divorced	11	6	5	3
Total number	4009	38952	1931	20317

* U.S. Bureau of the Census, "Money Income of Families and Persons in the United States," *Current Population Reports,* Series P-60, No. 129 (Washington, DC: Government Printing Office, Nov. 1981), Table 21, pp. 87-88, 91-92.

† U.S. Bureau of the Census, "Educational Attainment in the U.S., March 1979 and 1978," *Current Population Reports,* Series P-20, No. 356 (Washington, DC: Government Printing Office, Aug. 1980), Table 1.

‡ U.S. Bureau of the Census, "Marital Status and Living Arrangements," *Current Population Reports,* Series P-20, No. 333 (Washington, DC: Government Printing Office, May 1979), Table 1, pp. 8-9.

probability sample of the adult black and white population. The present study analyzes data on blacks and whites who were in their middle years (ages 45 to 59) and late years (ages 60 and older) in 1957, and blacks and whites who had attained similar ages in 1976. The 1957 sample is composed of 50 middle-aged and 32 older blacks, and 566 middle-aged and 455 older whites. The 1976 figures are 46, 55, 447, and 493, respectively. The

Health (Institute for Social Research, University of Michigan) (Ann Arbor: ISR Social Science Archive, Institute for Social Research, 1957, 1976).

black samples in both years were poorer, less educated, and less apt to be married than the white samples.

To assess use of the informal network and use of prayer as coping responses to distress, and to determine the persistence of these strategies from 1957 to 1976, respondents in both years were asked how they handled matters that were bothering or worrying them. They were also asked if they talked the problem over with anyone and, if so, with whom. The responses given fell into eight categories: informal help seeking, religious means (prayer being primary among such means),

FIGURE 1
DIFFERENCES IN TOTAL INCOME, EDUCATIONAL ATTAINMENT, AND
MARITAL STATUS OF BLACKS AND WHITES AT MID-(AGES 45 TO 64* YEARS)
AND LATE-LIFE (AGES 65 YEARS AND OVER

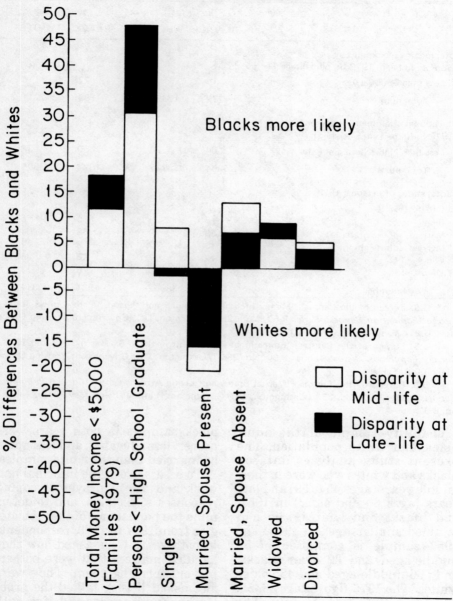

*Table 1 of this article.

denial, displacement, passive reactions, independent coping reactions, and "other" (this category included such reactions as sleep, drink, fantasy, and medication). These categories are listed in Table 2.

To determine racial and generational differences in patterns of help seeking within the informal network, those mentioned receiving informal help were placed into four additional categories: "spouse only"—respondent named a spouse and no one else; "single family member"—respondent named only a family member other than a spouse; "multiple family members"—respondent named two or more family members; and "friends"—respondent named friends, acquaintances, or neighbors (see Table 3).

SEEKING HELP IN
THE INFORMAL NETWORK

Whites in the *Americans View Their Mental Health* samples made greater overall use of the informal network at times of worry, both in 1957 and 1976, although older blacks and older whites were about equally likely to do so in 1976, as Table 2 indicates. The greater use of informal network members by whites was mainly because whites were much more likely than blacks, in both years and at both life stages, to seek help exclusively from their spouses (see Table 3). Whites were also more likely in each analysis year to seek help from one family member at a time. Blacks, on the other hand, were more likely than whites to seek help from friends in 1957 and from combinations of family members in 1976. Controlling for marital status, whites were still much more likely than blacks to discuss their worries with spouses

exclusively. Similarly, racial differences in single family member and multiple family member use within the informal network remained, after income, education, number of adults living in the respondents' household, and age were held constant.[5]

In sum, middle and late life blacks, in both 1957 and 1976, were less likely than their white counterparts to seek help in the informal network only from a spouse or from one family member. The model of reaching beyond single family members in times of need is evident among blacks in both years.[6]

Also evident in both years is that blacks select from a more varied pool of helpers as aging takes place; they substitute one type of helper for another. Blacks who were middle aged in 1957 seem to have shifted by 1976, when they were elderly, from use of friends in times of worry to use of multiple family members. In contrast, the whites who were middle aged in 1957 seem to have continued reliance only on spouses when possible and to hvae increased their use of single family members, presumably as a replacement for lost

5. We were unable, because of small numbers of blacks in the upper income and education categories, to apply adequate controls for these two variables. We instead analyzed racial differences within the lower income and education groups. It is unknown, then, whether higher-status groups, with respect to income and education, behave similarly.

6. Recognizing this help-seeking pattern of reaching beyond single family members as characteristic of women, and realizing that there were proportionately more older black women than older black men in our sample, we analyzed the sex data separately to determine whether these were actually sex, and not race, differences in use of the informal network. The numbers of black men in some of the age categories were too small for definitive statements, but black men seemed as

TABLE 2
DIFFERENCES IN WAYS OF HANDLING WORRIES BY YEAR (FIRST-MENTIONED RESPONSES ONLY, IN PERCENTAGES)

	1957 (N = 1035)				1976 (N = 988)			
	MID-LIFE		LATE-LIFE		MID-LIFE		LATE-LIFE	
WAYS OF HANDLING WORRIES	BLACK	WHITE	BLACK	WHITE	BLACK	WHITE	BLACK	WHITE
Informal help-seeking	8.3	24.8	7.1	18.7	20.5	33.0	23.5	21.6
Religious means (prayer, turning to the Bible, trusting in God)	66.7	18.9	50.0	24.2	27.3	15.8	54.9	22.5
Denial (trying to forget)	4.2	6.8	7.1	6.7	2.3	4.4	0.0	7.6
Displacement (engaging in activity, e.g., going for a walk)	6.3	13.1	10.7	11.0	9.1	5.6	2.0	6.7
Passive Reactions								
Nothing	2.1	9.4	10.7	15.1	9.1	10.0	2.0	14.3
Worry (e.g., until things work out)	4.2	5.7	10.7	5.3	9.1	4.6	5.9	6.0
Independent Coping Reactions								
Self-assessment	4.2	8.7	0.0	7.4	6.8	10.0	2.0	6.0
Immediate action (e.g., doing something about it)	0.0	6.7	3.6	5.0	4.5	8.6	0.0	6.7
Other (sleep, drink, fantasy, medication)	4.0	5.9	.1	6.6	11.3	8.0	9.7	8.6
	100.0	100.0	100.0	100.0	100.0	100.0	100.0	100.0

NOTE: N = total number of persons.

TABLE 3
DIFFERENCES IN SOURCES OF INFORMAL HELP FOR WORRIES BY YEAR (SPONTANEOUS MENTIONS) ONLY OF THOSE WHO SOUGHT HELP, IN PERCENTAGES)

SOURCES OF HELP	1957 (N = 728)				1976 (N = 770)			
	MID-LIFE		LATE-LIFE		MID-LIFE		LATE-LIFE	
	BLACK	WHITE	BLACK	WHITE	BLACK	WHITE	BLACK	WHITE
Spouse only	36.7	58.2	25.0	37.9	19.4	46.6	17.9	26.7
Single family member	6.7	10.9	12.5	26.8	8.3	9.6	17.9	25.8
Multiple family members	10.0	9.2	6.3	8.6	27.8	11.6	33.3	15.0
Friends, acquaintances, neighbors	40.0	16.7	56.3	21.4	44.4	28.8	28.2	25.2
Formal (e.g., doctor)	6.7	5.0	0.0	5.4	0.0	3.4	2.6	7.3
	100.0	100.0	100.0	100.0	100.0	100.0	100.0	100.0

spouses. They also increased their use of multiple family members, but not nearly so much as did their black counterparts.

The use of multiple family members for help with worries seems to increase as blacks move from middle to old age. Only one-tenth of the midlife blacks sought help from multiple family sources in 1957, while one-third of the late-life blacks did so in 1976 (see Table 3). The latter apparently increased the use of combinations of family members as they aged. Turning to various family members in times of need appears to be a growing phenomenon, particularly among elderly blacks; the increase in this pattern of help seeking was greater for this group between 1957 and 1976 than for any other race or age group.

In short, similarities in both analysis years suggest that a paradigm of seeking help beyond the narrowest range of helpers, and of increasing versatility in the substitution of types of helper as aging occurs and life circumstances and needs change, may be characteristic of blacks when they attempt to cope with worries.

PRAYER AS COPING

In line with conventional wisdom, black respondents in this study were much more likely than their white counterparts to react to worry with prayer. This holds true for the mid- and late-life samples in both 1957 and 1976. Prayer, in fact, remained the modal response of blacks in each of these years, suggesting that recourse to prayer may well have been one of blacks' tradi-

tional means of handling worries. Racial differences in the use of prayer remained when education and income were held constant.

The cohort of blacks who were middle aged in 1957 may represent a generation of blacks who regularly found relief from worry through prayer. A majority of this cohort turned to prayer in 1957 (two-thirds of the midlife cohort) and a majority did so in 1976 (55 percent of the late-life cohort). Presumably, this generation continued to find solace in prayer as they aged.

In spite of the fact that this group continued to use prayer as a means of handling worry, prayer became a less prominent source of relief to them as they aged. The decrease in the proportion who used prayer (from two-thirds in 1957 to 55 percent in 1976) may mean that, even among blacks who learned to respond to worry with prayer, prayer as a means of coping may be on the decline.[7] A further indication that prayer may be on the decline among blacks is that midlife blacks in 1976 were much less inclined than midlife blacks in 1957 to use prayer.

An interesting note is that suicide rates among the black and white elderly not only mirror income levels, as mentioned earlier, but also the likelihood of responding to worry with prayer. That is, elderly black women are least likely to commit suicide and most likely to use prayer as a coping response. Elderly white men are most inclined toward suicide and least inclined toward prayer. Elderly black men and elderly white women

likely as their black women counterparts to seek help from combinations of family members rather than from single family sources.

7. Prayer as a response to worries is also decreasing among all Americans. Joseph Veroff, Elizabeth Douvan, and Richard Kulka, *The Inner American: A Self-Portrait from 1957 to 1976* (New York: Basic Books, 1981), p. 483.

are ordered between these extremes.

This association between lower suicide rates and praying in times of need may be simply an interesting coincidence. Durkheim, however, suggests the incidence of suicide is lowest among those who are most strongly bonded to groups—the greater the degree of social integration, the less the tendency toward suicide.[8] And many authors have noted that blacks frequently pray together in times of need.[9] It may well be this communal aspect of prayer, the sense of prayer as a source of social support, that provides the logical link between prayer and lower suicide rates among older blacks.

Furthermore, Durkheim offers evidence that the greater the number of elements in a family grouping, the lower the incidence of suicide. As we observed earlier, older blacks tend to define their family groups broadly when seeking help; support may come from a number of family members. Older whites, on the other hand, limited their help seeking more to single family members. These findings suggest that blacks may be more and whites less bonded to groups of

helpers. It is possible that this greater and lesser bonding by blacks and whites, respectively, to multiple sources of help is related to their respective suicide rates. If lower suicide rates do indeed reflect better adjustment in old age, the bonding theory, though speculative, may explain more fully the role of the use of combinations of family members in the better adjustment of blacks to old age.

In sum, blacks were much more likely than whites at both middle and late life to respond to worry with prayer. This type of response is likely to have been a characteristic of blacks in the past, but it may now be on the decline as a coping strategy, even among the black elderly. The use of combinations of family members in response to worry, furthermore, seems to be increasing among older blacks as the use of prayer is decreasing. One may wonder whether multiple help seeking in the informal network will eventually replace prayer as the dominant mode of handling distress.

SUMMARY AND CONCLUSION

The blacks in our sample were poorer, less educated, and more likely to have experienced family disruption than the whites at both middle and late life and in both 1957 and 1976. If we assume that money, education, and nuclear family harmony serve to moderate stress, then blacks approach middle and late life less fortified against stress than whites.

Blacks were less likely than whites to rely upon single sources of family help in times of worry; in addition, blacks from middle to late life exhibited greater virtuosity

8. Durkheim explains further the role of family density in suicide, "The functioning of the family varies with its greater or lesser density, the number of its component elements affects the suicidal tendency. Where collective sentiments are strong, it is because the force with which they affect each individual conscience is echoed in all the others, and reciprocally. The intensity they attain therefore depends on the number of consciences which react to them in common." Emile Durkheim, *Suicide, A Study in Sociology* (New York: Free Press, 1951), pp. 201, 209.

9. See James T. Widgeon, "Differences in the Meaning of Religion for Blacks and Whites: Racial Differences on Indicators of Religiosity" (Unpublished manuscript, University of Michigan, Institute for Social Research, 1981).

than whites in substituting one type of informal helper for another, still within a paradigm of not limiting help seeking to single family members. This pattern among blacks of seeking help from a broader base of helpers increased with age.

Evident in both 1957 and 1976 were the tendencies of blacks to reach beyond single sources of support in the family and to interchange one informal helper for another, suggesting that these tendencies may represent long-standing patterns blacks have followed when coping with worries. From the present cross-sectional data, we cannot be sure that this is so. It is possible, however, that blacks, as they age, compensate for the diminution of other resources in a unique fashion—by increasing the variety of informal helpers from whom they may usefully seek help at critical transitional stages.

The data we examined showed that blacks, much more than whites, at both middle and late life turned to prayer as a response to worry. It appears, however, that prayer as a coping reaction to worry is on the decline among elderly blacks and even seems to decrease as they age. Blacks seeking help with their worries seem to be increasing the use of combinations of family members and decreasing the use of prayer.

In what ways might these unique strategies of older blacks, to call upon combinations of family members and to substitute one informal helper for another, promote greater adaptation to old age than is the case among whites? First, blacks may be more socialized to seeking help from combinations of family members and to substituting one type of informal helper for another. This help seek-

ing from a wider base and flexibility in substitution may even have been sensitive to changing circumstances and changing needs over life course, thereby helping blacks through critical stages.

Next, this greater socialization of blacks to use of a multiple-help paradigm with an overlay of flexibility might mean that as close family and friends are lost, they are more easily replaced by others from within the informal network. For example, blacks, having learned to draw from a larger pool of helpers, may be more likely in late life to have these helpers in place; and having rehearsed multiple use of family members and substitution of these helpers at critical life points, they may also be more likely to have well-oiled machinery in place to facilitate this selection and substitution of helpers. Having both helpers and the mechanisms in place may ease the transition of blacks into old age. Analogously, older whites, because they limited help seeking to single family sources and had little rehearsal in substituting a variety of informal helpers, may have more difficulty in replacing these single sources of help as they are lost. Thus the move into old age is less tranquil for whites than it is for blacks.

Finally, the multidimensionality of help received from informal network helpers may be an important consideration in the psychological survivorship of older blacks. For example, the help received from friends or combinations of family members may be different in quantity, type, or quality from the help received from a spouse or a single family member. If this assumption is true, than the quantity, type, or quality of help can be changed by changing the helpers. This method would be a benefit in coping with changing needs brought about by aging.

The decline of prayer suggests that it will not be the dominant coping strategy of elderly blacks in the future. Why is prayer as a coping reaction to worry decreasing among older blacks? First, resorting to prayer as a means of coping with problems may be inversely related to the size of the opportunity structure for blacks. As opportunities widen for blacks (as for example, they did between 1957 and 1976), more avenues to problem solving open, providing options other than prayer for use in solving problems— such as direct actions. This greater access to other modes of coping means that older blacks are better able to negotiate their environments and their family members are better able to arrange their environments as well—creating for older blacks less need to turn to powerful others for help and at the same time placing black family members in better positions to help their older family members. In other words, older blacks, their kin, and friends are more able to handle their problems directly. Extending the theory further, if positive outcomes are more often associated with direct actions than with prayer, these alternate strategies would become more rewarding and more motivating than prayer, and thus prayer as a means of coping with problems would begin to decline. An alternate explanation, of course, is that yesterday's prayers are being answered in today's empowerment and that older blacks' need for supplication has become less urgent and less global. If opportunities continue to widen for blacks and their family members, prayer as a coping strategy may eventually be replaced by help seeking in the informal net-

work. The present data suggest that this decline has already begun; that is, use of combinations of family members was observed to increase as the use of prayer decreased from 1957 to 1976.

We might argue, then, that lifetime rehearsal in using combinations of family members and friends; flexibility in interchanging these helpers at critical life points; and being able to manipulate the level, quantity, and type of help available by manipulating the helpers—coupled with the fact that blacks may also be more socialized to adapt to uncertainty and change within their lives—make up a dynamic coping package that is sensitive to life's changing circumstances and changing needs. This coping package, used at successive transitions, may become increasingly polished; those blacks who learn to use the package most effectively at previous stages overcome roadblocks more successfully at successive stages. These survivors thus arrive at the penultimate transition—old age—more fortified, more rehearsed, and better able to adapt to its exigencies, despite fewer economic and social resources. For blacks, then, the move into old age may be more transition than crisis. The critical issue of whether the strategies contained in this coping package are correlated with psychological survivorship remains open to question.

If the coping armamentarium of blacks is indeed different from that of whites and if it is this difference that accounts for the purported greater adaptation of blacks to old age, there needs to be a more precise analysis of the factors that constitute this coping package: its elements, the proportions of these elements that yield maximum effectiveness in coping, and its ability to change in response to life changes. If old age does indeed inherit what has gone before, is the ease with which individuals make the transition into old age predictable from the successful use of this package earlier in life? More importantly, are these adaptive strategies teachable?

If blacks have truly developed and used extraordinary coping repertoires that sustain them psychologically in old age, the mistake must not be made of thinking that this psychological well-being is an adequate substitute for economic and social well-being in old age. The goal of social policy, in fact, must be to strike a balance among the economic, social, and psychological components of well-being by attempting to equalize these factors in the lives of the black and white elderly. This equalization could be effected by strengthening the weaknesses of each group. If the adaptive strategies of blacks in old age are superior to those of whites, then the adaptive mechanisms of whites might be altered based on what is known about the successful strategies employed by blacks. Similarly, the economic and social resources of older blacks must be increased to levels that approach those of comparable whites. Such a balance would help to insure that the move into old age for blacks and whites alike will be more transition than crisis.

ANNALS, *AAPSS*, **464**, November 1982

Contemporary Grandparenthood:
A Systemic Transition

By JETSE SPREY and SARAH H. MATTHEWS

ABSTRACT: The transition to grandparenthood is presented as a stage in the family life cycle in which meaning comes from outside the boundaries of the original nuclear family unit through alliances initiated and produced by offspring. A demographic picture of grandparenthood is presented that shows that the transition is likely to occur in middle age and to overlap less with active parenting than was the case in the past, and that the ages of both grandparents and new parents are important variables affecting transition. Past research has focused on grandparenthood as a role and has largely ignored the effects of family systems on role performance. A systems perspective shows that the grandparent-grandchild bond is initially mediated by the parents. As time passes, however, the bond becomes more direct, although it continues to be negotiated within the extended family system, which is always in flux. Focus on role has obscured the nature of the transition to grandparenthood and the years immediately following it, viewing it as an extension of parenting and not characteristic of real grandparents.

Jetse Sprey, Ph.D., Yale, is professor of sociology at Case Western Reserve University. He is currently editor of the Journal of Marriage and the Family, *and has written extensively in the areas of family conflict and organization.*

Sarah H. Matthews received her Ph.D. from the University of California, Davis, and is assistant professor of sociology at Case Western Reserve University. She is the author of The Social World of Old Women: Management of Self Identity *and is currently engaged in research on friendship through the life course.*

MOST people spend their lives in various family settings. They are born and reared in a family of orientation, and travel afterward through a different family cycle that ranges from its inception—at marriage—to its final disappearance when its founding members are no longer alive. Social scientists have been interested in identifying specific stages or periods in the life course of families particularly relevant to the fate of their members.[1] Such stages are assumed to be associated with critical role transitions in the lives of those involved in them.[2] Looking at people in families over time in this manner provides a perspective within which the duality of the familial process can be understood analytically. The ongoing reciprocity between aging individuals and their changing family environment, each continuously confronting and influencing the development of the other, is elucidated within a family life cycle perspective.

The stages and their accompanying transitions that are significant in their effects on individual family members and the exact nature of their impact are empirical questions[3] that cannot be divorced from the historical period of which they are asked.[4] In consideration of this, grandparenthood and the transition to it will be dealt with in this article in such a way as to provide a framework that will prove conceptually fruitful in further research on intergenerational bonds in contemporary society.

In most research on the family life cycle, the boundaries of the family are set to include only two generations and to describe the ideal nuclear unit, which begins with a marriage and ends with the death of one of the spouses. To understand the complex nature of contemporary grandparenthood, the borders within which the family scenario takes its course must be extended so as to incorporate the bonds between grandparents and their adult children, mates, and offspring. The transition to grandparenthood, then, as visualized here, represents the entrance into a stage in which primary meaning comes from outside the boundaries of the original nuclear family unit. It is this element that adds to the fulfillment of any particular grandparental couple, but also brings outside encroachment into their own nuclear family unit. Furthermore, such exchanges with the outside continue to affect widowed grandparents as much as their still-married counterparts.

THE DEMOGRAPHICS OF GRANDPARENTHOOD

During this century both the number of persons and the proportion of the population who are quali-

1. Reuben Hill and Roy H. Rodgers, "The Developmental Approach," in *Handbook of Marriage and the Family*, ed. Harold T. Christensen (Chicago, IL: Rand McNally, 1964), pp. 171-211.

2. Joan Aldous, *Family Careers: Developmental Change in Families* (New York: John Wiley, 1978), p. 81.

3. Graham B. Spanier, William Sauer, and Robert Larzelere, "An Empirical Evaluation of the Family Life Cycle," *Journal of Marriage and the Family*, 41:27-38 (Feb. 1979); Steven L. Nock, "The Family Life Cycle: Empirical or Conceptual Tool?" *Journal of Marriage and the Family*, 42:15-26 (Feb. 1979); Steven L. Nock, "Family Life-Cycle Transitions: Longitudinal Effects on Family Members," *Journal of Marriage and the Family*, 43:703-14 (Aug. 1981).

4. John Demos, "Old Age in Early New England," in *Turning Points*, eds. John Demos and Sarane Spence Boocock (Chicago, IL: University of Chicago Press, 1978), pp. 248-87.

fied to become grandparents have increased significantly. Two demographic changes underlie this fact. In the first place, more infants survive long enough to become parents. This is the major consequence for grandparenthood of the declining death rate that has resulted in only minor improvements in survival rates once adulthood is achieved. The life expectancy for individuals who were 35 in 1900-2 was slightly over 74 years, while in 1974 it climbed to almost 75 years for that age category, a gain of less than one year.[5] Increased life expectancy, then, has occurred primarily because many more people survive the first years of life. Once the age of parenthood has been reached, individuals are likely to survive long enough to become grandparents or even great-grandparents. This situation has remained virtually stable since the beginning of the century, and it is not likely to change dramatically in the future. Also relevant is the fact that because of the steadily declining birthrate in North America, there has been a concomitant increase in the proportion of older persons. In 1900 only 4 percent of the United States population was 65 or older, while by 1980 this proportion had risen to approximately 11 percent.[6]

A second factor affecting the grandparent category in the population is that despite the overall reduction in average family size, more adult women become parents.

Approximately 23 percent of women born in the 1880s bore no children. The percentage of women who are child free has declined steadily in subsequent age groups so that in 1965 the percentage of women then in the middle of their child-bearing years who were expected never to bear children was only 10 percent.[7] The decline in the number of children per mother,[8] then, has been accompanied by an increase in the proportion of women who become mothers and who thereby create the foundation for grandparenthood. By the same token, a significant increase in the proportion of women who remain child free should result in an overall decline in the proportion of grandparents. Unfortunately, fertility rates are computed for women only, so that any prediction about changes in the number of men who become potential grandfathers must remain completely speculative.

Although the transition to grandparenthood is marked by the birth of the first grandchild, the transition process begins well in advance of that event. The ages at which parents become grandparents depend, first, upon the ages at which they themselves become parents and, second, upon the ages at which their children reproduce for the first time. Both of these are affected not only by personal choice but also by cohort and period effects with respect to the normative age at which marriage and child bearing occur.

Gender plays a minor but consistent part here. Males, on the average, tend to marry later than females,

5. Herman B. Brotman, "Life Expectancy: Comparison of National Levels in 1900 and 1974 and Variations in State Levels, 1969-1971," *The Gerontologist*, 17:12-22 (Feb. 1977).

6. R. Thomas Gillaspy, "The Older Population: Considerations for Family Ties," in *Aging Parents*, ed. Pauline K. Ragan (Los Angeles, CA: University of Southern California Press, 1979), pp. 11-26.

7. Paul C. Glick and Robert Parke, Jr., "New Approaches in Studying the Life Cycle of the Family," *Demography*, 2:193 (1965).

8. Paul C. Glick, "Updating the Life Cycle of the Family," *Journal of Marriage and the Family*, 39:8 (Feb. 1977).

and are most often older then their brides. Thus grandfathers as a category will be older than grandmothers and paternal grandparents as a category will be older than maternal ones at the onset of grandparenthood.

As noted earlier, almost all family demographers have used the life cycle framework with its focus on the "succession of critical stages through which the typical family passes through its life span."[9] Unfortunately, for the purpose of this article, its boundary is seen as the life span of the nuclear family unit, so that the birth of the first grandchild is incorporated in the family life cycle of a new family of procreation, rather than in that of the grandparents. Demographic data on the median age at which parents become grandparents for the first time are not available, but a fairly good estimate can be made. The median age of mothers in age cohorts at the birth of both the first and last child is available, as is the median age of mothers at the marriage of the last child. The median age of mothers at the marriage of the first child can be estimated from this information, and from this, the median age of grandmothers at the birth of their first grandchild.[10]

The age considered appropriate to marry and bear children fluctuates, but is always within biological limits.[11] Apparently the median age at which mothers become grandmothers has changed very little during this century. Women who married in the 1950s and 1960s can expect to become grandmothers at slightly earlier ages—42 or 43—but for all mothers who married in the twentieth century, the median age is only slightly higher, 45. The average age at which fathers become grandfathers, however, probably has changed slightly more, because the median age at which men marry has declined from 26.1 years in 1890 to 22.8 years in 1960, a difference of 3.3 years. The decline for women over the same period is 1.7 years.[12] Thus, becoming a grandparent at the present time is not, as some gerontologists suggest, "more a middle-age than an old-age event."[13] On the contrary, the average age at which parents become grandparents fluctuates within a small range of years and, at the present time, more grandparents are likely to live well into old age, long enough to see most, if not all, of their grandchildren mature and perhaps even have children of their own.

A grandparent cohort, which would include all parents who become grandparents in a given year, would be quite a diverse group, even with respect to age. As mentioned earlier, paternal grandparents are, on the average, likely to be older than maternal ones. Further significant variations would be associated with socioeconomic class. Children from higher socioeconomic backgrounds tend to marry at later ages than those from the lower part of the class structure.[14] The birth of the first grandchild, then, will occur at later ages

9. Ibid., p. 5.
10. Ibid., pp. 6, 8.
11. Alice S. Rossi, "Life-Span Theories and Women's Lives," *Signs*, 6:17 (Autumn 1980).

12. Glick and Parke, "New Approaches in Studying the Life Cycle of the Family," p. 189.
13. Lillian E. Troll, "Grandparenting," in *Aging in the 1980's: Psychological Issues*, ed. L. W. Poon (Washington, DC: American Psychological Association, 1980), p. 475.
14. James A. Sweet, "Demography and the Family," *Annual Review of Sociology*, 3:370 (1977).

more often for grandparents of higher socioeconomic status.

The ages of the children of such a grandparent cohort would also vary greatly and, in turn, result in different behavioral expectations associated with becoming grandparents. Parents who become grandparents at 45 because their 16-year-old daughter gives birth to a child face quite different responsibilities from those whose daughter is 25 at the birth of her first child. In the second instance, the behavior associated with the transition to grandparenthood may well be experienced as a great deal more voluntary than in the first one. The economic and emotional dependence of young parents on their parents will decrease with age and vary by class, educational status, and gender. It is thus only under quite specific circumstances that grandparents really can live up to the culturally held stereotype of happy, carefree grandparents and function as what a French author called *"parents à plaisanterie."*[15]

The more relevant demographic changes that have taken place during this century are not those that specifically affect the age at which parents become grandparents, but ones that are important to grandparenthood more generally. The number and spacing of offspring by parents who may at some future time become grandparents have changed. The average number of years between the births of the first and last child has decreased. For the cohort of mothers born in the 1880s, the average number of children was 3.9, and the length of time between the birth of the first and the last child, 9.9 years. For the cohort of mothers born in the 1950s, the corresponding figures are expected to be 2.5 and 6.9.[16] For grandmotherhood, and probably grandfatherhood as well, this means that the length of time in which mothers simultaneously have children at home and are grandmothers is much shorter at the present time than it was in the past.

The transition to the postparental stage of the family life cycle is likely to correspond more closely to the transition to grandparenthood than was the case in the past, especially for members of the higher socioeconomic strata who have lower overall fertility rates. This makes grandparenthood a distinct stage that, once entered, is likely to stretch well into the adult years of all of the grandchildren.

The transition to grandparenthood, then, marks the beginning of a period in the nuclear family life cycle in which outside connections increasingly dictate the challenges to which the formerly nuclear family must respond. Parents who become grandparents enter a stage, usually in middle age, in which they will participate in a family system that contains newly acquired in-law children, grandchildren, great-grandchildren and, very likely, stepgrandchildren and former in-law children as well.

DEFINING GRANDPARENTHOOD

Grandparents are parents' parents. Parents become grandparents not because of a decision they make but because their children reproduce. Therefore the relationship between grandparents and their grandchildren is an indirect one, in that it requires a mediating link

15. Hervé Le Bras, "Parents, Grands-Parents, Bisaïeux," *Population*, 28:18 (Jan./Feb. 1973).

16. Glick, "Updating the Life Cycle of the Family," pp. 6, 8.

through the parents.[17] This gives parents a great deal of control over the contacts between their children and their respective sets of parents. When the grandchildren grow older and become more independent of their parents, the mediated aspect of their relationships with their grandparents may disappear. When grandchildren are young, however, the link between grandparents and grandchildren is dependent on the actions of a mediating parent.

The actual transition to grandparenthood is a two-step process, since under ideal circumstances the birth of the first grandchild is preceded by the marriage of an adult child. This is not a trivial point, because it is the acquisition of the first in-law child that involves the parents in a newly extended family system of which their own family nucleus will remain an integral part for the rest of their lives. As in the case of grandchildren, the linkage to the in-law child is indirect and is initiated by their own child. It is potentially a very important bond because of the possibility that their child's marriage will terminate with custody of the grandchildren being awarded to the in-law child. This point is especially relevant for paternal grandparents, since in present-day American society, custody of the young children in case of divorce most often goes to the mother.

When the first grandchild is born, another link between the parents and their extended family is forged. This one, in contrast to the in-law tie, is biological or consanguineal. It redefines the existing bond to the in-law child, not by making it biological in the true sense, but by recognizing the parent as a vehicle, or intermediary, through whom the lineage of the grandparents extends itself one more step into the future. This is reflected in the conclusion of a recent study of kinship in which Spicer and Hampe suggest that the "presence of children is a functional equivalent for the marital bond in [a divorced spouse's] maintaining contact after divorce with affinal relatives."[18]

To explain and understand the realities of contemporary grandparenthood, therefore, it will not suffice to concentrate exclusively on the changing roles of individuals during the transition to grandparenthood. Viewing grandparenthood simply as a set of rules and norms that tell certain individuals how to deal with specific others cannot be very illuminating. Instead, it makes more analytical sense to consider grandparenthood as something that exists between sets of specific individuals. In other words, it is seen here not only as an individually held role but also as descriptive of a very specific and unique social bond. In this broader context the transition to grandparenthood becomes two dimensional in that it links persons horizontally with their expanding family system and vertically or diachronically with a new stage in their individual and familial life course.

STUDYING GRANDPARENTS

On the whole, the study of grandparents has been largely ignored by students of the family and gerontol-

17. Joan F. Robertson, "Interaction in Three-Generation Families, Parents as Mediators: Toward a Theoretical Perspective," *International Journal of Aging and Human Development*, 6(2):103-10 (1975).

18. Jerry W. Spicer and Gary D. Hampe, "Kinship Interaction after Divorce," *Journal of Marriage and the Family*, 28:118 (Feb. 1975).

ogists alike. Most existing work on grandparental behavior almost exclusively focuses on the nature and the meaning of their role performance. The concept of role was formulated by social scientists to help explain how individuals participate in social institutions. In and by itself, however, it is not sufficient to account for how the institutional order itself is structured and changes over time.

Grandparenting as role performance

Empirical research on grandparental role behavior has been reported by Albrecht, Neugarten and Weinstein, Wood and Robertson, Robertson, Boyd, and Kivnick.[19] Linda K. George concludes from her assessment of this research literature that "grandparenthood doesn't appear to be a high-impact life event. Normative guidelines are so few and so vague that individuals pursue the style of relationship they find most comfor-

19. Ruth Albrecht, "The Parental Responsibilities of Grandparents," *Marriage and Family Living*, 16:201-204 (Aug. 1954); Bernice L. Neugarten and Karol K. Weinstein, "The Changing American Grandparent," *Journal of Marriage and the Family*, 26:119-204 (Feb. 1964); Vivian Wood and Joan F. Robertson, "The Significance of Grandparenthood," in *Time, Roles and Self in Old Age*, ed. Jaber Gubrium (New York: Behavioral Publications, 1976), pp. 279-304; Joan F. Robertson, "Grandmotherhood: A Study of Role Conceptions," *Journal of Marriage and the Family*, 33: 165-74 (Feb. 1977); Rosamonde Boyd, "The Valued Grandparent: A Changing Social Role," in *Living in the Multi-Generational Family*, ed. Wilma Donahue (Ann Arbor, MI: Institute of Gerontology, 1969), pp. 90-106; Helen Q. Kivnick, Grandparenthood and the Mental Health of Grandparents," *Aging and Society*, 1:365-91 (Nov. 1981); Helen Q. Kivnick, "Grandparenthood: An Overview of Meaning and Mental Health," *The Gerontologist*, 22:59-66 (Feb. 1982).

table."[20] Lillian E. Troll reaches a similar conclusion: "the actual interactions between modern American grandparents and their grandchildren seem to be characterized more by idiosyncratic or personality-determined behaviors . . . grandparents are usually free to pick the style they wish."[21]

Conclusions like these which point to personal choice and, thereby, to the absence of a clearly defined social role, are suspect. To a significant degree, they are an artifact of viewing grandparental conduct as a role largely divorced from the family system that sets its parameters. For example, grandparents with divorced children are more likely than those without divorced children to see themselves as surrogate parents.[22] That this reflects a free choice or a quirk of personality seems unlikely. A better explanation is that this finding reflects the adjustment of the grandparent-grandchild relationship as an ongoing interpersonal bond to a drastically changed set of circumstances. In another example, Boyd sees the valued grandparent role as an extended parent role that presupposes "close and congenial relationships with one's children and in-laws." A prerequisite for its successful performance is "to be recognized and accepted as an active parent and grandparent."[23] Clearly, this kind of definition eliminates

20. Linda K. George, *Role Transitions in Later Life* (Belmont, CA: Wadsworth, 1980), p. 88.

21. Troll, "Grandparenting," p. 478.

22. Jetse Sprey and Sarah H. Matthews, "The Impact of Divorce on Grandparenthood" (Paper presented at the Gerontological Society of America Meetings, Toronto, Nov. 1981).

23. Boyd, "The Valued Grandparent: A Changing Social Role," p. 100.

grandparents who, for whatever reason, live far away from their grandchildren. Furthermore, it closes the door to any line of questioning directed toward finding out under what conditions grandparents are more accepted and/or active than other conditions.

In research that focuses on the style, type, meaning, or significance of the role of grandparent, their behavior is treated as a property of individuals only. Characteristics, such as age, gender, marital status, employment status, and friendship associations, are used to explain, for the most part unsuccessfully, the style or role of grandparents and/or the perceived significance of the grandparent role to the individuals in question. As suggested earlier, however, grandparenting does not take place in social isolation, nor is it a role performed indiscriminately toward all others. On the contrary, it derives its social and personal meaning from its reciprocity with a relatively small set of quite specific and significant others.

Even within this group of grandchildren, each separate grandparent-grandchild bond must be considered as unique. Most grandparents have more than one grandchild and often have sets of grandchildren, each linked to the grandparent through a different child and his or her spouse(s). To read, therefore, that three-fourths of all American grandparents see their grandchildren at least once every two weeks,[24] raises the question, Which ones are seen that regularly? All of them? Only the oldest daughter's? Or, perhaps, only one of them? Without ruling out the relevance of individual choice, it should be clear that factors, such as age, gender, geographic proximity, and

24. Troll, "Grandparenting," p. 476.

the life circumstances of grandparents, the mediating parents, and the grandchildren considered simultaneously, are essential components of the explanation of the meaning and role of grandparenting in general, as well as in the transition into that life stage.

Grandparenting within a systems context

The limitations associated with a strict role analysis of grandparental behavior do not invalidate such an approach completely, nor do they suggest that the quality of behavior is purely a function of situational contingencies. Such analysis, however, valuable as it may be, does not tell the whole story about the dynamics of grandparenting as an integral part of the contemporary family institution. A focus on the role alone, for example, cannot delineate the conditions under which it seems culturally appropriate and personally sensible to perceive and actually act a given formal, equalitarian, or patriarchal grandparent-grandchild role, to mention just a few options.

In one of the early treatises on grandparenthood, Apple attended to systemic parameters and hypothesized that "formality between grandparents and grandchildren is related to the association of grandparents with family authority."[25] This conclusion has been quoted widely, but its analytical thrust seems to have bypassed many students of contemporary grandparenthood. The point, however, seems quite simple. Individuals, when deciding how to act a given role, must operate within a finite set of

25. Dorian Apple, "The Social Structure of Grandparenthood," *American Anthropologist*, 58:662 (Aug. 1956).

FIGURE 1

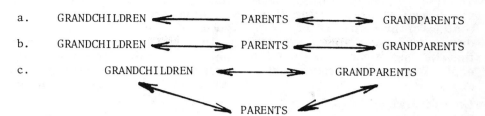

structural boundaries. Such constraints, which are dependent on the circumstances of specific situations, guide not only personal choices of style but also the manner in which participating grandparents perceive their identities within particular bonds.

There have been other attempts to place grandparental behavior within a structural framework. Kahana and Kahana, for example, suggest an approach in which grandparenthood "is viewed as part of a group process within the family involving relationships and interaction between the three or four generations, [and] considerations of power, control and influence in the framework of the kin network."[26] Unfortunately, in the figure that accompanies this description, the basic mediating position of the middle generation relative to the older and younger generation is ignored.

Since the nature of the ongoing reciprocity between grandparents and grandchildren changes over time, it seems instructive to diagram it for three stages: (1) when the grandchildren are infants and small children; (2) when the grandchildren are pre- and early teenagers; and (3) when the grandchildren are older teenagers and adults.

26. Eva Kahana and Boaz Kahana, "Theoretical and Research Perspectives on Grandparenthood," *Aging and Human Development*, 2:267 (May 1971).

The three resulting types are depicted in Figure 1. For very young grandchildren, then, contact with grandparents originates with the parents, while grandparental initiatives are also channeled through the parents. Only when children become quite independent are they in a position to bypass their parents completely. It is interesting to note that grandparents, in turn, also are in a position to mediate between their older grandchildren and the middle generations and between sets of grandchildren. Grandparents, of course, possess far less power in this type of mediation than do parents in their intermediary position vis à vis their parents and their children.

It is important to realize that social relationships in their interconnections possess a logic of their own. Age bonds, for example, are essentially asymmetrical between generations. They also are dynamic, that is, they change over time, which means that the balance between what is at stake for each side also may change considerably. Other relations, such as geographical distance, are symmetrical. Geography does affect each party equally, but its consequences for the lives of those involved may well differ depending on the impact of other variables, such as age or financial resources. The picture that emerges in this manner is quite complex because it is multivariate. To further explore its ramifications would lead well beyond the direct confines of this article. It does introduce a realm of analysis, however, that lies significantly beyond the explanatory power of role analysis.

Grandparenthood as a transition

The grandparent stage, then, is one during which existing relations with children, in-law children, former in-law children, grandchildren, and occasionally stepgrandchildren are continuously renegotiated and rearranged. The resulting equilibrium, if it exists at all, remains inherently unstable and reflects, at any given time, a balance between the various inputs and resources of all participants. This does not mean, however, that such complex, evolving sets of interlocking familial relationships are by necessity understructured, or inherently tenuous.[27]

When confronted with the necessity to maintain one's bonds with special others in the absence of cultural guidance, individuals create their own shared scenarios for dealing with each other and the outside world.[28] Despite the uniqueness of a family system, its ordering process may be quite predictable and recognizable both to its members and to outside observers. Even crisis events, such as separation or divorce, can be expected to have predictable consequences for the relations between members of different generations in different categories of families.

Individuals in each of the different generations, however, may deviate from the expectations the others in their respective families have about their behavior. Earlier, the timing of the birth of the first grandchild was identified as an event that could affect drastically the nature of the transition to grandparenthood. Teenage pregnancy, especially its out-of-wedlock variety, can force parents to severely downplay their ceremonial grandparental status and continue acting primarily as parents. Support for this statement can be found in Furstenberg's research on teenage parenthood. Almost 90 percent of the adolescents in his study lived with a parent or close relative during their first pregnancy, with 77 percent still in that living arrangement one year post-partum and 46 percent, five years post-partum.[29] Not all parents offer refuge and support to their teenage daughters, but the decision-making processes involved are neither random, nor strictly personal. Furstenberg, for example, also reports that

adolescents were more likely to remain in couple-headed households than in female-headed households. . . . The greater economic resources of the couple-headed families either were used to purchase childcare services or enabled the grandmother to remain at home while the young mother resumed her education.[30]

27. Gunhild O. Hagestad, "Problems and Promises in the Social Psychology of Intergenerational Relations," in *Aging: Stability and Change in the Family*, eds. Robert W. Fogel, Elaine Hatfield, Sara B. Kiesler, and Ethel Shanas (New York: Academic Press, 1981), p. 18.

28. David Kantor and William Lehr, *Inside the Family* (San Francisco: Jossey-Bass, 1976), pp. 6-22.

29. Frank Furstenberg, "Implicating the Family: Teenage Parenthood and Kinship Involvement," in *Teenage Pregnancy in a Family Context*, ed. Theodora Ooms (Philadelphia: Temple University Press, 1981), p. 136.

30. Ibid., p. 140.

Most students of the early pregnancy phenomenon simply ignore the fact that the parents involved also have been transformed into grandparents. Ladner's study of black lower-class adolescent girls, many of whom had become mothers in adolescence without marrying, is a case in point. Mothers of teenage girls remain mothers even after the birth of the grandchild, as is clear from the following:

Rarely were young mothers who remained in the home of their parents expected to take complete charge of these responsibilities. Most of them could always get their mothers and grandmothers to baby-sit for them and to take care of many of the major tasks associated with child-rearing.[31]

Grandmothers in such situations also seem to remain frozen in their statuses. To Ladner, the difference between mothers and grandmothers of teenage mothers is simply one of age, since both seem to function conjointly as surrogate parents. It may be that this somewhat circular perception by family members and social scientists alike accounts for the comment cited previously, "grandparenthood doesn't appear to be a high-impact life event."[32] When the transition does cause a major impact, the individuals in question remain identified in their own minds, and in those of outsiders, as parents rather than as grandparents. Since most of the more traumatic and problematic transitions are likely to be associated with early grandparenthood, it becomes less puzzling that happy, carefree grandparenting is linked traditionally to old age.

31. Joyce Ladner, *Tomorrow's Tomorrow: The Black Woman* (New York: Doubleday, 1971), p. 228.
32. George, *Role Transitions in Later Life*, p. 88.

A view of the transition to the grandparental stage as normal thus depends on the degree to which the first grandchild's parents are in step with the behavioral expectations associated with their membership in a given age cohort. The actual content of such prescriptions is, in its turn, a function of a range of additional factors, for example, social class, religious affiliation, race, and degree of formal education. In addition to teenage pregnancy, the significant postponement of the birth of the first child also will have lasting consequences for the quality of grandparent-grandchild relations. This reproductive pattern, possibly associated with a growing proportion of dual-work marriages, will tend to increase the age differentials between grandparents and their grandchildren. The older the new parents are, the more independent from their parents they are likely to be, thereby increasing the probability that the new grandparents will participate purely on a ceremonial level. The timing of parenthood, then, has significant consequences for two generations of grandparents. Individuals who postpone parenthood not only affect the transition to grandparenthood of their parents, but also of themselves.

Finally, the high divorce rate in the United States has its major impact on grandparenting in the years immediately following the transition. Most separations and divorces still occur during the early years of marriage when most offspring are quite young and many couples still are economically vulnerable. At that point, many grandparent couples are middle-aged, especially the maternal ones. Such grandparents, on the average, will have access to valuable resources to offer their divorcing child.[33] Furthermore, they will be, in all likelihood, young enough to become actively involved with the care of their grandchildren if deemed necessary. On the other hand, at that stage in the life cycle many grandparents still may be working full-time and be active in a range of community and other social activities. All these factors may give rise to basic conflicts of interest and a need for renegotiation and restructuring of existing relationships. In addition, it may be necessary to come to terms with relatively new components within the family system, such as former daughters-in-law who are custodial parents, and step-grandchildren. The transition to grandparenthood cannot be conceived, therefore, as a one- or even two-step process. It is, especially during the first 15 years or so, a process of differentiation and change during which the existing equilibrium between all participating generations will be continuously open to challenge.

SUMMARY AND CONCLUSION

Becoming a grandparent has been a middle-age transition since the beginning of this century. The demographic changes identified in the preceding pages point to more people in contemporary American society becoming grandparents but to a declining number of grandchildren per grandparent. Grandparenting, as a stage in the life cycle, is increasingly associated with the empty nest stage of the family life cycle, and a growing proportion of grandparents will see all of their grandchildren grow into adulthood.

33. Hans Von Hentig, "The Sociological Function of the Grandmother," *Social Forces*, 24:389-92 (Mar. 1946).

The family event that clearly seems most influential on the transition to grandparenthood, and its subsequent life career, is the timing of the first grandchild. Of great importance also is the spacing of the additional grandchildren. Both sets of reproductive behaviors lie beyond the immediate control of the grandparents themselves, but do significantly influence the course of their grandparental careers. Indeed the only voluntary aspect of becoming a grandparent is the decision to become a parent.

Grandparenthood as a social phenomenon remains very much neglected both by gerontologists and family sociologists. Most research has focused on the manner in which grandparents perform their culturally prescribed social role. The grandparental role, however, is blurred and highly stereotyped in American culture, so that such studies, important as their findings may be, fail to explain the part grandparents play within the extended networks of their families. Thus terms like "role loss," for example, not only seem somewhat irrelevant but also potentially misleading, since they provide labels rather than explanations. Structurally, there is no loss during the transition to grandparenthood, but only gain, since the newly acquired bonds literally branch out and enlarge the intimate network of the original nuclear family. It is in this context that a most relevant change in grandparenthood is identified. Nuclear families are becoming smaller, but at the same time, members of more generations are alive at one time and share a greater part of each other's life spans. It is this potential for direct, voluntary interaction between young adult grandchildren and their grandparents that seems an important added interpersonal resource, not just to the individuals involved, but also to the family and present-day society.

Contemporary grandparents are confronted with a range of situational circumstances, some of which are so new that conventional wisdom simply does not offer normative solutions. Despite the absence of culturally defined role models, there is no reason to assume that the interaction between grandparents and the others in their families necessarily becomes unstructured or a mere reflection of idiosyncratic personal choices. Rather, the negotiated order that is observed in such instances reflects a different quality of structuring than that which characterizes the more bureaucratically organized segments of society.

Anticipating Transitions:
Possible Options in "Family" Forms

By GORDON F. STREIB and MADELINE HAUG PENNA

ABSTRACT: Three major trends affecting family life are an increase in households composed of unrelated persons, an increase in single-parent families, and an increase in divorce. These trends indicate the need for forms of living arrangement other than the traditional nuclear family, especially to confront two major sets of problems faced by many mid-life women: economic and socioemotional. Two prototype living arrangements—"families"—are proposed: (1) adaptation of the concept of the halfway house and (2) utilization of a cooperative living arrangement that has operated successfully with older persons. Since these prototypes have been somewhat successful in dealing with primary group environments of the young and the elderly, such models might be adapted on an experimental basis for midlife women who need added social supports and an increased array of choices from which to plan new directions in their lives.

Gordon F. Streib is graduate research professor, Department of Sociology and a faculty associate of the Center for Gerontological Studies, University of Florida, Gainesville. He received his Ph.D. from Columbia University and was a member of the faculty of Cornell University. His current research is on shared living arrangements for older persons, and a comparative study of retirement communities.

Madeline Haug Penna is an assistant professor of sociology at Florida Atlantic University. While a graduate student at the University of Florida, she was Gordon Streib's research assistant and coauthored with him an earlier report on mid-life women for the Select Committee on Aging. Her other writings include: "Miami's Garment Industry and Its Workers," to appear in Peripheral Workers, *volume II of* Research in the Sociology of Work, *1982.*

THE records of human cultures show clearly that life transitions are significant social and psychological events. Many cultures have marked the transition points—dedication of the infant, puberty, marriage, widowhood, and death—by important public and family events. In 1909 Arnold L. Gennep was the first writer to give a systematic account of some of these transitions in his book, *Les Rites de Passage*.[1] Gennep and other writers—anthropologists, psychologists, and journalists—have directed their attention primarily to the early transition points. Only recently has focus been directed to transitions in adult life. Marjorie Fiske Lowenthal and her colleagues have provided one of the most systematic and detailed accounts by describing and analyzing what happens to men and women at four stages of adult life: high school seniors, young newlyweds, middle-aged parents, and older persons about to retire.[2] Lowenthal and other contemporary writers about middle- and late-life transitions have concentrated upon personal adaptation to the transition points.[3]

1. See Arnold L. Gennep, *Les Rites de Passage* (Paris: E. Nourry, 1909).
2. See Marjorie Fiske Lowenthal, Majda Thurher, David Chiriboga, *Four Stages of Life* (San Francisco: Jossey-Bass, 1975).
3. See Douglas C. Kimmel, *Adulthood and Aging*, 2nd ed. (New York: John Wiley, 1980); see Daniel J. Levinson, *The Seasons of a Man's Life* (New York: Knopf, 1978); Bernice L. Neugarten, "The Awareness of Middle Age," in *Middle Age and Aging*, ed. Bernice L. Neugarten (Chicago: University of Chicago Press, 1968), pp. 93-98; Bernice L. Neugarten and Gunhild O. Hagestad, "Age and The Life Course," in *Handbook of Aging and the Social Sciences*, eds. Robert H. Binstock and Ethel Shanas (New York: Van Nostrand Reinhold, 1976), pp. 35-55; see Gail Sheehy, *Passages: Predictable Crises of Adult Life* (New York: Dutton, 1976); see George E. Vaillant, *Adaptation to Life* (Boston: Little, Brown).

These writers were concerned with the psychodynamics of middle- and late-life transitions—areas psychological or sociopsychological in their focus.

The orientation of this article is more sociological, in that it is concerned with the larger social and cultural factors that determine the transition points and processes. Thus the focus is on the instabilities and changes that mark the larger culture, and on the way in which social factors mark the turning points, particularly in terms of negative cultural determinants.

This analysis centers on current living arrangements and marital status of midlife persons, primarily women. A voluntary type of family is then discussed, with particular attention to how it offers supports to meet economic and socioemotional issues of the mid- and late-life transitions.

It is assumed that persons engage in problem solving. They seek to maximize rewards and to avoid costs so as to consolidate their gains. Choices are made from available options. The traditional rational economic model of human behavior is not considered relevant, for in studies of family life in natural settings, the problem-solving person confronts the realities of the complexity of the culture and the sociopsychological pressures involved in the everyday experience. Thus the attention of this article shifts from the macro-level—culture and society—to the smaller units of living—the micro-environment where most people carry out their daily lives. Various kinds of living arrangements, or pseudo-families, may become real options for persons at crucial transition points to consider and accept as ways by which to cope with their circumstances. Descriptions of these shared living arrangements, or intentional families, are presented. Such families may provide ways to generate new choices and responses that help overcome the imperatives of the turning points.

Elder has said: "Turning points in retrospect have much in common with a mirage; the closer one's approach the more elusive they become."[4] This may be the view of the outsider, the detached analyst. But from the standpoint of the insider, the person at a crucial point in the life cycle, they are not mirages; they are situations involving difficult choices for which society and the local community might provide resources to facilitate the transitions.

CURRENT LIVING
ARRANGEMENTS AND
MARITAL STATUS OF
MID-LIFE WOMEN

In an advance publication on 1980 population characteristics, the Bureau of the Census reported that since the last census the number of family households rose nearly 9 million. Almost one-half of this increase, however, was because of the growth of households headed by either men or women with no spouse present. Increases also were registered for the numbers of persons living alone or with nonrelatives. During the same time period, the growth in number of family households was 17 percent, while the growth for nonfamily households was 85 percent.[5]

Thus more Americans are experiencing solitary or fragmented family living arrangements, and many of these people are in mid or later life. Of the population living alone, 65 percent were persons 45 years of age or older.[6] In years past, the period of mid-life transition was marked by the married couple's celebration of their children's maturation. During the last two decades, however, this time of celebration has been marred by increasing rates of divorce for mid-life couples, with the result that some mid-life individuals find themselves living as solitary heads of families or as solitary individuals.

Family researchers traditionally have looked upon mid-life as a period in which the married couple move inward toward each other as they launch their children from the family nest into the outside world. This, however, is no longer the case for many individuals, and this departure from tradition is more acute for women than for men. For example, among today's mid-life population, only 70 percent of women are married and living with their spouses in comparison with 83 percent of men. As they advance toward the latter portion of mid-life (ages 55 to 64), the difference between the sexes is accentuated— 67 percent of women are married with their spouses present in the home in comparison with 84 percent of men.[7] Thus the family and living arrangements of more midlife

4. Glen H. Elder, Jr., "Approaches to Social Change and the Family," in *Turning Points: Historical and Sociological Essays on the Family*, (Supplement to *American Journal of Sociology*, vol. 84), eds. John Demos and Sarane Spence Boocock (Chicago: University of Chicago Press, 1978), p. S5.

5. U.S. Bureau of the Census, *Current Population Reports*, Series P-20, No. 367,

"Households and Families by Type: March 1981 (Advance Report)" (Washington, DC: Government Printing Office, Oct. 1981), p. 1.

6. U.S. Bureau of the Census, *Current Population Reports*, Series P-20, No. 365, "Marital Status and Living Arrangements: Mar. 1980" (Washington, DC: Government Printing Office, 1981), p. 4.

7. U.S. Bureau of the Census, *Current Population Reports*, Series P-23, No. 111,

TABLE 1
PERCENTAGE IN EACH FAMILY STATUS AMONG WOMEN IN
EACH AGE GROUP, MARCH 1980

	AGE GROUPS			
	40-64	40-44	45-54	55-64
In families	87.5	94.2	90.5	80.7
Wife of head	69.6	74.0	72.2	64.4
Head	14.0	17.1	14.9	11.3
In related subfamily	.6	.9	.7	.5
Other	3.3	2.3	2.7	4.5
In unrelated subfamilies*	.1	.2	.1	.1
Not in families	12.4	5.6	9.4	19.2
Nonfamily householder †	13.3	4.6	8.1	18.1
Other persons in household ‡	.9	.8	1.0	.8
In group quarters	.2	.2	.3	.3
Total percentage	100.0	100.0	100.0	100.0
Total number of women, in thousands	28,659	5956	11,669	11,034

SOURCE: U.S. Bureau of the Census, *Current Population Reports,* Series P-20, No. 365, "Marital Status and Living Arrangements: March 1980" (Washington, DC: Government Printing Office, 1981).

* Previously defined as secondary families.

† Previously defined as primary individuals.

‡ Previously defined as secondary individuals in households.

women than midlife men (both absolutely and relatively) have been affected by current divorce and remarriage trends and mortality rates. Consequently, we focus more directly on the situation of women than men.

These two trends concerning mid-life women—greater numbers as heads of families or as solitary individuals—are evident in Table 1. Four million, or 14 percent, of mid-life women were classified as family heads in 1980. Female-headed families had the highest rate of growth of all family types during the decade of the 1970s, and in the 1980s 43 percent of the heads of such families are

women 45 years of age or older.[8] The percentages of mid-life women who head families drop with age. As age increases, however, greater percentages of these women find themselves living outside of family settings. In 1980, over 12 percent of all mid-life women reported nonfamily status, while for the 55 to 64 age group, 19 percent did so. As the categories in Table 1 indicate, most of these women are nonfamily householders, or put more simply, they live alone.

These two factors—women living alone and women living with families with no spouse present—point to

"Social and Economic Characteristics of Americans During Midlife" (Washington, DC: Government Printing Office, June 1981), p. 3.

8. Steve W. Rawlings, *Current Population Reports*, Series P-23, No. 107, "Family Maintenance by Female Householders 1970-1979" (Washington, DC: Government Printing Office), p. 5.

the need for some type of alternative living arrangements for mid-life women. The husband-wife household continues to remain the dominant form of living arrangement for mid-life women. The latest census figures, however, suggest that many women in this age group are living in some type of household that deviates from the traditional nuclear family structure. Moreover, if current trends continue, greater percentages can be expected to do so in the future.

Changes in the living arrangements of mid-life women are largely a result of changes in their marital status. Between 1970 and 1980 the divorce ratio (number of divorced persons per 1000 married persons) in the United States increased by 89 percent, compared with a 34-percent increase for the decade from 1960 to 1970. Moreover, women have a higher divorce ratio than do men (120 versus 79 per 1000), a fact that reflects a longer average period between divorce and remarriage for women and their lower likelihood of remarriage. For mid-life females the divorce ratio has increased from 53 per 1000 in 1960, to 66 per 1000 in 1970, to 112 per 1000 in 1980. Comparable figures for mid-life men indicate that their divorce ratio increased from 39 per 1000 in 1960, to 40 per 1000 in 1970, to 72 per 1000 in 1980. Thus while divorce has become a more common form of marital status for both mid-life men and women, the divorce rate for men is still only 65 percent of that for their female counterparts.[9]

Thus changes in the marital status of mid-life women are largely changes in the percentages and numbers of those who are divorced. While the greatest changes in the divorce ratio in recent years have occurred among younger age cohorts, all age categories have witnessed substantial increases. Moreover, there is no indication that this trend will decrease. If predictions concerning a 31-million increase in population size for the 45 to 54 age group between 1980 and 2010 are correct, an increase in the numbers of divorced women in this age group can be expected as well.[10]

The distribution of marital statuses of women between the ages of 40 and 64 seems to parallel the distribution of living arrangements. As of 1980, approximately 74 percent of the women in this age group were classified as married with husband present (see Table 2). This status was less common, however, among older midlife women, with only 67 percent of those between the ages of 55 and 64 so classified. Approximately 11 percent of all midlife women were widows in 1980, but 19 percent of those between the ages of 55 and 64 were, compared with about 3 percent of those between the ages of 40 and 44. Divorce, on the other hand, is more characteristic of younger mid-life women. Although at present approximately 9 percent of all midlife women are divorced, only about 7 percent of those between the ages of 55 and 64 are divorced, compared with about 11 percent of those between the ages of 55 and 64. In addition, approximately 4 percent of mid-life women are married with husband absent, with younger groups

---

9. Compiled from Table C, U.S. Bureau of the Census, "Marital Status and Living Arrangement p. 3.

10. U.S. Bureau of the Census, "Social and Economic Characteristics of Americans During Mid-Life," p. 1.

TABLE 2
**PERCENTAGE IN EACH MARITAL STATUS AMONG WOMEN IN
EACH AGE GROUP, MARCH 1980**

	AGE GROUPS			
	40-64	40-44	45-54	55-64
Single (never married)	4.6	4.8	4.7	4.6
Married, husband present	74.0	76.7	75.0	67.1
Married, husband absent	3.7	5.0	4.1	2.8
Separated	3.0	4.3	3.3	2.0
Other	.7	.7	.8	.8
Widowed	10.7	2.8	7.0	18.9
Divorced	8.5	10.6	9.2	6.7
Total percentage	100.0	100.0	100.0	100.0
Total number of women, in thousands	28,661	5957	11,670	11,034

SOURCE: U.S. Bureau of the Census, *Current Population Reports,* Series P-20, No. 365, "Marital Status and Living Arrangements: March 1980" (Washington, DC: Government Printing Office, 1981).

more likely to fall into this category (see Table 2).

In summary, the effects of changing cultural determinants on the living arrangements of the American population in general are reflected also in the living arrangements of mid-life women. Compared with earlier periods, mid-life women are now more likely to live alone, to live with nonrelatives or to be heads of families. Presently there are over three and one-half million women in the United States between the ages of 40 and 64 who live alone, and another four million who are heads of households (see Table 1). It is important to note that despite the recent attention given to the increasing incidence of cohabitation among nonmarried individuals, so far it is an uncommon solution to the problems of mid-life. While the number of individuals sharing living quarters with persons of the opposite sex more than doubled between 1970 and 1980, these adults represent only miniscule proportions of the mid-life population. The experience of cohabitation and its recent increase are more common among younger age groups.

What these census figures suggest is that the phrase "women alone" aptly describes almost 30 percent of women who are now in mid-life transition. Increasing incidence of divorce has left these women as heads of families or as individuals who live alone in a culture that is geared toward the needs of married couples and families. For both groups of women, the socioemotional adjustments of mid-life transition are confounded by the structural circumstances in which they find themselves. Both groups face economic problems as well. Thus far, however, the community has offered no alternative living arrangements to replace the companionship and economic reciprocity of traditional family structures.

THE VOLUNTARY FAMILY:
WHY IT IS NEEDED AND
WHAT IT CAN OFFER TO
MID-LIFE WOMEN

Underlying any attempt at social intervention is the rationale that the intervention measure will lead to some type of positive change—either for the individual, or society, or both. For example, such programs not only require expenditures of public funds, but may increase dependency in some cases. Nevertheless, serious economic and socioemotional difficulties are faced by some mid-life women. The next two sections will focus on these problems and on the possible solutions that alternative family and living arrangements can provide.

Economic issues

An examination of the living conditions of unattached women and their families points to one of the most obvious problems of their lives: their economic condition. The median family income of U.S. families in 1978 was approximately $17,640; however, most female-headed families or women living alone did not enjoy such an income level. The median income of female householder families was $8540, approximately 48 percent of the figure for families in general.[11]

The figures suggest that the economic situation of unattached mid-life women and their families in relation to the economic situation of other mid-life categories is quite dismal. Among those in mid-life, women's earnings were 56 percent of men's earnings. While 6 percent of all families headed by a person in mid-life lived below the poverty level, 20 percent of those maintained by a woman with no husband present did so. Moreover, 10 percent of mid-life women compared with 6 percent of mid-life men lived below the poverty level in 1978.

The monetary problems of mid-life women compared with those of men are a reflection, in part, of the relatively disadvantageous competitive position of women. Approximately 50 percent of mid-life women were in the labor force in 1979, while 83 percent of men were. Labor force participation rates for mid-life women decline with age; only 40 percent of those between 60 and 64 are currently active. Thus mid-life women are more likely than men not to be working outside the home. If they find outside employment, their most probable occupations will be in clerical or kindred positions, categories with relatively low income levels. This situation, in part, is because of women's relatively low education levels. While more mid-life women than men are high school graduates, greater percentages of mid-life men currently hold college or advanced degrees. Thus if mid-life women seek employment outside the home, they are fairly likely to find themselves in lower-paying occupations. Should they lose their job, they will most probably be unemployed for a longer period of time than will mid-life men.[12]

The employment situation of mid-life women undoubtedly reflects their familial situation in

11. Rawlings, "Family Maintenance by Female Householders 1970-1979," p. 33.

12. U.S. Bureau of the Census, "Social and Economic Characteristics of Americans During Mid-life," p. 9.

many cases. Over 62 percent of all female-headed households in 1979 had at least one of their own children under the age of 18 present in the home. Among mid-life (ages 45 to 64) female householders, 38 percent headed families with at least one child under 18 in their home. The constraints that child-care responsibilities can place upon women alone are manifested in their responses to queries concerning their labor participation. When part-time women workers between the ages of 25 and 54 were asked why they had not chosen full-time work, 59 percent mentioned household responsibilities as a constraining factor and 22 percent indicated that they could not find full-time work. Similarly, when nonworking women in the same age category were questioned about their lack of labor force participation, 87 percent replied that household responsibilities keep them from working.[13] Thus it seems reasonable to conclude that the economic problems of mid-life women are, in part, a function of the constraints arising from familial arrangements and their reactions to these constraints.

An additional source of difficulty, primarily for divorced women, is the precarious nature of their income. At least one-half of the divorced women who depend on alimony as a major source of income—approximately 15 percent of divorcees have been awarded alimony—receive it either rarely or irregularly.[14] Not only is the income

received meager but it also does not offer economic security.

Another major source of income with a precarious basis for female-headed families with children is Aid to Families with Dependent Children (AFDC) payments. Approximately three-fifths of families receiving AFDC payments depend on some type of additional welfare assistance.[15] Although AFDC payments are less variable than alimony, they generally provide only a minimum level of income. Thus social mobility or economic security are goals beyond the reach of most women receiving AFDC payments.

The major issue which some mid-life women must face is therefore economic—lack of an adequate and secure income. These problems are most severe for divorced women and less severe for widows and never-married women, although women in all three categories generally are less well-off economically than their male counterparts.

The first positive and probably most needed consequence of voluntary familial arrangements for women would be economic. Women would pool their resources and cooperatively share the burden of supporting a household. Nontraditional familial arrangements would offer these women the chance of improving their economic conditions. If vocational training and counseling were included as part of each program, family members would have the opportunity to upgrade their labor market skills.

13. U.S. Bureau of the Census, "Money Income in 1976 of Families and Persons in the U.S.," *Current Population Reports*, Series P-60, No. 114, Tables 59 and 60 (Washington, DC: Government Printing Office).

14. National Commission on the Observance of International Woman's Year, "To Form a More Perfect Union" (Washington,

DC: Government Printing Office, 1976), p. 102.

15. R. Brandwein, C. Brown, and E. Fox, "Women and Children Last: The Social Situation of Divorced Mothers and Their Families," *Journal of Marriage and the Family*, 36:498-514 (Aug. 1974).

The sharing of familial tasks, particularly child care, would also create the conditions that would allow these women to hold and competently perform in full-time jobs. Studies of AFDC mothers have demonstrated that many of them preferred to work, but they chose to remain at home because of the lack of available child-care facilities. This problem has been particularly acute for divorced women who work. Not only did marital dissolution result in the loss of a mate, but in many cases it also resulted in the need for a new source of child care.[16] A voluntary family would provide a source of alternative child-care arrangements allowing women to pursue either vocational or academic training or full-time employment.

Although child care is a need which pertains, for the most part, to women in early mid-life, communal child-care arrangements may have positive consequences for older women as well. Because older divorcees and widows are likely to have lower educational and occupational skills than younger ones, they may be less able to engage in outside employment. In addition, the widowed may be receiving pension or social security benefits that would give them the option of choosing to be employed or not. It is quite possible that older members of the family may find the assumption of a part-time child-care role a more attractive method of contributing to the voluntary family than outside employment. In this case, age integration of women would allow the age groups to pursue the forms of activity with which they are more comfortable.

Economic benefits would also accrue for society, for instance, a possible reduction in the number of female families on welfare rolls. In calculating net savings, however, one must include the initial cost of starting and operating such a program, compared with any reduction that might occur in the number of welfare recipients. Nevertheless, it seems reasonable that alternative family types would create the conditions making such a reduction possible.

A second economic consequence for society would be a consolidation of social services. At present, a series of government and community programs are serving the needs of mid-life women—that is, counseling and career training, public housing, day-care centers, work-incentive programs, and financial assistance. The coordination of these services with a viable living environment for mid-life women would undoubtedly reduce the overall cost by curbing duplication of services and reducing the need for counseling or therapy.[17]

A third possible benefit that would affect the local community would be the recycling of large, older homes. Halfway houses and wife-abuse centers have, for the most part, been located in large, already-existing private houses. Therefore, particularly in communities that are concerned with preserving their historical legacy, alternative living environments for mid-life women would once again restore large, older facilities to a place of usefulness in the community.

---

16. Ibid., pp. 498-514.

17. An example of the coordination of these activities is the Maryland Center for Displaced Homemakers. See P. Bujarski-Green, "Starting Over: A Guide for the Displaced Homemaker," *Family Circle* (July 1978), pp. 14, 20, 25, 28.

The negative economic consequences of alternative family arrangements are much less apparent.
For individual women, a possible
negative consequence might be to
prolong a state of economic dependency. If women are not encouraged
to actively rearrange their economic conditions, then these living
arrangements might become institutionalized and lose their status as
voluntary group living. Therefore
the emphasis in such a program
must be on creating conditions that
facilitate economic independence of
the group and of the individual
members.

Socioemotional issues

Discussions of mid-life focus on
two types of problems or crises that
can occur at this stage in the life
cycle: (1) maturational crises or
developmental stresses that have a
tendency to be manifested intermit-
tently throughout adult life; and (2)
situational crises or extraordinary
events that only affect selected individuals in any age group.[18] Thus
almost all women, married or
unmarried, experience some stress
at some time during the middle
years; however, the divorced and
widowed must cope additionally
with the situational crises of marital
dissolution.

Coupled with these maturational
crises are the questions and doubts
particular to mid-life women who
are alone or who are single parents.
One counselor of women at the
American Institute for Family
Relations in Los Angeles has suggested from her years of experience
that women alone, regardless of how

uncomplicated their lives may seem,
suffer from some type of adjustment
problems.[19]

Thus the experience of being
alone and being 40 poses not only
economic problems for women but
socioemotional ones as well. In addition, the situational crisis that exa-
cerbates the already existing
maturational problems for widowed
and divorced women singles out these
two groups as the most likely to benefit from the voluntary family.

Research on the effects of divorce
and widowhood on women suggests
that these processes are similar but
not identical. Typically, both categories of women express feelings of
unhappiness, fear of being alone,
loss of self-esteem, and a lack of self-
confidence.[20] The problems of
adjustment, however, are usually
more severe for the divorcee, for she
is less likely to receive the same sympathy and support as that directed
toward widows.[21] In addition, the
divorcee is more likely to experience
feelings of rejection or failure, particularly if the divorce was proposed
by her husband.

Although divorce, separation,
and widowhood are traumatic experiences, the extent of the socioemotional problems that result is
dependent on a number of factors.
Those women who experience the
most difficulty are the ones who find
their lives at a standstill—they
either lack social support systems to
reintegrate themselves into the routine of daily living, or they refuse to
take part in activities. Thus one

18. J. S. Stevenson, *Issues and Crises
During Middlescence* (New York: Appleton-
Century-Crofts, 1977); pp. 127-33.

19. S. Gorney and C. Cox, *After Forty*
(New York: Dial, 1973), pp. 140-44.

20. J. Burgess, "The Single Parent Family: A Social and Sociological Problem," *Family Coordinator*, 19:137-44 (Apr. 1970).

21. V. Rose and S. Price-Bonham,
"Divorce Adjustment: A Woman's Problem?"
Family Coordinator, 22:291-297 (July 1973).

counselor admits that the most useful advice she gives mid-life women in transition is to keep living by developing a variety of activities and friends and some type of social life.[22] The importance of a viable friendship network cannot be overestimated. Studies of widows have found that friends are active ingredients in the social support system,[23] and that having a friend or a confidant eases the grief process for both widows and divorcees.[24]

Those divorced women who experience high degrees of trauma are those who continue to be dependent on and attached to their former spouses.[25] Whether this attachment is a result of lack of alternative relationships is not known, but surely the lack of institutional arrangements for divorcees has some effect.

The socioemotional problems of mid-life women who are alone are reflected in their responses recorded in the 1976 National Opinion Research Center (NORC) General Social Survey.[26] Divorced, separated, never married, or widowed women between the ages of 40 and 60 were more likely to express dissatisfaction with their recreational activities and familial

situation than were their married counterparts. For example, about a fourth of unmarried mid-life women reported that they gained little or no satisfaction from their leisure activities, while only 12 percent of married women did so. Similarly, over 26 percent were only "fairly" or "not at all" satisfied with their friendship network, compared with less than 12 percent of married women. It is, however, the family situation itself that seems to separate married from unmarried mid-life women. Approximately 20 percent of the unmarried women reported that they received little or no satisfaction from their family life, while only 3 percent of married women gave this answer. These differences by marital status are attenuated in estimations of overall happiness. For unmarried women, about 25 percent responded that overall they were "not at all" happy. Married women, on the other hand, were less likely—nearly 9 percent—to report such unhappiness.

The major socioemotional problem of mid-life women in transition appears to be a lack of services or caring persons. A living environment geared toward mid-life needs would undoubtedly alleviate much of the loneliness and isolation of these women. The environment would offer a friendship network, consisting of individuals with similar problems, and the family could function as a mutual self-help group. Finally, an existing environment toward which women could turn would offer them a sense of emotional security and possibly the self-confidence to reorganize their lives. For some women the voluntary family may be a temporary arrangement functioning as a brief transitional stage in their process of reorganization. For other women,

22. Gorney and Cox, *After Forty*, pp. 142.

23. H. Z. Lopata, "The Meaning of Friendship in Widowhood," in *Looking Ahead*, eds. L. Troll, J. Israel, and K. Israel (Englewood Cliffs, NJ: Prentice-Hall, 1977), pp. 93-105.

24. Stevenson, *Issues and Crises During Middlescence*, p. 204.

25. Rose and Price-Bonham, "Divorce Adjustment: A Woman's Problem?" pp. 291-97.

26. Data were collected for this survey by the National Opinion Research Center from a national cross-section sample of U.S. adults aged 18 and over. Data were made available through the Inter-University Consortium for Political and Social Research, University of Michigan.

however, particularly the never married and widowed who are less likely to remarry, the voluntary family may be a more permanent arrangement that allows them to live in a familial-type environment of reciprocal support.

For society as a whole, alternative family types may very well be a step toward establishing the institutional arrangements which have thus far been lacking for unattached individuals. In addition, surrogate families may provide an excellent atmosphere for both formal and informal group counseling—a method of reciprocal help that has been found quite effective. Not only is group counseling generally effective but in a family setting it would be more economical and efficient as well.[27]

Thus alternative family arrangements for mid-life women may be helpful in coping with the problems many of them face. More importantly, however, because of the need for such alternatives to be integrated into the community, they could serve to educate the public about the problems and issues confronting mid-life women, thus counteracting some of the stereotypical conceptions of them.

The negative social and individual consequence of alternative family forms for mid-life women would most likely relate to their needs for privacy and their willingness to surrender recently won power and independence (for the divorced or sometimes the widowed). Cooperative living arrangements require the sharing of resources and of oneself.[28] A major problem for partici-

27. L. Walters and B. White, "Helping Each Other," in Troll, Israel, and Israel (eds.), *Looking Ahead*, pp. 186-91.

28. Rose and Price Bonham, "Divorce Adjustment: A Woman's Problem?" pp. 291-97.

pants and community groups is the provision of both privacy and reciprocity. In addition, such a living arrangement may create resentment among friends and relatives and among members of the community because it is seen as unconventional.

Thus in order not to seem threatening to existing kin networks or to the institution of marriage and men-women relationships, the innovative family forms will need to be open, in some sense, to public inspection. This will undermine the group's sense of family, but it may be necessary if these living arrangements are to become alternative in the existing family system, rather than being viewed as a reaction or in opposition to the traditional nuclear family.

PROTOTYPES FOR
ALTERNATIVE LIVING
ARRANGEMENTS

The discussion thus far has considered trends and consequences in terms of economic and socioemotional issues. In this section two alternative living arrangements are proposed as substitutes for the traditional nuclear family, for they may ameliorate some of these strains. The two alternative family forms—halfway houses and cooperative family groups—are proposed as viable possibilities because they have quite successfully assisted other individuals who, although bereft of traditional family supports, require some kind of primary group life. These models offer alternatives that may enable mid-life women to reach personally rewarding decisions about their life course; in the long run, the outcomes may also be beneficial to the community. One of the problems is that mid-life women with economic or socioemotional difficulties often have very limited choices in their interpersonal and intergroup exchanges. With a little societal input, the possibilities may be substantially enlarged, with many positive results.

Although halfway houses and Share-A-Home arrangements for the elderly were not designed to serve the needs of mid-life women, their organizational structures serve as prototypes of what can realistically be expected in this area.

Halfway houses: prototype for alternative living environments

The main impetus for halfway house development for both men and women in the United States emerged within the correctional system in the 1950s. Initially, houses were started by private groups, but by 1961 the federal government had begun to establish Federal Pre-Release Guidance Centers. Estimates of the numbers of halfway houses currently in existence vary, but as of 1973, the National Institute of Mental Health listed some 806 homes for the mentally ill and for alcoholics.[29]

The organizational structures of halfway houses are designed to serve various types of needs. Houses vary in size, location, required length of stay, source of funding, and so on. While houses range in size from 6 to 140 residents,[30] the optimum recommended capacity is usually set at 20 to 25.[31] Typically, the house is located in an urban or suburban area where residents can take advantage of the variety of available community services. The required length of stay usually depends on the type of clientele and the nature of their problems. Members of correctional after-care homes average about 12 weeks in residence,[32] and 3 to 4 months is recommended as the ideal length of stay. The support of halfway houses stems primarily from four sources: religious groups, state or federal government, private community groups—for profit and nonprofit purposes—and the residents themselves. The source of funding, as well as the cost of running a halfway house, depends on the type of residents who are served.

In regard to starting and operating halfway houses, all types of homes seem to face two major problems: funding and obtaining community support. These two problems are interrelated in that often community groups provide resources in cash and in kind for local houses. State and federal correctional administrators have begun to persuade community agencies and groups to start homes.[33] Houses operated by community groups appear less costly and in better position to obtain public donations from local agencies, groups, and businesses. Regardless of the group operating the home, the importance of establishing good community relations is continuously

29. National Institute of Mental Health, *Halfway Houses Serving the Mentally Ill, United States, 1973*, DHEW Publication No. (ADM) 76-246 (Washington, DC: Government Printing Office, 1975), pp. 2-12.

30. Richard Seiter et al., *Halfway Houses*, Summary Report, National Institute of Law Enforcement and Criminal Justice (Washington, DC: Government Printing Office, 1977).

31. Richard Rachin, "So You Want to Open a Halfway House," in *Community Based Corrections*, eds. G. R. Perlstein and T. R. Phelps (Santa Monica, CA: Goodyear, 1975), pp. 161-74.

32. Seiter et al., *Halfway Houses*.

33. E. E. Miller, "The Halfway House: Correctional Decompression of the Offender," in *Corrections In the Community*, eds. E. E. Miller and R. R. Montilla (Reston, VA: Reston, 1977), pp. 211-231.

emphasized. For example, in describing how to start a halfway house, one expert insists that forming a community relations committee is "in a nutshell . . . probably the single most important task facing new program administrators."[34] Community support should be solicited at the very conception of a halfway house program, and organizers need to be aware of local zoning ordinances.

Using halfway houses as a prototype for alternative living environments for mid-life women presents some difficulties. First, their success or failure is still in question because of the paucity of evaluative research. However, existing studies point to the fact that, in general, halfway houses have been at least as successful as, or more successful and more economical than, traditional programs. The second problem is that most community-based programs, particularly in the correctional field, have been designed for men. Thus they tend to be oriented toward the needs of men, and they fail to realize that women in such facilities usually face two major problems—adjusting to their dual roles of family breadwinner and homemaker.

Two programs currently in existence serve as examples of the types of facilities and services most applicable to community-based, residential environments for women. Hopper Home, founded in 1844 in New York, has been described as the most sophisticated halfway house in this country for women. It has a capacity of 18 persons and provides a comprehensive set of services, including medical care, vocational training, academic education, emo-

tional counseling, and a special staff for the sole purpose of helping the women adjust to their roles as mothers.[35]

A program of more recent origin is the Wife Abuse Center started in 1978 by a local women's group in Florida. Although the program handles abused wives only, organizers plan to expand their services to include displaced housewives and women in distress. The program is located in a large, rented home and currently houses 4 women and 10 children. The success of any such program depends not only on the organization of the home but also on its relation to the surrounding community, as well as on local support, enthusiasm, and approval.

Share-A-Home: another pragmatic model

Another alternative living experiment that could be adapted to the mid-life woman is Share-A-Home. This is a new and ingenious concept developed in Florida that has been successful in providing a solution to the problems of housing and family life for ambulatory elderly persons.[36]

In 1972 Share-A-Home Association, Inc. was founded as a nonprofit tax-exempt organization chartered under the laws of the State of Florida. It has a board of 11 directors chosen from the community. While the association does not control or supervise the daily life of the families in an institutional sense, it does provide information and assistance

34. Rachin, "So You Want to Open a Halfway House," pp. 161-74.

35. Miller, "The Halfway House: Correctional Decompression of the Offender," pp. 211-31.

36. G. F. Streib, and M. Hilker, "The Cooperative 'Family': An Alternative Lifestyle for the Elderly," *Alternative Lifestyles*, 3:167-84 (May 1980).

when new families are formed and while they are in operation. For example, it lends funds to families for basic repairs or for furnishings that might be necessary to get a family started or to provide more comfortable surroundings. Share-A-Home has a coordinating function in relation to the families. In a sense it performs a kind of surrogate parent role for the 10 families now in operation.

The concept is that nonrelated senior adults form a family that shares a household and divides up the expenses of running it. At present, families are housed in already existing structures, ranging from large private residences to unused college buildings. The cost averages around $400 a month, depending on the costs of each unit and whether or not the person shares a room. This makes it a far less expensive solution than nursing homes for the isolated elderly person who cannot afford to keep his own household or does not want to live alone. A salaried manager and staff handle finances and housekeeping and are responsible for providing food, transportation, laundry services, and the like. The family has the privilege of retaining or dismissing the management.

The Share-A-Home concept meets three important sociopsychological needs: (1) free choice, (2) association with others who give affection and concern, and (3) feelings of dignity and autonomy. While Share-A-Home has been developed for older persons, the concept as a practical form of living arrangement could be adapted to the needs and situations of midlife women. Shared expenses and available concern and support as the basic idea of a cooperative living arrangement are important advantages for all age groups. The adaptation of existing

structures makes the idea more economical, feasible, and practical than planning and constructing new buildings.

Another practical advantage of the Share-A-Home concept is that a paid manager can more effectively run a household for unrelated individuals. Moreover, a paid staff provides continuity in leadership and support, since turnover of family members will inevitably occur. The use of paid staff also enables mid-life women to obtain education and retraining, or permits them to hold full-time jobs. Living together in a cooperative voluntary family could provide the possibility of companionship, emotional support, and security for mid-life women who must cope with new patterns and find new directions.

CONCLUSION

In the contemporary United States some mid-life women are confronted by special economic and socioemotional problems because of the breakdown of traditional family environments. It is proposed that if these mid-life women are offered an enlarged set of choices, some of these problems might be ameliorated.

A traditional view of human behavior assumes that all members of society have equal opportunities to make choices, and that family arrangements are a personal matter. A realistic appraisal, however, indicates that there is considerable variation in the kind and number of choices available to individuals, and in the family problems that they face. In a complex industrialized society, familial matters are not just an individual's personal problem but are to some degree community and societal concerns, as demonstrated by the variety of existing health and welfare plans.

One may ask why shared living arrangements are discussed principally in relation to women. Is there also a need for men in mid-life transition to consider such family groups? Prototypes such as Share-A-Home do show that at the end of the life cycle some men who are seeking housing arrangements are willing to become residents of shared living facilities, and the women welcome their presence as a sort of head of household. The situation of the mid-life woman, however, is more complicated; her set of socioemotional problems is different from those faced by women at the end of the life cycle. The barriers of integrating unrelated adults to the intimacy of shared living at mid-life poses a new set of problems.

In addition, there is not the same economic need for such arrangements for men, for their average income is about twice that of women in mid-life. Men generally have fewer responsibilities for child care than women. Furthermore, men tend to remarry sooner than women and therefore do not experience as extended a period of socioemotional stress. In addition, there is always a certain proportion of men who are loners, who shun any kind of group living and who prefer to live in a single room. Their mid-life transition sometimes involves an escape from family life of any kind.

These differences in the mid-life situation of men and women explain why alternative family arrangements are needed primarily for women. Society has responded to the needs of children and the elderly with innovative programs, but the needs of mid-life women have largely been ignored. Since the two prototypes described have been somewhat successful in dealing with primary group environments of the young and the elderly, such models might be adapted on an experimental basis in urban and small town settings for mid-life women who need added social supports and an increased array of choices from which to plan new directions in their lives.

ANNALS, *AAPSS*, **464**, November 1982

Retirement: Leaving the World of Work

By ROBERT C. ATCHLEY

ABSTRACT: The process of retirement begins with attitudes toward retirement, retirement policies, and factors in the decision to retire. Currently, high levels of desire for retirement and poor health cause most retirements to occur at or near the minimum age for retirement. The retirement transition has varying effects, depending on how the individual arrives at retirement. Those who retire voluntarily have little or no difficulty adjusting. Those who are forced out by mandatory retirement policies tend to be dissatisfied at first, but eventually they adjust. And those who retire because of poor health are understandably the most dissatisfied, although retirement improves health for many of them. Retirement itself has no predictable negative effect on physical health, self-esteem, or life satisfaction. It does tend to reduce activity level. A good adjustment in the retirement years depends on having a secure income, good health, meaningful activities and high marital satisfaction. Given income and health, most retired persons adjust well. However, retirement income systems and health care financing systems in America are losing ground, and gaps in coverage are widening. This situation poses a serious threat to the future of retirement.

Robert C. Atchley is director of the Scripps Foundation Gerontology Center at Miami University in Oxford, Ohio. He has directed four large-scale studies of retirement and is author of The Sociology of Retirement. *He is also author of* The Social Forces in Later Life, *an introductory text in social gerontology that is now in its third edition.*

RETIREMENT is the withdrawal of an individual from employment, along with entitlement to income that is based on having been employed over a period of years. From the point of view of the individual, retirement is a means of coping with health problems that make employment arduous. It is also a legitimate way to drop one's job responsibilities in order to lead a life of one's own choosing. For employers, retirement is a means of creating job turnover, reducing the size of the work force, or getting rid of undesirable employees, so defined either because of age prejudice or poor performance. For society, retirement is a way to reduce unemployment and to reduce poverty among the elderly. For unions, retirement is a way to get more out of management and to create job opportunities. Thus retirement serves many purposes and points of view.

We tend to view the retirement of individuals as a rather simple matter that involves leaving the work force at around age 65 and living on a pension. However, in America there is not one retirement system, but many. There is a multiplicity of retirement income systems, including Social Security, various civil service retirement systems (federal, state, and local), private pensions, Individual Retirement Accounts, and so on. Each of these systems has different rules concerning the minimum age for retirement, the number of years of service required, the means used to determine pension amounts, and provisions for disability retirement. They vary tremendously in terms of the adequacy of the retirement incomes they provide.

There are also various routes people take to arrive at retirement.

Some people retire because of poor health. Others retire because they are eligible to retire and want to do so. Still others retire because they have lost their jobs and have been unable to find new ones. A small proportion of people retire because they are forced to by mandatory retirement policies. The timing of retirement also varies. Some retire early, some retire at the customary age of 65, and others retire late.

Finally, all these factors vary systematically by sex and social class. For example, compared with men, women are less likely to be covered by pensions in addition to Social Security,[1] they are more likely to retire early or late rather than around age 65,[2] and they are more likely to retire for health reasons.[3] These same variations apply to working-class people in comparison with the middle class.[4]

Given these sources of variety, it is obviously ill advised to speak of retirement as a single type of transition that has only a narrow range of effects. It is a complex of various types of transitions that can have a very large number of effects. But having said this, we can also say that the majority of individual retirements have positive outcomes in terms of health and enjoyment of living.

1. Gayle B. Thompson, "Pension Coverage and Benefits, 1972: Findings from the Retirement History Study," *Social Security Bulletin*, 41:3-17 (Feb. 1978).

2. Robert C. Atchley, "The Process of Retirement: Comparing Women and Men." in *Women's Retirement*, ed. Maximiliane Szinovacz (Beverly Hills, CA: Sage, 1982).

3. Erdman Palmore, "Why Do People Retire?" *International Journal of Aging and Human Development*, 2:269-83 (Nov. 1971).

4. Robert C. Atchley, *The Social Forces in Later Life* (Belmont, CA: Wadsworth, 1980), pp. 138-45.

In this article we will look at attitudes toward retirement in the preretirement period and at the factors that affect the decision to retire. We will then look at the retirement transition and its effects. We will conclude with a brief look at what factors are related to well-being in the postretirement period.

ATTITUDES TOWARD RETIREMENT

The retirement process begins when individuals recognize that some day they will retire. How younger people view the prospect of retirement has a bearing on how they assess their retired friends and more importantly, perhaps, on how they themselves fare when retirement comes. In general, people's ideas about retirement are very favorable. In a study of adults ranging in age from 45 on up, I found that the concept of retirement had four separate dimensions: activity, physical potency, emotional evaluation, and moral evaluation.[5] On all four dimensions the concept of retirement was very positive, regardless of the age or sex of the respondent. The only variation from this very positive view of retirement occurred among retired people who would have liked to have continued on the job. These people felt that retirement was unfair and bad, but their overall attitude was still favorable. Most adults expect to retire (less than 10 percent do not), and most of them expect to retire early.[6] Only a very few say that they dread retire-

ment.[7] Generally, the individual's attitude toward retirement is closely allied to his or her financial situation. The higher the expected retirement income, the more favorable the attitude. About two-thirds of employed adults envision no financial troubles in retirement, although most expect retirement to reduce their incomes by up to 50 percent from their preretirement levels.

The relationship between income, education, and occupation on the one hand and attitudes toward retirement on the other is complex. People with high incomes realistically expect to be financially secure in retirement, although they tend to estimate their income requirements at a level substantially below their present incomes. People with a college education are more likely than others to plan an early retirement.[8] Those at higher occupational levels, with the exception of professionals, executives, and government officials, tend to see retirement more favorably than do people in lower occupational groups.[9] Workers at the higher occupational and educational levels not only have higher earnings and more favorable attitudes toward retirement, but they also find their jobs more interesting and in actual practice are less prone to retire.[10]

5. Robert C. Atchley, "The Meaning of Retirement," *Journal of Communications*, 24:97-101 (Autumn 1974).

6. Louis Harris, "Pleasant Retirement Expected," *Washington Post*, 28 Nov. 1965.

7. George Katona, *Private Pensions and Individual Savings* (Ann Arbor, MI: Survey Research Center, 1965), p. 15.

8. James N. Morgan, *Income and Welfare in the United States* (New York: McGraw-Hill, 1972), p. 163.

9. Wayne E. Thompson, "The Impact of Retirement." (Doctoral dissertation, Cornell University, Ithaca, NY, 1956); Ida H. Simpson, Kurt W. Back, and John C. McKinney, *Social Aspects of Aging* (Durham, NC: Duke University Press, 1966), p. 80.

10. Matilda White Riley and Anne E. Foner, *Aging and Society*, vol. 1; *An Inventory of Research Findings* (New York: Russell Sage, 1968), p. 445.

People at lower occupational levels have less income and anticipate more financial insecurity in retirement. These people favor retirement, but dread poverty. Here the question is money. Apparently, few people at the lower occupational levels continue to work because they love their jobs. At the middle occupational level, positive orientation toward retirement is at its peak. These people anticipate sufficient retirement income and at the same time have no lasting commitment toward the job.

Age may also be related to attitudes toward retirement. Early studies found that the older a person becomes, the more likely he or she is to dread retirement.[11] More recent research findings suggest that retirement is becoming more accepted over time within various age groups and that younger age groups are more accepting of retirement compared with older ones.[12] Finances are probably important in the relationship between age and attitude toward retirement.[13] For example, if adequate income could be assured, the proportion who would retire increases steadily with age from 21 to 64 years of age.[14] The increase in positive attitudes over time among all cohorts is probably the result of substantially improved retirement incomes over the last 15 years.

THE RETIREMENT DECISION

The decision to retire is influenced by the desire for retirement, and attitudes toward retirement indicate that in the United States desire for retirement is generally high. In addition, individual factors such as unemployment and health problems have an important bearing on the decision. Factors such as employer policies about minimum retirement age, mandatory retirement age, and early retirement incentives are also involved. There are also informal influences on the retirement decision, such as occupational norms about whether retirement is desirable and if so at what age, attitudes of family and friends about retirement, and informal pressures at the work place.

An individual may decide to retire because he or she cannot find a job. Hiring policies, particularly in manufacturing, tend to discriminate against hiring older workers. Almost the only jobs that are not hard to find as one grows older are jobs that pay badly, or jobs for which there is a chronic labor shortage. This pattern has been found in the United States, West Germany, and Japan, and it probably applies to most industrial nations.[15]

When asked to defend their hiring policies, employers usually say that older people cannot meet the physical or skill requirements of the jobs. There is apparently no foundation for these allegations; neverthe-

11. Katona, *Private Pensions and Individual Savings*, p. 15.

12. Gordon F. Streib and Clement J. Schneider, *Retirement in American Society* (Ithaca, NY: Cornell University Press, 1971).

13. Judith Robinson and Robert C. Atchley, *Attitude Toward Retirement and Distance from the Event* (Oxford, OH: Scripps, 1982), p. 2.

14. Riley and Foner, *Aging and Society*, vol. 1, p. 445.

15. Robert C. Atchley, *The Sociology of Retirement* (Cambridge, MA: Schenkman, 1976), pp. 39-52; Barbara Fülgraff, "Social Gerontology in West Germany: A Review of Recent and Current Research," *The Gerontologist*, 18:42-58 (Feb. 1978); Erdman Palmore, *The Honorable Elders* (Durham, NC: Duke University Press, Feb. 1975), pp. 54-78.

less, they are acted on as if they were true.

Retirement is encouraged by employer policies that allow employees to generate entitlement to early retirement. Early retirement plans usually allow employees to retire before they become eligible for a Social Security retirement pension by providing supplemental pension payments. Such supplemental payments keep pensions at an adequate level until the retired person becomes eligible to collect Social Security.

Early retirement is popular among dissatisfied factory workers, who want to retire as soon as it is economically feasible,[16] and among employers, who see early retirement as an effective way to deal with technological change, mergers, plant closings, and production cutbacks.[17]

A third factor involved in the retirement decision is mandatory policies that require retirement at a specific chronological age. Virginia Reno found that 36 percent of the men and 23 percent of the women who retired in the last half of 1969 reported a compulsory retirement age on their most recent jobs.[18] The most common age was 65 (68 percent of the cases) followed by 70 (20 percent of the cases). The existence of compulsory retirement fluctuated a great deal by occupation. For example, 56 percent of men with professional and technical jobs were subject to mandatory retirement, compared with only 23 percent among service workers.

James Schulz estimated that in a group of retired men only about seven percent were retired unwillingly at a mandatory retirement age and unable to find new employment.[19] A national longitudinal study found that only four percent of over 2000 retirements fit this category.[20] Women were even less likely to be affected by mandatory retirement which usually occurred in conjunction with private pensions.[21] Thus, numerically, mandatory retirement affected a small minority of workers who tended to be relatively advantaged in terms of retirement income.

Nevertheless, mandatory retirement has not been popular. Louis Harris and Associates[22] found that 86 percent of both the older population and the general public felt that people should not be forced to retire solely because of age if they wanted to continue and were still able to do the job. Accordingly, in 1978 Congress amended the Age Discrimination in Employment Act to abolish mandatory retirement in the Civil Service and generally to raise the mandatory retirement age to 70. Several states had earlier abolished mandatory retirement for state civil

16. Richard E. Barfield and James N. Morgan, *Early Retirement: The Decision and the Experience* (Ann Arbor, MI: Institute for Social Research, 1969), p. 3.

17. Harold L. Sheppard, *Industrial Gerontology* (Cambridge, MA: Schenkman, 1970), p. 131.

18. Virginia P. Reno, "Compulsory Retirement Among Newly Entitled Workers," *Social Security Bulletin* 35:3-15 (Mar. 1972).

19. James H. Schulz, "The Economics of Mandatory Retirement," *Industrial Gerontology*, 1:1-10 (Jan. 1974).

20. Herbert S. Parnes and Gilbert Nestel, "The Retirement Experience," in *Work and Retirement*, ed. Herbert S. Parnes (Cambridge, MA: MIT Press, 1981), pp. 155-97, p. 158.

21. Reno, "Compulsory Retirement Among Newly Entitled Workers," pp. 3-15.

22. Louis Harris and Associates, *The Myth and Reality of Aging in America* (Washington, DC: National Council on the Aging, 1975), p. 213.

servants. However, because only a relatively small proportion of people are affected adversely by mandatory retirement, the overall impact of this change is apt to be minimal.

Unfortunately, the debate over mandatory retirement obscured a more important policy issue: the gradual decline of the minimum retirement age. All sorts of evidence indicates that most workers retire as soon as it is financially feasible. Thus policies governing the minimum age for retirement have a much more direct effect on the level of retirement (proportion retired in the population) than mandatory retirement policies do. This effect is amply illustrated by the fact that as soon as Social Security retirement benefits became available to men at age 62 rather than 65, the typical age of retirement under Social Security quickly went from 65 to 63, even though early retirement meant reduced benefits.

Disability is also related to the retirement decision. Most jobs in American society are full-time. There is no mechanism for adjusting conditions of work to fit the capacities of older workers. This problem is no doubt related to the fact that applications for disability benefits under Social Security increase dramatically with age. Well over half of the men and women who apply for disability benefits are over 50. In addition, the proportion of applicants who are awarded disability benefits increases from 32 percent under age 30 to 68 percent at ages 60 to 64.[23]

The issue of health pressures toward early retirement is cloudy. On the one hand, both disability data and survey data on reasons for retirement indicate that there is a substantial health component in the decision to retire. However, among those who retire before age 60, health seems to be declining in importance.[24] In addition, people sometimes cite health as the reason they retired, because they see it as more socially acceptable than simply a desire for retirement.[25] A national longitudinal study found that 38 percent of white men and 47 percent of black men who retired had reported job-related health problems prior to retirement.[26] Variations in working conditions over the life course are important determinants of the extent to which poor health is an actual factor in early retirement.

An individual's decision to retire can also be influenced by informal norms. For example, most professionals are probably discouraged from retiring by the attitudes of their colleagues, since retirement tends to be viewed negatively among professionals. On the other hand, assembly-line workers generally have favorable attitudes toward retirement and indeed show a growing tendency toward early retirement. Two individuals anxious to retire quite obviously do not face the same decision in these two quite different occupational areas.

Attitudes of friends and family also probably play an important role in retirement decisions. One man's children may want him to retire,

23. Mordechai E. Lando, "Demographic Characteristics of Disability Applicants," Social Security Bulletin, 39:15-23 (1976).

24. A. William Pollman, "Early Retirement: A Comparison of Poor Health to Other Retirement Factors," Journal of Gerontology, 26:41-45 (Jan. 1971).

25. James H. Schulz, The Economics of Aging (Belmont, CA: Wadsworth, 1976), pp. 57-8.

26. Parnes and Nestel, "The Retirement Experience," p. 159.

another's may not. One woman's husband may want her to retire, another's may not. One man lives in a neighborhood where retirement is sneered at, another lives in a leisure community where retirement is the rule rather than the exception. If we retire, then the characteristics our friends and family impute to retired people will be imputed to us. All of these factors may encourage or discourage retirement.

Employers sometimes exert pressure on employees to retire. This may be done by suggestion or by job transfers or job classifications that substantially alter the employee's working conditions. There are countless ways that employers can apply pressure to retire. As yet we have no basis for estimating what proportion of older workers experience such pressures, but three-fourths of the complaints of age discrimination in employment concern conditions of employment other than hiring or firing.

Most people want to retire and to do it while they are still physically able to enjoy life in retirement. The small proportion that does not want to retire can expect to find it increasingly easier to stay on as long as they can still do the job. The decision to retire is more a question of when to retire than whether to retire. The timing of retirement appears to be influenced primarily by the minimum age of eligibility for socially adequate retirement income. Desire for retirement and poor health combine to produce a situation in which most retirements occur shortly after the minimum age.

This general analysis of decisions to retire is based primarily on research from the United States. Ethel Shanas and her associates found that Americans were more likely to retire voluntarily than either Danes or Britons.[27] However, Chris Phillipson found that retirement has become increasingly attractive in Britain, even though pensions tend to be low.[28] Older Danes tend to retire at the minimum age of pension eligibility, which is higher than in the United States.[29] Barbara Fülgraff reported that when the minimum retirement age went down in West Germany, so did the average retirement age.[30] Thus the sensitivity of decisions on timing of retirement to policies on minimum retirement age seems to be widespread among industrial societies. Health pressures to retire understandably vary cross-nationally with minimum retirement age. The higher the minimum retirement age, the greater the prevalence of health pressures to retire. Other cross-national variations relate to the cultural acceptability of retirement. Retirement is viewed very positively in the United States;[31] at the other extreme, it is seen as social death in France.[32]

IMMEDIATE REACTIONS TO RETIREMENT

The person's route to retirement has a significant bearing on what life is like immediately after retirement and, in turn, on how the person reacts. People who plan their retire-

27. Ethel Shanas et al., *Older People in Three Industrial Societies* (New York: Atherton, 1968), p. 290.

28. Chris Phillipson, *The Emergence of Retirement* (Durham, England: University of Durham, 1977), pp. 43-48.

29. Henning Olsen and Gert Hansen, *Retirement from Work* (Copenhagen: Danish Institute for Social Research, 1977), pp. 102-16.

30. Fülgraff, "Social Gerontology in West Germany," pp. 42-58.

31. Atchley, "The Meaning of Retirement," pp. 97-101.

32. Anne-Marie Guillemard, *La Retraite: Une Mort Sociale* (Paris: Mouton, 1972).

ment well in advance may go through a honeymoon phase in which they are quite active or they may go through an R and R (rest and relaxation) phase of recuperating from the stresses and strains of employment. But by the end of six months, most people who plan their retirement have settled into a routine of activities that is satisfying and long-lasting. Herbert Parnes and Gilbert Nestel found these people to be slightly more satisfied with various aspects of life than their nonretired age-mates. People who are forced to retire by their employers are not very numerous, but the potential for stress in their situation is often high. Parnes and Nestel found that these people were much more dissatisfied than those who retired voluntarily. But those who retired because of ill health were by far the most likely to be dissatisfied with life in retirement, and not just in terms of their poor health. Those with health-related retirements also tended to be much less satisfied with their housing, standard of living, and leisure activities.[33]

Those who retire gradually or who retire after lengthy unemployment probably experience very little sudden change in their lives as a result of retirement, and their reactions could be expected to be muted accordingly. However, this is a guess and needs to be researched.

I found that activity levels did go down substantially after retirement, which means a lot of people fit the R and R model, since nearly all had planned to retire. But by three years after retirement, activity levels tended to be as high as in the preretirement period. The dip in activity level was not accompanied by a drop in life satisfaction—it increased steadily.[34] The major deterrents to establishing a satisfying and active routine in retirement were disability and low socioeconomic status, both factors that limit the individual's capacity to enjoy the freedom that retirement represents.

Retirement is widely thought to have an adverse effect on health. Everyone seems to know people who carefully planned for retirement only to get sick and die shortly after leaving their jobs. However, the crucial question is whether people retire because they are sick or whether they get sick because they retire. If people retire because they are sick, then it should not be surprising that some of them remain sick and some soon die. The decisive test of the impact of retirement on health is the state of health following retirement, compared with just preceding retirement. Data from a large longitudinal study of people both before and after retirement showed that health declines are associated with age, but not with retirement.[35] That is, retired people are no more likely to be sick than people of the same age who are still on the job. In fact, unskilled workers showed a slight improvement in health following retirement. A study of nearly 4000 rubber tire workers before and after retirement found that preretirement health status was the only significant predictor of mortality within five years after retirement.[36]

33. Parnes and Nestel, "The Retirement Experience," p. 185.

34. Atchley, "The Process of Retirement: Comparing Women and Men."

35. Streib and Schneider, *Retirement in American Society*, pp. 69-73.

36. Suzanne G. Haynes, Anthony J. McMichael, and Herman A. Tyroler, "Survival After Early and Normal Retirement,"

A good deal of research has been devoted to the impact of retirement on mental disorders, but no definite effect has yet been found.[37] Several studies point to a higher incidence of mental impairment among retired people, but the association between retirement and mental illness has been found to be mainly a function of poor health, low social activity, and unsatisfactory living arrangements rather than of retirement in itself.[38]

Much of the research on the personal consequences of retirement concerns the impact of retirement on social adjustment. The broad category of social adjustment includes such factors as acceptance of retirement, life satisfaction, morale, self-esteem, age identification, and job deprivation. It has been generally assumed that retirement has a negative impact on social adjustment, but research has disproved this assumption.

Morale and life satisfaction are two concepts that have been used to assess overall emotional reaction to one's life at a given point in time. Morale has been found to be generally unconnected to retirement.[39] Morale is influenced more by health, family situations, and other personal factors than by retirement. High morale is associated with independence between generations in the family and with a functional, home-based pattern of activities within the older couple. The only work-related factor associated with morale is the tendency for those with orderly work histories to have high morale in retirement. Retirement produces no significant change in life satisfaction,[40] and there is a great degree of longitudinal consistency in morale during the retirement transition.[41]

Apparently, no matter how the subjective reactions to the retirement life situation are measured, retirement makes little difference. The proportion with a high degree of satisfaction depends more on factors such as family situation, job history, and other personal factors, for example, health, than on retirement itself.

Another area of interest concerns the self. Several aspects of the impact of retirement on self have been studied. Kurt Back and Carleton Guptill identified three dimensions of self-concept; involvement, optimism, and autonomy.[42] They found that the involvement scores for retired people were considerably lower than for people in preretirement, regardless of socioeconomic characteristics. However, retirement had very little effect on the optimism or autonomy dimensions. They concluded that the decline in perception of self as involved results almost entirely from loss of job. Their findings indicated that an individual who was healthy, had a middle- or upperstratum occupation, and had a high

Journal of Gerontology, 33:269-78 (Mar. 1978).

37. Theodore Nadelson, "A Survey of the Literature on the Adjustment of the Aged to Retirement," *Journal of Geriatric Psychiatry*, 3:3-20 (Fall 1969).

38. Marjorie F. Lowenthal and Paul L. Berkman, *Aging and Mental Disorder in San Francisco* (San Francisco: Jossey-Bass, 1967), p. 214.

39. Simpson, Back, and McKinney, *Social Aspects of Aging*, p. 129.

40. Streib and Schneider, *Retirement in American Society*, pp. 107-16.

41. Linda K. George and George L. Maddox, "Subjective Adaptation to Loss of the Work Role: A Longitudinal Study," *Journal of Gerontology*, 32:456-62 (July 1977).

42. Kurt W. Back and Carleton S. Guptill, "Retirement and Self Ratings," in *Social Aspects of Aging*, eds. Simpson, Back, and McKinney, pp. 120-29.

number of personal interests would feel a minimal loss of sense of involvement brought on by retirement. Nevertheless, even these people did not successfully fill the gap left by the loss of their jobs. Yet self-esteem in retirement tends to be quite high, much higher than among high school students. Retirement has no effect on self-esteem.[43]

In retirement most people continue to do the same kinds of things they did when they were working. About a third increase their level of nonjob-related role activities to fill the gap left by retirement. About a fifth of the retired population experience a decrease in activities; however, gains or losses in activity are a relative matter. For someone who was uninvolved prior to retirement, leaving the job can result in an increase in activities and still leave gaps of unfilled, unsatisfying time. On the other hand, for an overinvolved professional, retirement may reduce the net amount of activity, but at the same time bring the level down to a point more suitable to the person's capabilities and desires.

A great deal of attention has been paid to the impact of retirement on leisure participation. According to one school of thought, leisure cannot legitimately be engaged in full-time by adults in Western societies without resulting in an identity crisis for the individual and a social stigma of implied inability to perform.[44] At one time, and in some cultures more than in others, this set of assumptions may have been widely applicable. In fact, much of the retirement research done in the United States in the early 1950s supports such a view. However, there is growing evidence that in recent years the leisure of retirement—to the extent that retirement brings leisure rather than a new set of obligations—is viewed both by retired people and by society at large as an earned privilege and opportunity.[45]

WELL-BEING IN THE POSTRETIREMENT PERIOD

Most people probably underestimate the number of years that they will spend in retirement. Yet in 1980, men who were age 65 could be expected to live an average of 14.3 years and women an average of 18.7 years. Income security, marital satisfaction, meaningful activities, and good health are the major factors that promote well-being among retired persons.

Financial security for retired people is always a vulnerable area because retired persons have little power to increase their incomes through employment. As a result, they tend to become more anxious over inflation and perceived threats to Social Security than does the general population. In order to retire without a loss in level of living, it is necessary to replace about 60 percent of gross earnings before retirement. In other words, about 40 percent of the average worker's gross income goes for taxes and expenses connected with employment that do not carry over into

43. W. Fred Cottrell and Robert C. Atchley, *Women in Retirement: A Preliminary Report* (Oxford, OH: Scripps, 1969), p. 33.

44. Stephen J. Miller, "The Social Dilemma of the Aging Leisure Participant," in *Older People and Their Social World,* ed. Arnold Rose (Philadelphia: F. A. Davis, 1965), pp. 77-92.

45. Robert C. Atchley, "Retirement and Work Orientation," *The Gerontologist,* 11(1):29-32 (Feb. 1971); Gayle B. Thompson, "Work Versus Leisure Roles: An Investigation of Morale Among Employed and Retired Men," *Journal of Gerontology,* 28:339-44 (May 1974).

retirement. Currently, Social Security retirement benefits are replacing about 58 percent of preretirement earnings for married couples. However, the earnings replacement level is only about 38 percent for individuals currently retiring. In addition, people who have been retired a long time have much lower pensions because average earnings were very much lower at the time they were generating their entitlement to Social Security, and Social Security benefit levels are tied to earnings averaged over a large number of years.

Private pensions in addition to Social Security are not available to most American workers. In 1970 only 49 percent of men and 21 percent of women workers were covered by employer pensions in the private sector.[46] While the number of workers covered by private pensions has increased dramatically since 1950, the percentage is leveling off, and the prospects for large future gains in coverage are not bright.

About 80 percent of government workers are covered by government pension plans. But many of these plans are unfunded, which means that no funds have been set aside for payment, which in turn means that pensions must be paid out of current tax revenues. Harold Sheppard and Sara Rix think that many of these plans represent fiscal time bombs for many state and local governments, as well as for the federal government. When the time comes to meet their obligations, many governments may not have the resources to do so, and the result will be a drastic loss in retirement income security for government workers.[47]

The current federal vogue is to call on employees to plan for their own retirement income security through Individual Retirement Accounts and the like. But past research has shown that working people are simply not able to save enough from their hard-pressed incomes to save adequately for retirement.[48] The result is large numbers of elderly people living in poverty. Responsible national policy should be based on what is possible; therefore there needs to be a strong federal commitment to income security for retired Americans, regardless of the type of employer they worked for. The system we have now, with its multiple levels and gaps in coverage, is widening the gap between the retirement income of the haves and the have-nots.

As long as both members of the couple are reasonably healthy, marital satisfaction increases as the couple grows older. Most retired couples have high marital satisfaction. The major threats to marital satisfaction are inadequate income and disabling illness in one or both members of the couple. Lack of income reduces marital satisfaction by overly constraining the couple's choices with a corresponding increase in tension. Physical illness reduces marital satisfaction as a result of the physical and emotional drain that long-term caring for a spouse can represent.

46. Thompson, "Pension Coverage and Benefits, 1972," pp. 3-17.

47. Harold L. Sheppard and Sara E. Rix, *The Graying of Working America: The Coming Crisis in Retirement Age Policy* (New York: Free Press, 1977), pp. 116-34.

48. Alicia H. Munnell, "Possible Responses to Social Security's Long-Run Deficits," *New England Economic Review*, 25-34 (Jan./Feb. 1982).

Most retired people are quite active, and activity in retirement is associated with high life satisfaction. For men, it is also important to have numerous personal goals.[49]

Finally, good health is a major enabling condition for a satisfying life in retirement. Good health is necessary for activity and marital satisfaction, both of which affect life satisfaction. In addition, poor health has obvious direct effects on outlook.

The keys to good health in retirement are prevention of disabling conditions and rehabilitation to restore unavoidable losses. Unfortunately, preventive and rehabilitative health services are not widely available for retired Americans. Medicare and other third-party health care financing systems generally do not provide for preventive services, and rehabilitative services are usually tied to the prospect of future employment, which for

49. Atchley, "The Process of Retirement: Comparing Women and Men."

retired persons is not an appropriate issue. As a result, these very important services are generally available only for the well-to-do.

In spite of these problems, most retired Americans are leading satisfying lives today because they have not fallen through the gaps. But the gaps are getting wider, and this is an issue about which all currently employed people should be concerned. We do not want to create a situation in which the 1970s are seen as a golden age of retirement, followed in the 1980s and 1990s by a steady deterioration of living conditions for the retired.

Another approach is to say that individuals do not have a problem with retirement as a life transition now, but that society is beginning to have a problem with retirement as a social institution. And unless we begin now to straighten out the social institution it will not be long before large numbers of individuals begin to have problems with retirement as a life transition.

ANNALS, *AAPSS*, **464**, November 1982

Divorce and Remarriage
at Middle Age and Beyond

By DONNA HODGKINS BERARDO

ABSTRACT: Recent societal trends have led to simpler divorces, a growing acceptance of divorce, greater personal freedom, and increased gainful employment for women, as well as a general weakening of institutional norms. The occurrence of divorce at mid-life brings losses and adjustments. Divorce at older ages causes similar losses and adjustments, as well as others associated with old age. In addition, the elderly experience divorce indirectly through the divorces of their children. Beyond divorce or widowhood, there are problems associated with remarriage that arise from age, previous marital status, sex ratios, geographic residence, and kinship relationships. The success or failure of a second marriage depends on many factors and is affected by a lack of institutionalized norms fitting the situation. As expectations change regarding the permanency of marriage, and as the family adapts to changes in its structure, desirable goals will include the establishment of normative behavior patterns for the transitions from married, to divorced or widowed, to remarried; clarification of roles and relationships; ways of easing role transitions; and help in the preservation of long-term marital relationships.

Donna Hodgkins Berardo is on the faculty at Florida Junior College in Jacksonville, Florida, where she teaches sociology. Her major research areas are marriage and the family and social gerontology. She is currently working on an analysis of dual-career families in the United States.

I N the past two decades a grow-ing number of trends have favored divorce in American society. The divorce rates have risen not only among the young but also among those marriages that had endured 15 years or more. The impact of marital breakdown at mid-life and beyond is more devas-tating than in youth, the recovery process may be more tenuous, and finding a new partner can be more difficult for older age groups. This article examines the effects of divorce trends on mid-life and older people, factors related to successful remarriage, and the implications of divorce and remarriage at later ages on the society as a whole.

SOCIETAL TRENDS FAVORING DIVORCE

The increase in the divorce rates in the United States appears to be associated with several societal trends.[1] First, a number of states established no-fault divorce laws, which have not only reformed and liberalized the divorce process, but have also made marital dissolution easier to obtain. Added to this legal change has been a second factor, an attitudinal change toward a grow-ing acceptance of divorce as a reasonable or even desirable alter-native to an unhappy marriage. Husbands and wives who had for-merly faced an adversary court sys-tem and a social stigma attached to divorce have found it easier in recent years to end unsatisfactory or em-bittered relationships.

A third trend influencing divorce among mid-life and older couples is

1. Ruth Albrecht, "Correlates of Marital Happiness among the Remarried," *Journal of Marriage and the Family*, 41(4):857 (Nov. 1979).

the changes in traditional roles of women. The women's movement of the 1960s and 1970s encouraged women to seek greater personal freedom and employment outside the home. Some working wives and mothers with their own paychecks became less dependent upon hus-bands and felt secure enough to leave unsatisfactory relationships. For others, the shifts in life-style and balance of power, because of women working, caused strife in the home. The steady increase in labor force participation of women suggests that they are unlikely to return to traditional roles. In addition, the decline in fertility rates also increases women's labor force par-ticipation and thereby increases their economic independence.

Fourth, we appear to be in a period of challenge to basic societal institutions and values that in the past have been supportive of fam-ilies. Increasing emphasis on indi-vidualism, a pervasive liberalism resulting in a loosening of mores, and a changing ideology sparked by the women's liberation movement are just a few of the many factors that have served to undermine the strengths of traditional norms. However, institutional accommoda-tion to these changes is far from complete.

Older couples today have more time alone than in the past because of a number of factors, including increased longevity, compression of the childbearing period, and a longer empty nest period after the children have grown and left home. Coping with individual change and growth as well as the changes in one's mate over time is difficult for many people, especially those who have had little or no development of interpersonal skills.

DIVORCE AS A
MID-LIFE CRISIS

Over 350,000 people were affected by middle-aged divorce in 1975.[2] This figure represents a steady increase in the number of divorces among marriages of longer duration, that is, 15 to 29 years. The usual readjustments that occur after divorce may indeed reach more dramatic proportions for those who have been entangled in a web of family and friends for many years. Losses and adjustments following divorce often include:

—the loss of contact with former in-laws as well as couple friends;

—financial losses through dividing property and other resources;

—the loss of a partner to help in parenting teenagers;

—the loss of identity of mate's position, such as doctor's wife or stockbroker's husband;

—the need for many women to develop new labor market skills;

—the need for men and women to increase their financial resources to offset the high costs of alimony, child support, and loss of the partner's income.

Individually, these losses and adjustments are traumatic, but their cumulative effect can be devastating. The real losses of significant people and financial resources are often accompanied by psychological adjustment, such as (1) coping with a sense of failure of a lengthy personal investment, (2) dealing with an individual identity after being part of a unit, and (3) reentering the dating game only to discover that the mores have changed. There is a double standard in mate selection with respect to age norms in American society now: the marriage of older men to younger women is tolerated, whereas the marriage of older women to younger men is looked upon with disapproval. This double standard of eligible partners often means that middle-aged women must compete with younger women for men in their age group. Successful readjustment to the mid-life crisis of divorce is easier for those with greater personal resources, including money, a strong kin network, higher educational levels, and single friends or friends with whom one interacts on an individual basis.

IMPACT OF DIVORCE
ON THE ELDERLY

The impact of divorce on the elderly can be described in both direct and indirect terms. The divorce rate for couples over age 65 is less than three percent, a figure much lower than for younger age groups.[3] Therefore only a small number of couples must directly experience adjustments that may well be even more difficult than those faced by middle-aged people. However, the rising divorce rates of younger age groups indirectly affects the lives of couples over 65 by altering their parent-child and grandparent-grandchild relationships.

2. Michael A. Smyer and Brian F. Hofland, "Divorce and Family Support in Later Life," *Journal of Family Issues*, 3:66 (Mar. 1982).

3. Peter Uhlenberg and Mary Anne P. Myers, "Divorce and the Elderly," *The Gerontologist*, 21:276-82 (June 1981).

Gerontological studies have noted that the elderly often can survive on fixed incomes only because they have already paid for their houses and other major consumer durables. To divide this property upon divorce could plunge both individuals into precarious economic positions and increase the need for welfare or kin support. In addition, the divorced elderly appear to have lower life chances than the married elderly, that is, they express lower family satisfaction, show poorer mental health, lower satisfaction with relationships, and higher mortality rates. All these factors suggest inadequate support networks for the divorced elderly.

Beyond the divorce adjustments that have been outlined for middle-aged people, the elderly must often cope with the physical impairments of aging, decreasing physical mobility that restricts one's opportunities for finding another partner, and, for older women, a lack of available partners because of the uneven sex ratio for those over 65. In short, older people may find themselves left without a partner when partners are hard to find and when the physical and mental energies needed to search for a new companion are declining.

The divorced elderly do not receive the social support that widows experience. The relationships prior to divorce are often characterized by tension and hostility, and unlike widowhood, the contact often must be continued after the loss of the partner because of family obligations. The social stigma surrounding divorce may well be greater for the elderly, since they and their peers were socialized in an era when divorce was an unacceptable alternative to an unhappy marriage.

A growing number of older people are experiencing the problems of divorce indirectly through the divorce of their own children. The roles of grandparents may be strengthened or weakened depending upon individual situations, geographic proximity, and involvement in or style of grandparenting. Relationships between grandparents and their in-law children are often cemented by the financial and emotional security they can provide upon divorce. One study noted a tendency for families to grow closer when their own daughter had custody of the grandchildren.[4] Given the emphasis on biological ties in the United States, Sprey and Matthews express doubt that families would accept the term "exgrandparent." Rather than eliminating old kin ties, the tendency appears to be the addition of new positions upon remarriage of children. New relative positions that are created out of remarriages may include "stepgrandparent" or "former-in-law child."[5]

REMARRIAGE

In the early part of this century death usually set the stage for remarriage, whereas at present the stage is primarily set by divorce. In the early 1900s most remarriages followed the death of a partner. By 1975, 84 percent of all brides and 86 percent of all grooms were remarrying after divorce, while only 16 percent were remarrying after widowhood. The numbers who remarry decline for older age groups.

4. Jetse Sprey and Sarah Matthews, "The Impact of Divorce on Grandparenthood" (Paper presented at the Annual Meeting of the Gerontological Society of America, Nov. 1981), p. 4.
5. Ibid.

The differences in remarriage rates for middle-aged people and those over 65 reflects age-related values and the availability of new partners. The divorced are more likely to remarry than the widowed because they are generally younger and they may have life circumstances predisposing them to remarry. For example, (1) there may be young children for whom the divorced person needs to make a home; (2) the divorced are not obliged to defer remarriage out of respect for the deceased; (3) they may be more liberal; and (4) their plans to remarry may have precipitated the divorce.[6]

Those who remarry following divorce or widowhood often have some similar and some quite different experiences. Losing a partner through divorce or widowhood usually means both bereavement and adjustments to being without the former mate. The widow who receives support from family and friends may feel even stronger ties to her network of relatives, while the divorced may actually experience a loosening of ties with society.

Adjustment to remarriage should be easier if the bereavement process following the loss of a mate has been completed. The widowed have a tendency to sanctify their former mates, remembering all their positive qualities and forgetting the negative.[7] In contrast, the divorced person often retains negative feelings toward the former mate, which means that the second mate may feel less competition with the first mate.

The second partner of a widow or widower may feel that he or she is indeed a second choice and that if the former partner were living, the mate would be with that person.

Both the widowed and the divorced may experience feelings of guilt associated with remarriage.[8] These feelings may be rationalized by noting that the second marriage involves a different and more mature love. The guilt of marrying again may be fostered by children who feel competition for their parent's affections with the new spouse. Older children may be concerned about the destiny of their inheritance. The new partner may be treated as an intruder or compared with the first mate by children, friends, and relatives.

The divorced often must face the additional complications of relationships with the expartner and the social stigma still attached to divorce. Middle-aged couples who have teenage or younger children may become involved in assisting them in working out visiting relationships with the noncustodial parent. In addition, continuing relationships with grandparents and establishing associations with new relatives become a challenge.

Age and previous marital status are not the only factors affecting remarriage. Among older age groups, men are five times more likely to remarry than women. Because there are more women than men over 65, the men have more potential mates available to them. In addition, about 20 percent of the older grooms choose a bride under 55 years of age who has never married. There are more age-discrepant marriages involving

6. Judith Treas and Anke Van Hilst, "Marriage and Remarriage Rates among Older Americans," *The Gerontologist*, 16:134 (Apr. 1976).
7. Helena Z. Lopata, "Widowhood and Husband Sanctification," *Journal of Marriage and the Family* 43(2):439 (May 1981).

8. Robert Bell, *Marriage and Family Interaction*, 5th ed. (Homewood, IL: Irwin, 1979), p. 563.

an older groom and a younger bride than vice versa, suggesting a double standard of aging.[9]

Another factor promoting remarriage among the elderly appears to be geographic residence, that is, those living in the South and West are twice as likely to remarry as those in the northeast and north central states. The larger population found in the South and West because of their retirement communities, or the mobility promoted by the warmer climate of these regions, may be responsible for these differences.[10] For older age groups the likelihood of remarriage is greater for those who are mobile, are in good health, have adequate financial resources, and whose children do not oppose the match.

Success of remarriages

When the children are grown and no longer part of the household, second marriages take on the characteristics of first marriages in that the major adjustments are those of everyday living as a couple. The complex family structure that evolves following remarriage when children are present creates strains and stresses for all family members. Added social roles of stepparents and stepchildren are taken on and children are often linked to two or more households. The lack of institutionalized norms for resolving many of the everyday problems of the blended family often results in conflict and confusion.[11]

Besides the impact of children on a second marriage, the problems for

couples take on a different order of importance. As one study noted, the order of problems in first marriages was

—infidelity,

—lack of love for each other,

—emotional,

—financial,

—physical abuse.

The order of problems in second marriages was

—financial,

—emotional,

—sexual,

—spouse's former marriage, and

—problems with in-laws.[12]

It is possible that expectations are different the second time around. The first-order position of financial problems associated with second marriages may be a reflection of the difficulty of dividing property and maintaining two households upon divorce. For the elderly, the lack of partners available to women may cause some to choose partners who are less well-off than they are.

A few specific factors associated with the stability of remarriage for those over age 60 have been identified by Walter C. McKain.[13] First, as in first marriages, those who had known each other for a long period of time before the marriage were more successful. Second, those who had been able to adjust to the role changes of aging had stayed remarried. Third, the approval of friends and relatives appeared to be impor-

9. Treas and Van Hilst, "Marriage and Remarriage Rates," p. 133.

10. Ibid.

11. Andrew Cherlin, "Remarriage as an Incomplete Institution," *American Journal of Sociology*, 84(3):637 (Nov. 1978).

12. Ruth Albrecht, "Correlates of Marital Happiness," p. 857.

13. Walter C. McKain, "A New Look at Older Marriages," *Family Coordinator*, 21:61-69 (Jan. 1972).

tant to the success of the second marriage. Fourth, success was associated with adequate incomes. In Ruth Albrecht's study, those couples reporting religious affiliation and those married to regular church attenders expressed higher satisfaction with their second marriages. Respondents in Barbara Vinick's study of 24 remarried couples aged 60 to 84 were more likely to report marital satisfaction if they had been able to predict, with some degree of accuracy, what their life would be like following the marriage.[14]

IMPLICATIONS OF DIVORCE AND REMARRIAGE FOR FAMILIES AND SOCIETY

If we project the current rise in divorce statistics into the future, we can expect further increases in the numbers ever divorced and the numbers of divorces after age 65. Expectations regarding the permanency of marriage may be changing. In the future, more people will have either seen or experienced divorces, making them less extraordinary. It is to be hoped that a development of normative behavior patterns will help to accommodate individuals making the transitions from married, to divorced or widowed, to remarried. An accepted terminology for stepkin and former kin networks might help clarify roles and relationships. Therapeutic enrichment seminars and workshops in local communities may be developed to ease role transitions and help prevent marital relationships from wearing out because of the sheer exposure caused by longevity.

The family must adapt to the changes in its structure caused by divorce and remarriage. Significant family ties become a source of support to the elderly. If a spouse dies or divorces an elderly person, a part of their support network may be lost. The question has been raised as to what support adult children will assume for elderly stepparents.[15]

If we project the decline of remarriage of ever-divorced since 1967 to the future, there may be more elderly without a spouse to provide emotional, physical, and fiscal support. The family will most likely be called upon to pick up the slack and meet the needs of related individuals. Where there are insufficient family services, other forms of assistance will come from other segments of society. Divorce may increase the need for welfare for some individuals, as well as for other forms of support, such as transportation, recreation, and counseling needs.

The transition into a successful remarriage has the potential for easing the pressure on the individual's small kinship group to provide companionship and support services. For example, the incorporation of new kin through remarriage expands the available network of relatives who might be able to meet some of the socioemotional and economic needs of the couple.

Finally, we may note that some have proposed that the age norms governing mate selection in American society are becoming less restrictive. If this is true, we may find that the concept of an increasingly age-irrelevant society proposed by Bernice Neugarten will have some applicability to divorce and remarriage among our older population.[16]

15. Uhlenberg and Myers, "Divorce and the Elderly," pp. 276-82.

16. Bernice L. Neugarten, "Time, Age, and the Life Cycle," *American Journal of Psychiatry*, 137(7):889 (July 1979).

14. Barbara Vinick, "Remarriage in Old Age," *Family Coordinator*, 27:362 (Oct. 1978).

For example, older women searching for a mate will have greater opportunities for success if allowed to widen the field of eligibles to include younger men. Indeed, mid-life and older remarriages should receive more encouragement since we know that married people are generally happier than singles and have overall better mental health.

Clinical Issues of Middle Age
and Later Life

By BOAZ KAHANA and EVA KAHANA

ABSTRACT: Mental health problems of middle and late life are the focus of this article. Among topics discussed are adjustment reactions to mid-life, late-life transitions, and stressful life events. Emerging mental health problems during this period are considered as a function of increased stress that is not mediated by social supports or effective strategies in coping. Sex differences in adjustive tasks during mid-life and the later years are presented. The impact of family dynamics on mental health is considered. Age-related differences in specific types of mental disorders, including organic problems, schizophrenia, and depression, are reviewed. Sexual problems, substance abuse, and psychosomatic problems are reviewed in the context of clinical problems during middle and late life. Diversity and individual differences in responses to the stresses of life transitions are emphasized while psychosocial strengths of older persons that promote mental health are portrayed.

Boaz Kahana, Ph.D., is professor of psychology at Oakland University, where he served as chairperson for five years. He is director of the Mental Health and Aging Training Program at Wayne State University's Institute of Gerontology. Dr. Kahana is a consulting clinical psychologist, specializing in work with older adults.

Eve Kahana, Ph.D., professor of sociology and director of the Elderly Care Research Center at Wayne State University, received an M.A. in clinical psychology from City University of New York and a Ph.D. in human development from the University of Chicago. She has held a career development award from the National Institute of Mental Health.

I T is generally agreed that mental illness in late life is based on multiple causative factors. Organic-biological factors have been traditionally recognized as playing important roles in mental illness. In addition, both physical illness and history of previous mental illness have been found to be important predictors of mental illness in late life. However, in late life, more so than in earlier parts of the life cycle, psychosocial factors also play a very important role in contributing to the onset of clinical problems. Thus personal stresses and vulnerabilities are often cited as responsible for clinical problems of late life. Social orientations and attitudes also contribute to the development of psychological problems.

ETIOLOGY AND EPIDEMIOLOGY
OF MENTAL ILLNESS
IN LATE LIFE

The prevalence of specific mental health problems during middle and late life provide cues to the magnitude and importance of a given problem during these periods of the life span. Establishing statistics reflecting the frequency with which these problems occur requires reliable methods for identifying and registering such cases. It is generally assumed that there is underreporting of mental health problems in late life with an attendant decrease in resources directed toward treatment and amelioration.

In addition to clinical judgments by mental health professionals, cases may also be diagnosed through structured psychiatric interviews, self-administered psychiatric rating scales, assessments of functional status, or a combination of these. Recent literature has begun to report specific rates for psychiatric disturbance and illness for the

elderly, that is, those over the age of 65. There are few data, however, that single out midlife psychiatric illness. Furthermore, reliable data on adjustment reactions or mental health problems that do not require hospitalization are difficult to obtain.

Specific studies focusing on psychiatric illness in late life have typically been conducted at a given point in time, revealing the rate or frequency of a disease per 100,000 of the population. Although studies have differed in method, the rates of diverse forms of severe psychiatric impairment in the elderly living in the community have been estimated to be between 5 and 10 percent, with an additional 10 to 40 percent of the elderly exhibiting milder forms of psychiatric impairment. Percentages of impairment are much greater for the aged in institutional facilities. Substantial differences exist between the types of mental illness and impairment found among elderly residents in mental hospitals and nursing homes or other long-term care facilities. Those with psychiatric problems are far more likely to be admitted to mental hospitals, whereas those exhibiting confusion and other cognitive impairments are more often found in nursing homes.

In considering age-related differences in rates of psychiatric illnesses a number of studies have found that the prevalence of neuroses declines with age. Interestingly, most of these have been relatively early studies, and this observation has not been made in studies during the last 15 years. Research in both the United States and Britain have nevertheless pointed to overall increases in psychiatric symptomatology as one moves from mid-life to late life. In distinguishing different types of mental illness it has been noted that incidence of schizophrenia declines with age whereas incidence of psychosomatic complaints and of organic brain syndromes increase with age.

In considering mental health problems of late life, it is important to note that the vast majority of the very old are women who are increasingly outliving men. Hence special attention must be paid to mental health problems unique to elderly women. Poverty, which is a major risk factor in mental health problems, is especially prevalent among this group. Women are also more likely to be widowed and socially isolated and hence are often deprived of support necessary for maintaining good mental health as they are aging.

The issues of clinical problems in midlife and late life may be explored from an epidemiological stance without the need to invoke developmental explanations. Thus it has been found that certain mental illnesses peak during midlife while the prevalence of others appears to be greatest during late-life periods. Differential incidence and prevalence rates for emotional problems or abnormal behavior patterns do not imply, however, that developmental factors are necessarily responsible for their occurrence.

Assuming a more direct causal relationship between aging and mental health, development transitions may be viewed as potential sources of emotional and psychological distress. Such relationships between aging and psychopathology are at times seen as biologically determined. Thus menopause has been viewed as a period of hormonal changes that have been associated with emotional or psychological vulnerability. Brain syndromes of late life also provide examples of clinical problems that have age-related organic etiologies. Developmental psychologists and other social scientists focus on the linkages between aging and clinical problems. They note that as the individual moves along the life span he/she must cope with new and different adaptive tasks and handle them successfully. Not only are the environmental demands placed on the aging person changing, but his/her own orientations, personality, and values may be undergoing parallel or, at times, orthogonal changes.

A stress adaptational framework

The relationships among life events, stress, and physical and mental problems of the elderly has been examined on a very limited basis.[1] It has been argued that the elderly may be more susceptible to stresses because they undergo many negative life events and experience many losses during a period of concurrent physical decline. Thus they experience special demands for adaptation at a time when their capacities are diminishing.

Chiriboga and Dean[2] studied life transition in a sample of adult men and women ranging in age from 21 to 72. Younger adults generally reported more life events than did the older adults, and women reported more life events than men.

1. For a review of research on stress and mental illness, see B. Dohrenwend and B. Dohrenwend, *Stressful Life Events: Their Nature Effects* (New York: John Wiley, 1974); C. Eisdorfer and F. L. Wilkie, "Stress and behavior in aging. Issues in mental health and aging," *Proceedings of the Conference on Research in Mental Health and Aging*, 1:60-66 (1979).

2. D. Chiriboga and H. Dean, "Dimensions of stress," *Journal of Psychosomatic Research*, 22:47-55 (1978).

However, the sheer frequency of events provided only partial evidence concerning the potentially disruptive effect of life events. Personal stresses were apparently more intrusive in the lives of middle-aged individuals and retirees. Such stresses were least intrusive in the lives of newlyweds. Household stresses did not prove disruptive for younger men and women, but played an important role for both older men and women. Younger and older men alike shared work-related stress as a dimension with considerable impact on their lives. The most salient stresses for older women were financial and marital stresses, and were associated with decreased life satisfaction and increased incidents of depression.

One important life change, relocation from one residence to another or from the community to the institution, has been extensively studied.[3] Success in coping with the stress of moving has been found to depend on: (1) the degree of choice the aged individual had regarding the relocation, (2) the extent of predictability of the environment after relocation, and (3) the degree of control the individual had regarding the relocation.

Both external and internal resources have been posited as palliative in the reduction of stress. The resources that have been found to mitigate the effects of stress include physical health and availability of adequate medical assistance. Social resources include actual and potential social supports that the older adult could draw upon in mediating stress. Psychological resources include coping mechanisms developed and used by the older adult in dealing with past and present stresses.

ADJUSTMENT REACTIONS ASSOCIATED WITH MIDLIFE TRANSITIONS

The middle aged have been identified as a population at risk from both physical and mental health perspective. Studies of mid-life transitions have identified a number of impediments for the middle aged in their efforts to cope with life course changes that confronted them as they were aging. Stress reactions associated with the mid-life empty nest period have included depression, alcoholism, and divorce.

A middle-age crisis has been postulated to take place between early maturity and middle age.[4] This is seen to occur around age 40, somewhat earlier for women and later for men. These crises have been described as accompanied by a sense of uneasiness or anxiety, or feeling of being trapped by life and often result in acting out behavior on the part of those experiencing the crisis. The most frequent behavioral manifestation has been reflected in marital problems, usually infidelity, initiated by one of the marital partners not as much in response to an unhappy marriage as in response to a middle-age restlessness. The crisis has been defined as a period of major shift in attitudes and personality brought about by internal and external pressures.

Some have associated middle-age crisis with the hormonal background of the climacterium, or loss of reproductive potential. For women this period is more clearly

---

3. R. Schulz and G. Brenner, "Relocation of the Aged: Review and Theoretical Analysis," *Journal of Gerontology*, 32:323-33 (1979).

4. B. Fried, *Middle Age Crisis* (New York: Harper & Row, 1965).

demarcated and ends with menopause, the cessation of menstruation. Nevertheless, there is evidence of slower but parallel male hormonal changes resulting in reduced sex drive and reduced reproductive capacity. It is noteworthy that the psychological changes or crises tend to antedate demonstrable hormonal changes.

Middle-age crises are also associated with special stresses within the family life cycle. The middle generation is simultaneously confronted with caring for aging parents and demands by adolescent children. One's fantasies about inheriting a senior position both within the family and in the world of work with all the attendant responsibilities also materialize during this period. This puts the middle-aged person in a position to face his own mortality for the first time during the life cycle. Erikson[5] identified the conflict of mid-life as the crisis of generativity. This period is considered as one of account taking when an individual surveys what he or she has accomplished or generated and judges himself to be productive or stagnant.

The restlessness, boredom, dysphoric affect and acting out behaviors that have been cited as the more extreme manifestations of mid-life crises may also be viewed as clinical problems. When such symptoms appear in mid-life the clinician is faced with a task of differential diagnosis to distinguish potentially dangerous mental health problems from transitory reactions to midlife stress.

A comprehensive study[6] of men entering middle age and a compari-son group of men in their twenties did not confirm readily identifiable mid-life crises for males. Data, however, did point to work-related problems of mid-career and to the importance of men's emotional involvements in their family during mid-life.

The empty nest syndrome

There has been considerable controversy regarding the existence of a special crisis associated with the cessation of child rearing. Psychologists and psychiatrists tend to emphasize adverse reactions by parents to the departure of children from the household. In contrast, recent studies by sociologists have failed to identify adverse reactions associated with the empty nest period.[7] While negative reactions to the empty nest may not be normative, extreme adverse reactions have been observed by mental health professionals. These are relatively infrequent reactions, and information about their epidemiology is not available. They are defined as temporal associations of clinical depression with the cessation of child rearing. They may also go along with an inability of the parent to cope with demands of everyday living.

Investigations of major life transitions have found that women typically have positive anticipation regarding the departure of their children. Greater happiness was found among women whose children had left home than among women of similar ages whose children were still at home. Negative images of the

5. E. Erikson, *Childhood and Society* (New York: Norton, 1963).

6. M. Farrell and S. D. Rosenberg, *Men at Midlife* (Boston: Auburn, 1981).

7. M. F. Lowenthal and D. Chiriboga, "Transition to the Empty Nest: Crisis, Challenge or Relief?" *Archives of General Psychiatry*, 26:8-14 (1972).

postparental period for women have been attributed to the ideology of motherhood in Western society. It may be argued that important sex differences in reponse to the empty nest period exist with fathers having far more unfavorable reactions to children leaving the home. This may be due to the lack of frequent and meaningful interactions between fathers and their children in modern U.S. society. While the postparental period may be a natural outgrowth of parenting for mothers, it may present a sudden and abrupt recognition for the father, who had little time for his growing children, that he has missed the opportunities of fatherhood. This observation runs counter to arguments by psychiatrists and psychologists that mothers react more adversely to the departure of children since they have depended more heavily upon their parental roles as a major source of satisfaction and identity.

Adverse reactions during the postparental period have also been attributed to ambiguity in family roles during this period. Marital conflicts are seen as resulting from the loss of social roles that had been highly valued by society. Launching of children has also been associated with anxieties that may be disruptive of family life.

Reemployment of empty nest women has been cited as one coping strategy that mitigated the negative consequences—especially depression—of the empty nest period. The experience and resolution of empty nest on time rather than off time, that is, too early or too late, also appear to mitigate negative psychological consequences. Family therapy, anticipatory socialization, and rational emotive therapy have been cited as useful in the treatment of adjustment reaction during the empty nest period.

Sex differences in adjustment reactions of midlife

Sex differences are generally greater than life stage differences and prevail in many areas of personality and behavior. To the extent that life course trajectories of the two sexes do not parallel each other, one may expect different clinical problems to exist during middle and late life. In a study of life transitions in teenagers, young adults, middle-aged, and retirement-age people,[8] middle-aged women were found to express a great deal of stress-related preoccupation. Regardless of the actual stress they experienced in their lives, they appeared far more preoccupied with it than were their middle-aged male counterparts. Middle-aged women also had far more psychiatric symptoms than any other subgroup across the four life stages, and they also showed poorer patterns of adaptations. They also reported significantly more marital problems than their male counterparts or older preretirement-age women.

Data from other investigations, however, paint a more stressful picture of midlife for men. When general evaluations of middle age by fathers and mothers were compared in a study of middle-aged parents of college-age children,[9] some interest-

8. M. F. Lowenthal, M. Thurher, and D. Chiriboga, *Four Stages of Life* (San Francisco: Jossey-Bass, 1975).

9. B. Kahana and J. Meznek, "Life Events and Middle Age—An Approach to the Study of Middle Age Change. Perspectives of Parents and Adult Children" (Paper presented at the American Psychological Association Meetings, August 1976).

ing differences were observed. Whereas only 12 percent of mothers evaluated middle-age changes as negative, a considerably greater proportion of fathers gave an overall negative evaluation to middle age. This difference is also reflected in the greater proportion of mothers than fathers evaluating middle-age changes as overwhelmingly positive.

Menopause and climacteric

The terms "menopause" and "climacteric" (change of life) are often considered to be interchangeable designations for mid-life women. Although these two concepts are related, they do denote different phenomena. The climacteric refers to years surrounding the menopause when endocrine, somatic, and psychic changes take place to varying degrees, with the actual menopause being one discrete landmark during this time. In terms of psychological manifestations of clinical problems during this period, the medical and psychiatric literature refers to signs of irritability, insomnia, depression, and anxiety. Improvements in these symptoms have been reported subsequent to estrogen therapy,[10] but neither the symptoms nor the effects of estrogen on psychiatric symptoms have been well-documented beyond clinical case studies.

Because it symbolizes the end of reproductive life, menopause has often been considered a threat to the woman's feminine identity and an experience requiring great readjustment. However, studies of menopause typically have not confirmed reports of clinical problems or psychiatric distress for the vast majority of women interviewed. One explanation for this may be that society's labeling of menopause as a highly stressful event is based on stereotyped notions offered by persons who have not experienced this event. Middle-aged women are far more likely to provide positive evaluations of middle-age changes than are persons in younger age groups. The majority of middle-aged women attribute little discontinuity in their lives to the climacterium and many believe that the woman herself has some control over her symptoms. In a study considering the perceived role of menopause among other life events, Kahana et al.[11] found that women rate menopause as requiring little readjustment when compared with other life events. Interestingly, men were found to view the climacterium as a major life change, supporting earlier findings that men evaluate mid-life in more negative terms than do women.

Work-related stress reactions during mid-life

Various stresses confronting individuals in the work environment have been associated with ill health, mental strain, job dissatisfaction, absenteeism, and job turnover. Work-related stresses may include heavy work loads, role ambiguity or conflict in the work place, dissatisfaction with coworkers or supervisors, and lack of job security or

10. J. Jones, E. Cohen, and R. Wilson, "Clinical Aspects of Menopause," in *Menopause and Aging*, eds. K. Ryan and D. Gibson (Bethesda, MD: U.S. Public Health Service, National Institute of Child Health and Human Development, 1971.)

11. E. Kahana, A. Kiyak, and J. Liang, "Menopause in the Context of Other Life Events," in *The Menstrual Cycle*, eds. A. Dan, E. Graham, and C. Beecher (New York: Springer, 1980).

opportunities for advancement. Many of these stresses affect workers of all ages but some have been identified as representing particular risk factors for the middle aged. Work-related psychological problems during mid-life or late life may be viewed as a function of special stresses in the work place for the older worker and special vulnerabilities for coping with stress during these periods in the life cycle. Effects of stresses experienced in the work setting are also more likely to be exacerbated when other pressures, for example, in the family arena, impinge on the individual.

One of the most extensively documented personal risk constellations relevant to work stress in midlife has been the identification of the Type A personality, that is, the individual at a high risk for heart disease.[12] Persons exhibiting aggressive, competitive behavior and high achievement orientation are far more likely to develop heart disease than those with the opposite pattern of work commitment and behavior. Special problems of the middle-aged worker include the recognition that career advancement is likely to be slowed and to become more limited. For some middle-aged workers these insecurities are also combined with the fear of obsolescence.

In a study of life transitions conducted by Lowenthal[13] and her colleagues, work-related problems were found to be very salient for middle-aged men, primarily in terms of the pressures of producing sufficient retirement income. Notably, these men had considerable job security and about 10 years to work until retirement. We interpret these concerns as reflecting strain, boredom, and anxiety, which we see as placing middle-aged men at high risk for developing mental health problems. Lowenthal also suggests that different typologies of stress reactions for men may exist in mid-life wherein some men show signs of psychological distress and vulnerability whereas others, approximating Type A personalities, show little psychological distress but develop significant somatic problems.

Career shifts in mid-life increasingly represent real options for both men and women. There have been suggestions that both career and marital instability represent mid-life adjustment reactions or even signs of psychopathology. Nevertheless data comparing emotional adjustments of middle-aged men who were identified as career shifters and those who were stable in their career patterns did not reveal any significant differences in functioning.

FOCUS ON LATE LIFE

A variety of issues and problems are associated with transitions into late life. These include mental health concerns, family dynamics, sexuality, psychosomatic disorders and hypochondria, and substance abuse.

Emotional problems and adjustment reactions in late life

Mental health problems are typically distressing and even debilitating, but are often transitional and seldom require psychiatric hospital-

12. M. Friedman, "The General Causes of Coronary Artery Disease," *The Pathogenesis of Coronary Artery Disease* (New York: McGraw-Hill).

13. Lowenthal, Thurher, and Chiriboga, *Four Stages of Life.*

ization. They may range from interpersonal or sexual difficulties to
experiencing negative emotions,
anxieties, or worries. They would
not be classified, however, as forms
of mental illness.[14]

The multiple losses experienced
by older persons in terms of declining health and death of loved ones
make demands on them to both
grieve and cope with their losses in
socially acceptable ways. At the
same time, changes in personality
may result in diminished affect and
even tendencies for emotional and
psychological withdrawal. Grief
and mourning are necessary emotional responses that help the older
person accept the reality of his or her
losses and to make peace with the
unalterable reality. The emotional
distress of grieving is often accompanied by physical symptoms, including insomnia and digestive
upsets. Rates of physical illness
and even death have been shown
to increase subsequent to bereavement.

In addition to interpersonal problems and losses, personal illness, disability, and sensory impairment are
also likely to elicit adverse emotional reactions among older persons. Hearing losses represent a
prevalent sensory impairment
affecting about 30 percent of older
persons. This problem is particularly troublesome to older persons,
often reducing reality testing, which
leads to suspiciousness and even
paranoia. Connections between
hearing loss and depression have
also been observed. Visual loss can
also lead to emotional and mental
health problems, making older people more fearful of their environment and resulting in poor
orientation.

There is a general loss of a sense of
control and mastery over one's self
and environment as a person
reaches old age. Fear, anxiety, and
even rage are common emotional
responses to such loss of control.
Ameliorative efforts to deal with
such problems have ranged from
environmental aid to supportive
psychotherapy and in some cases
drug therapy. Group therapy helping older persons learn to cope more
competently with their environments and establish a sense of control has also been found useful.

Family dynamics and mental health

The role of the elderly in the family has received increasing attention
in recent years.[15] In studies published on the three-generational
family, stereotypes of complete lack
of communication and abandonment of the older generation by their
children have been shattered. Studies generally indicate that adult
children represent important supports for their aged parents, especially in times of illness or crises.

The single most important source
of support for the aging person
within the family context comes
from the marital unit. Older persons
with a living spouse have consistently been found to require fewer
services and to exhibit better health
and higher morale than their
widowed counterparts. Yet the marital unit can also be a source of friction and conflicts as people move
through life transitions. Retirement

14. For a more extensive review of emo-
tional problems in late life, see R. Butler and
M. Lewis, *Aging and Mental Health* (St.
Louis: Mosby, 1982).

15. G. Streib, "Old Age and the Family,"
in *Aging in Contemporary Society*, ed. E. Shanas (Beverly Hills, CA: Sage, 1970).

typically alters life-long patterns of interaction for the couple, with the man being in the house, often seeking to fill his leisure time with activities around the house. This in turn interrupts the customary freedom of the older wife who had grown accustomed to her household autonomy. Marital friction results during this period.

Special stresses of a far more serious kind await spouses when one partner becomes seriously ill or has to be placed in a nursing home. Chronic illnesses of late life are frequently of long duration, severely taxing coping abilities of the caretaking spouse. Feelings of guilt, anger, and depression are common emotional problems experienced by persons caring for an ill or dying spouse.

Although it is socially desirable to report satisfaction in the grandparental role, it is clear that grandparents are marginal members of the family and that the role does not carry much intimacy.[16] Grandparents are expected to fulfill an expressive function, but are discouraged from playing an instrumental role because of the great premium we place in the U.S. and Western culture on independence of families. Noninterference in grown-up children's family life is a commonly expressed norm along with the desirability of giving love and help to grandchildren. When grandparents continue to treat their adult children in a dependent fashion, family friction often results, with subsequent discouragement by the parent generation of involvement by grandparents. It has been argued that the grandparent role may also be diminished in the egalitarian, permissive U.S. family because there is no great need for grandparents to mediate conflict between the middle and youngest generation.

In a recent study of the effect of intergenerational living,[17] the presence of an older family member in the household did not foster an increase in conflict, anxiety, or neurotic symptoms nor did it foster an over-dependence of the aged, as has been previously suggested by psychiatrists and family practitioners. On the contrary, more positive attitudes toward the aged and more frequent parent-child communications were reported in families that included an aged person. It has been aptly stated that Americans live in a split-level family, that is, children and adults go about their business in the company of their peers, usually people of the same age, race, and social status. This is in contrast to many other cultures where closer generational interactions prevail. Yet social contact between old and young serves important functions. Surveys of college students show that those students who had a grandparent living at home with them at some point during the first 15 years of their lives had far more favorable attitudes toward the grandparent than students who did not have this kind of contact.

Some important changes in family structure in the United States have been occurring in recent years that have implications for mental health of elderly family members. There has been a dramatic increase

16. For a review of grandparent-grandchild relations, see E. Kahana and B. Kahana, "Theoretical and Research Perspectives on Grandparenthood: A Theoretical Statement," *Aging and Human Development*, 2:4, 261-268 (1971).

17. B. Bresver, "Intergenerational Living and Mental Health" (Ph.D. dissertation, University of Toronto, Toronto, Ontario, 1973).

in recent years in the number of multigeneration families and in the ratio of elderly to young family members. In addition, middle-aged women who usually represent the major family caretakers have been increasingly returning to the labor force. Accordingly, a crisis may be developing in terms of unavailability of caretakers of the mentally and/or physically frail elderly in the family context.

Sexuality in late life

Investigations of sexuality among the aged have awaited a greater climate of acceptance and frankness about sexuality in society at large. Nevertheless, while taboos against sexuality among adolescents and adults have been liberalized, taboos against sex in old age are still prevalent.

Some decline in sexual function has been documented among older persons.[18] Men past 60 are slower to be aroused sexually, slower to develop erections, and slower to achieve ejaculation. Women over the age of 60 also show diminished physiological response to sexual stimulation. Interestingly, capacity to reach orgasm does not diminish, especially among women who had regular sexual stimulation. Thus from a physiological point of view there appears to be no time limit attached to sexuality in women. Studies have also shown an abrupt lessening of sexual activity among persons over age 75 due to frequent and chronic illness in both the aged respondents and their spouses.

Many of these very old persons express sexual interest despite the absence of sexual activity.[19]

Two major factors have been recognized as interfering with the sexual functioning of older persons. One relates to illness or fear of illness, while the other is based on negative attitudes by society, family members, or professionals. In terms of fears of illness, some elderly are afraid they may suffer a heart attack during sexual relations. However, their fear is exaggerated. Diabetes of old age may be responsible for impotence in men, but the latter can be ameliorated if the diabetes is controlled. Prostate gland surgery may induce impotence; however, recent surgical approaches have reduced such adverse effects. Hysterectomies do not produce physiologically induced declines in sexual desire. When decline occurs it is usually psychological. Mastectomies and other surgery that may be viewed as disfiguring may lead to concerns over sexual indulgence. Therapy aimed at one's self image can be beneficial, as can mutual support groups, for example, colostomy or mastectomy support groups. Although therapists report a lower success rate in dealing with sexual problems of older people, this is because of longer duration of the problem and stronger taboos on sexuality that were instilled in members of the older generation as they were growing up.

The second problem relates to cultural stereotypes that older people no longer have sexual needs and should not portray such interest. Thus older people describe sexual

18. B. Kahana, "Social and Psychological Aspects of Sexual Behavior Among the Aged," in *Aging and Reproductive Physiology*, ed. S. E. Hafez (Ann Arbor: Science Publisher, 1976).

19. R. N. Butler and M. Lewis, *Sex After 60, A Guide for Men and Women for Their Later Years* (New York: Harper & Row, 1976).

desires, but are embarrassed over their feelings. In those cases where elderly widows or widowers indulge in sexual expression, their adult children may induce guilt feelings in them. For the widowed elderly and in particular for older women whose chances for remarriage are slim, absence of available partners constitutes a major barrier to sexuality. Homes for the aged do not provide privacy and nursing staff often become upset when older persons express their sexuality. In view of these considerations, sex education for the elderly is important, but must be complemented by a more accepting social climate for sexual expression in late life.

Psychosomatic disorders and hypochondria

Psychosomatic disorders are changes in body function due to psychological causes—for example, excessive stomach acidity and spastic colon—whereas hypochondria refers to unwarranted concern and anxiety over one's body functions, with little somatic basis—for example, cancer phobias and fear of sudden heart attack or stroke. Clinicians have reported considerable hypochondriacal concern among the aged.[20] It appears that there is no appreciable age-related increase in hypochondria and psychosomatic disorders within the age range of 18-60. Beyond this age an increase in symptoms is evident, but it is difficult to demonstrate conclusively that these symptoms are hypochondriacal or psychosomatic as opposed

to having a medical cause—for example, excessive urination and skeletal-muscular pain.

When hypochondria is definitively diagnosed in the aged, it may symbolize underlying feelings of depression or unresolved grief over loss of spouse or other family members.[21] At times a flareup in hypochondria occurs around the anniversary of the death of a loved one ("anniversary reaction") or in anticipation of the death of a terminally ill family member ("anticipatory grief reaction"). In treating these conditions, clinicians report good results with antidepressant medications for those cases where hypochondria is symptomatic of depression. Antianxiety drugs may also be useful for hypochondria based on anniversary reactions or anticipatory grief. Supportive therapy and provision of an opportunity for elderly patients to vent their feelings have proved to be very useful in alleviating these concerns.

Substance abuse during middle and later life

There has been increasing public attention turned toward personal and social problems caused by substance abuse—in particular, drug abuse and alcohol addiction—among young people. Only recently have mental health professionals recognized that substance abuse also poses important mental health concerns during late life. During the middle years problems of substance abuse are usually considered as symptoms of mid-life adjustment

20. W. D. Gentry, "Psychosomatic Issues in Assessment," in *The Clinical Psychology of Aging*, eds. M. Storandt, I. Siegler, and M. F. Elias (New York: Plenum Press, 1978).

21. J. B. Nowlin and E. W. Busse, "Psychosomatic Problems in the Older Person," in *Psychosomatic Medicine*, eds. E. D. Witkower and H. Warnes (New York: Harper & Row, 1977).

reactions or of depression. Yet there are few specific discussions of alcoholism or drug addiction as accompanying mid-life transitions.

Alcoholism is a serious problem among the elderly and the problem is increasing as the elderly population is growing. Yet it is seldom recognized or treated.[22] The highest frequency of alcoholism occurs in the 35-50 year age group with a subsequent decline with increasing age. This, however, is due in no small part to the earlier death of alcoholics due to a variety of causes, such as cirrhosis, cancers of the mouth, accidents, and suicide.

Laboratory studies have shown that older animals metabolize alcohol at a slower rate than younger animals, show greater change in brain chemistry in response to alcohol, and portray greater decline in behavior.[23] Among humans, older alcoholics show greater impairment on neuropsychological tests than younger alcoholics. This difference is greater than the difference between younger and older persons who do not consume alcohol. When older and younger people are both given equal doses of alcohol, there is a higher blood level of alcohol in the older individuals. Autopsy studies also show differences in brain chemistry between young, middle-aged, and older alcoholics that are greater than the difference among their normal counterpart groups. Of additional concern is the fact that this group takes more medication than other age groups, and these medica-tions may interact unfavorably with alcohol.

Some researchers have distinguished between chronic elderly alcoholics and reactive-situational alcoholics. The latter group took to alcohol in reaction to loss of a spouse, retirement, or loneliness. Treatment of the situational alcoholic involves helping the person to cope better with these emotional reactions to loss. Chronic alcoholism is more difficult to treat and is characterized by a life-long history of problems in employment, in marital and family instability, problems with the police, and a high incidence of psychopathology, including underlying depression.

Continued overindulgence in alcohol over the years—which is often accompanied by continued malnutrition—results in pathological nervous system changes above and beyond those changes seen with normal aging. Among normal social drinkers continued intake of the same dosages of alcohol over the years may become problematic because of reduced tolerance of alcohol with aging. Alcoholism in the aged often goes undetected. It is therefore important for physicians and other health care workers to be particularly alert when dealing with aged clients and to include a diagnostic workup for alcoholism.

Overuse and abuse of drugs has not been specifically cited as a mid-life problem. It has been consistently identified, however, as an important problem during the later years. While older persons comprise only about 11 percent of the U.S. population, they consume about 25 percent of the medicine sold in this country.[24] Much of this medication is

22. W. Gibson Wood, "The Elderly Alcoholic: Some Diagnostic Problems and Considerations" in *The Clinical Psychology of Aging*, eds. Storandt, Siegler, and Elias.

23. B. Mishara and R. Kastenbaum, *Alcohol and Old Age* (New York: Grune and Stratton, 1980).

24. W. Poe and D. Holloway, *Drugs and the Aged* (New York: McGraw-Hill, 1980).

either unnecessary or unlikely to correct the problem for which it is being used. On the contrary, overuse and misuse of drugs may be viewed as an important cause of illness among the elderly. Unfavorable reactions to drugs occur in about 12 percent of hospitalized older persons. Not infrequently psychological side effects occur, such as restlessness, anxiety, depressive symptoms, and agitation. In addition, the multiple and chronic health problems of the aged along with the lack of needed social and personal supports to deal with them often make medication and pill popping a ready crutch.

The average person age 65 and over takes four different medications. As the number of diseases increases so does the number of drugs used and the likelihood of potential adverse reactions. The implication is that drugs must be used judiciously and appropriately. The physician must be aware of all medication being used, including over-the-counter drugs. It is important to determine the optimal level of drug dosage for effective results for a particular patient and to make periodic adjustment in drug dosage based on frequent patient observation.

MENTAL ILLNESS IN MID AND LATE LIFE

Substantial numbers of older persons suffer from mental disorders in late life. These include organic brain disease, schizophrenia, depression, and suicide.

Organic brain disease

Organic brain disease limits or impairs functioning in the community and is often responsible for admission to psychiatric hospitals and nursing homes.[25] The brain, like other organs, undergoes an aging process. Organic brain syndrome is, for the most part, an affliction of the elderly and generally does not present itself in mid-life. Exceptions include presenile dementia, Pick's disease, and Huntington's disease. Common symptoms of the various organic brain syndromes are increased forgetfulness, decline in intellectual ability, diminished orientation as to one's environment, and unstable emotional functioning. The course of decline may vary in duration ranging from rapid decline occurring within several months in the presenile dementias to extended duration of many years in the senile dementias. Despite differences in causes of these disorders, the symptoms often overlap sufficiently so as to present a serious problem in diagnosis. Accordingly, different types of brain changes may produce the same general end result in terms of behavior. Further complicating the picture, a number of organic syndromes may coexist in the same individual, for example, Alzheimer's and Parkinson's diseases, arteriosclerosis, and reversible organic brain syndrome. Advances in radiographic techniques—C.A.T. scans and more recently, P.E.T. scans—have resulted in greater diagnostic accuracy, but these techniques are not without their margin of error.

Because of difficulties in confirming diagnoses during the life of the patient, many patients are misdiagnosed even by competent neurologists. Such misdiagnoses result in

25. M. Reskind, "The Organic Mental Disorders," in *Handbook of Geriatric Psychiatry*, eds. E. Busse and D. Blazer (New York: Van Nostrand, 1980).

undue optimism or pessimism in the mangement of an elderly patient. Older persons suffering from depression may frequently portray symptoms characteristic of Alzheimer's disease. If properly diagnosed, such patients could be more successfully treated with antidepressant drugs and therapy.

Some organic brain disorders may be reversible. These reversible conditions have been referred to as delirium in the medical literature and they are typically associated with some form of acute physical illness. Frequently they develop over a short period of time and last a few hours to a few days. If diagnosed and treated in time these conditions are reversible. Examples include organic brain syndromes due to infection, dehydration, and excessive use of alcohol and other drugs.

Among the chronic, irreversible forms of organic brain disease, senile dementia of the Alzheimer's type[26] has been termed the most personally devastating and socially costly of the physical afflictions of late life. Patients suffering from this disease fill many of the psychiatric beds occupied by the aged and the senile wards of nursing homes. Considerable resources of the mental health profession have been turned in recent years toward developing treatments for Alzheimer's disease.

Strokes, ministrokes, and arteriosclerosis in the brain are also responsible for cognitive and behavioral decline in the later years, and sometimes in the latter part of the middle years. Strokes are distinguished behaviorally from Alzheimer's disease by a rather sudden decline in functioning, and frequently in paralysis. Some patients suffer from both Alzheimer's disease and arteriosclerosis of the brain.

There are numerous additional organic diseases affecting the elderly that range from rare virus infections to genetically caused disorders and diverse forms of arteriosclerotic disease. All of these conditions share in common overlapping symptoms of cognitive deterioration, poor prognosis, and difficulties in making a definitive diagnosis. Therapeutic efforts are currently limited to palliative care.

A good deal of scientific activity has been focused in recent years on developing a better understanding of etiologies of diverse brain diseases afflicting older person. The roles of slow-acting viruses, changes in the immune system over the adult years, genetic factors, and chemicals in the environment are being considered. Mental health professionals are hopeful that the convergence of scientific interest will result in some major breakthroughs in understanding and combating these conditions.

Schizophrenia in middle age and old age

Schizophrenia is a disorder characterized by the inability to function due primarily to a breakdown in one's logic and ego functioning. Delusion and hallucinations are cardinal symptoms and reflect the underlying disorder in thought processes. According to earlier studies the age range of schizophrenia is from the late teens to the early forties, with the modal age being early twenties. There is strong support for a biological and genetic basis for schizophrenia, as demonstrated by a

26. R. Katzman, R. D. Terry, and K. L. Bick, eds., *Alzheimer's Disease: Senile Dementia and Related Disorders* (New York: Raven Press, 1978).

series of studies of twins and by adoption studies.[27] However, there is also support for the role of stress in precipitating schizophrenic disorders. According to some authors, there are two distinct groups of schizophrenics during early and middle adulthood. Early onset schizophrenia, which occurs in the early twenties, primarily affects males, in contrast to a somewhat later onset schizophrenia, which appears more likely to affect females during the 30s. In explaining these sex differences, stress-related interpretations have been put forth, contending that men are more stressed in their early twenties in attempting to establish their work identities and becoming economically autonomous whereas women are more saddled by child-rearing and family responsibilities during their thirties.

In contrast to the generally poor prognosis of childhood and young adulthood schizophrenia, later onset schizophrenics are considered to have a better prognosis. Nevertheless, there is still controversy among researchers and theoreticians with regard to the etiology and prognoses of schizophrenia occurring at different points of the lifespan.

Schizophrenic-like reactions have also been observed in late life and have been referred to as paraphrenia or senile schizophrenia. These diagnoses are especially prevalent in the clinical literature in Europe. While these conditions share many of the symptoms of schizophrenia, there is considerable controversy as to whether they are true forms of schizophrenia. Late onset schizophrenias often come about among persons deprived of social contact and among the deaf elderly. Paranoid symptoms tend to predominate. In addition to these late onset schizophrenias, many elderly have been chronic schizophrenics—since young adulthood—who received little treatment and who have spent many years on back wards of mental hospitals.

Depression

It had long been believed that women in mid-life are particularly susceptible to depression associated with the menopause, that is, involutional melancholia.[28] Researchers, however, have found no correlation between menopause and major depression independent of age. There is an increase in major depression after the age of 45. This increase is found more so in the lower class than the middle class, in those who are currently unmarried, and in women more so than men. However, alcoholism, which is seen by some authorities as the male equivalent of depression, is more frequent among men than women. Alcoholism is seen as taking the place of depression in men since men have been conditioned not to express feelings of depression. Psychological theories of depression focus on the theme of loss. In mid-life the loss is related to perceived loss of attractiveness and desirability, in taking stock of oneself and feeling that one's life will not improve significantly, and that one has achieved most, if not all, of which one is capable of achieving. Writers on depression focus on the impor-

27. D. W. Kay and M. Roth, "Environmental hereditary factors in the schizophrenia of old age, *Journal of Mental Science*, 107:649-86 (1961).

28. P. Bart, "Depression in Middle Aged Women," *Transaction*, 8:69 (1970).

tance of previous adaptation in determining midlife depression.[29] Women who developed depressions in mid-life were frequently found to have lost their own mothers in childhood. Specific life events have been recognized as potential precipitants of depression and suicide in mid-life. These include marital disruptions, difficulties at work, and death of a close family member.

The increase in hypochondriacal concerns among those aged 60 may also reflect a disguised depression. The slight decline with age in an extroverted orientation toward the environment along with a shift from active mastery to passive mastery of the environment are congruent with findings of increased depression with age. Despite these findings, the increased availability in recent years of alternative life-styles, of new careers after retirement, of relocation to new environments, and of greater options in general may all serve to change the current picture of the aged with regard to depression.

Psychotherapy of a supportive type has been found very useful for both mild and moderate depressions. The advent of antidepressant drugs has contributed significantly to the alleviation of depressive symptoms. Thus the tricyclic antidepressants are reported to be successful in 70 percent of patients coming for treatment. In supportive psychotherapy it is important to offer the patient the opportunity to express anxieties and concerns and to learn to cope better with both feelings and realities that confront the individual.

Suicide

Persons in the 50 and older age group represent that segment of the population at highest risk for suicide.[30] While persons over age 50 comprise only about 23 percent of the U.S. population, they account for 40 percent of all suicides. Suicide rates have been found to be highest for white men, with older blacks having remarkably low suicide rates. The peak rate of suicide for white women appears during middle age. Suicide rates for women, however, are on the increase, with older women showing the greater increase. Although suicide has been identified as a major mental health problem among older persons, attention has only recently been focused on this phenomenon along with greater recognition within society of mental health problems in late life. In considering the meaning of suicide in young and old, it must be noted that those attempting to commit suicide in late life typically fully intend to die. Thus while only one in seven young persons attempting suicide succeeds in taking his/her life, one in two older persons succeeds in doing so.

29. W. Zung, "Affective Disorders," in *Handbook of Geriatric Psychiatry*, eds. E. and Blazer.

30. For a more detailed discussion, see J. Weiss, "Suicide in the aged," in *Suicidal Behavior*, ed. H. C. P. Resnick (Boston: Little, Brown, 1968).

Depression has been identified as an important contributory factor in suicide of late life. The suicide rate of depressed patients is at least 25 times higher than that of the general population and is substantially higher than that of other psychiatric patients. While the dynamics of suicide and depression apparently overlap, they are not identical. Many depressed older individuals never attempt suicide while others who show no clinical signs of depression, do. It has been noted that the elderly undergo many extreme stresses and that major readaptations may be required of them just when their adaptive capacities are diminished. Exposure to death and separation may represent particularly important stresses for older persons, and some may be unable to cope in any other manner than by attempting to end their lives. Butler and Lewis[31] have postulated that ageism and the severe loss of status it causes for white men may be responsible for their excessive suicide rates. For older persons who feel a total loss of control over their lives due to ill health or social circumstances, suicide may represent an attempt to exert control at least over their deaths. It is not unusual to find a combination of mercy killing of a spouse and suicide among elderly couples where one or both parties suffer from debilitating and painful physical illnesses.

In addition to active suicides just discussed, interest has recently also been directed at indirect self-destructive behaviors in late life.[32] Thus older persons have often been observed to stop eating and taking medication or to expose themselves to undue dangers, for example, as victims of crime. Indirect self-destructive behaviors particularly have been frequently found among older persons living in nursing homes or other long-term care facilities. Mental health professionals involved with the aged argue that suicide rates would be substantially higher if indirect attempts at self-destruction would be added to single and dramatic acts of suicide.

Among men the suicide rate increases with age from childhood to above the age of 80 when it reaches its peak, especially with the white elderly. Suicide rates among men are consistently higher than for women in each decade throughout the lifespan and range from two times to ten times the women's rate. Among women the suicide rate gradually escalates with increasing age up to the decades of the 40s and 50s where it reaches its peak and thereafter declines with each succeeding decade, a pattern very different from that of men.

CONCLUSION:
MENTAL HEALTH IN
MID AND LATE LIFE

Having reviewed the variety of clinical problems that afflict middle-

31. Butler and Lewis, *Aging and Mental Health.*

32. N. Farberow and S. Moriwaki, "Self Destructive Crises in the Older Person," *The Gerontologist,* 15:333-37 (1975).

aged and older persons as they progress through the life cycle, perhaps we reaffirmed an impression sometimes prevalent in the gerontological literature: as people age, they become vulnerable and dependent beings, "uselessly dangling at the end of the life cycle." The mental health professions as well as researchers concerned with clinical issues have typically focused their attention on problems in functioning. Consequently, far better definitions of mental illness than of mental health exist.

Mental health problems related to life transitions, on the whole, result from human difficulties in coping with overwhelming demands for adaptation. After focusing on impairments in functioning or affective states reflecting such failures in adaptation, we invite the reader to step back and consider the impressive resiliency with which people for the most part do cope and adapt to environmental and interpersonal demands posed by life transitions.

Successful aging or mental health through normal life transitions involves biological, social, psychological, and economic factors. In considering the import of aging in these diverse areas the effects of disease must be differentiated from those of normal aging. Accordingly, apparent intellectual or emotional changes of aging often turn out to be effects of diseases that occur with greater frequency in late life. Longitudinal studies of normal elderly have generally resulted in an optimistic view of late life, revealing few emotional or cognitive deficits that are simply results of normal aging.

Gerontologists have attempted to provide criteria for successful aging in diverse research endeavors. Considerable controversy has surrounded alternative theories of activity versus disengagement as representing modes of optimal aging.[33] Although the beneficial roles of activity and involvement in enhancing well-being in late life are generally recognized, students of aging also note that numerous typologies of successful aging may be possible. Social integration is generally known to provide a sense of well-being while social isolation is seen as contributing to mental health problems in late life.

Changes occurring within older persons are generally viewed by gerontologists as negative or detrimental, whereas stability is considered to be the most positive response to the aging process. Furthermore, when changes do occur, they are generally seen as outside of the older person's control and volition. These trends generally reflect the view that change is problematic. The concept of ego integrity has been used as one useful concept in explaining aging.[34] Such integrity has been suggested to come about when older people resolve three crises. These include abandonment of work preoccupation, body tran-

33. E. Cumming and W. E. Henry, *Growing Old* (New York: Basic Books, 1961).

34. Erikson, *Childhood and Society*.

scendence, and ego transcendence, that is, an emphasis on one's contributions to others. The importance of contributory roles for successful aging has also been stressed by Midlarsky and Kahana[35] based on studies of altruistic behavior among older persons.

The lively controversy regarding stability versus change in human personality is still raging, providing social scientists and the public with frequent evidence of both.[36] Recent longitudinal studies specifically focusing on late life have emphasized stability of personality into old age. Thus evidence of stability has been reported for diverse traits ranging from extroversion-introversion t neuroticism and to a lesser exter even an openness to new experienc(and excitement-seeking.[37] It has been argued that data that may be interpreted as evidence of stability by some may also be viewed as evidence of change by others. Some consider stability of personality to reflect stagnation and suggest that one cannot be a true developmentalist without a concern for human potential for growth and change.

Closely related to considerations of the impact of change during the

later years is the question of personal desirability of change and the concept of futurity. Older persons have been found to project themselves into a much more limited time frame than younger persons when asked to describe important future events in their lives. The general consensus among gerontologists has been that older persons lack futurity. This position is based in part on the limited probability that older persons would live a substantial number of additional years in good health. A perception of this limited futurity of the aged has been cited as a reason for not investing major resources in older persons by society.

In contrast to the prevailing view on the generally negative impact of change in older people, a few researchers have recognized the potential value of personal and environmental change during late life. They have suggested that deliberate cultivation of flexibility after age 50 as part of preparation for retirement may enhance adaptation to new roles in late life. In spite of well-documented role losses during the later years, old age can also provide a period of new role opportunities. Given health, some social support, and personal innovation, it is possible to alter role-sets in later maturity.

In exploring criteria for mental health in late life, one cannot focus only on the reduction in social roles and interpersonal involvements characterizing the older person. Instead, reverse patterns of seeking engagement, involvement, and

35. E. Midlarsky and E. Kahana, "Altruism and Helping among the Aged: A Conceptual Model," *Interdisciplinary Topics in Gerontology* (Winter 1982).

36. D. Levinson et al., *The Seasons of a Man's Life* (New York: Knopf, 1978).

37. P. Costa, R. McCrae, and D. Arenberg, "Enduring Dispositions in Adult Males," *Journal of Personality and Social Psychology*, 793-800 (1980).

stimulation during the later years must also be considered. Self-initiated environmental change by the aged may provide them with a possible and meaningful avenue toward extending themselves in the future, finding meaningful new stimulation and roles, and may enhance their general satisfaction during late life.

Our recent studies[38] of older persons undertaking long-distance moves have considered older persons voluntarily relocating from one community to another. Rather than a traditional focus on the vulnerable aged, this research focused on the competent and well aged. Instead of fitting the stereotypes of being disengaged and unable to form any new attachments, older persons choosing to relocate to distant regions assume a great deal of control over their environment. Adventurous older persons often seek discontinuity in order to establish new life-styles. Voluntary relocation results in high levels of satisfaction for most aged undertaking such moves in spite of the major readaptation required from them. Positive attitudes and expectations serve as important determinants of coping with long-distance relocation.

Recognition of alternative patterns of late-life adjustment should broaden our view of the range of aging experiences and patterns of successful aging. Acknowledgment of a more hopeful pattern of responses to later life may also provide an incentive to many older persons who have been led to believe that their options were severely limited. They may look toward expanded life-styles, being aware that a sense of futurity may be as much a liberating frame of mind as a limiting sense of reality.

The later years may be viewed as posing new opportunity for freedom from obligations and role prescriptions, affording older people with a second career in living. This may be a chance to get in shape, fight for one's favorite cause, or even try to make the world a little better place to live. The adventurous aged, in fact, may be seen as embodying and giving substance to the adage, "Life begins at 60." While the search for new life-styles exemplified by this group may be relatively infrequent among the elderly, they pose a challenge to gerontologists to reexamine our stereotypes and to consider alternative pathways to integrity in the later years.

SUMMARY

Overall increases in psychopathology have been observed as one moves from middle to late life. Diverse forms of mental illness show different patterns of age-related changes. While incidence of schizophrenia and neuroses decline with age, depressive and organically based psychiatric disorders show

38. E. Kahana and B. Kahana, "Environmental Continuity, Discontinuity, Futurity and Adaptation of the Aged," in *Aging and Milieu: Environmental Perspectives on Growing Old*, eds. G. Rowles and R. Ohta (New York: Academic, 1982).

age-related increases. A wide variety of factors have been cited as responsible for age-related differences in mental health problems including biological factors and changes in social conditions and roles that predispose individuals to mental illness and personal vulnerabilities or inability to cope with life events and transitions. Sex differences in mid-life do not show consistent patterns, but in old age women face multiple jeopardies predisposing them to mental health problems.

Adjustment reactions precipitated by life transitions tend to be transitory and amenable to environmental intervention. More severe forms of mental illness typically have both biological and environmental etiologies and are treated by drugs and psychotherapy. In spite of increased vulnerability to mental health problems in late life, many older persons exhibit psychosocial strengths and cope successfully with the developmental tasks of late life.

ERRATA

Please note the following corrections to "The Federal Courts Under Siege" by Charles McC. Mathias, Jr., which appeared on pages 26-33 of the July 1982 issue of THE ANNALS:

Page 31, Note 27 should read: "Quoted in *Documents Illustrative of the Formation of the Union of the American States.*"
Page 31, Note 29, the correct title is *Supreme Court Review.*

ANNALS, *AAPSS*, **464**, November 1982

Death and Survivorship:
The Final Transition

By RICHARD A. KALISH

ABSTRACT: In spite of some recent increases in services for bereaved persons, the availability of such services is minimal. The process of grieving itself takes place in time in several ways: the extent to which the death is sudden, expected, and timely; the passage of time from the beginning of anticipatory grieving before the actual death through the diminishing effects of the loss over an extended period of time; and the age and stage in life of the grieving persons. During the grieving process the survivors often develop physical and health problems, face psychological and emotional distress, encounter difficulties with social relationships, and must cope with numerous practical issues. The subsequent adjustment of widows and widowers appears to be related to the extent to which there had been the opportunity for open communication. Whether widows fare better than widowers after the death is uncertain; research has provided conflicting results and equally conflicting interpretations of the results.

Richard A. Kalish is a social psychologist who has spent the last dozen years as a self-employed author, researcher, teacher, speaker, and consultant. His writings have included a dozen books on topics such as aging, death and loss, and general psychology, as well as over 100 journal articles and 20-25 book and film reviews. After finishing his Ph.D. in psychology at Case Western Reserve University, he took a teaching position in psychology at the University of Hawaii, followed by a similar position at California State University, Los Angeles. From 1966 through 1971 he was associate professor of Public Health at UCLA and head of that program's gerontology center. He is presently about to reenter the academic marketplace.

RELATIVELY little has taken place during the past quarter century to alter the perceptive insights of Marion Langer in *Learning to Live as a Widow*.

You had no training, no preparation to help you handle this crisis [of widowhood] in your life. You did not know what you could reasonably expect of yourself and other people.[1]

The transition from wife to widow, from husband to widower, is still as distressing as ever, and it still leaves the survivor just as lonely, confused, uncertain, depressed, and financially vulnerable as ever. This is not to say that the status quo has prevailed in the availability of services and in the general professional awareness:

—widow-to-widow support groups have been established all over the country;

—a useful, albeit modest, flow of research and writing has provided insight to service-providers and to widows themselves;

—the fact that more women are familiar with work and careers has undoubtedly served to reduce a little of the stress of the transition;

—crisis intervention centers provide significant services.

Each of these is helpful, facilitative of better physical, mental, emotional, social, and spiritual well-being, but all taken together, they still do not invalidate Ms. Langer's point.

WITH TIME ON THE ABSCISSA

Time is a factor in the transition from the role of spouse to that of

1. Marion Langer, *Learning to Live as a Widow* (New York: Gilbert, 1967), p. 12.

survivor in at least three ways. The first is the way in which the death occurs in time: the extent to which it is sudden, expected, and timely. Second, as the death approaches, then occurs, and finally recedes in time, the feelings of grief, the status of the bereaved, and the rituals of mourning all change. And third, the way in which transition to widow(er)hood occurs differs as a function of the age and of the stage in life of the individual experiencing the transition.

Sudden, expected, and timely

People die suddenly and they die slowly and in all stages in between; their deaths can be expected, unexpected, and all stages in between; they can have timely deaths, untimely deaths, and all stages in between. And each of these continua will affect the kind of transition experienced by the survivor.

In thinking of sudden versus slow deaths, the assumption is frequently made that the slow death is necessarily a painful death, while the sudden death is not painful. This is often, but not always, a valid assumption. If the sudden death is instantaneous, such as a gunshot or sudden coronary causing either immediate death or a comatose state until death, then there is no pain; if the slow death is from cancer in a particularly painful site, then there is intense pain.

Sudden death, especially when it is also unexpected, leaves the survivors unprepared and often precludes the dying person's making appropriate arrangements for survivors. Victims of sudden, unexpected death have no time to get their financial affairs in order, no opportunity to explain to their spouses how the household works or where important documents are, and no chance to make arrangements to see family members or to offer or receive absolution for long-past deeds that have produced family schisms. In short, I view sudden deaths as being the cruelest for the survivors. One study of 80 widows has shown that sudden death does, in fact, lead to stronger grief reactions than death following a more prolonged illness; in this instance, sudden death was defined as occurring fewer than five days from the onset of symptoms.[2]

Although sudden deaths are frequently also unexpected deaths, and although unexpected deaths by definition cannot be prolonged, sudden and unexpected are not by any means synonymous. A man has a coronary at age 48 and recovers; in his fifties he has several strokes that slightly incapacitate him; at 60 he has a massive coronary and dies. A middle-aged woman, depressed, makes a serious suicide attempt that is thwarted; six months later she succeeds in committing suicide. Both of these deaths are sudden; neither can be considered unexpected. The spouse of a man with a life-threatening coronary problem or of a woman who is depressed and potentially suicidal lives in a very different family system than someone living with a spouse with terminal cancer or multiple sclerosis.

Deaths are often seen as untimely when they occur either too soon or too late in terms of a person's career, family relationships, fame and prestige, and so forth. The death of someone with significant responsibilities for work or family or someone whose creativity is still developing is often viewed as untimely; conversely, we may think that an elderly person has lived too long when he or she lives to see the deaths of children and grandchildren, or the disintegration of values held dear, or the deterioration of a business or farm that had been part of his or her life. Both kinds of death are out of sync. In the former, the spouse undoubtedly suffers a great deal; in the latter, the surviving spouse is likely to welcome the death.

Grief is not static

The grieving process is far from static. A spouse legally and statistically becomes a widow(er) in a moment, but the same person may begin the psychological role of widow early in the marriage or even before being married, through fantasizing the meaning and feelings associated with that role. This rehearsal for widow(er)hood is reported more frequently by women than by men.[3] Grieving, in a more familiar fashion, often begins with anticipatory grief, when the spouse who will survive learns that the husband/wife is now going to die in a foreseeable and moderately predictable future.

When does grieving end? Certainly not a week later, by which time the survivors are expected to return to work, school, housekeeping, and similar roles. The variability in duration is immense: a year or, more probably, two years will be needed to recuperate from the grief, and some people never fully cease grieving. Although the trend is for feelings of grief to become less intense and for episodes to become less frequent over time, this is not a

2. Justine F. Ball, "Widow's Grief: The Impact of Age and Mode of Death," *Omega*, 7(4):314-15 (1976-77).

3. Richard A. Kalish, "Sex and Marital Role Differences in Anticipation of Age-producted Dependency," *Journal of Genetic Psychology*, 119:53-62 (Jan. 1971).

simple linear trend; a recent report showed that some widows have a second depressive reaction some years after the death, and that this is often more intense than their depression at the time of death.[4]

Grieving, it must be emphasized, is not a point but a process, one that changes constantly and, to a modest extent, predictably over a period of time. Various attempts to delineate stages of grief have been made, one of which proposed four stages: numbness, pining, depression, and recovery.[5] These stages are not to be seen as rigid, irreversible, or universal, but they do describe modal behavior that can be viewed across time.

Mourning behavior, the rituals associated with the state of bereavement and the feelings of grief, is more readily given boundaries. In a Los Angeles study roughly one-third of the respondents stated that the bereaved person should feel free to remarry within six months of the death, could return to work within one week of the death, and could start going out with other men/women within a month after the death.[6]

Grieving as a function of age and stage

Time is also on the abscissa when we consider the transitions caused by the death of one's spouse, as these transitions are affected by the age of the survivor and the stage of life of

that survivor. Although the use of a life-span perspective to view human behavior is gaining acceptance in the behavioral and social sciences, it is still more widely ignored than integrated into research and writing in these fields. The application of life-span perspectives to policy and programs is even more tenuous.

It is immediately obvious that the transitions encountered by the 25-year old widower differ in a variety of ways from those met by the 45-year-old widower, the 65-year-old widower, and the 85-year-old widower. Recent research[7] on adult developmental stages suggests that men at different ages are also at different stages in the ways they see themselves, their work and career, and their families. The death of a spouse would enter dynamically into the equation along with these other factors to produce a very different kind of transition to widow(er)hood as the result of age and related stage.

Not only will this transition differ because of the psychological factors just outlined, but it will also differ because of the sociological factors. The younger man is just beginning a career; the middle-aged man may well have children in both high school and college; the elderly man is likely to have some chronic health condition for which his wife provided ministering.

Adult development research findings on women are just beginning to filter in, but there is no doubt that the age and stage of women will also influence the meaning of their transition. A 40-year-old widow may be earning considerably less and have

4. Carol J. Barrett and Karen M. Schneweis, "An Empirical Search for Stages of Widowhood," *Omega*, 11(2):98 (1980-81).

5. C. Murray Parkes, *Bereavement: Studies of Grief in Adult Life* (New York: International Universities Press, 1972), p. 7.

6. Richard A. Kalish and David K. Reynolds, *Death and Ethnicity: A Psychocultural Study* (Los Angeles: University of Southern California Press, 1976; reprinted New York: Baywood, 1981), pp. 212-13.

7. For example, Daniel J. Levinson, *The Seasons of a Man's Life* (New York: Knopf, 1978) and George E. Vaillant, *Adaptation to Life* (Boston: Little, Brown, 1977).

less earning potential than her 40-year-old male equivalent, so she faces a different financial stress than does the widower. Similarly, a 50-year-old widow may have finished her formal education only a decade or so before and may have had only a handful of years climbing the career ladder, while a man of the same age has probably been pursuing his career for 25 years or more. Thus both age and stage will influence the meaning of the transition to widowhood.

THE GRIEVING PROCESS

Grieving, as I have emphasized, is a dynamic process and not a static occurrence. Having said that, I want to discuss a variety of concerns that develop immediately following the death—and frequently preceding it—and that continue, although often with diminishing intensity and frequency, for an extended period of time. These are physical and health changes, psychological and emotional distress, social and relational concerns, and practical issues.

*Physical and
  health changes*

In his now-classic article on grief, Erich Lindemann described numerous physical changes that occur in the very early stages of grief: somatic distress occurring in waves of 20 minutes or more, tightness in the throat, choking and shortness of breath, need to sigh, empty feeling in the abdomen, lack of muscular power.[8] Other symp-

toms have also been observed, including lack of physical strength, loss of appetite, reduced sexual drive, and restless and aimless hyperactivity.[9]

Immediately after the death some people feel the pangs of grief just described, while others experience a numbness that appears to be comparable to a state of shock, leaving the widow(er) without the anticipated feelings of or physical responses to grief. This stage will pass, normally within a few days.[10]

Several studies have shown that health problems accompany grief. In one study 80 widows ranging in age from very young to age 75 were interviewed between 6 and 9 months after the death of their spouses. The physical symptoms that were most frequently mentioned were sleeping problems (71 percent); restlessness (68 percent); fatigue (61 percent); loss of appetite (61 percent); and drug usage (48 percent). For the first three symptoms listed, 29 percent or more indicated that their symptoms were severe or occurred often; for the latter two, 14 percent described the symptom as severe or frequent.[11]

Two other investigations offer further confirmation. The recently bereaved were found to suffer from such symptoms as headache, dizziness, muscular ache, menstrual irregularity, loss of appetite, sleeplessness, fainting spells, skin rashes, indigestion and vomiting, chest pains, and heart palpitations. In fact, it appears that as many as 40 percent of widows consulted a physi-

8. Erich Lindemann, "Symptomatology and Management of Acute Grief," *American Journal of Psychiatry*, 101:141-42 (Sept. 1944).

9. Parkes, *Bereavement*, pp. 34, 50.
10. Ibid., p. 39.
11. Ball, "Widow's Grief: The Impact of Age and Mode of Death," pp. 318-25.

cian within eight weeks following their bereavement.[12]

The evidence points to a definite increase in both illness and death rates of widows and widowers within the six months following their bereavement.[13] We cannot be certain, however, how much of this increase arises from the changes in health practices during the period before the death, since those caring for dying spouses often neglect their own health; how much is due to the stress that accompanies the death and related losses; and how much is a function of the new and often unanticipated stresses that face recent widow(er)s as they attempt to adapt to their new roles and circumstances.

Psychological and emotional distress

The health problems just discussed are undoubtedly also indications of emotional distress. Sleeplessness, for example, or loss of appetite can be caused directly by physical illness or indirectly by the reactions of the body to stress and distress. Psychological and emotional responses to grief are not limited to those with identifiable somatic correlates. Lindemann listed "an intense subjective distress described as tension or mental pain"[14] among the symptoms he observed.

In a Minnesota study of 434 widows and widowers, substantial percentages indicated confusion about the future (30 percent), depression and unhappiness most of the time (20 percent), a lack of feeling that life was worthwhile (18 percent), and difficulty in concentration (11 percent). At the same time, many respondents also described changes in a positive direction. Since the death, they had become more appreciative of others (41 percent), more sensitive to the feelings of others (35 percent), and warmer toward others (27 percent).[15] It appears that although widows and widowers feel severe loss and distress, they also view their losses as having led to personal growth, particularly in terms of relationships with others.

Social and relational concerns

It is not surprising to learn that loneliness is the most significant problem experienced by recent widow(er)s.[16] Even loneliness, however, is not always a totally negative experience. Many widows and widowers come to appreciate the new autonomy that comes from not having anyone at home who requires care. There seems nothing inconsistent in grieving deeply for the deceased spouse and simultaneously welcoming opportunities to explore new roles and relationships and reduced responsibilities. This would be especially true for persons whose spouse required a great deal of care and

12. Ira O. Glick, Robert S. Weiss, and C. Murray Parkes, *The First Year of Bereavement* (New York: John Wiley, 1974), Chap. 4; David Maddison and A. Viola, "The Health of Widows in the Year Following Bereavement," *Journal of Psychosomatic Research*, 12:297 (Dec. 1968).

13. K. F. Rowland, "Environmental Events Predicting Death for the Elderly," *Psychological Bulletin*, 84(2):349-72 (Nov. 1972).

14. Lindemann, "Symptomatology and Management of Acute Grief," p. 141.

15. Greg Owen, Robert Fulton, and Eric Markusen, "Death at a Distance: A Study of Family Survivors" (Paper presentation to the Midwest Sociological Society, Omaha, NE, 14 Apr. 1978), pp. 16-18.

16. Ball, "Widow's Grief: The Impact of Age and Mode of Death," p. 324; Raymond G. Carey, "Weathering Widowhood: Problems and Adjustment of the Widowed During the First Year," *Omega*, 10(2):169 (1979-80).

attention over a lengthy period of terminal illness.

The widow(er) is still obviously in need of ongoing social relationships to provide nurturance, to satisfy intimacy needs, and to offer companionship and stimulation. These can be satisfied through friends, relatives, work associates, organizational involvement, service-providers, and—at a somewhat different level—God, pets, self, fantasies, and the deceased spouse.[17]

Friends and relatives would normally present the most available pool for establishing or maintaining relationships, but interactions with these people often undergo a noticeable change. Friendships have likely been established on a couple-to-couple basis, and most widow(er)s and divorced people are familiar with the difficulty in continuing these relationships as a threesome. It may be true that "old friends are the best friends," but widow(er)hood often requires the development of new friendships. Previous friendships established on a one-to-one basis are probably more likely to continue.

Relationships with relatives—children, brothers and sisters, parents, and perhaps cousins—are likely to continue and even to grow stronger. In-laws provide another source of relationships, but many of these people are doing their own grieving and may not have the ability to be supportive at this point. Also, once the surviving spouse begins to move into a new life, perhaps seeking new relationships that will replace the lost relationship, in-laws can feel threatened and displaced.[18]

Work associates and people met through social, political, recrea-tional, or religious organizations may offer social relationships. Relationships established in these ways may compensate to some extent for the loss, but they seldom provide the needed kinds of nurturance and intimacy. Service-providers supply limited forms of relationship, but while appreciated, they cannot take over the role of family member or friend. Interestingly enough, and in spite of their bad press, funeral directors often receive warm commendations for their important support, exceeding those for physicians, nurses, chaplains, social workers, clergy, and neighbors.[19]

The ongoing relationship with the deceased spouse deserves special mention. The presence of the dead person is felt on numerous occasions. Rather than being viewed as pathological, this experience needs to be understood as normative, since it occurs with great frequency.[20] In some instances the surviving spouse reports an awareness of the presence of the dead person in such terms as "I felt he was close to me, and it was like I heard his voice, although I didn't," or "I was dozing off to sleep and I felt her next to me." On less frequent occasions the occurrence is that of actually seeing, hearing, smelling, or being touched by the dead person. The experience is almost always a positive one. Although research evidence is lacking, it seems likely that these encounters offer support and solace to the widow(er) and may be facilitative of a normal response to bereavement.

The feeling of presence is not the only way that widows and widowers

---

17. Carol J. Barrett, "Intimacy in Widowhood" (Mimeograph, circa 1978). pp. 3-13.
18. Ibid., p. 6.

19. Ibid., p. 8; Carey, "Weathering Widowhood: Problems and Adjustment of the Widowed during the First Year," p. 172.
20. Glick, Weiss, and Parkes, *The First Year of Bereavement*, Chap. 8; Parkes, *Bereavement*, p. 57 ff.

maintain the dead spouse in their lives. Over one-third of a large sample of such persons agreed that "everything around me seems to remind me of [the deceased]."[21] Another familiar kind of statement is "I still find myself waiting for his key in the lock at 5:30 each afternoon," or "I sometimes set two places at the table without thinking anything of it."

The sexual relationships of widow(er)s have received very little attention. It is as though the death eliminates all sexual needs, which initially seems to be the case for some widows who described a period of early avoidance of sex and of disgust with men, followed by a period of acute sexual needs and fantasies.[22] Widows often receive sexual advances from men who take it upon themselves to satisfy what they see as the obvious sexual needs of the poor, deprived widow. It is not unusual for the man who makes such an advance to be a close friend of the husband or the husband of a close friend of the recent widow. Sometimes companionship, love, and comfort accompany the proposition; often it is a blatant proposal for direct, immediate, and presumably rapid sex.

Although once again the literature is devoid of research, it is highly likely that extremely few of these early sexual overtures are accepted by recent widows—whether the situation for widowers is comparable is more problematic. Nonetheless, widows, like divorced women, are often seen by the still-married women as threats to their marriage. The assumption seems to be made,

often implicitly and perhaps unconsciously, that a formerly married woman, especially one whose sexual needs have presumably been satisfied until recently, will entice husbands into affairs. This dynamic undoubtedly adds to the tendency of couples to withdraw friendship from the recently widowed.

The practical issues

Recent widows and widowers face innumerable practical problems, created or exacerbated by the death. If the dead person had contributed a large share to the family income, financial problems will loom large, with insurance often being insufficient to compensate for the loss or compensating only for a limited period of time. If the dead person had been primarily a housekeeper, rather than directly producing income, the survivor must either take over those chores or pay someone to do them. In the event that small children remain in the home, the surviving spouse virtually always must work outside the home, and care for the children becomes a major logistical and financial problem.

Household chores are also a practical issue. Whether the household tasks had been divided along traditional sex-role lines or more egalitarian bases, the loss of a spouse diminishes the tasks to be done by very little and leaves the performance of the tasks to one person. Children, of course, may be helpful in taking up the slack if they are old enough and still living at home, but if they are not old enough to help—or if the widow(er) does not know how to incorporate them into performing household tasks—they merely add to the practical difficulties, even

21. Owen, Fulton and Markusen, "Death at a Distance: A Study of Family Survivors," p. 16.

22. Barrett and Schneweis, "An Empirical Search for Stages of Widowhood," p. 98.

though they may offer emotional support and companionship.

Schools, churches, and other public and private organizations still work on the assumption that adults come in pairs and that children have two functional parents. Although this is slowly changing and although many churches have developed groups for single persons, usually emphasizing the divorced, activities are often planned with little regard for single parents or single persons. Making matters worse for widows, the fear of criminal victimization will often keep single women home, especially at night, further restricting their involvement in activities. This seems to be particularly true for older people.

Other practical issues also emerge, as time, money, energy, and patience are found to be in short supply, with one person now having to accomplish most of what two people had been accomplishing. Some examples include getting ready for holidays (also depressing for many widow(er)s, especially Christmas and birthdays); arranging for home/car/appliance servicing (telephone installers and plumbers continue to assume that someone in the household is going to be home anyway, and that it does not matter if the appointment is early, late, or postponed for the day); finding care in case of illness or disability; finding companionship for a movie, concert, or Sunday stroll; moving the household to a new home and neighborhood.

FACTORS INFLUENCING THE TRANSITION

Factors influencing the stressful nature of the transition to widowhood are obviously numerous, including the ego strength of the survivor, the nature of the previous relationship, the availability of support from others, the perception of the effectiveness of the health professionals and health facilities, and the secondary losses that accrue as a result of the death, such as loss of income, change in parenting requirements, anticipated loneliness, and consideration of relocating.

The nature of the illness itself and of the death trajectory is also a factor, although not widely discussed in the literature. One available study compared widows whose husbands died from cancer with those whose husbands died from cardiovascular problems. Compared to the latter, those women who were widowed through a cancer death (1) perceived the illness as more stressful, (2) felt their role was more passive and that they were forced to watch suffering, (3) experienced more anxiety and saw their own role as wives as less essential, (4) were more angry with the health-care system and ruminated more about health care, and (5) had more nightmares about the final illness.[23]

Predicting later adjustment

Most of those who write about the concerns of the dying and the bereaved have speculated that the ability to maintain an open communication system concerning the terminal prognosis would make the dying process easier. Recently a study of widows of cancer patients found that this shared communica-

23. Mary L.S. Vachon, K. Freedman, and S.I.J. Freeman, "Cancer and Bereavement" (Paper presented at the Symposium on Coping with Cancer, Toronto, 24-26 Apr. 1977), pp. 7-8.

tion did make it easier to cope with the subsequent grief.[24] This result fits with the finding, discussed earlier, that the grief from sudden death was more intense than the grief following a more prolonged death:[25] when the death occurs suddenly, there is much less opportunity—and sometimes no opportunity at all—to talk together and to share feelings and concerns.

In one well-known study, 68 young widow(er)s were interviewed shortly after the bereavement and then again a year later. Those who were adjusting least well had experienced a short terminal illness and had had no opportunity to talk and share feelings and fears with the dead spouse, again confirming the findings mentioned previously. They were also the people who, in the initial interview, were most likely to (1) indicate high anxiety, (2) express a strong yearning for the deceased, (3) feel no one cared about them, (4) welcome their own death, and (5) describe themselves as feeling empty.[26] All of these expressions could be readily translated as indicating not only considerable fear and anxiety, and perhaps a reduced capacity to cope with the demands of the world, but also a high level of depression.

Differences between widows and widowers

Are widowers better off or less well-off than widows? The answer is partly a function of how one reads the research and observational find-

ings and how one decides what makes someone better off than someone else. Thus a British study showed that widows are more likely to be living with relatives, usually their children (46 percent versus 29 percent), while widowers are more likely to live alone (65 percent versus 49 percent).[27] Is the widow better cared for? Is the widower more autonomous and better off financially? Answers may be in the eye of the beholder.

Findings from several comprehensive studies of elderly widows and widowers are relevant here. In two studies widowers were found to be more likely to participate in social organizations, to reach out more to friends, and to be less likely to say they were lonely.[28] Conversely, in another study, widows were found with great consistency to have greater resources and less overall need than widowers, with the latter experiencing lower morale, greater loneliness and dissatisfaction with life, less adequate diet, and more negative attitudes toward community services.[29] Clearly we need to be cautious before coming to conclusions when the research findings are still so inconclusive.

A study of somewhat younger persons (median age of 57), concluded that widowers were better adjusted than widows, and the author speculated that this was because of (1) the loss of identity that

24. Ibid., p. 5.

25. Ball, "Widow's Grief: The Impact of Age and Mode of Death," pp. 314-15.

26. C. Murray Parkes, "Determinants of Outcome Following Bereavement," *Omega*, 6(4):303-23 (1975).

27. Ann Cartwright, Lisbeth Hockey and John L. Anderson, *Life Before Death* (London: Routledge & Kegan Paul, 1973), p. 203.

28. Robert C. Atchley, "Dimensions of Widowhood in Later Life," *The Gerontologist*, 15(2):177 (Apr. 1975); Carey, "Weathering Widowhood: Problems and Adjustment During the First Year," p. 169.

29. Carol J. Barrett "Sex Differences in the Experience of Widowhood" (Paper presented to the American Psychological Association, 1 Sept. 1978), p. 6.

the wife suffered, because her identity was more involved in her husband's than vice versa; (2) the greater difficulty widows have in remarrying; and (3) the greater stress generated by the practical problems of making decisions, handling money, and so forth.[30]

Experience and logic suggest numerous differences between widows and widowers. Compared with widows, widowers will

—be older and, therefore, less healthy;

—be less numerous and, therefore, have more difficulty in finding older men with whom to establish friendships, but will find it easier to remarry or to develop relationships with women;

—have more money;

—be less capable of accomplishing the traditional female tasks of housekeeping and child care, but more capable of accomplishing the traditional male tasks of earning money and home maintenance. It seems possible that fewer of these advantages will accrue to the widower in old age, since the occupational role has normally ceased anyway;

—have developed fewer social and verbal skills and be less willing to reach out for help;

—be more likely to drive and to be willing to be out after dark; they are also more likely to be willing to go places alone;

—have had more experience in making financial and related decisions.

There are undoubtedly other differentiating characteristics that might be hypothesized, but two conclusions seem apparent from these assumptions. First, the determination as to whether widows or widowers do better after bereavement depends on which variables one examines; and second, other factors, such as age, social class, and income, interact with gender in determining the relative problems of coping with the death of a spouse.

CONCLUDING COMMENTS

This article has not attempted to prove anything or to make a specific point. Its purpose has been to examine the effects of the transition from wife to widow, from husband to widower, and to describe some of the processes and events that accompany this transition. Certainly there is always the temptation, during the summing up, to call for more research. The call is just as valid for this topic as for most others, although it is important to recognize that the research cited here is only a sample selected from a much larger body of work now available.

Perhaps the issue is not so much more research as research that recognizes differences in age, sex, education, ethnicity, income, and health. Certainly a life-span perspective seems essential. And if the criteria of physical, mental, emotional, social, and spiritual well-being are applied to topics to determine their worthiness for conducting research and for creative, constructive thought and writing, the topic of widow(er)hood will be a popular one for at least the remainder of this decade.

30. Carey, "Weathering Widowhood: Problems and Adjustment During the First Year," p. 167.

ANNALS, *AAPSS*, **464**, November 1982

Transitions and Models of Intervention

By PHYLLIS R. SILVERMAN

ABSTRACT: All transitions are associated with change. People, basically conservative by nature, tend to resist change. Any intervention needs to consider that reactions to a transition are affected by prior experience, by the way transitions are viewed in an individual's social network, and by what learning opportunities are available. Responses can be viewed as typical under the circumstances, with rites of passage and helpers available to guide people in coping; or they can be viewed as a result of deficits in the individual for which treatment is prescribed. To facilitate change, seen as an expected event, individuals need to be linked to resources and information. They need role models and legitimation of their feelings. Learning, at such times of stress, seems to be facilitated by the availability of a peer, in the sense that the helper has had a similar experience. This help is available in mutual help groups. However, many kinds of help need to be available. The goal of any help is to empower the individual to cope in ways that promote growth and change.

Phyllis R. Silverman is on the faculty of the Institute of Health Professions, Massachusetts General Hospital. She holds an appointment in the Department of Psychiatry, Harvard Medical School. Dr. Silverman developed the concept of the Widow-to-Widow Program and did the research that demonstrated its effectiveness. She has served on several task forces on bereavement and primary prevention convened by the National Institute of Mental Health; and she has consulted with agencies across the nation and internationally on similar issues. She holds a Ph.D. from Brandeis University, a Sc.M. Hygiene from Harvard School of Public Health, and an M.S.S from Smith College, School of Social Work.

I NHERENT in the concept of transition is the idea that a change is taking place. Change implies a need to modify, transform, or alter. James Tyhurst, a pioneer in the study of transition states, observed that not only should the focus be on the change itself but also on the state of change—the going from one situation to another.[1] He was concerned with the social and psychological circumstances that make change possible. In this context the purpose of any intervention offered to someone in transition should be to enhance the competency with which the person traverses such a period.

Change takes place over time, and the time periods can be divided into stages. At each stage the individual has different needs with different tasks required of him or her; to a large extent, moving on to the next phase depends upon completing some of the work of the preceding stage. Ultimately an accommodation is achieved, rather than a return to an earlier level of functioning. Since the work of a transition is to move from one stage to the next, any help offered has to facilitate this movement. To do this, the help has to be responsive to the point the individual has reached in the transition, as well as to sustain the individual between stages. Many kinds of help ideally should be available to respond to the variety of needs and tasks associated with each stage.

Appropriate forms of intervention will be examined in this article, which is divided into three sections. The first section discusses the work of transition, identifying factors that have impact on people's responses; the second represents some data on what qualities of a helping experience will enhance coping with change; the third looks at sources of help available today.

THE WORK OF TRANSITION

Following Tyhurst's thinking, I characterize a transition in three parts: (1) there is a disequilibrating event, or series of events; (2) a role change is involved; (3) change takes place over time.[2]

Disequilibrating events

There is an event or series of events that have a disruptive effect on those involved, causing stress. Individuals experience stress because they can no longer function, at least not as fully as before. While the onset can be gradual or sudden, anticipated or unanticipated, change is always involved and stress is typically and unavoidably associated with change. It is not a question of avoiding stress, but of recognizing it as appropriate and learning what responses can moderate and alleviate it. To understand any individual's response, it is essential to determine how prepared he or she is to manage change. This preparation depends not only on previous personal experience with change but also on knowledge about the nature of the current transition state, and on the attitudes, values, and rituals in their larger social network that affect how individuals perceive and react to their situation.

1. James S. Tyhurst, "The Role of Transition States—Including Disasters in Mental Illness," in *Symposium on Preventive and Social Psychiatry*, (Washington, DC: Government Printing Office, 1958), pp. 149-69.

2. Phyllis R. Silverman, "Services for the Widowed During the Period of Bereavement," *Social Work Practice* (New York: Columbia University Press), pp. 170-89.

Individuals' past experience shapes their view of their life cycle, and it can provide perspective with which to approach a new situation. Clearly, if an individual has experienced a change and managed it successfully, in principle he or she may find a new situation less threatening. Everyone has gone through many transitions over the formative years of childhood with some degree of success in order to arrive at adulthood and later life. Often, however, they have not articulated the process and do not generalize from one period to another. Ideally, individuals should develop a schema for dealing with an evolving sense of self that would include a repertoire of responses when change is required. This repertoire has to include a vocabulary for describing and understanding change, as well as an ideology that gives meaning to the event. Ideologies and language have an integrating function.[3] They define an event as manageable or as overwhelming, and they mediate the stress associated with change. For example, a transition can be defined as a problem or as an expected occurrence. Grief, if defined as an illness, becomes a condition for which treatment and a cure are sought. On the other hand, grief can be defined as a natural reaction to death, an inevitable human experience with which everyone must cope. In the latter situation, mourners recognize themselves to be in a state of transition. They expect, then, to participate in socially established rituals that facilitate mourning. These rituals provide ways of coping with stress and extreme feelings; in addition, they provide guidance for making an accommodation.

Ideology and language are in part transmitted by the larger culture, so that this sense of self and the repertoire of responses individuals develop cannot be separated from the values and attitudes current in the larger society in which their lives are embedded. If the focus in that society is on maintaining a closed system with fixed parameters, then members of that society will have a less difficult time learning to cope with a transition. Such a society may have rules, customs, and rituals governing behavior at such times, directed at change in an acceptable context. In a review of grief and mourning in cross-cultural perspective, Paul C. Rosenblatt, R. Patricia Walsh, and Douglas A. Jackson describe the role of ritual specialist.[4] Specific people in the role of teacher are assigned to individuals in transition to guide them, to show them how to behave and how to manage their feelings, and to prepare them to enter a new role. In a more open system, such ideologies are less likely to exist, and people may be without guidance. In contemporary Western society few rituals exist for helping people cope. For example, the funeral is currently criticized as too costly, and its function as the last public act that honors the deceased and provides the mourners with a forum for acknowledging their loss and their grief is ignored. The success of Gail Sheehy's *Passages* reflects the searching for ways of viewing and reacting to change over

3. Silvio Arieti and Jules Bemporad, *Severe and Mild Depression* (New York: Basic Books, 1978).

4. Paul C. Rosenblatt, R. Patricia Walsh, and Douglas A. Jackson, *Grief and Mourning in Cross Cultural Perspective* (Human Relations Area Files Press, 1976).

the life cycle that is current in our larger society today.[5]

Adaptation involves learning, and the adaptive strategies people develop are affected by the learning opportunities available to them.[6] A similar observation related effective coping with transitions connected to major illness or life-cycle role change to the availability of pertinent information.[7] The Community Support Systems Task Force of the President's Commission on Mental Health found that access to guidance and information is essential in order to cope effectively with problems of daily living as well as with a major transition.[8] Learning opportunities need to be available that provide the person in transition with pertinent information. Given the proper tools, most people are capable of dealing with any transition state. The lack of customs and rituals are reflected in a dearth of learning opportunities for providing the proper tools.

Role changes

Most transitions generally involve status changes for the affected individuals, necessitating a redefinition of the roles they per-

form in their social networks.[9] Letting go of familiar roles is not simple. Peter Marris noted that in every change there is a loss, if not actually a death, in the need to give up an old, inapplicable role and to develop a new, appropriate one. He observed people's reluctance to relinquish the past, the familiar; he labeled this wish for things to remain constant as "the conservative impulse."[10] The individual, however, does let go by integrating some aspect of the past into the new role or changed situation. This integration resembles the cognitive process identified by Jean Piaget. Children who tried to apply formerly workable strategies to new situations learned that the present would not assimilate certain aspects of the past because they were no longer applicable. Ultimately, in such situations an accommodation is achieved, and a new schema can be identified for dealing with the new situation; within this schema there are remnants of the prior schema.[11]

The same process applies to adult learning as well. In responding to a death, therefore, the individual mourner should not be expected to give up the past, but instead to find ways to incorporate aspects of past relationships into the present and future.[12] Symbols that provide immortality to the dead supply several means of remembering.[13] It has been observed that people let go

5. Gail Sheehy, *Passages: Predictable Crises of Adult Life* (New York: Dutton, 1976).

6. Robert W. White, "Strategies of Adaptation: An Attempt at Systematic Description," in *Coping and Adaptation*, eds. G. V. Coelho, David A. Hamburg, and John E. Adams (New York: Basic Books, 1974), pp. 47-68.

7. David A. Hamburg and John E. Adams, "A Perspective on Coping: Seeking and Utilizing Information in Major Transitions," *Archives of General Psychiatry*, 17:277-84 (1967).

8. President's Commission on Mental Health, *Commission Report*, Vol. II (Washington, DC: Government Printing Office, 1978).

9. Rhona Rappaport, "Normal Crisis, Family Structure and Mental Health," *Family Process*, 2:68-80 (1963).

10. Peter Marris, *Loss and Change* (New York: Pantheon, 1974).

11. Jean Piaget, *The Construction of Reality in the Child* (New York: Basic Books, 1954).

12. Lily Pincus, *Death and the Family* (New York: Random House, 1975).

13. Robert J. Lifton, "Symbolic Immortality," in *The Patient, Death and the Family*.

when some of the past can be assimilated into the present.[14] The incorporation of elements of the past into new roles and schema helps to bridge the gap between past and future.[15]

When a death occurs, the living must be psychologically committed to passage from old conditions to new ones.[16] Another perspective on factors that make this role difficult has been provided by Helena Z. Lopata.[17] She observed that the less well-defined the role is to which an individual must aspire, the more difficult the shift will be. For example, the role of wife for most women has traditionally been an honorable and desirable one.[18] The role of widow in this society is ill-defined and puts a woman in a marginal position. There is little honor in being widowed or, for that matter, in being retired or old. In practice, these are roles that place people on the edge of society, so that the ease with which an individual accepts the need to learn a new role is inversely related to the intensity of the stigma associated with that role.

Some researchers have speculated that women have an easier time with transitions associated with aging because they occupy so many roles over a lifetime. Yet data from studies on widowhood indicate that women have a particularly difficult time changing roles because they see no alternative to the role of wife. They define themselves in terms of their relationships to others. Difficulty in changing roles may relate to how much that role frames an individual's identity. Help, then, during this period has to enable people to see that change is part of the human condition and to find ways of altering or giving up old roles. Not only do people need to learn to add new roles, but they also may have to create these roles for themselves in a new mold that legitimizes and destigmatizes them.[19]

Change over time

Adaptation to any change takes place over time and this same process applies to a transition state.[20] It has been observed that the widowed become dismayed when they experience their relatives' impatience with their continued grieving,[21] and the widowed were not prepared for the length of time necessary to achieve an accommodation. They hoped, like their relatives, that mourning would end in a matter of weeks. It has been noted that in societies with established rites of passage, time periods are well marked with established rituals for helping people cope.[22]

To a certain extent in every transition there is a beginning and an end; between them the individual does the work of the transition. Most people need to learn what this work

eds. Stanly B. Troup and William A. Greene (New York: Scribner, 1974), pp. 21-36.

14. Marris, *Loss and Change*.

15. Pincus, *Death and the Family;* Daniel J. Levinson with Charlotte W. Darrrow et al., *The Seasons of a Man's Life* (New York: Knopf, 1978).

16. Rosenblatt, Walsh, and Jackson, *Grief and Mourning*.

17. Helena Z. Lopata, "Loneliness: Forms and Components," *Social Problems*, 17:248-61 (1969).

18. Phyllis R. Silverman, "Widowhood and Preventive Intervention," *The Family Coordinator*, 21:95-102 (1972).

19. Phyllis R. Silverman, *Helping Women Cope with Grief* (Beverly Hills, CA: Sage, 1981).

20. White, "Strategies of Adaptation."

21. Silverman, "Widowhood and Preventive Intervention."

22. Rosenblatt et al., *Grief and Mourning*.

involves. The work of transition can be divided into phases, each with its own tasks associated with it. Tyhurst and John Bowlby described transitions as involving three stages: impact, recoil, and accommodation.[23] Others have extended these to four or five stages.[24]

For our purposes three will suffice. During impact the individual is numb or dazed. The sense of disbelief in the reality of change, which stems from most people's reluctance to relinquish the past, is very strong. Behavior appropriate to the past role still dominates.

The second stage, recoil, is characterized by a growing recognition of the reality of the change and by a growing frustration and tension that result from the inability to continue to live as if no change has taken place. As the individual realizes it is no longer possible to live by the old rules, a crisis in meaning develops.[25] Stress is caused by the vacuum that exists when new rules have not yet replaced the old, inapplicable ones. As the range of their feeling and the realization of changes required becomes clear, people need specific information about what they are experiencing. They need to feel legit-

imated, to see that it may be safe to change their relationship to the deceased, and to understand that their stress is normal. They need to identify their choices for other roles they can develop. They need opportunities to practice assuming, at least in part, a new identity that can involve new behavior patterns.

An accommodation is achieved when the individual finds a new direction and in part assumes a new identity. The goal of accommodation as an end stage is not acceptance, as has been interpreted by some observers.[26] Acceptance is a part of the process only as it applies to the need for change. Avery Weissman noted that people who did not quietly accept their imminent death from cancer, but strove to maintain an involvement in living and a hope for the future, had a higher survival rate.[27] There can be no script for accommodation except that an individual must find a way to live in a changed situation. This process could be the opportunity for dramatic growth or a quiet reorientation, depending on the nature of the transition and the way the work of transition proceeds.

FACILITATING CHANGE

Implicit in the preceding discussion is the observation that no one copes with a transition entirely alone. Many types of help and relationships are required in order to make an accommodation, but little is known about what qualities facilitate learning in a time of change.

23. Tyhurst, "The Role of Transition States"; John Bowlby, "Process of Mourning," *International Journa of Psychoanalysis*, 42:329 (1961).

24. Robert S. Weiss, "Transition States and Other Stressful Situations: Their Nature and Programs for their Management," in *Support Systems and Mutual Help*, eds. Gerald Caplan and Marie Killilea (New York: Grune & Stratton, 1976), pp. 213-32; Elizabeth Kubler-Ross, *On Death and Dying* (New York: Macmillan, 1969).

25. Sam M. Silverman and Phyllis R. Silverman, "Parent Child Communication in Widowed Families," *American Journal of Psychotherapy*, 32(3):428-41 (July 1979); Colin M. Parkes, "Psycho-Social Transition: A Field of Study," *Social Science and Medicine*, 5:101-15 (1971).

26. Roxanne L. Silver and Camille B. Wortman, "Coping with Undesirable Life Events," in *Human Helplessness*, eds. Judy Garber and Martin L. Seligman (New York: Academic, 1980).

27. Avery Weissman, *Coping with Cancer* (New York: McGraw-Hill, 1979).

Much recent interest has been focused on the buffering qualities of support provided by social networks.[28] Support is seen as a mediator of stress, and the availability of support relates positively to people's sense of well-being. The following is a more specific statement about those aspects of support that contribute to people's well-being:

The significant others help the individual mobilize his psychological resources and master his emotional burdens: they share his tasks; and they supply him with extra supplies of money, materials, tools, skills and cognitive guidance to improve his handling of the situation.[29]

Parallels to these aspects of support can be found in the needs of people in transition described in the first section of this article. Other aspects of support include guidance, feedback, and social participation.[30] Gerald Caplan describes the family in terms of its supportive qualities, as a haven for rest and recuperation, as a reference and control group, and as a source and validator of identity.

Support, as just defined, can be used to maintain a system or the status quo, as well as to facilitate change. Little is known about how support differs, depending on its source, or on how aspects of support make change happen. John Eckenrode and Susan Gore recognized this problem when they tried to identify what affects a network's ability to mobilize support. They emphasize the need to look at the context and its constraints.[31]

Ronald Havelock and Mary Havelock, in looking at change on a broader level, talk of the need for change agents, catalysts whose main function is establishing linkages between people in need and resources and information.[32] Linking agents can also demonstrate how to use resources and information in a manner similar to the role of ritual specialist, described earlier in this article. What qualities in the contexts in which a transition is played out become central to achieving an accommodation? What are the characteristics of linking agents that make them most effective? One body of data emphasizes the special value of helpers who have been through a similar experience. There is evidence that learning in crises or emotionally laden situations is enhanced in a peer context.[33] Reporting on a study of affiliative tendencies in college students during periods of anxiety, Stanley Schacter observed that subjects chose to be alone under stress rather than with people who did not share their experience.[34] He

28. Benjamin Gottlieb, "Social Networks and Social Support in Community Mental Health," in *Social Networks and Social Support*, ed. Benjamin H. Gottlieb (Beverly Hills, CA: Sage, 1981).

29. Gerald Caplan, "Support Systems," in *Support Systems and Community Mental Health*, ed. Gerald Caplan (New York: Basic Books, 1974), p. 6.

30. Manuel Barrera, "Social Support in the Adjustment of Pregnant Adolescents: Assessment Issues," in Benjamin H. Gottlieb, *"Social Networks,"* p. 69-96.

31. John Eckenrode and Susan Gore, "Stressful Events and Social Supports: The Significance of Context," in Benjamin H. Gottlief, *Social Networks*, pp. 43-68.

32. Ronald G. Havelock and Mary C. Havelock, *Training for Change Agents* (Ann Arbor: University of Michigan Press, 1973).

33. Albert Bandura, *Social Learning Theory* (Englewood Cliffs, NJ: Prentice-Hall, 1977).

34. Stanley Schacter, *The Psychology of Affiliation* (Stanford, CA: Stanford University Press, 1959).

concluded that whatever the needs aroused by anxiety, it seems that satisfaction demanded the presence of others in a similar situation. In a small sample of members of three mutual help groups—Kidney Transplant and Dialysis Association, the Cured Cancer Club, and the Spina Bifida Association of Massachusetts —I found that people who joined these groups did so out of a pressing need to find someone else who had had a similar experience with whom they could share feelings and discover new ways of coping.[35]

From a follow-up study of the original Widow-to-Widow program, data were available on every new widow under the age of 65 in the Boston community in which the program operated over a two-and-one half-year period, and in particular on those women who refused the offer of help.[36] I found that most of those who had refused had friends or relatives who were widows.

Roxanne Silver and Camille Wortman noted that peers—in the sense of having been through the same experience—are unique sources of help for people in stress.[37] They are more understanding and patient, and their expectations are more appropriate. The impact of learning from peers as an important source of information, experience, and assistance with transition needs

to be appreciated and further examined. As a child grows, we recognize his or her need to learn from peers who serve as role models or with whom they explore ways of coping with their common needs.[38] Children who have role-model peers do not feel alone, unique, or isolated; they feel legitimated. This type of relationship probably pertains to an entire lifetime and not just to adolescence.

Not only is the need to find someone like oneself central to making a critical transition, but the opportunity to change roles and become a helper may be important as well. A survey was conducted of the members of a group called Mended Hearts and of heart surgery patients not affiliated with the organization to determine how participation in the group affected adjustment to their illness.[39] It was found that significant differences appeared between the two groups only among retired men who were active in the organization. Those who became helpers made the best adjustment to open heart surgery. The role of helper tends to foster competency in the helper. In addition, receiving help from a peer tends to minimize a sense of weakness or incompetence in the person needing help.[40] I am suggesting that during periods of transition when people must obtain relevant new information in order to cope, their ability to use this information is affected by the availability of someone who has gone

35. Phyllis R. Silverman and Diane Smith, "Helping in Mutual Help Groups for the Physically Disabled," in *Mental Health and the Self-Help Revolution*, eds. Alan Gartner and Frank Reissman (New York: Human Science Press, in press).

36. Phyllis R. Silverman, "Anticipatory Grief from the Perspective of Widowhood," in *Anticipatory Grief*, ed. Bernard Schoenberg (New York: Columbia University Press, 1974).

37. Silver and Wortman, "Coping with Undesirable Life Events."

38. Zick Rubin, *Children's Friendship* (Cambridge, MA: Harvard University Press, 1980).

39. Morton Lieberman and Leonard Borman, eds., *Self Help Groups for Coping with Crisis* (San Francisco: Jossey-Bass, 1979).

40. Phyllis R. Silverman, *Mutual Help Groups: Organization and Development* (Beverly Hills, CA: Sage, 1980).

through the experience with whom the individual can identify. In addition, the opportunity to change roles from recipient to helper further enhances the accommodation. The context in which help occurs is critical in terms of the personal experience of the helper and the opportunities within the helping framework for mutuality and role mobility.[41] When role mobility is considered it is important to look at the dynamic issues in any helping exchange. Since transitions take place over time, available help must change over time also.

Robert Lifton, in a study of experiences of returning Vietnam veterans, identified factors in the helping situation that facilitate coping with a transition. He found a three-part progression: the first is that of affinity, the coming together of people who share a particular—and in this case overwhelming—historical personal experience, along with a basic perspective on that experience, in order to make some sense of it. The second principle is that of presence, a kind of being there or full engagement and openness to mutual impact—no one ever being simply a therapist against whom things are rebounding. The third was that of self-generation, the need on the part of those seeking help, change, or insight to initiate their own process and conduct it largely on their own terms; even when calling in others with expert knowledge, those who seek help retain major responsibility for the shape and direction of the enterprise. Affinity, presence, and self-generation seem to be necessary ingredients for making a transition between old and new images and

values, particularly when these relate to ultimate concerns, to shifting modes of symbolic immortality.[42]

One of the few places where expetise in coping with transitions is concentrated in today's society is within mutual help organizations. When people meet formally to find or exchange solutions to common problems, they form mutual help groups. Mutual help groups are highly specialized agencies focusing generally on a single issue that their constituents have in common. Such groups become organizations, regularize practice, and formalize membership. Members control the resources of the group and plan and carry out their programs.[43] In mutual help organizations members obtain pertinent information from others who have had similar experiences; they find role models, legitimization for their feelings, and a direction for change and accommodation. Helpers in mutual help groups also fulfill linking functions of change agents. They amass bodies of necessary information required by people in transition and know where and how resources are available.

A parallel can be drawn between the unfolding of a mutual help exchange and the stages of transition. Drawing this parallel seems a good way of summarizing the unique aspects of mutual help in aiding people through transition

41. Ibid.

42. Robert J. Lifton, *Home from the War* (New York: Simon & Schuster, 1973).
43. Marie Killilea, "Mutual Help Organizations: Interpretations in the Literature," in *Support Systems and Mutual Help: Multidisciplinary Explorations*, eds. Gerald Caplan and Marie Killilea (New York: Grune & Stratton, 1976); Alan Gartner and Frank Riessman, *Self Help in the Human Services* (San Francisco: Jossey-Bass, 1977); Phyllis Silverman, *Mutual Help Groups: A Guide for Mental Health Workers*, ADM 78-646 (Rockville, MD: NIMH, 1978).

and of demonstrating how helping relationships must change over time.

The first stage of a transition is the impact/affinity/recovery stage. People are preoccupied with a desire to reject the new situation. Ability to make an accommodation depends upon allowing the numbness to lift and recognizing at some level that a new reality exists. This becomes easier to do when someone is available who has been in the same situation, is now living a normal life, and is even able to help others. An affinity develops that makes it possible for a bond to grow between seeker and helper. New members are then less fearful about their new situation.

For new members, willingness to talk with such a helper is an indication of readiness to consider making a transition, to learn to accept a new status and role designation. For example, a woman who agrees to talk about her widowhood with another widow begins to cast off her feeling of numbness and to see that this designation may apply to her. Although she still may not be ready to call herself "widow" and to accept the full meaning of her husband's death for her current life, she will find guidelines in the new exchange. The first question she will ask is, "What happened to you? How did you get here?" The helper must be prepared to retell her story.

In the recoil/presence stage, the second phase of transition, help consists of the provision of specific information about the condition and/or new role and about how to deal with it effectively. The person in transition is able to accept this information because of the presence or unity that has developed.

Either in one-to-one contact or at group meetings advice is offered about how to deal with a problem or what to expect from the situation that the sufferer is experiencing. A framework is provided for the problem. Not only does he learn to understand the current experience, but he may receive anticipatory guidance about problems that will arise. For example, a newly bereaved woman does not know that she will ever be able to stop crying or ever feel joy again. She learns how others have dealt with the problem, and they share with her their tricks of the trade.[44] Such interactions serve to expand her coping repertoire and options.

The content of the help will inevitably differ with the problem. The information offered has to relate to the specific transition, but once people have found a way of talking to each other, what is it that is talked about? Much of what mutual aid is about is the small things. It's not the big deal, the surgery (that is, the important lifesaving experience or whatever else it might be), it's the small survival kind of things . . . it is the small things that make up the essence of daily life.[45]

Accommodation/self-generation is the third stage of transition. Accommodation is a period in which the individuals' feelings have quieted down, and they are beginning to integrate all the knowledge they have obtained into new identities. They use this time to practice new behavior patterns, new ways of dealing with themselves and the world. Accommodation can be likened to an active apprenticeship period. During this time the moral support of the group may be essential for suc-

44. Erving Goffman, *Stigma: Notes on the Management of Spoiled Identities* (Englewood Cliffs, NJ: Prentice-Hall, 1963).
45. Edith Lennenbert, Personal Communication, 1971.

cess as individuals integrate the past with the present.

In this period the new member moves out of the new-member status and becomes aware of and responsive to other people's needs. The option of becoming a helper is now available to him. In order to be helpful in turn, either in an informal exchange or as part of an organized effort, the helper has to control resources and be able to integrate the knowledge gained from the experience into the helping activity. The context in which the help is offered becomes critical. It is not only the type of help itself which distinguishes mutual help from other kinds of help but it is also the setting in which the work is carried out and the helper's relationship to that system.

How are these aspects of the helping process reflected in other helping modalities available today?

SOURCES OF HELP

In her book, *Passing through Transition,* Naomi Golan developed an amalgam for presenting resources available in any community:[46]

—self/natural help system: family, friends, and neighbors;

—mutual help system: informal and formal;

—nonprofessional support system: voluntary organizations, community, care givers, and paraprofessionals; and

—professional helping system: persons with special training that qualifies them to help with psychological and social problems.

This kind of continuum reflects proximity of the helping system to the daily lives of people in transition[47] and the degree of control they can exercise over these resources. Clearly the interaction with self and with family and neighbors is continuous, and ties are usually strong. Help is available because people are obligated to each other; it is generally offered without solicitation and with the expectation that there will be opportunity to reciprocate. There are no entrance requirements in order to receive assistance. Nor does help from this system imply deviance or unusual need. It is this type of interdependency that makes meaningful life possible. At the opposite end of the spectrum, help available from the professional system is intermittent, generally based on a fee for service. The recipient had to enter the system and apply for assistance with no expectation of reciprocity, personal obligation to the helper, or ability to control the resources.

Golan correctly observes that most people are able to cope with change by themselves. As noted previously, however, this self-reliance does not mean that the individual had no assistance, but instead that none was solicited from a formal system. More needs to be known, in such instances, about how the helping networks of these people functioned, what kind of help was available, what experience people had who made themselves available, and how the help was mobilized. Caplan observed that families are sources of information, perspective, shared rituals, and experience from

46. Naomi Golan, *Passing Through Transitions: A Guide for Practitioners* (New York: Free Press, 1981), p. 242.

47. Benjamin Gottleib, "Lay Influences on the Utilization and Provision of Health Services: A Review," *Canadian Psychological Review,* 17 (2): 1197-1199 (Oct. 1976).

which to model coping strategies.[48] In a study of widows, many who refused assistance reported that there were other widows in their existing network with whom they shared their grief. Self-reliance is not to be taken literally, but instead it implies that the individual is part of a network that supports and legitimates, that provides opportunities for finding new identities and opportunities to engage in reciprocal helping relationships. There is no need to look beyond the network for additional resources.

Deborah Belle has found that for some, the cost of help from natural networks is very high and needed help is not available.[49] The network members may have a restricted view of a situation. The price they may exact for their help is to insist that the individual maintain himself or herself in a role that is familiar and comfortable for the network.[50] For any change to occur, other help and support need to be mobilized and available to replace that of the existing network. Even if the network is supportive, it may not contain the needed resources.

To supplement what kith and kin can provide in most communities, there exists a wide range of fraternal and voluntary associations. People who affiliate accept the obligations of membership to help each other and/or to provide service to their larger community. This type of association is the model for mutual help organizations mentioned earlier.

The formal professional helping system, in contrast, clearly delineates helpers and recipients. Helpers are licensed after having earned special credentials. To qualify as a consumer of their services an individual has to meet their entrance requirements and be willing to declare himself in need. For the most part, the institutions these helpers represent provide services that represent an essential division of labor needed to maintain communal life in contemporary society. These institutions are mandated by law to provide education and health care, religious guidance, employment opportunities, law and order, and welfare for the indigent and infirm. Society needs its experts, people who concern themselves fulltime with solving problems, be they politicians, physicians, social workers, scientists, or funeral directors. In this formal helping system is embedded an extensive mental health and human service system. The mandate of this mental health system is to help people with emotional problems and mental illness, and to decrease psychological and social disability.

The recent diagnostic manual (DSM III) developed by the American Psychiatric Association labels almost every reaction associated with the normal developmental cycle as a symptom of a potential psychiatric illness.[51] They extend their responsibility for care and treatment to all these conditions. As noted in the first section of this article, choice of descriptive terms

48. Gerald Caplan, "The Family as Support System," in Caplan and Killilea, *Support Systems and Mutual Help*.

49. Deborah Belle, "Social Stress and Social Support," in *Lives in Stress*, ed. Deborah Belle (Beverly Hills, CA: Sage, 1982).

50. Carol Stack, *All Our Kin* (New York: Harper Colophon, 1974).

51. American Psychiatric Association, *Disorders*, 3rd ed. (Washington, DC: American Psychiatric Assoc., 1980).

becomes critical in the way the transition is viewed. In the human service system, these reactions are defined as problems needing therapeutic interventions and requiring the assistance of well-trained experts. Never before have so many of the problems related to the human condition been assigned to the care of secularly trained specialists.[52] What are the implications of continuing to defer to professionals in mental health and human service systems as the primary source of help when discussing transition work?

If primary help comes from treatment-oriented institutions, such as mental health centers, psychiatric clinics, or social agencies, then any reactions to the transition will be viewed as a result of deficits in the individual. The focus is on treatment, not learning. The focus of control is with the expert. In this context dependency and a sense of ineffectuality can be fostered as a result of being assigned a diagnostic label and being placed in the role of patient in what should be viewed as a normal reaction, albeit painful and disruptive, to a transition state.

Other sources of knowledge, such as life experience, are considered less valuable in this system and overall in the larger society; they are not prized and therefore not used.[53] Yet there is evidence that expertise gained from successful experience may be the most effective source of knowledge to help people in transition develop strategies for managing change.

Professionals have been aware of the limitations of the medical model. There are many new efforts being made to make help more relevant to consumer populations. The Community Mental Health Center Act (1976) mandated the development of consultation and education programs. In these programs practitioners are developing new roles for themselves as consultants and educators. They are experimenting with ways of collaborating with new systems.[54] Articles are appearing in the news media about transition. Volunteers and paraprofessionals are being employed in the system to help bridge the gap between the community and the agency. As trained staff become aware of support systems and the value of learning from peers, professionally led educational and support groups are being offered. Robert Weiss's seminars for the separated are an example of a model followed in groups now being developed for children with elderly parents, for people facing retirement, for the widowed, and so forth. Learning in this context seems effective as long as the tasks of each stage are clearly outlined and learning from each other among group members is facilitated. As professionals reach beyond their system, they are learning to work with consumers as peers and collaborators.[55] Helpers in this system, however, are not going to provide service based on their own life experience, but on professional knowledge.

52. Silverman, *Mutual Help Groups: Organization and Development.*

53. Thomasina Borkman, "Experimental Knowledge: A New Concept for the Analysis of Self-Help Groups," *Social Service Review* (Sept., 1976), pp. 445-56.

54. Phyllis Silverman, "The Mental Health Consultant as Linking Agent," in *Community Support System and Mutual Help: Building Linkages,* eds. David Beigel and Arthur Naparstek (New York: Springer Press, 1982).

55. Golan, *Passing Through Transitions,* p. 259.

Some professionals are formalizing a role for themselves as a linking agent between the professional system and the mutual help system. There are a number of self-help clearing houses sponsored by community mental health agencies, whose main purpose is to link potential members to groups and to each other. In New Jersey the clearing house has a listing of several hundred groups on a computer. They respond to an average of 2000 calls a month. These services, since they do not produce a fee for service, are in jeopardy in a period of declining financial support.

We should not overlook interventions that are designed to facilitate competency in coping, interventions that can reach people before a transition in order to help during removal of architectural barriers, housing, displaced homemaker services, and so forth. People can learn to anticipate needs over a lifetime and plan appropriately for their changing social and emotional, as well as economic, needs. No amount of advanced preparation, however, can substitute for the work that needs to be done at the time of the transition. Prior orientation notwithstanding, some help still needs to be available.

We are talking about a range of help over a period of time. We are not concerned here with what to do when coping fails, but with what should be available to prevent failure through the promotion of competency. Helping networks should be fluid and changing so that an individual interacts in different ways at different times with different helpers. Any network should be composed of kith and kin, informal caregivers, ritual specialists, and mutual help opportunities playing alternate roles as transition work proceeds. If the network is effective, the need for professional mental health intervention should be unnecessary. The goal is to empower the individual to cope effectively in any transition by engaging in mutual help exchanges and interdependent relationships that promote growth and change.

Book Department

INTERNATIONAL RELATIONS AND POLITICS

RICHARD K. BETTS, ed. *Cruise Missiles: Technology, Strategy, Politics.* Pp. 612. Washington, DC: Brookings Institution, 1981. $32.95; Paperbound, $15.95.

For anyone who wants one complete information source on cruise missiles, the search is over. Richard Betts has compiled in *Cruise Missiles* fifteen different essays grouped under the general headings of Technology, Strategy, and Politics.

Each essay addresses one aspect of the cruise missile story—its inception during World War I, its development into a sophisticated and superb weapon, the intra- and interservice rivalries surrounding its development, and the agenda for the SALT negotiations. Mr. Betts has done a remarkable job of assembling within 612 pages the brilliant thoughts of the Who's Who in the cruise missile business—academicians, think task consultants, and military officers.

For the neophyte in the world of cruise missiles, it will serve them well not to attempt to read this book in any particular order. This is not a novel. Rather one should select chapters at random, following one's instincts, and digesting this book in small bites. Once you have done this, then I suggest you expand your horizons further into the three topical areas mentioned above. You may first want to read Chapter 4: "Program Costs and Comparison," then Chapter 8, "The Tomahawk and General Purpose Naval Forces." These are two good starting points, particularly the latter, which relates the recommissioning of the battleship New Jersey to the deployment of the Tomahawk cruise missile, an evolution of some familiarity to newspaper readers.

Cruise Missiles is not a book you read in one sitting. One must first become familiar with the acronyms and military jargon normally associated with a subject of this kind. Once past this hurdle you find yourself rereading almost every chapter, each of which is full of dates, figures, and facts.

There are some interesting conclusions to be drawn from *Cruise Missiles*. First, as Richard Betts notes, "cruise missile policy is a bucket of worms." I echo his sentiments. It is almost impossible to comprehend that with the problems inherent to any weapons system based on uniformed service commonality, it will even be ready to deploy in its initial stages by December 1982. With interservice territorial and development strategies working at crosspurposes, funding problems, and strategic employment in both a conventional and nuclear mode, it is surprising the concept ever left the drawing board. Furthermore, one conclusion is inescapable—the threshhold decisions on the development and employment of the cruise missile were made with regard to politics and not technology.

The great merit of *Cruise Missiles* is that if you care to spend the effort and time digesting this encyclopedia of facts and knowledge on our most advanced weapons system, you will be justly rewarded. It is to these hearty patrons of weaponry that I recommend *Cruise Missiles*.

RICHARD E. JOHE
St. Johns University
New York City

BRUCE CUMINGS. *The Origins of the Korean War: Liberation and the Emergence of Separate Regimes, 1945-1947.* Pp. xxxi, 606. Princeton, NJ: Princeton University Press, 1981. $40.00; Paperbound, $14.50.

The Korean War, like all international conflicts, was rooted in events, policy choices, and conflicts that long preceded the actual cataclysm. Bruce Cumings has undertaken a massive study and effort to demonstrate that the separation of North and South Korea and the resulting conflict stemmed from the earliest American decisions and activities in Korea. He pointedly laments the impact of those decisions on the budding post-Japanese-surrender reformist movement and the consequent denial of political and economic liberation of long oppressed (both by the Japanese colonial system and the centuries' old feudal structure) Korean peoples.

The final evaluation of this study will have to await a promised companion volume as this unit deals only with the 1945-47 era and its conflicting nationalist developments. The ultimate weaving together of the threads that led to the international conflict will presumedly be made in the subsequent book.

There is much to be said for this study. It is comprehensive and well-written. Cummings has over 100 pages of chapter notes and an overwhelming bibliography. He provides a wide variety of statistical and documentary data. In fact, one wonders if the author was not overwhelmed by his data sources at times, especially as he also is obviously attempting to validate his personal conviction that significant reform was not only desirable but inevitable if American policy makers had not been so obtuse, parochial, and fearful of Soviet intentions. His access to hundreds of declassified documents, official and private memoranda, and statements of the disenchanted enabled a near polemical verbal overkill in his zeal to demonstrate his points.

His later chapters, which deal with Soviet behavior in the newly emerged and separate North Korea, are developed on the basis of a much more limited set of data that provide insight into the political dynamics and internal conflicts in North Korea. Consequently, the thrust is essentially laudatory and almost apologetic when excesses are recognized.

In the final chapter a much more balanced and consequently insightful appraisal is made. He recognizes that the probability of the American leadership choosing other alternatives was very unlikely and that even different choices in the South would not have led inevitably to the desired end of a nonviolent but massive reform movement. He gives only passing recognition to the fact that, essentially, American policy did achieve its political end (containment) even if it compromised local Korean interests.

Despite the points just made, this book is a valuable source document and is certainly thought-provoking. Its analysis is essentially acceptable, and scholars like Cumings, whose approaches to scholarship sometimes get stilted by their political values (or at least they do not disguise them as well as others), need to be heard from and to be considered.

They provide the intellectual leaven that allows all of us to rethink our own positions on the past.

ARVIN PALMER

Northland Pioneer College
Holbrook
Arizona

JOHN LEWIS GADDIS. *Strategies of Containment: A Critical Appraisal of Postwar American Security Policy*. Pp. xi, 432. New York: and Oxford: Oxford University Press, 1982, $25.00.

In *Strategies of Containment* Professor Gaddis examines the different phases of U.S. postwar foreign policy and finds that to a great extent Washington was preoccupied with the challenge caused by Soviet expansionism. Between 1947 and 1979 a number of strategies of containment were developed to contain Soviet ambitions.

Containment of the Soviet Union was, in effect, also the strategy of President Franklin Roosevelt, who sought to ensure a stable postwar order by offering the Soviet Union a prominent place in it. It was a strategy of containment by integrating Moscow into a postwar security system. In hindsight it is easy to recognize the failure of this approach; however, contemporaneous observers such as U.S. Ambassador to Moscow W. Averell Harriman and General John R. Deane, head of the American military mission there, realized long before the end of World War II that the Soviet Union intended to impose unilateral settlements in Eastern Europe and to dominate their surroundings. Their warnings fell on deaf ears.

President Truman continued FDR's efforts to accommodate Moscow, but eventually he recognized that Soviet behavior could neither be influenced by trust nor pressure. A revision of American strategy commenced with the famous long telegram dispatched by George F. Kennan in February 1946 from Moscow. It initiated the first of five phases or codes of postwar U.S. foreign policy, as distinguished by the author. All of these codes pursued as their main objective the containment of Soviet expansionism. Professor Gaddis discusses the different phases both in terms of content and implementation, that is, the best methods for dealing with Moscow. There appears the perennial concern with the distinction of what constitutes vital or peripheral interests, or if U.S. policy should be symmetrical or asymmetrical. The original architects of symmetry and asymmetry, Paul Nitze and George Kennan respectively, are still debating the virtues of their proposed strategies.

Tensions between the Kremlin leadership and the international communist movement did not lead, as expected, to a weakening of Soviet control, and U.S. policy makers apparently did not anticipate Moscow's willingness to use force to keep its empire together.

President Carter's policies, based on the rejection of America's preoccupation with the containment policy and the assumption of the inevitability of Soviet expansionism, was short-lived. Soviet actions throughout the world negated Carter's new approach. Soviet expansion in sub-Sahara Africa and in the Near East relied largely on Cuban proxies, and the direct use of Soviet troops in December 1979 in Afghanistan finally changed the President's perception of Soviet intentions.

Professor Gaddis made extensive use of recently declassified documents in his outstanding study of America's postwar foreign strategies.

ERIC WALDMAN

University of Calgary
Alberta, Canada

V. KUBALKOVA and A. A. CRUICK-SHANK, *International Inequality*. Pp. 293. New York: St. Martin's Press, 1981. $29.95.

The matter of equality is a potent, exciting, and necessary ingredient in almost all political discussions and investigations. At the level of international concern the reality of inequality, the protection of hierarchies, and the protest against domination form the core of political debate and political behavior.

The authors of this volume take the reader through a series of perspectives and arguments concerning the causes of and place of inequality in international relations. No one seriously denies that we inhabit a world that is profoundly unequal. But, as one would intuitively expect given that we are talking about relations between individuals and nations with interests, there is considerably less than agreement about things from this observation onward. Some—dependency theorists, Marxists and neo-Marxists, world systems types—point out the decidedly unnatural and therefore illegitimate nature of international inequality. Others—realists, conservatives, some liberals, some patriots, and some religious theologians—press the case that the world by its very nature is constituted by nation-state actors of uneven assets, capabilities, and desires. These varying and often antagonistic viewpoints are the stuff of Kubalkova and Cruickshank's able presentation.

The format of the book allows the reader to set one perspective about international inequality against other views. Included in the work are discussions of the nature of the equality-inequality debate; the dependency-third-world perspective; the views of the Soviet Union and the Chinese; and conservative, liberal, and radical Western perspectives. Basically I found the treatment to be fair and helpful, although I do have some reservations and criticisms.

One criticism—I hope that it is not unfair—concerns the fact that examples of the modes of explanation for international inequality are absent. It would have been of great benefit had the authors provided us with brief examples of how the various perspectives presented sought to explain real specific events or circumstances. The contours and indeed the character of the debate between contending viewpoints is often lost or diminished owing to the lack of case studies. It also means that this is not a good book for beginners—one had best know considerable history beforehand or the debates outlined are not meaningful.

I also found the discussion of Marxism and neo-Marxism to be thin and mechanical. The presentation of the neoconservative and indeed patriotic theology (for example, people like Robert Tucker) was also thin and will allow those who are unaware of the issues to believe that there is more of substance involved in these arguments than there is in reality.

The authors conclude that "we discover at the end of our survey that the debate on international inequality turns out to be nothing more or less than a debate about world politics." This should not be news to anyone who has kept up with world events.

CARL F. PINKELE

Ohio Wesleyan University
Delaware
Ohio

ROBERT L. MESSER. *The End of an Alliance: James F. Byrnes, Roosevelt, Truman, and the Origins of the Cold War*. Pp. viii, 292. Chapel Hill, NC: University of North Carolina Press, 1982. $19.95.

Franklin Roosevelt cast a long shadow that extended into the Truman era. American-Soviet developments reflect this as they merge into the cold war. One of the tangible reflectors was James T. Byrnes, senator, supreme court justice, and "assistant president for the home front," who became Truman's secretary of state. As Dr. Messer depicts the triple relationship, it is a fascinating narrative. Little can be said about the Roosevelt-Truman side, which was superficial and distant. Byrnes's relationship with Roosevelt and Truman is Messer's story.

This lucid book systematically uses available sources, accompanied by cogent analysis of motivations of three superb professional politicians. The kernel shows how their political perceptions materialized in hard-ball actions that hurt one. This was Byrnes.

Politicians have a subtle code, and the line between manipulation and deceit is thin. Interpretations may vary. From his evidence the author concludes, like some before him, that Roosevelt, dumping Wallace, encouraged Byrnes to enter the 1944 vice-presidential race intentionally to get the party's liberal wing to accept Truman as a compromise. Dusting off Byrnes, Roosevelt included him in the Yalta conference delegation for his influence on the senate and as public lobbyist for what agreements would be reached there. Byrnes did not attend the very crucial military discussions. He attended the plenary sessions and was active upon the UN voting formula problem and liberated areas declaration. On Far East dealings with the Soviet Union, Byrnes was kept in ignorance by Roosevelt, and he left the closing formulation of that secret protocol. His mission was public advance man to sell Yalta (as he knew it) before the president's return. Byrnes's reputation as Yalta expert, which he did not discourage, was, along with his prominence, an important factor in Truman later naming him as secretary of state. His imperfect knowledge and his stance brought strong criticism when the Far East agreement surfaced. This contributed to Truman-Byrnes frictions.

Truman, initially the junior foreign affairs partner, finally adjusted to his job and humanly resented Byrnes, who had sheparded him as a new senator, whom he had volunteered to nominate at the 1944 convention, and who still loomed as Mr. Democrat.

That Byrnes sought political style compromises at the postwar conferences with the Russians, brought mounting criticism that he was soft in dealing with them. American public and congressional views hardened as the Russians consolidated Eastern Europe, and there and elsewhere did violence to American concepts.

Byrnes, aware of Truman's intention to lead, privately submitted his resignation in April 1946, to take effect after concluding the peace treaties. This did not come until year's end. Truman had General Marshall available and waiting.

An intriguing feature of the Truman-Byrnes relationship is the attempts of both to alter the record. The author diagnoses the famous January 5, 1946 Truman memorandum, allegedly discussed with Byrnes and later fodder to justify his dismissal. He concludes it was not really discussed and was written, if about that date, with a history-conscious eye to show a prescient executive troubled by Soviet moves and the need for strong American reaction. The State Department later wanted Byrnes's records on the Postdam conference. Byrnes altered his aide's hitherto unknown diary of the conference to conform to a tough attitude toward the Soviets.

Politics is life intensified, and practitioners can rapidly grow unseemly warts, which should not detract from their human outlines. None should expect a responsible politician on a major issue, as to substance and timing, to utter his death knell: "I was wrong."

ROY M. MELBOURNE
Chapel Hill
North Carolina

MICHAEL WALLER. *Democratic Centralism: An Historical Commentary.* Pp. 155. St. Martin's Press, 1981. $20.00.

"*Tout commence*," wrote Péguy, "*en mystique, et finit en politique.*" Michael Waller, Senior Lecturer in government at the University of Manchester in England, has indited a paean to mystique without offering the empirical evidence to give substance to his *profession de foi*, the point of which is to preserve the glowing icon of democratic centralism from the dross accumulated from any real experience, particularly as that doctrine is realized in the Soviet Union. It is arguable, he asserts, that there is somewhere another variety of democratic centralism, "a dialectical unity of centralism and democracy." He searches for it high and low among selected groups of Bolsheviks, among the Trotskyists, and among West European dissident Communists. He suggests that the term originated with the Mensheviks and was shortly adopted by both factions of Russian Social Democracy at the Unity Congress of 1906. By taking a special case as a general guide to Lenin's organizational thought and by ignoring the polemic of the Liquidators who wished to terminate Bolshevik conspiratorial activity, Waller depicts Lenin as a democrat who only put democracy aside when compelled to do so by hostile circumstances. "The Party," he argues, "was competitive because it was *forced* to be so." Referring to the Democratic Centralist opposition at the Ninth Congress (1920), he forebears from mentioning Trotsky's name, whose advocacy of militarizing labor was one of the sources of complaint. He notes the close connection between democratic centralism and the prohibition of active political subgroups within the Party, banned in 1921 as fractional. Foreign communist parties accepting the 21 Conditions for entering the Comintern (1920) would be subject to "'iron discipline, bordering on military discipline.'" Fleeting references to a Leninist simile comparing the Party to a healthy body and opposition to its leadership as sickness, if combined with Antonio Gramsci's attribution to the Party of *organicitá*—"a continual adaption of the organization to the real movement, a matching of thrusts from below with orders from above"—might, as an ideal combination of civil militarism plus organicism, be interpreted as a Leninist groping toward proletarian fascism, but the author is too controlled to permit a spasm of originality. What he has produced is a short commentary from an apparent Trotskyist standpoint of aspects of the concept without empirical evidence—although with generous italicizations—of the practical operation of democratic centralism in any real party other than the CPSU in concrete political circumstances. It will primarily interest specialty collectors of political commentary by the trendy left.

DALE LaBELLE

Reading
Massachusetts

I. WILLIAM ZARTMAN and MAUREEN BERMAN. *The Practical Negotiator*. Pp. xiii, 250. New Haven, Yale University Press, 1982. $20.00.

The second half of the twentieth century has become the age of negotiations for international labor relations, for business, for financial affairs. The importance of the delicate art of negotiation is further evidenced by the number of excellent new books on negotiation as both theory and practical process that have recently appeared. Among the best of these is *The Practical Negotiator* by William Zartman, of the School for Advanced International Studies at Johns Hopkins, and Maureen Berman, of the International League for Human Rights.

This volume grew out of the Academy for Educational Development's extensive study of both the scholarly and hands-on approaches to negotiation. The yawning gap between these two approaches was to be bridged by reference to their respective strengths and by seeing how the two traditionally discrete approaches could build off each other and produce a more effective solution, or group of solutions, to the problems that are faced in the negotiation process.

Through extensive interviews with experienced international negotiators, including George Ball, Arthur Goldberg, Phillip Jessup, and Averell Harriman, the authors have sought to focus more clearly on the factors that are needed in a successful negotiator—empathy, patience, self-assurance, ingenuity, and stamina. While these traits seem obvious, Zartman and Berman have given them color and life by discussing them in terms of specific negotiating experiences. The use of illustrative examples in this volume is demonstrated in a lengthy discussion of the different stages through which most important international negotiations pass. From the crucial recognition by the relevant parties of the necessity to negotiate a particular dispute, to the evolution of a formula for solving it and the implementation of the relevant detailed provisions, the authors make the point that some notion of justice is important to the conclusion and effective continuation of a particular negotiation.

As part of their analysis of different negotiating techniques, the authors discuss the importance of timing in granting concessions, the grounds for establishing trust and credibility, and the risks involved in devising too overbearing an opening position. Although each of these ideas is discussed in terms of particular international disputes (indeed such discussions are one of the best points in the book), the authors could have had a greater impact by expanding the examination of such examples rather than relying on brief vignettes. It would have been quite helpful to discuss two or three negotiations in all of their ramifications, in addition to the illustration approach used by the authors. Professor Louis Henkins's recent book, *How Nations Behave*, was particularly good at this technique.

The Practical Negotiator is not designed merely as a step-by-step primer on how to be a better negotiator. The aim of the authors is a bit more ambitious, that is, to demonstrate that negotiators can grow to meet the increasingly heavy demands placed on them by learning the nuances of fact situations rather than by slavishly following a predetermined procedural method. The book also shows its

ambitions by undertaking to demonstrate that "one of the eternal paradoxes of negotiations is that it allows the weak to confront the strong and still come away with something which should not be possible if weakness and strength were all that mattered." What matters in this book is that the authors have maintained a fine balance between theory and practice and have done so with considerable insight.

JAMES R. SILKENAT
Member of the
    District of Columbia Bar
Washington, D.C.

AFRICA, ASIA, AND
LATIN AMERICA

ALAIN DE JANVRY. *The Agrarian Question and Reformism in Latin America.* Pp. xvi, 311. Baltimore, MD: Johns Hopkins University Press, 1982. $27.50; Paperbound, $8.95.

What is the answer to the agrarian question as to why the world's poor become ever more poor despite land reform and other public policies in agriculture? The root of rural poverty, according to de Janvry, lies in what he has termed "functional dualism." Cheap food policies for the peasantry in Latin America have composed one side of a dual agricultural development. Under land reform, peasants were expelled from the haciendas and hired as wage earners. They became a transitory fraction of a class within capitalism. While they delivered cheap labor to the capitalist sector, they continued to raise food for their own households in order to survive. The other side of dualism has been the development of agricultural products for export under capitalism.

State policies have sustained cheap labor by repressing worker demands and manipulating the terms of trade against most wage foods. At the same time, the state has favored large landowners with institutional rents and has sought foreign capital and technology for their benefit. Labor has come to see this as exploitation and hence militates against the existing political-economic system, rather than working toward social-democratic settlements.

The author's discussion of land reform from the political and economic angles has a disturbing conclusion: "Both the problem of deficient and uneven production performance in agriculture and the persistent problem of rural poverty increasingly arise from the first determinant of stagnation—cheap food." This determinant lies beyond the scope of land reform. Whatever the type of reform, one factor remains constant. The subsistence sector as the necessary source of cheap labor is untouchable.

So, with agrarian land reform at a standstill, the agrarian programs of the 1970s turned to rural development projects. Their political role was to reinforce and expand the upper fringe of peasants to act as a buffer class in rural conflicts. Their economic role was to perpetuate cheap labor under functional dualism. The status quo was to be maintained by supplying basic needs to the peasant sector. These projects directed at commercial agriculture developed the forces of production at the political cost of increased landlessness and proletarianization.

De Janvry criticizes the top-down and paternalistic nature of the rural development projects supported by international aid agencies and outlines what he believes should be attempted. Because the agrarian question is fundamentally nonagrarian, "its solution lies in social and structural changes at the level of the total social formation." The rapidly emerging rural semiproletariat and landless labor should be transformed into wage buyers. In order to effect this structural change there would have to be social change.

Since growth does not remedy basic inequalities, the peasants would have to mobilize to establish mass-based democratic regimes. Only class struggle

would bring them land reform and rural development programs for social change which are by and for the peasants. Further, a state of class consciousness as proletarians would have to be created which would allow them to see beyond petty bourgeois demands. Finally, an alliance between this proletarianized segment of the peasantry and the workers would have to be achieved.

These very arguments were heard by this reviewer in the northeast of Brazil at the height of peasant revolts in the early 1960s. In 1964 the United States government supported a revolution that counteracted advancing reforms and extinguished the leaders of the Peasant Leagues. On reading this book, one would hope that Professor de Janvry would inspire many students in his courses at Berkeley to serve in future official policymaking for Latin America so that, in coming revolutions, the real issues of the agrarian question might be understood.

VIRGINIA FREEHAFER
West Chester
Pennsylvania

EARL H. KINMONTH. *The Self-Made Man in Meiji Japanese Thought: From Samurai to Salary Man.* Pp. xii, 385. Berkeley: University of California Press, 1981. $28.50.

Since the late Tokugawa period the Japanese have actively sought a success ethic to guarantee elite status to those who subscribed to it faithfully. Although the nature of the goal changed through the years as society changed, one thing remained constant—the determination to find a group formula for individual success. Professor Kinmonth has explored, among other sources, a wide variety of the Japanese self-advancement literature. He has reconstructed the development of the concept of *risshin shusse*, or personal advancement, from the early Meiji idea that the state equaled the sum of individual energies and efforts, to the modern "examination hells" whose intense competition guards the citadels of elitism today.

The fascinating part of Mr. Kinmonth's story lies in this transformation of *risshin* from its earlier implication that study, application, and perhaps audacity would exalt every student with ability into a cabinet minister or corporate executive, to the recent idea that conformity is the best road to success. He sees Japan as unusually egalitarian in potential for advancement, having no natural elite based on race, religion, or area of residence. Thus there is inherently a high ratio of people to possible opportunities. This provides a great pool of nearly identical but disappointed seekers for elite status standing below every successful candidate and letting the latter know that he could be replaced at any moment without a ripple. This, Kinmonth suggests, makes the modern, successful salary man very likely to eschew any marks of individuality or deviation, and to conform as completely as possible to what he interprets as the employer's wishes. The author sees this as a possible explanation of the intelligentsia's timidity in opposing militarism in the 1920s and 1930s.

The Self-Made Man is an interesting work and provides a number of correctives to earlier generalizations about the Japanese success ethic. It is certainly, however, a long road from Mr. Kinmonth's samurai to his salary man. While his succinct and sprightly introduction and conclusion demonstrate his considerable talents at interpretation and with the language, his overlong analysis, particularly of the self-help literature itself, is often just plain tedious. It is necessary to ask, is overkill of this sort justified in order to turn what might have been a sparkling article into a book-length work?

R. KENT LANCASTER
Goucher College
Baltimore
Maryland

RICHARD CURT KRAUS. *Class Conflict in Chinese Socialism*, Pp x, 243 inc. notes, index. New York: Columbia University Press, 1981. $22.50.

Class struggle is a basic concept of Marxist social theory. No less so is it basic to Chinese communism and to Mao Zedong's own analysis. Richard Kraus has examined Chinese class theory, and has placed the rather complicated problem in some perspective. His analysis in this short book (183 pages with notes and index) is seen from three foci: class relationships in a socialist society, adaptation of Marxist social theory to Chinese conditions, and Mao's role as a critic of inequality.

In the discussion that follows, Kraus outlines the two stratification systems that the Chinese have adopted: classes that were dominant before the revolution and that based their power on ownership of private property, and postrevolutionary classes that based their power on bureaucratic position.

The hierarchy of the former system consisted of more than 60 class designations ranging from good—poor and landless peasants and workers—to bad—landlords, rich peasants, and capitalists. With the advent of liberation, land reform, and socialist transformation, these bad classes were eliminated, and there arose a class stratification system based on a hierarchy of work grades in an extensive bureaucracy. For government employees 30 grades of cadres were developed, 12 for professors, 25 for education administrators, 8 for engineers; writers, actors, opera singers, and many others all received appropriate work grades that stipulated their salaries, precedence, and perquisites.

Kraus goes on to describe class struggle following the elimination of the elites in the property-based class system. He traces Mao's revival of class conflict in which Mao admonished his followers never to forget class struggle, and to treat it as the key link. This in spite of many senior party members who believed that class struggle ended with socialist transformation. Both Liu Shaoqi and Deng Xiaoping were among these leaders and were purged as a consequence of their heresy. Mao led a movement to revive the old class designations to catch some who had previously escaped, and this included the children of the class enemies. This was especially true during the Cultural Revolution's Remember Past Bitterness campaign when blameless children were branded with the designations of their parents.

So too were new enemies found and labeled as counterrevolutionaries, bad elements, rightists, ghosts and monsters, revisionists, and eventually "people in the Party taking the capitalist road." None could be certain to escape criticism. A good pedigree was no guarantee of safety since Mao rejected the theory of natural redness. Neither was party position considered safe, as criticism was directed at "capitalist roaders within the Party."

Kraus concludes with the thought that class conflict in China will continue as various classes seek to regain, retain, or improve their positions in the hierarchy. He believes that Marxist social theory is broadly adaptable, and hence will continue to be useful. Finally, Kraus considers Mao Zedong as a critic of class conflict, and concludes that Mao's analysis will be valuable to whatever new directions Chinese ideology may be heading.

Richard Kraus's *Class Conflict in Chinese Socialism* is a most useful contribution toward an explanation of Chinese social theory, and sheds light on some of the bizarre events in China since the establishment of the People's Republic.

JAMES D. JORDAN

Alexandria
Virginia

SIMON LEYS. *Broken Images: Essays on Chinese Culture and Politics*. Trans. Steve Cox. Pp. 156. London: Allison & Busby, 1979. $8.95.

SIMON LEYS. *The Chairman's New Clothes: Mao and the Cultural Revolution*. Trans. Carol Appleyard and Patrick Goode. Pp. 272. London: Allison & Busby, 1981. $8.95.

Pierre Ryckmans, the Belgian Sinologist better known by his pseudonym of Simon Leys, prefaces *The Chairman's New Clothes* with an untranslated quotation from the Han dynasty historian Ssu-ma Ch'ien: "The assent of a thousand men is unequal to the honest criticism of a single scholar." This aphorism embodies Ryckmans's conviction that Westerners have habitually displayed far too much acclaim for, and far too little informed judgment about the state of post-1949 Chinese politics and culture. Ryckmans sought to correct this perceived imbalance in his widely read 1974 polemic *Chinese Shadows*, establishing himself in the process as one of the most caustically controversial antagonists of Mao Tse-tung's new order in the Western literary world. The two books under consideration fully accord with this approach, but can hardly be expected to have the same impact in view of the volte-face in China itself during the past half-dozen years. As the author acknowledges, China's post-Maoist leadership has frequently validated his worst opinions and owned up to Mao's more egregious errors, notably the horrors of the Cultural Revolution. The appearance of both volumes in English translations at this juncture is therefore less productive of revelations than of elaborations or further confirmation of Ryckmans's already well-publicized views.

The Chairman's New Clothes is a lengthy, rather disjointed book: part historical prelude to the Cultural Revolution (the most interesting portion of the work), part documentary appendices illustrating a number of key episodes connected with P'eng Te-huai's disgrace in 1959 and the protest movements of the late 1970s, and the principal narrative, which presents a detailed and cogent account of the movement itself from 1967 to 1969. Since its initial publication in Paris in 1971, however, the book has not been substantially revised. *Broken Images*, on the other hand, is a collection of Ryckmans's trenchant, often witty reviews, articles, and essays dating from 1975 to 1978, several of which were previously unavailable in English. The selections range over such varied topics as a fascinating analysis of the great twentieth-century litterateur Lu Hsun, brief sketches of the roles of Chiang Kai-shek and Mao in modern Chinese history, a scathing critique of Roxane Witke's biography of the now reviled Chiang Ch'ing, a disquisition on the Orwellian fate of museums in the People's Republic, and the title essay, a disturbing series of impressionistic vignettes on contemporary Chinese life based on refugee interviews.

If there is a central theme running through both books, it is the author's undisguised admiration for the Chinese high culture anathematized by Mao's Cultural Revolution, coupled with his sympathy with Chinese citizens suffering under what he considers an only nominally socialist totalitarianism. Ryckmans sees the Cultural Revolution as a fraudulent contradiction in terms, neither genuinely concerned with culture (except as a tactical pretext to sanction power struggles between Mao and his detractors) nor revolutionary in any legitimate sense of the word. He minimizes the extent of long-standing ideological differences among the leadership, and maximizes the idiosyncratic, cynically manipulative character of Mao's erratic stewardship during the 1960s. Mao emerges as a latter-day Ch'in Shih-huang (the ruthless first emperor of China whose policies proved his own undoing); he outlived his usefulness and earlier political genius, becoming a dangerous nuisance whose visionary schemes and anachronistic rustic mentality crippled China's quest for modernization. As any serious student of Chinese politics will recog-

nize, such characterization of both a complex event and the equally complex man behind it involves more than a little distortion and oversimplification.

While nodding in recognition of the positive achievements of the People's Republic, Ryckmans views the regime in humanistic terms as a revolution manqué. His avowed spiritual mentor is, appropriately enough, Lu Hsun, whose cultural pessimism and critical engagement Ryckmans brilliantly describes. While Lu Hsun fictionalized the pathologies of precommunist China, Ryckmans seeks to expose the all-too-real maladies of the present political dispensation. In both instances dispassionate objectivity becomes a casualty in the pursuit of significant truths, and there is enough evidence of the latter in both these books to justify the attention of readers concerned with contemporary China.

ROBERT P. GARDELLA
U.S. Merchant Marine Academy
Kings Point
New York

CLEMENT HENRY MOORE. *Images of Development: Egyptian Engineers in Search of Industry.* Pp. xi, 252. Cambridge: MIT Press, 1980. $25.00.

Images of Development is a critical study of the role of engineers in the development and modernization process of contemporary Egypt. It tests the conventional wisdom that a society's modernization is defined mainly by the proportion of its well-educated professionals.

The author looks at the role of engineers in three perspectives: as professionals, as members of a new middle class (state bourgeoisie), and as agents of technical rationality. Corresponding to such a division, the modernization process itself is analyzed in terms of the development syndrome of differentiation, equality, and capacity.

Part 1 of this book deals with engineers and their professional development; it examines the extent to which Egyptian engineers measured up to the general principles of professionalism. The discussion begins with the foundation of the Royal Society of Egyptian Engineers in 1920 and moves through the rise of Professional Engineers' Syndicate, the political maneuvering to gain greater professional recognition for Egyptian engineers, and the ethic of professionalism in the engineering profession in contemporary Egypt. Although the increased emphasis on industrialization and technical development during the Nasser era raised the demand for engineers and enhanced their prestige, by the late 1960s the situation was changing drastically. Engineering fell from number one in terms of professional prestige in 1961 to number four in 1976. Part of the reason was Nasser's systematic politicization of the engineers' syndicate. With its dependence on political connections and an enlarging public sector, the profession lost much of its self-respect. The government's "habit of making a price list of school certificates and diplomas"—its practice of assigning a certain salary and grade to a diploma encouraged Egyptian parents to push their children into engineering degrees. This, along with Nasser's decision to make all high school graduates eligible for university education, resulted in overcrowded classrooms, greater demand for teachers, dilution of academic standards, and inevitable degree inflation. All of these had disastrous consequences for the technical competence of Egyptian engineers and their professional prestige. Inadequate employment opportunities and a sagging economy compounded these problems.

Erosion of academic quality was not confined only to undergraduate engineering education; it affected engineering research as well. Due to political considerations, many of the high-level research and scientific administration positions, such as the head of the Atomic Energy Commission, were given to military or personal friends of the regime who did not possess the necessary technical qualifications for the job. The politicization of research establishments and the alienation of highly qualified researchers, many of whom emigrated to other countries, resulted in mediocre engineering research and prolonged Egypt's dependence on foreign technology.

Part 2 of the book deals with engineers and social change. As in many other poor countries, engineers in Egypt came mainly from the urban bourgeoisie. Nasser regime's egalitarian rhetoric notwithstanding, the politicization of engineering education, along with an expanding public sector and a paternalistic ruling oligarchy reinforced each other to maintain their class-orientation. It is true that a large number of women entered, and graduated from, engineering schools during this period. However, only a small number of them were selected for postgraduate special training opportunities, and therefore the rate of their professional growth was significantly slower than that of their male counterparts. The author does not find any evidence to suggest that engineering education in Egypt during Nasser-Sadat regimes grew out of its bourgeois male character.

In Part 3, the author examines engineers in the context of their relations with the political order. Although Egyptian engineers were not active politicians, they were victims of political changes. They were courted by both Nasser and Sadat into political ranks at least partly to legitimize their regimes, and probably partly due to a military leader's preference for doers over talkers in politics. At any rate, this cooption of engineers into political ranks posed serious problems for their professional standing. The inevitable conflicts between their political roles and professional judgments eroded their professional credibility and rendered their influence on the government rather weak and transitory; they were only as influential as the political system that fostered them.

The Egyptian engineer that emerges from the study is very much a part and, at the same time, a victim of political networks. His image is far from that of the prototype that Emile Durkheim visualized in a modernizing industrial society. The author's conclusion that Egyptian engineers failed to practice theoretical modernization—that they contributed little to the development syndrome of social differentiation, equality, and administrative capacity seems to be valid. However, engineers do not deserve all the blame for it. Any attempt on their part to achieve their potential identities as professionals was always stymied by lack of economic opportunities and an impoverished political system that produced inconsistent policy-making in the areas of education and scientific research.

The book is not very well organized nor is its style particularly appealing. Many of its conclusions on the role of Egyptian engineers in modernization and development may be valid for higher education in general, both in Egypt and in many other underdeveloped countries. In fact, that seems to be its strength; the study seems to validate some of the strong suspicions raised by development economists in recent years on the correlation between higher education and economic development.

P. I. MATHEW

U.S. Coast Guard Academy
New London
Connecticut

TIM NIBLOCK, ed. *State, Society, and Economy in Saudi Arabia.* Pp. 314. New York: St. Martin's Press, 1981. $27.50.

MICHAEL CURTIS, ed. *Religion and Politics in the Middle East.* Pp. x, 406. Boulder, CO: Westview, 1981. $19.95.

Tim Niblock, deputy director of the University of Exeter's Centre for Arab Gulf Studies, has assembled an able, articulate, interdisciplinary team of Middle East experts. Drawing upon their respective specialties, the center has constructed what was not claimed to be, but nevertheless succeeded in becoming a fairly comprehensive delineation of state, society, and economy in Saudi Arabia.

The commonly held notion of Saudi Arabia as an oasis fabulously rich and serenely stable amidst the swirling turbulence of Arab rivalries and revolutionary discontent is naively mythic. To be sure, in demonstrating the linkage between townsmen and Bedouin nomads anterior to formation of the present Saudi state, Niblock dispels the classic thesis of a traditionalism-modernism dichotomy. Yet it becomes abundantly evident that following World War II, with the unremitting exploitation of petroleum deposits, many dislocations and vexing issues ensued. The impact of motor vehicles upon pastoral life has been profound. The detribalization, the break up of families, the lure of the towns; exposure through contact with Lebanese, Palestinians, and Pakistanis to Westernized Islamic ways; the heightened craving for material goods; the incrementalized liberation of upper-class women; and the subtle challenges to Wahabbi puritanism have cumulatively eroded ancestral mores. With the advent of a petrodollar economy sharp socioeconomic cleavages have begun to undercut the rough egalitarianism of the desert kingdom. Sheer opulence and dissipation in the royal ambience, affluence in commercial circles, prospective penury and restiveness at the base—this is the brew from which revolution is compounded. To this trouble in paradise add Shi'ite sectarianism emanating from Iran, antimonarchism mounted by radical Arab regimes, simmering disputes with Gulf sheikhdoms, relentless subversion by the USSR—and there crystallizes a mood of foreboding.

Among the most valuable papers in the collection are those providing a careful analysis of the Saudi economy—in banking, petroleum, petrochemicals—with particular attention to the role of the United States, Japan, and Korea. At the very heart of Saudi growth is the almost inevitable generation of tensions: a Saudi technical intelligentsia whose incipient secularism menaces the entrenched religious fundamentalism; a limited labor force augmented by indispensable foreign migrants who might become a Trojan horse; the employment of oil pricing as a policy tool, while yet desiring a strong West as a counterpoise to Communism rampant. To appreciate these seemingly irresolvable oppositions is to reject a simplistic proposition advanced by more than one contributor—that the Palestinian dilemma constitutes the major unstabilizing factor for Saudi Arabia's future.

The second collection is also interdisciplinary, but without the input of economists. Its geographical scope is obviously broader, and it combines the talents of Christian, Jewish, and Muslim scholars. Many of the articles previously appeared in *Middle East Review*, *Middle East Journal*, and other authoritative publications. Michael Curtis, the editor, is well-schooled in comparative politics and political theory, and displays sound judgment in the papers culled for this enterprise. He personally authored a trenchant introduction, and arranged for the inclusion of a bibliographic essay and glossary.

The opening chapters of the volume explore the revitalization of Islam and seek to unravel the interrelationships of ethnicity, socialism, and religion. The question is also raised, but goes unanswered, whether Islam can coexist in peace with Christianity and Judaism. What emerges clearly is that Christian Arabs, who once held significant leadership roles in Arab nationalist movements, have little to expect from the future.

As the reader moves from state to state, reviewing the empirical analyses, he finds Islam serving both to unify and destabilize. Ultrafundamentalist groups, ever vigilant to detect secularizing instrusions, upbraid the political authorities for alleged lapses. They have menaced the Egyptian leadership, attempted to assassinate Nasser, and succeeded with Sadat. They have glowered in Saudi Arabia at Western inroads upon Wahabbi conservatism. They have pushed Libya's Qadhafi into offering reassurances that his socialism is entirely consistent with the shari'a. Meantime, equally zealous Muslim sectarianism has bedevilled Iraq, Syria, the Sudan, and especially Lebanon. The ultimate step in promoting the paramountcy of Islam (though of the Shi'ite variety) has been taken in Iran, with Khomeini's theocratic republic. What is perhaps equally noteworthy, one discovers even in secular Turkey a residual sacral component legitimating the state.

Some observers of the contemporary Middle East have conjectured a resurgent pan-Islam. Divisive parochial interests in the immediate present seem to block its consummation. Nevertheless, this volume renders it compellingly transparent that political and social action in the Middle East, whenever indifferent to the power of Islam, are reduced to fatuous miscalculations.

ELMER N. LEAR
Pennsylvania State University
Middletown

STANLEY ROSEN. *Red Guard Factionalism and the Cultural Revolution in Guangzhou (Canton).* Pp. xv, 320. Boulder, CO: Westview, 1982. $32.50.

JOHN H. FINCHER. *Chinese Democracy: The Self-Government Movement in Local, Provincial and National Politics, 1905-1914.* Pp. 276. New York: St. Martin's Press, 1981. $27.50.

Most books on the Cultural Revolution (CR) in China are macrostudies dealing with the larger issues of intraparty conflicts and college students. Stanley Rosen's book *Red Guard Factionalism and the Cultural Revolution in Guangzhou (Canton)* is a microstudy of the Red Guard movement in one city—Guangzhou, with focus on middle school students. It examines the mass level and politics within the mass organizations. The chief objective of the book is to identify the causes of factionalism among Red Guards.

Rosen's main sources of data are Chinese materials, including Red Guard publications and interviews with former Red Guards and students in the Guangzhou area. The book begins with a description of the Chinese middle school system from 1960 to 1966 before the CR. This provides the reader with a background knowledge of the cleavages among middle school students on the eve of the CR. This is followed by an analysis of factionalism among the Red Guards during the CR. Finally, an epilogue briefly discusses the structure of education in China in the late 1970s. Although dealing primarily with the Red Guard movement in Guangzhou, the book links local developments to national politics.

The major finding in this book is that factionalism in the Red Guard movement in Guangzhou is caused by the emphasis on the students' family class origin. Students of good family class origin, such as revolutionary cadre and revolutionary military, joined the conservative organization while students of less desirable family origin, such as intellectual middle class, workers, and peasants, joined the rebel organization. Students of bad family class origin, such as former capitalists, landlords, and Nationalists, did not actively participate in the CR. Furthermore, Red Guards were more active in elite and good schools than in the ordinary and poor schools. They were more active in senior high than in junior high schools.

The book contains many detailed accounts by former Red Guards or students of their personal experience during the CR. The attention paid to detail contributed to the strength as well as the weakness of this book. The minute details make the book tedious and repetitious in some parts. There are too many unnecessary lengthy quotations, especially in the first three chapters.

Another problem with this book is its overemphasis on the factor of class origin in analyzing the political behavior of middle school students who are teenagers, many in their early teens.

Undoubtedly class origin was the most crucial factor in determining a student's political behavior during the CR. But this should not obscure the fact that these students were young children and were not politically sophisticated, although they were more politicized than their counterparts in Western societies. Most of them lived at home. They must have been influenced by their families and their teachers in their formative years. A more indepth treatment of the influence of family, especially parents, and teachers on the political behavior of the young people may shed some new light on political socialization in China. Besides class origin, some nonpolitical factors may also have influence on the political affiliation of students, such as friendship, hobbies, sports, and proximity of their residences.

The book did not assess the impact of the CR on the political behavior of the young people in China after the CR except to mention that they were disillusioned because they were sent to the countryside to be rusticated or to the factories. This nationwide turmoil has had an enormous effect on the CR generation in terms of their political outlook, experience, activism, national integration, and leadership training. Rosen's book is very useful in providing factual information on Red Guards in middle schools, an area not adequately researched by scholars of Chinese affairs.

John H. Fincher's *Chinese Democracy* examines the development of democracy in China immediately before and after the 1911 revolution that ended the imperial system in China. His main purpose is to demonstrate that China did develop democratic institutions and had some degree of political participation by the people, especially at provincial and local levels between 1905 and 1914. Furthermore, the author attempts to use a comparative perspective to show that in certain aspects China was more democratic than other Asian countries such as Japan and India. Fincher also tries to illustrate that in a historical perspective China did not fare too badly in developing democracy compared to some Western countries during a comparable period of development.

Although the book has not added anything new to our knowledge of China, it provides a detailed account of the development of democratic institutions in China. It emphatically reminds the reader that a democratic experiment did take place in China at the turn of the twentieth century.

Fincher's attempt to examine the Chinese democratic experience in a comparative perspective is very desirable in the study of Chinese politics, but his comparison is rather casual, unsystematic, and superficial. He did not have any conceptual framework concerning the key issues of democratization in traditional societies to compare the Chinese experience with that of some other major countries. Moreover, in his examination of the development of democratic institutions, the author did not pay enough attention to the socioeconomic-cultural dynamic forces in China that created the demand for political participation.

The contribution of Dr. Sun Yat-sen and his revolutionary alliance—the Tongmenghui, organized in 1905—to the 1911 revolution and the democratization of China during this period are not given the kind of recognition they deserve in this book. Although Sun's revolutionary activities did not lead to a mass movement in China during this period, his "Three Principles of the People" developed by 1905, his influence overseas, especially among Chinese students in Japan, and the propaganda work of his followers in China certainly contributed to revolution and democratization in China. The very fact that Sun was elected as the first president of the republic after the revolution of 1911 clearly indicated his prestige and influence among the Chinese people. Yet Sun and his revolutionary alliance were mentioned only very briefly in a few places in this book. This is an unfortunate deficiency.

GEORGE P. JAN

University of Toledo
Ohio

STEVEN E. SANDERSON. *Agrarian Populism and the Mexican State: The Struggle for Land in Sonora.* Pp. xx, 290. Berkeley and Los Angeles: University of California Press, 1981. $22.75.

How was the populist pact formed in Latin America? Why did it break down? Steven Sanderson's revised doctoral thesis (Stanford, 1978) asks these questions, and finds convincing answers from a case study of agrarian reform policy in Sonora, Mexico.

In the first part of his book Sanderson reviews agrarian policies from the liberal midnineteenth century up to the Revolution of 1910. He then contrasts the early postrevolutionary land reforms, which aimed at increasing the number of small property holders, with the policies of President Lázaro Cárdenas after the Depression, which represented the fullest expression of the populist pact. Cárdenas mobilized the rural masses against corrupt politicians and reactionary landholders, and proclaimed the state's responsibility for ameliorating inequities, protecting the underclasses, and arbitrating class conflicts. He coopted peasants and workers into state-linked organizations such as the CNC and the CTM. He also began land distributions in Sonora's fertile river valleys, and extended credit to the peasants' collective ejidos. At the same time Cárdenas enlarged the state's responsibility for promoting capitalism, in the sense of stimulating public finance and investment, and building infrastructure.

The renewed economic crisis of 1938 and capital flight ended the redistributive emphasis of Cardenás's agrarian reform, and substituted production and conservation as new priorities. In the 1940s a "general anti-Communist, antifascist" fervor and close trade ties with the United States turned Cárdenas's successors away from populism, and in the direction of frankly bourgeois policies to change the peasants into proletarians. In Sonora, more heavily mechanized, irrigated private farms dominated production, and the resulting economic miracle ended the government's concern for supporting peasants against large landowners.

But Sonoran peasants did not forget the revolution's promises. They suffered from mechanization and crises in capitalist growth, particularly the inflation and weakened peso of the 1970s, results of the policy of financing import-substituting industrialization through foreign loans and deficit financing, without fiscal reforms to increase taxes. They reacted by invading and claiming lands.

To reduce rural tensions, President Luis Echevarría tried to revive the populist pact, with new agrarian laws favoring small ejidos. Echevarría bought back the ejidos' alienated lands, and stimulated rural education and credit. He also used Cardenás's tactic of pitting peasants against the agricultural bourgeoisie. But in the 1970s the bourgeoisie, backed by the powerful Monterrey industrialists, was too strong, while the peasants, split into various competing organizations, remained heavily dependent upon state recognition and favors. As a result, the peasants' land invasions were violently repressed. When Echeverría bid to regain peasant support by distributing lands and expanding ejidos, his eleventh-hour reforms were largely nullified as soon as he left office.

In a persuasive final chapter Sanderson restates his points as contributions to a theory of Mexican populism. The Mexican state moved from a role as liberal nightwatchman guarding private property, to a populist role of promoting capitalism while arbitrating class differences and claiming to protect the underclasses. But these two roles were ultimately incompatible: capitalism presumes the bourgeois expropriation of the means of production and the values produced by the workers, while social justice demands the more equitable distribution of these means and values. Thus the Mexican state now tends to become "merely the gendarme of the bourgeoisie," and "the agrarian reform as a genuine allocation of national wealth and a call to the masses for allegiance is dead."

One can question what Sanderson means by "genuine." A Marxist alternative, given the author's use of concepts developed by Gramsci, Maurice Dobb, and James O'Connor, and especially his affinities with Roger Bartra, seems implicit. Certainly his well-documented and forceful criticism of agrarian policy since the revolution will help the reader understand contemporary Mexico.

PETER L. EISENBERG

Universidade Estadual de
    Campinas
São Paulo, Brazil

THOMAS C. WRIGHT. *Landowners and Reform in Chile: The Sociedad Nacional de Agricultura, 1919-40.* Pp. xix, 249. Urbana: University of Illinois Press, 1982. $21.00.

This book of 212 text pages consists of an introduction, 8 chapters, 9 pages of appendices, 15 pages of helpful bibliography, and a lengthy index. There are 17 tables and one helpful map. The material is well-documented, with between 60 and 120 notes at the end of each chapter. The detail and laborious documentation perhaps are unmistakable evidences of the work of the trained historian, but the author is a skillful writer with a good eye for facts. Consequently, the book moves along at a fairly lively clip and for the most part avoids being boring.

The first four chapters are devoted to the time between 1869 and World War I. The *Sociedad Nacional de Agricultura* (SNA) was founded in October 1869 "as a voluntary association dedicated to the progress and development of agriculture." It had as its purpose the combatting of outmoded and inefficient practices in agriculture. During the first several decades there were only a few hundred members, nearly all of whom were wealthy owners of very large estates. Chile was almost totally a feudal society until the 1880s, when large-scale nitrate exports began.

It was the crash of the nitrate industry immediately following World War I that constituted the first major crisis for the organization, because agricultural exports also tumbled to pitifully small magnitudes. With surging unemployment and balance of payments crises, a movement got underway in the major cities and even in the countryside to identify causes of the problems and effect corrections.

Chapter 5 is on "The Struggle over Food Price Inflation," which occurred approximately between 1919 to 1940, a time span also included in Chapters 6 and 7, "Landowners and Agrarian Reform," and "Landowners and Rural Labor." During this time, and in the 1930s especially, the oligarchs and their feudalism were revealed to be the great incubus to national progress. They dominated the political and economic life of the country and restrained production increases and progress to match what some othe countries such as Argentina and Uruguay were achieving, and what appeared to be possible. The SNA acquiesced to limited agrarian reforms, and maintained effective domination of national life. But they were branded by much of the organized middle class as decadent, and they could not prevent the rise of multitudes of organized rural labor, which became ever more militant. The organization must be judged as successful in attainment of its announced goals until World War II.

The final chapter contains the material of greatest interest to most readers, "Epilogue: Landowners and Politics, 1941-79." From 1964, with the election of Eduardo Frei, the agrarian reforms moved with an almost inexorable thrust. Frei proved to be too timid, and the 1970 election saw almost all of the left and much of the center rally to Salvador Allende, who promptly set about socializing the Chilean economy. This volume does not attempt an assessment of Allende, but does note that many urban interest groups did not abide socialism. Allende was overthrown with deliberate approval and support of the SNA, which thereby gave up its claim that it supported Chilean Democracy.

FLOYD B. McFARLAND
Oregon State University
Corvallis

EUROPE

TOM GARVIN. *The Evolution of Irish Nationalist Politics.* Pp. xii, 244. New York: Holmes & Meier, 1981. $39.50.

History, even political history, is more than past politics. Utilizing a framework that encompasses social, cultural, geographic, and economic phenomena, the author examines the origins and development of Irish nationalist politics with emphasis on public opinion, political organizations, and governmental institutions. Garvin's chronological canvas extends from eighteenth-century antipathy for the Ascendancy to contemporary party alignments in the Irish Republic. Possessed of a data base as broad as its scope, this volume exploits evidence from sources that range from the oral traditions disseminated by itinerant storytellers to quantitative correlations revealed by computers. Garvin, employing an organizational structure that is both conceptual and chronological, depicts an Irish political history defined by its continuities.

Even a cursory meditation on the Irish past evokes images of turbulence—Defenderism, the rising of 1798, the Ribbon Society, O'Connell and the struggle for Catholic emancipation, the abortive insurrections of 1848 and 1867, Fenianism, Parnell and the Irish National League, Hibernianism, de Valera and the Easter rebellion, the IRA. Strife, however, is not always a harbinger of abrupt transitions. According to Garvin, opposition to British imposition placed most Irish politicians in the same nationalistic continuum, regardless of differences between constitutionalists and revolutionaries. Nationalism emphasized Irish or group freedom. Thus, argues Garvin, aspirations for individual social and economic rights were refracted through the prism of Irish nationalism. Moreover, due to the dominance of Ireland by non-Catholics, no rigid dichotomy emerged between popular religion and nationalism. Despite leadership provided by urban politicians, the Irish countryside rendered nationalism a mass movement. Given the essential conservatism of agrarians and the rural tradition of distrust toward outsiders, Garvin labels Irish nationalism evolutionary. Organizations self-consciously built usable pasts, linking themselves to earlier groups. Ignoring its inheritance from British forms, for example, the Irish Republic proclaims itself heir to a quasi-mythical Gaelic state of antiquity. Since nationalism spawned past agitation, Garvin deems the political stability of the independent republic a natural outgrowth of Irish consciousness prior to the 1920s.

Garvin does not find Ireland's political development unique. Although Irish exceptionalism—early and remarkably enduring colonial rule, ethnic identity defined by religious affiliation, and an unusual physical proximity between the conquered and the empire's nucleus—exists, indigenous coloration ought not to obscure "the system's resemblances to post-colonial systems elsewhere." With a history of cultural suppression and a poverty unknown to other Western European democracies, Garvin's Irish Republic exhibits a political style, based on pragmaticism, consensus, and patriotic symbolism, common to postcolonial states.

In the absence of sustained empirical comparisons between the politics of Ireland and that of emerging Third World nations, Garvin's thesis is more intriguing than persuasive. Nevertheless, Garvin demonstrates that myriad variables complicate Seymour Martin Lipset's correlation between advanced economic development and liberal

democratic government. And adroit analysis illuminates the relevance of the past to Ireland's present and future.

WILLIAM M. SIMONS
State University of New York
Oneonta

WILLIAM M. JOHNSTON. *Vienna Vienna. The Golden Age 1815-1914.* Pp. 332. New York: Clarkson N. Potter, 1981. $30.00.

In recent years the study of Viennese cultural history during the late nineteenth and early twentieth centuries has developed into a growth industry. Given the wide range of important figures still meriting further study, however, few historians have attempted a synthetic analysis of Viennese culture during the last years of the Habsburg monarchy's existence. Among those who have, two are Americans. In 1972 William Johnston of the University of Massachusetts published *The Austrian Mind: An Intellectual and Social History 1848-1938*, in which he devoted particular attention to Viennese thought, and in 1980 Carl Schorske of Princeton published his long-awaited *Fin-de-Siècle Vienna: Politics and Culture*, a collection of seven brilliant essays united by a perceptive introduction and a common interpretive scheme. Precisely because these two books approach a similar topic from differing points of view, both are important contributions. For his part, Schorske has concentrated upon the latter part of the nineteenth century and the innovative response of intellectuals to the failures of Austrian Liberalism associated with the economic crisis of 1873 and the subsequent rise of mass political parties. In contrast, Johnston has studied a broader time period and has stressed continuity between the thought of the early and the late nineteenth century.

Against the background of this scholarly disagreement and of Johnston's critical review of *Fin-de-*

Siècle Vienna in the Spring 1981 issue of *The American Scholar, Vienna Vienna. The Golden Age 1815-1914* is a disappointment. Written for the general reader, the book is lavishly illustrated but adds little to what Johnston has previously written, while it lacks an adequate bibliography and provides no footnotes. Nevertheless, it would be wrong to dismiss the book as one suited only for the coffee table. Professor Johnston has written three lively essays on successive periods of Viennese culture and provided each with an album of fine illustrations. The first essay covers the period from 1815 to 1848 and defines Viennese Biedermeier culture as a middle-class version of the aristocratic baroque. The second begins with a discussion of domestic and external disasters sustained by the Habsburg Monarchy between 1848 and 1890 and continues with a harsh criticism of Viennese architectural historicism. The third concentrates upon those thinkers who between 1890 and 1914 stripped away from art and society the facades that had gratified the previous generation.

Johnston states his major thesis succinctly toward the conclusion of his first essay. "Vienna's Golden Age begins and ends," he maintains, "with a withdrawal from politics into art. In between came a brief two decades of muted confidence in man-made remedies." Unfortunately, the essays are too sketchy to generate confidence in this emphasis upon an essential continuity in Viennese cultural history. Least satisfactory is the opening essay, which many readers will find superficial in its treatment of Biedermeier politics and culture. Better informed is the second essay, although Johnston's gibes at the middle class for espousing historicism, a movement by no means unique to Vienna, will disturb those acquainted with recent interpretations in architectural history. Ironically, the accompanying photographs of exteriors and interiors along the Ringstrasse tends to refute rather than sustain the author's negative assessment of the aesthetic value of the period's architecture. The most rewarding essay is the third, which offers a valuable analysis of Viennese impressionism and an informative discussion of Sigmund Freud's debts to Vienna. Yet even here there are weaknesses. By stressing continuity, Johnston minimizes the similarities between specifically Viennese thought and general intellectual trends after 1890, when disillusionment with the hollow achievements of Liberalism produced creative critiques of bourgeois values throughout Europe. Furthermore, Johnston misses an opportunity to strengthen his thesis of continuity by overlooking the direct influence Biedermeier simplicity exerted upon architects and designers at the end of the century.

It is, of course, easy to find fault with a book that undertakes a formidable assignment. Despite its shortcomings, moreover, *Vienna Vienna* serves the useful purpose of jolting specialists out of complacency. Even when he is least convincing, Johnston stimulates thought; at his best, he offers keen insight. Above all, the illustrations are splendid and will delight the eye of the general reader. Serious students of European intellectual history will necessarily give primary attention to Johnston's *The Austrian Mind* and to Schorske's *Fin-de-Siècle Vienna*, from whose diverging interpretations they will profit. They will also, however, wish to consult *Vienna Vienna*, especially for its reproductions of contemporary paintings, drawings, and lithographs, and for its third essay, before passing the book on to their students for reading, viewing, and debating.

RONALD E. COONS
University of Connecticut
Storrs

MAARTEN ULTEE. *The Abbey of Saint-Germain-des-Prés in the Seventeenth Century.* Pp. ix, 210. New Haven: Yale University Press, $20.00.

The abbey of Saint-Germain-des-Près was not only Paris's oldest monastery in the seventeenth century, it was also one of France's wealthiest. Furthermore, it was an important seat of Benedictine scholarship and a vital member of the Parisian community. For these reasons and many others, it makes an admirable subject for historical inquiry, particularly considering the staggering wealth of its archival remains.

Professor Ultee's concern is clear: "Without losing sight of the strong religious fervor of the Maurists [who reformed Saint-Germain in 1631], we strive for an understanding of the abbey within a social and economic context." That concern, though, is vast, and in the absence of a strong argument to structure the evidence and bind the work together, the volume reads as a collection of nearly independent essays. Professor Ultee moves through studies of the abbey's life and concerns in the seventeenth century, the demography of the Congrégation de Saint-Maur, the abbey's revenues and expenditures, the journal of the monk Claude Coton, the ways in which Saint-Germain sought to separate itself from the world, and its roles within the city of Paris; he provides some comparative evidence along the way.

Some of the chapters are quite good. The chapter on the abbey's revenues is particularly strong, showing the intelligence with which the monks not only overcame momentary crises but also increased their revenues through the century. The chapter, "Closed Community," is wide-reaching and imaginative and goes well with that on the abbey's finally unsuccessful struggle to maintain temporal and spiritual jurisdictions independent of the Châtalet and the archbishop of Paris.

Much in the volume begs for development into unifying arguments. For instance, although Professor Ultee traces the difficulties attendant upon the reformation of the abbey by the Congrégation de Saint-Maur, speaks of the amount of internal dissent at Saint-Germain, discusses the monks who escaped, describes the strong Jansenist undercurrents at the abbey, refers to the abbots' connections at court, provides us with the names of many of the abbey's creditors (largely from the class of royal officials), locates the social origins of many of the monks (often in the families of royal officials), and returns regularly to the monastery's battles with rival jurisdictions, he does so only at widely separated points; he does not consider or explore possible connections among this tantalizing collection of subjects. Professor Ultee's work is, one hopes, one of many yet to come that will exploit the great richness and variety of evidence on Saint-Germain.

WILLIAM A. WEARY
Abington Friends School
Jenkintown
Pennsylvania

UNITED STATES

RONALD H. BAYOR, ed. *Neighborhoods in Urban America.* Pp. ix, 238. Port Washington, NY: Kennikat, 1982, $27.50.

This anthology, with one exception, is composed of reprinted articles. The single original article—"The Neighborhood Invasion Pattern"—was written by the editor who explained in the preface that the absence of a collection of readings on neighborhoods was the reason for this volume.

Chapters are devoted to the neighborhood and the city, neighborhood groups, government and neighborhoods, neighborhood cycles, and neighborhood renewal and rehabilitation. Articles either deal with the subject in general or are case studies, such as Black Rock in Buffalo or the Tremont Street district in Boston. The articles are multidisciplinary, drawing upon works by geographers, political scientists, sociologists, and historians. The historical articles are particularly useful in providing a framework in which to view current neighborhood conditions, but the reader is provided with little assistance in understanding the current process of change in urban neighborhoods.

This collection suffers from the disparate nature of the articles and the lack of good introductory essays integrating the articles. As an anthology of reprints, one does not find in the collection the results of the latest research on neighborhoods.

To sum up, *Neighborhoods in Urban America* contains several good articles and is useful primarily as a set of supplemental readings in academic courses that place some emphasis upon neighborhoods.

JOSEPH F. ZIMMERMAN
State University of New York
Albany

DAVID J. BELLIS. *Heroin and Politicians: The Failure of Public Policy to Control Addiction in America.* Pp. xx, 239. Westport, CT: Greenwood, 1981. $27.50.

David Bellis has been around. He has used heroin and methadone, has worked with over 2000 heroin addicts, has been a consultant to drug treatment programs, has been a faculty member at two universities, and is currently a city councilman. This considerable experience from different vantage points plus Bellis's persuasive style make *Heroin and Politicians* a credible polemic against current heroin treatment and law enforcement policies.

The work is divided into two major parts. Part I covers the history of governmental attempts to control heroin use, emphasizing the war on heroin during the Nixon administration, and the physiology and politics of methadone maintenance. Part II is a detailed review of the research on the results of the major treatment modalities: methadone maintenance, detoxification and counseling, residential programs, and therapeutic communities. The last two chapters review the vested interests involved in the drug-abuse industrial complex and spin out a scenario of the future of heroin and other addictions in the next hundred years.

The hitch is that the book is a polemic; it was apparently written to advance the beliefs that treatment of heroin addicts is bound to fail, regardless of the treatment method, as are attempts to eliminate the traffic in heroin. The huge treatment and legal structures whose manifest purpose is to eliminate heroin use exist only to employ and provide profit for the entrepreneurs of the drug-abuse industrial complex.

The book is challenging because it presents far more than rhetoric. The arguments are heavily and appropriately documented with references to scientific studies. The irritating quality of the work is that, in his desire to draw a particular conclusion, the author goes beyond the data he presents. A few examples will illustrate this point.

Bellis correctly deplores the absence of control studies comparing the effects of different treatment modalities with one another and with no treatment at all, but frequently implies that particular treatment programs have unacceptably low success rates without reference to either the outcomes of competitive modalities or to any cost/benefit analysis. The absence of a standard of success on any of the criteria employed to evaluate treatment programs, makes the statements regarding success or failure read more like rhetoric than scientifically derived conclusions.

Most of the clients of methadone maintenance programs are poor, poorly educated, and unskilled. The finding that heroin addicts transferred from heroin to methadone do have poor job histories after the transfer should not be surprising. An expectation that methadone would, by itself or with a little counseling, turn such a population into educated, skilled, experienced, and ambitious citizens is preposterous, yet that is the apparent standard of success Bellis wishes to impose on the employment outcomes of methadone programs.

The bias against methadone maintenance is further illustrated by the discussion regarding the impact on criminality among heroin addicts transferred to methadone. He cites no data on the impact of methadone maintenance on crime patterns of heroin users who began or increased their criminal activity after they became users, principally to support their habit; yet he concludes that "criminality is not significantly affected by oral methadone maintenance." He discounts the evidence on the undifferentiated majority of transferees showing that arrest rates after entry into methadone maintenance are lower than arrest rates before entry. Methadone should be evaluated solely on its capacity to safely and effectively wean people from heroin addiction, and its capacity to render people who committed crimes to support their addiction available for legitimate activities, not on the unreasonable expectation that it will change people's personalities, social skills, or economic status.

Bellis's review of the evidence on the safety and effectiveness of methadone maintenance is informative and troubling because it presents conflicting reports, some of which claim serious side effects of methadone. The important question of whether methadone is more or less harmful than heroin is not answered with hard evidence. The alternative treatment methods—counseling, residential programs, and therapeutic communities—are readily discredited by the consistent findings that they have negligible long-term benefits of any sort and are prohibitively expensive. The informally acquired knowledge among program directors of this pattern of outcomes has resulted, understandably, in little enthusiasm for objective evaluation and few reliable studies of these kinds of programs.

The chapter on the drug-abuse industrial complex raises the question of why so much money is spent in patently unsuccessful efforts to cure heroin addicts and suppress the heroin traffic. The answer offered is that these attempts are not intended to accomplish their manifest purposes because success would destroy an industry upon which too many drug manufacturers,

treatment specialists, and law enforcers depend for their livelihood. The argument is clearly and compellingly presented, though perhaps more emphasis than necessary is given to corruption within the industry. The success of current treatment and law enforcement efforts would not be substantially improved even if all participants were scrupulously honest, were treatment and law enforcement strategies to remain unchanged.

Heroin and Politicians is interesting and important reading and a good place to start for anyone who wants to learn why government action and medical treatment have failed to eliminate heroin use.

JOSEPH E. JACOBY
Bowling Green State University
Ohio

THOMAS E. CRONIN, TANIA Z. CRONIN, and MICHAEL E. MILAKOVICH. *U.S. v. Crime in the Streets.* Pp. x, 212. Bloomington: Indiana University Press, 1981. $17.50.

In 1968, in response to spiraling crime rates and citizen fears about crime, Congress passed the Omnibus Crime Control and Safe Streets Act. The Safe Streets Act created the Law Enforcement Assistance Administration (LEAA) and earmarked large amounts of federal funds in an all-out war against crime. Twelve years and some $8 billion later, crime rates are still increasing, and LEAA is a recognized failure. Why LEAA failed is the topic of Cronin, Cronin, and Milakovich's informative book, *U.S. v. Crime in the Streets.* Drawing on detailed interviews from congressional aides, justice department workers, and recipients of LEAA funds, the authors give an excellent history and analysis of the politics of the national war on crime from the 1960s to the 1980s.

As the authors show, although the Safe Streets Act was intended by Lyndon Johnson to be a progressive piece of social engineering, it emerged from Congress in a virtually unrecognizable form. Much to their credit, the authors build a rich history of the political context of the modification of the Safe Streets Act: escalating crime rates, civil rights and Viet Nam protests, and the growing strength of the right wing of the Republican party. They show how Johnson was under strong political pressure to do something about the growing crime problem, and how a conservative congressional coalition of Republicans and Southern Democrats used the Safe Streets Act to limit the power of the attorney general, strengthen the police, and funnel anticrime funds directly to the states.

A large part of the book is devoted to a detailed analysis of what LEAA was intended to do and what it did. Cronin, Cronin, and Milakovich are blunt in their criticism of LEAA. Indeed, the authors conclude that "mostly what we have learned through the LEAA experiment is what doesn't work." They are careful in their criticism, however, explicitly outlining LEAA's history of mismanagement, neglect, and fiscal abuse. The reasons the authors give us for the failure of LEAA are convincing. One of the primary difficulties LEAA had was that there was very little supervision of the spending of funds. Although the Johnson Administration wanted a strong federal-state alliance on combatting crime, the final bill allowed for the dispensing of anticrime monies through almost unsupervised block grants to the states. It was intended that each state present a master criminal justice plan to LEAA for review and eventual funding. What happened, however, was that, in the first few years of its existence, LEAA was under pressure to dispense grant monies quickly, and was less concerned with ascertaining how and on what the money was being spent. As a result, although of poor quality, very few state plans were modified and none was outright rejected. LEAA administrators were of little help to states in providing planning guidelines or standards. This problem, in turn, reflected a larger difficulty within LEAA itself, a failure of leadership. LEAA was crippled at the outset by the administrative troika specified by the original Safe Streets Act. Even when the troika was abandoned in favor of one administrator, some presidents left the position vacant for long periods of time, creating a leadership vacuum. An additional difficulty was that the philosophy of the chief administrator fluctuated from one favoring accountability and evaluation of programs to one favoring demonstrated evidence of crime reduction to another who perceived the agency's main goal as one of giving money and not interfering in state and local criminal justice affairs. As a result, LEAA had no coherent principle guiding its operation.

In sum, what Cronin, Cronin, and Milakovich give us in their book is a lesson in the political manipulation of the crime issue, the limits of federal intervention in state and local criminal justice institutions and the mismanagement of LEAA. The book is well written and well documented. In reading this excellent history one cannot help but get a sense of frustration and irritation at the chicanery of politicians in using the fear of crime for political purposes, and the greed and ineptitude of LEAA grant recipients. Just as exposes of the Viet Nam War may prevent another foreign policy blunder, the authors will have written an important book if we may learn and grow from our experiences with the other war we lost.

RAY PATERNOSTER
University of South Carolina
Columbia

PAUL R. DOMMEL and Associates. *Decentralizing Urban Policy: Case Studies in Community Development.* Pp. xi, 271. Washington, DC: Brookings Institution, 1982. $24.95; Paperbound, $9.95.

Enthusiasm for decentralizing federal assistance to cities has steadily grown since it started under President Nixon's proposal for a new federalism. On the assumption that local communities know best how to deal with their problems, the new federalism promised to revitalize local government and wean federal officialdom from excessive involvement in local affairs. This was to be spearheaded by shifting federal assistance from categorical grants-in-aid for specific purposes to more widespread use of block grants allowing localities greater discretion over the use of federal funds. Several programs enacted during the 1970s put this idea into practice and President Reagan has committed his administration to extending the decentralization of federal aid to cities.

In *Decentralizing Urban Policy* a group of scholars led by Paul R. Dommel at the Brookings Institution provide a very balanced assessment of one of the major new federalism initiatives—the 1974 Community Development Block Grant (CDBG) program—and, in this reviewer's view, raise serious questions about the wisdom of such reforms. CDBG consolidated a number of separate categorical programs of the Department of Housing and Urban Development (HUD) into a single program that distributes grants on a formula basis to entitlement localities; this consolidation includes urban renewal, model cities, the neighborhood development program, water and sewer projects, and other categorical programs related to community development. At the request of HUD, the authors examined the impact of this programmatic shift through a network of field researchers in 61 communities across the nation; they combined these findings with case studies of five communities, including Phoenix, Houston, Chicago, Allegheny County, Pennsylvania, and CArbondale, Illinois, during the first few years of the block grant program.

This volume focuses on the case studies which report how the various localities shifted to the more flexible block grant program, detailing changes and continuities in the federal presence, local decision making, and community participation, as well as an assessment of the substantive policy outcomes, particularly alterations in the distribution of resources to competing social groups and programs. All this is evaluated in the light of the changing national politics of CDBG from its inception to 1981.

Employing a common framework, most of the case studies provide a rich body of evidence that is nicely summarized in one of the concluding chapters assessing the lessons of CDBG. In general, the authors find that this program evoked more common patterns of local response than diverse outcomes resulting from the peculiarities of local politics. As intended by its supporters, CDBG did result in a vastly diminished federal role in guiding community development, particularly under Republican administrations seeking to restrain HUD's supervisory function. Further, the influence of general local governmental institutions was enhanced by this program, which bypassed local agencies created under earlier categorical programs and had become important rival sources of political power.

Nevertheless, this pattern of revitalization often came at significant cost to the disadvantaged groups who had been major beneficiaries of federal assistance under the old categorical arrangements. Their power was diluted as the more open-ended federal initiative created an enlarged local bargaining arena with widespread competition among varied community interests, including better-off neighborhood groups. Most important, CDBG demonstrated a tendency for cities to shift federal assistance away from programs targeted at the poor to more general community conservation measures that could be expected to be far less redistributive in their impact on the community.

While these and other themes are carefully reported in this book, they are often obscured by the authors' apparent reluctance to probe the larger social and political implications of their analysis.

In particular, they fail to connect the CDBG experience to the way America's federal system works to promote the interests of particular groups. Like many other studies of CDBG, the evidence reveals that the bias of local politics often discourages efforts at redistribution in preference to programs to enhance the city's economic base. Cities must compete with other cities in the struggle for growth. In contrast, federal officials are often less sensitive to these concerns and are more permissive of measures to target resources to the disadvantaged, a fact born out by the national debate over CDBG in past administrations. This book should be about federalism and the way it works, not just about grants-in-aid, in order to assess the meaning of CDBG. Nevertheless, those interested in the future of our governmental system will find this an insightful description of an important program.

PAUL KANTOR

Fordham University
Bronx
New York

DWIGHT L. FRANKFATHER, MICHAEL J. SMITH, and FRANCIS G. CARO. *Family Care of the Elderly: Public Initiatives and Private Obligations.* Pp. xvii, 123. Lexington, MA: D. C. Heath, 1981. $17.95.

Senator Birch Bayh once observed that government has not been able to fashion a substitute for the family. If government efforts have failed, so have private initiatives. This is not to say that hospitals, nursing homes, day care centers, and a variety of other institutional arrangements for the care of disabled elderly Americans do not have their place. Obviously, they do. But public policy probably has called upon institutionalization too often; roughly 90 percent of public support for chronically disabled elderly men and women in America pays for the purchase of institutional care.

Family Care of the Elderly provides a description of the Family Support Program, a research and service demonstration project conducted by the Community Service Society of New York from October 1976 through September 1979. The Family Support Program sought to examine policy issues in a two-tier entitlement strategy to serve the disabled elderly at home. One tier involved public assumption of full responsibility for the care of disabled elderly persons who had no families. The other tier involved disabled elderly persons with families, using publicly financed services that complement family efforts. The FSP served 96 families for at least six months and served 48 families for at least two years.

Family care of the disabled elderly is often accomplished by families only with considerable financial, emotional, and physical stress. Job interruptions, lost sleep, restricted freedom, and heavy demands on one's time can impose great stress on family members as they provide needed care. Services provided by family members range from food preparation and shopping, bathing and grooming, making trips to the welfare office, doing a disabled person's taxes, balancing a checkbook and paying bills, shoveling snow from a sidewalk, appliance and home repairs, and catering to idiosyncratic preferences and whims. Disagreements can often arise among family members on arrangements for care and division of responsibility. In all, family members in the program displayed remarkable persistence in caring for a disabled family member, and the withdrawal of family support that might be feared when public services are provided to supplement family efforts did not materialize.

In addition to providing an account of the Family Support Program, *Family Care of the Elderly* analyzes issues involved in home care for the disabled elderly, and provides recommendations for public long-term care policy. While it seems evident that there clearly is a strong case to be made for increased public support for home care for the disabled elderly, it also is clear that many issues have yet to be resolved, and that any move toward increased public support for such care will be implemented only incrementally. *Family Care of the Elderly* is a clear-eyed description and examination of the benefits, problems, issues, and possible directions needed for home care of America's disabled elderly persons. It provides a masterful balance of social work's zeal to provide help where it is needed, with the policy researcher's recognition of political, social, financial, and administrative realities.

GEORGE R. SHARWELL

University of South Carolina
Columbia

WALTER J. FRASER, Jr., and WINFRED B. MOORE, Jr., eds. *From the Old South to the New: Essays on the Transitional South.* Pp. xiii, 286. Westport, CT: Greenwood, 1981. $35.00.

This stimulating collection of essays grew out of the 1978 and 1979 Citadel Conferences on the South. Divided into eight sections, it touches on race relations, elites, urban structure, law and disorder, southern mythology, and reform. The period covered is equally broad: from the antebellum years through the 1960s. Given its thematic and temporal range, the volume is somewhat lacking in cohesiveness. But editors Walter Fraser and Winfred Moore manage to keep a few unifying threads in the reader's mind through their brief but intelligent section introductions. Similarly, the disturbing mixture of formal and informal styles, characteristic of books comprised of oral presentations, is offset by the uniformly high quality of the writing.

Some of these essays are clearly important, most are at least informative. Perhaps the most noteworthy is David Donald's article suggesting that the imposition of Jim Crow laws in the 1890s stemmed less from heightened concern over black assertiveness than from the compulsive desire of the aging Civil War generation to bequeath to its descendants a racially well-ordered society. Based loosely on generational theory, Donald's thesis is merely sketched in this paper. But it is an intriguing one, sure to fuel future debate.

On the issue of continuity and change—a central theme in this book—separate essays by William Barney, John Radford, and Don Doyle effectively highlight the way in which both rural and urban southern elites rejected economic innovation as too disruptive and too Yankee. On the other hand, David Carlton's essay on the growth of the South Carolina textile industry indicates that in some areas, at least, power did pass to new, commercially oriented leaders. Dan Carter's witty overview of continuity and change in the New South critiques all those who have attempted to generalize on this fundamental question, indicating that there is still room for further study.

Other cautions against overgeneralization are sounded as well. David Bodenhammer, for example, argues against a monolithic image of southern violence by pointing out significant differences in the nature and frequency of antebellum crime within urban and rural areas. Yet James Burran, who analyzes urban race riots during World War II, finds the southern pattern consistent and distinctive. There, disturbances were almost always begun by whites protesting against perceived black advancement, while disturbances in the north were generally a product of black frustration.

Most of the essays in this book, including Burran's, suffer from brevity. Averaging under fifteen pages of text apiece, few of these papers leave the reader truly convinced by the author's argument. The editors would have been better off eliminating some of the weaker sections and encouraging the remaining writers to elaborate on their ideas and to present more supporting evidence. Likewise, a strong concluding essay or epilogue would have helped to pull the volume together. Nevertheless,

From the Old South to the New is an attractive and informative book, clearly testifying to the creative work being done on this topic.

LAURA L. BECKER

Clemson University
South Carolina

DAVID HAMLIN. *The Nazi/Skokie Conflict: A Civil Liberties Battle.* Pp. 184. Boston: Beacon, 1981. $12.95.

David Hamlin, former executive director of the Illinois American Civil Liberties Union, has written more than a book detailing his side of the controversy surrounding Frank Collin's attempt to stage a rally in Skokie, Illinois. He has also written a passionate defense of a virtually absolutist interpretation of the First Amendment. He tells this story with restraint so that the larger moral and political issues clearly occupy the center of our attention. Only the logic of his central position fails to compel.

Collin headed the National Socialist Party of America, a Chicago-based neo-Nazi organization dedicated to the establishment of a master race. Collin wrote to the nearby village of Skokie, home of a large community of holocaust survivors, to declare that he and 250 followers would stage a demonstration on Sunday, 1 May 1977, in uniform, with swastikas. When the survivors learned of Collin's intention, individual members swore that they would not allow any form of Nazism to raise a voice under any circumstances whatsoever. They cried, "Never again!" The village council replied to the threat of public disruption with a series of restrictive ordinances.

Collin called upon the American Civil Liberties Union for legal assistance. In justifying the decision to defend Collin, Hamlin tells the story of the falling away of a large part of the ACLU's membership, of conflicts within the ACLU's offices, of the anguish of the survivors, of differences between the Anti-Defamation League and other Jewish establishment groups.

The ACLU considered this to be a "classic First Amendment case" that "tested the very foundations of Democracy." The effort of the village of Skokie to enjoin speech before it had occurred, they maintained, whatever one felt about the content of the speech, "violates the very essence of the amendment." Hamlin argued that "every citizen has the absolute right to disagree with the actions of government and every citizen has the right, within legal limits, to make that disagreement public." The ACLU had to act to prevent the village from engaging in a form of prior restraint that was "pure political censorship."

Publicity about the march galvanized the community and brought the involvement of people from outside the village who promised to physically prevent a demonstration. Hamlin argues that it was the Skokie council's theory that the demonstration could be legally prevented "because the audience—not Frank Collin—might break the law." This "primary line of defense" lay with the theory known as the heckler's veto: though there was nothing illegal in Collin's proposed demonstration, the law would nevertheless be broken by the audience, and therefore the audience's reaction to the speaker could be grounds for censoring the speaker.

At the hearings, Hamlin rejected as irrelevant testimony the high emotion and fear that gripped a substantial portion of the community: "At the very heart of Skokie's argument lay an obvious, but ultimately useless fact: the residents of the village of Skokie lay especially vulnerable to the hatred which Collin fused." Above all, Hamlin takes care to demonstrate that the personal views of Collin, and the political contents of his speech, were irrelevant. Neither Skokie nor anyone else could put ideas on trial. Courts simply were not allowed to stop speech before it takes place. By far the most frequently used argument against permitting the neo-Nazis to demonstrate was based on the doctrine of falsely shouting "fire!" in a crowded theater. Hamlin argued that "fire" is a "*post*-speech doctrine, one intended not for prior restraint but for after-the-fact law." To shout fire is prohibited, for the shout invokes censorship of the other point of view: "Wait! There is no fire." Since, Hamlin argues, in Skokie ample opportunity existed for the presentation of the other point of view, there was no justification for prior restraint.

Yet opponents of the march feared not what Collin would do that afternoon in Skokie but rather the potential of his ideas and of his movement. They pointed out that the Nazis began small but grew quickly. Toleration by the authorities, they argued, expressed by their permission of the demonstration would aid in the legitimation and spread of the movement. This would be the real message that would cause surprise and panic, the endorsement of the cry of fire. This toleration by the government might well then panic a captive audience of the citizenry. Toleration of Nazi rights by the government increases the possibility that the error of the Nazi position might not be corrected, for more is involved than simply the expression of a second point of view. To think that ideas are valued because of their intrinsic truth is naive. Good citizens seek signs of public or governmental approval. Ideas spread because people believe them to be authoritative or legitimate.

In his virtually absolute defense of the First Amendment Hamlin argues that "no speech ever broke a bone . . . the mere . . . uttering of an idea without action is not a crime." This again raises the classic question of whether ideas ever lead to action, and whether Hamlin can maintain his position because he feels that ideas are harmless.

Not everybody will agree that freedom of speech is the highest good. Freedom of minorities from persecution, security of life, freedom from torture, imprisonment, and harassment are greater personal and social objectives. Ordinarily, freedom of speech and other First Amendment freedoms are essential to these ends. Ordinarily, when these highly desirable objectives conflict, we weigh and measure and balance one off against the other. Thus it does make sense for a civil liberties organization to work for one who would eradicate them. Because it is difficult to revoke Collin's right to speak without revoking the rights of others as well, the ACLU was probably correct to defend Collin. The greatest protection for minorities undoubtedly does come from general principles that can be supported by the majority, or in the pluralistic conception by a majority of minorities. In contemporary America the judicial decisions that protect the neo-Nazi right to march in Skokie undoubtedly offer the best protection to the survivors and other Jews who threatened to break the law because of their perception of an external menace.

These arguments, however, do not rest upon a belief in the absolute sanctity of freedom of speech but upon a complicated social calculus. Despite his apparent commitment to abstract principles, Hamlin's position is also embodied in a calculus of social assumptions. The three elements of that calculus are (1) his faith in American democracy, (2) his perception that the greatest danger to democracy came from the entrenched politicians of Chicago's establishment; and (3) his judgment that Frank Collin was a pathetic man and that his organization did not endanger anybody.

Hamlin's profession of faith in American democracy while admirable is not the only answer. "It can happen here," the survivors charged. Hamlin declares, "I insist that we are, as a people, far too wise to accept what Frank Collin offers."

Hamlin does not offer his beliefs abstractly. He embeds them in a practical assessment of the nature of the neo-Nazi menace. The book does not start with a general defense of civil liberties. The book begins by informing us that the image of Collin as a charismatic dynamo is an illusion, that Collin is a "hopeless leader with a helpless cause." Hamlin ends his book with the information that Frank Collin—whose FBI records disclose as Jewish, whose real name is Frank Cohn, and who is the son of a survivor of the Nazi holocaust—ended by being arrested in 1980 and sentenced to seven years in jail for "taking indecent liberties with underage boys." The real enemy, according to Hamlin, lay in the city of Chicago's political machine, which "has always understood once the Nazis are free to communicate, the Republicans will probably try it too."

Hamlin undoubtedly had a better grasp of the social realities than did those who tried to stop the Nazi demonstration. And yet at the end of the book, when Hamlin recounts their elation at the court victory that ordered the Collin demonstrated to be allowed to proceed, he relates his sense that the "principles at stake in the legal controversy, which we had fought so hard to protect, could all too easily explode if Collin actually demonstrated and anything—anything at all went wrong . . . if that happened, the precious victories that the First Amendment had finally enjoyed would not mean a damn thing, for all of Skokie's fears would be realized and the law would turn to mush."

Idealism should be made of sterner stuff.

IRVING LEONARD MARKOVITZ
Queens College
Flushing
New York

BERNARD JOHNPOLL and LILLIAN JOHNPOLL. *The Impossible Dream: The Rise and Demise of the American Left.* Pp. xi, 373. Westport, CT: Greenwood, 1981. $29.95.

For more than 150 years a varied and vocal array of radical leftists have assailed almost every aspect of American society. And for more than 150 years they have been ignored by many of the very people they have attempted to reach. But their revolutionary crusades have not been wholly in vain; many of the political and social reforms enacted since the 1820s have stemmed from American leftist agitation. For the first time the entire historical panorama of significant American leftist leaders, movements, and ideologies is presented in one objective, nonpolemical, and truly fascinating book.

The Impossible Dream begins with the seventeenth-century radical Mennonite John Plockhoy, and ends in the excesses of the New Left. It focuses on the era between 1820 and 1920, when the foundation of American radicalism was really formed and the movements were the most influential. This volume introduces readers to such groups as the Owenites, the Individualists, the Workies, the Perfectionists, and the Wobblies, and to leaders and theorists from Burnette G. Haskell and Edward Bellamy to Johann Most and Daniel De Leon. Powerful political movements such as the Populists, Socialists, and Communists are described, as are smaller radical groups like the German 48ers. In each case the ideological basis for a movement or group is discussed, as well as the practical effects of its political efforts.

The American labor movement of the early nineteenth century was more involved in political than economic activity. Occasional strikes were held and a few contracts were negotiated, but the chief interest of organized workingmen was the election of prolabor men to legislatures and the furtherance and support of communistic and socialistic enterprises of a Utopian character.

The primary aim of Fourierism was a more efficient capitalist society; its chief purpose was to avoid working-class revolution. It was essentially an interlude in American history that emphasized the inability of intellectuals to comprehend the needs and aspirations of the working class. It was only after the Civil War had ended and America again faced the primary issue of industrial labor versus capital that the radical left revived.

Revolutionists in the United States have historically allowed their emotions to dominate their reason to the detriment of the revolution they purported to favor. The Socialist Labor Party, unable to attract the support of native-born Americans, remained through the 1880s an insignificant, impotent, and alien organization. All of its efforts aimed at winning support from the broad masses of American labor had failed miserably.

The nationalist movement was a major factor in the early years of the populist movement which swept the country in the early 1890s. Religion played a key role in the development of the American left: the roots of the earliest socialist and anarchist movements were to be found in the radical utterances of the Old Testament prophets and the social teaching of Jesus. With the rise of industrial America, especially between 1870 and 1940, an increasing number of clergymen turned to socialism as the answer to the social problems of the times.

The socialist trade and labor alliance remained a small organization of De Leonites until 1906, when it was, for a short time, amalgamated into the Industrial Workers of the World.

The New Left, the radical movement that dominated the 1960s, was a short-lived phenomenon lasting only five years. The rhetoric of the New Left was a compound of Lenin, Trotsky, Stalin, Mao, and Marcuse. Nowhere was socialism a reality in 1906, nowhere is socialism a reality in 1982, and on the basis of empirical historical evidence, it seems irrefutable that nowhere will socialism be a reality in the year 2056.

Remarkable for its objectivity, *The Impossible Dream* is also uniquely authoritative. It is the first history of the American left based almost exclusively on original sources. The authors examined manuscripts, letters, minutes of meetings, radical journals, newspapers, and pamphlets to create a truly accurate portrait of radical movements and leaders. *The Impossible Dream* is a seminal contribution to

American political history and vital reading for teachers, scholars, and students interested in the growth of American politics.

CLAUDE M. URY
Kansas State University
Manhattan

P. M. KAMATH. *Executive Privilege versus Democratic Accountability: The Special Assistant to the President for National Security Affairs, 1961-1969.* Pp. xvi, 362. Atlantic Highlands, NJ: Humanities Press, 1982. $30.75.

In many ways *Executive Privilege versus Democratic Accountability* is a maddeningly frustrating effort, leading the reader down many paths, each of which turns out to be unpromising. First, the title misleads. This is not a book about executive privilege and democratic accountability. It is largely composed of institutional and historical description plus familiar case studies of the Bay of Pigs-Cuban Missile Crisis-Tonkin Gulf-Vietnam events. The technical, legal, constitutional, and ideological emanations of executive privilege are really only dealt with in the short, penultimate chapter of the 300-plus-page study. In principle, titles aside, this is not a bad choice of priorities. But what of the book it really is?

At the most ambitious and interesting level, the book purports to analyze the evolution of the position of the presidential Special Assistant for National Security Affairs as a major force in foreign policy decision making. The method is to concentrate on the aforementioned crisis cases in which Bundy and Rostow played undeniably large roles. The book does not—perhaps cannot—increase our perception of the relative extent of impact vis à vis the other actors involved. The major conclusion that the National Security Council (NSC) staff system "came to acquire the essence [whatever that means] of the decision making in the crucial crises" is simply not supported by the preceding reports of events. Kamath's more general observation that the Bundy-Rostow stewardships probably prepared the way for the Kissinger coup is well taken. Indeed the needed investigation will address the Kissinger mode of dominance in routine foreign policy planning and choice making. This book, though published in 1982, does not peek at events much after the early 1970s.

One must note, however, that though the subject is rather constrained by the narrow focus, within that focus the homework was done. In fact there is a mountain of labor here. Apparently every case study, commentary, significant journal article, historical analysis, or document relevant to these events is consulted and cited. Above and beyond, presidential library archives, White House files, oral histories, and other primary sources are reported. Regrettably, all of this industry does not pay off sufficiently for two major reasons. First, it does not seem to add much, even by nuance, to our prior understanding of the events or personalities (which may not be the author's fault). Second, however, there is an indiscriminate tendency to weigh each piece of evidence equally. Thus a summary statement drawn from a doctoral dissertation equals a presidential journal entry equals a popular journalistic opinion. Standards of analysis and interpretation are unclear. In the end the trees of recounted detail seem to overwhelm the forest of broader meaning and interpretation.

A final uncharitable note should be made of the unforgivably bad editing—spelling, syntax, grammar, typographical errors, and the like—which is evident on most pages of a book priced by no means cheaply.

CHARLES E. JACOB

Rutgers University
New Brunswick
New Jersey

HANS H. LANDSBERG and JOSEPH M. DUKERT. *High Energy Costs: Uneven, Unfair, Unavoidable?* Pp. xiii, 104. Baltimore: Johns Hopkins University Press, 1981. $12.50; Paperbound, $4.95.

High Energy Costs is a very readable and incisive summary of a Resources for the Future-Brookings Institution conference on energy and equity held in 1980. Readers will be impressed with the rigor and scholarship displayed by the authors—drawing upon the contributions of conference participants—an admirable characteristic of virtually all Resources for the Future publications.

Most of the book is devoted to carefully identifying the impact of rising energy prices upon the poor. Attention is devoted to measuring the impact of both direct and indirect energy expenditures upon those at varying economic levels. The finding that the poor spend proportionately more of their income on energy than the middle class or rich is not new or novel, but the extent to which the authors are able to quantify the energy expenditure-income relationship is a significant contribution to the literature. Based upon the best data available, the authors conclude that as a national average, the poorest U.S. families in 1979 were required to spend nearly half of their reported income to pay for the direct and indirect costs of energy. They also demonstrate that national averages conceal substantial regional price variations. Residential energy expenditures in the Northeast, for example, are nearly twice as high as those in the West. Considerable attention is devoted to carefully detailing the limitations of the data, and in explaining the ambiguities attendant the subject (e.g., defining "the poor"). In fact, the book's strongest recommendation is for better data and a clearer conceptual underpinning.

This book will not appeal to everyone since it is an inordinately dispassionate treatment of a highly controversial and emotional issue. The authors come down on the side of removing all price controls on energy, while advocating compensation (primarily cash) to those most seriously affected by rising energy prices. While this recommendation satisfies energy economists, it often suffers in implementation. Aside from the inefficiencies and inequities in government welfare programs, the commitment to reimburse the poor sometimes gets lost. Congress, for example, in 1980 passed a nonbinding resolution proposing that 25 percent of the net proceeds from the Windfall Profits Tax be reserved for low-income energy assistance; yet tax receipts targeted for this purpose have fallen far short of this goal. The authors are cognizant of the pitfalls and difficulties associated with all forms of low-income energy assistance, but offer little insight into possible new approaches. They claim there is "reason for concern" if low-income energy assistance is turned over to the states through a block grant—a Reagan Administration proposal. Despite prescriptive shortcomings, this is an excellent basic summary of impacts and issues.

JACK N. BARKENBUS
Oak Ridge Associated Universities
Tennessee

PAUL C. LIGHT. *The President's Agenda: Domestic Policy Choices from Kennedy to Carter.* Pp. ix, 246. Baltimore: Johns Hopkins University Press, 1981. $17.95.

The literature on the presidency over the past decade has reflected an important change in the American political process and that institution. Whereas previously the growth and extension of presidential power was almost a foregone conclusion, duly noted and analyzed, the years since Nixon have provided considerable evidence that the president is increasingly limited in the scope and penetration of his power, a development carefully examined in recent studies. This slim but pithy book is an admirable contribution to this literature and provides a perspective on how issues, alternatives, and priorities are dealt with in White House decision making.

On the basis of data gathered in interviews with 126 former White House staff members and information collected from OMB legislative clearance records, Light analyzes the process of domestic policy formulation and implementation from 1961 to 1980, and offers some tentative comments on the initial months of the Reagan Administration. Central in his argument is the contention that the presidency is quantitatively different today from that of a generation ago.

The result, concludes Light, is the No Win Presidency, wherein "presidents are caught in a stream of cross pressures," and forced to balance the early years of their tenure when they tend to be more influential against the final years of their term when influence wanes but effectiveness rises. This has meant, in the author's view, that presidents have a difficult time determining whether to act quickly when they have the influence or wait a bit until they have the effectiveness, while throughout casting a wary eye toward reelection. The net result, Light argues, has been no win on both counts, further circumscribing both presidential power and effectiveness.

The causes for this diminution are several: more competition from Congress; increased complexity of policy-making at the federal level; the declining influence of the office itself; the increased scrutiny and surveillance of executive activities by the Congress; and most importantly, the changed nature of the issues the institution must deal with, which are now essentially constituentless. In short, Light's case is that the price for effective policy-making by presidents has risen in recent decades, while the resource base the chief executive needs to draw on for payment has actually shrunk.

What to do? Light's recommendations are innovative and, given their

variance from the norm of recommendations usually encountered in such works,
should engender considerable
discussion and debate. He argues that if
presidents are interested in legislative
success, reelection, and the development
of feasible programs, they need to focus
their attention on eight facets of agenda-
setting and policy implementation:
move quickly at the outset of the term—
"move it or lose it"; leave learning to
later in the first term; take the first
alternative that meets the established
criteria in making a policy choice; avoid
the myriad of details, leaving the
substance of legislation to staff; place
the highest priority on reelection; accept
the fact that cabinet government as
ideally conceived is antithetical to
effective decision making; and finally,
be careful how authority is delegated
and controlled among staff.

Several of these recommendations
will strike the knowledgeable reader as
odd, or perhaps even somewhat
blasphemous given the traditional view
of the presidency. This is not, however, a
traditional treatment of the subject, and
offers a fresh—if contentious—view of
the institution. No doubt it will be of
much interest not only to political
scientists, but potential aspirants to the
office.

KENT MORRISON
University of Utah
Salt Lake City

ARTHUR S. LINK et al., eds. *The Papers
of Woodrow Wilson*, vol. 37, 1916.
Pp. xxiv, 566. Princeton, NJ: Princeton University Press, 1982. $30.00.

The editors believe that "as this
volume ends [August 7, 1916], Wilson
faces the direst crisis of leadership in his
political career up to this point." The
threatened railroad strike, however,
seems closer to Wilson himself than to
the nation. Germany had yielded in May
to Wilson's demands on submarine
warfare. England peremptorily
maintained its freedom of action at sea,
limiting American rights, and enforced

a harsh boycott on Germany, but the
British were no serious threat to
American peace. Uneasy relations with
revolutionary Mexico troubled the man
in the street more directly than did the
conflict 3000 miles away. At worst, no
dire results could come of Mexican
guerrilla threats. And yet Wilson, touted
as a man of peace, and constantly appealing for peace and reason, was to ask for
massive war no more than eight months
later.

His 27 May address to the League to
Enforce Peace, which young Walter
Lippmann thought one of the greatest
utterances since the Monroe Doctrine,
assumes American willingness to join
"any feasible association of nations
forced to realize . . . [peace] objectives."
Yet it is England, fostering the League
of Nations, which worries over Wilson's
desire to maintain as inviolate "security
of the highway of the seas." Wilson is
outraged, but outraged as one who,
somewhat secretly, favors England's
cause. This fact can be dug out of Colonel
House's numerous pronouncements,
upon which Wilson leans heavily. They
involve an alarming confidentiality
toward Sir Edward Grey who, after all,
wants only to win for England. But that,
House urges, would not be a good thing
for England, since it would tear
Germany apart, and make a stable peace
afterward difficult. House sees Wilson's
neutrality stance and his Federal
Reserve Act as weighing equally in the
coming elections. He views Charles
Evans Hughes, Wilson's Republican
challenger, as the "German" candidate,
and his criticism of Wilson's foreign
policies as "tantamount to a criticism of
America." He sees "the fires of liberty
and democracy" as burning as brightly
in England as in America.

Wilson quotes Napoleon as having,
finally, concluded that force had never
accomplished anything permanent. Had
Wilson been able to maintain the
"relentless neutrality" the journalist
David Lawrence urged upon him, it
would have changed the world's history.
But Wilson in fact believed Germany
must be defeated: a belief he did not
share with the people whose servant he

claimed to be. So one must ponder the dynamics that enabled the president soon after to declare Germany a menace to civilization, and its defeat urgent.

Although Wilson writes as a modern man, downgrading as a back number any president who would not recognize great sections of the population such as organized labor, he is clearly conservative in his premises. He wants the vote of women in the dozen states where they have the suffrage, but his Democratic program wants this done by states, not constitutional amendment. His famous endorsement of Louis D. Brandeis for the Supreme Court is in part done to help gain the independent vote. Ray Stannard Baker, famous as a muckraker and later to become Wilson's biographer, finds Wilson overwhelming in his clear, scientific approach to problems; but Wilson shows up better with his human frailties than as a towering pacific figure. That he is better remembered for his ideals of peace than are such figures as Romain Rolland abroad and Norman Thomas at home, who better exemplified the above-the-battle approach, is a vagary of history.

This volume, like all the preceding volumes, has its numerous human nuggets. The president sits for a distinguished bust by the sculptor Jo Davidson. He leads the Preparedness Parade in Washington in civilian clothing, carrying an American flag. Theodore Roosevelt does not figure in the Wilson papers, and must be sought elsewhere to fill out the picture of prewar preparedness. Wilson's British Ambassador Walter Hines Page's blatant racism is nowhere better expressed than in his 12 May letter to Wilson. The so-called Porto Rican Bill, which made that island's inhabitants American citizens, is so casually noted as to remind us of how important events often make small appearance on the larger stage.

LOUIS FILLER

Ovid
Michigan

JONATHAN MOORE, ed. *Campaign for President: 1980 in Retrospect.* Pp. xxiii, 304. Cambridge, MA: Ballinger, 1981. $12.95.

By the time the campaign and election of 1980 and its inevitable immediate post-mortems had ended, this reviewer, like many others, had reached a saturation point. Now, a year later, with my system cleansed of its overdose of politics and political analysis, I approached the opportunity to read *The Campaign for President* with great enthusiasm. I was not disappointed.

This book is, in essence, the transcript of a series of meetings during the first weekend of December 1980. These sessions were moderated by well-known representatives of the media who had followed the campaign closely, and included 26 participants from nine different presidential campaigns. As editor Moore points out in an introduction that both sets the context of the conference and presents his own analysis and interpretation, not every critical player was present. Among the most conspicuous absentees were Hamilton Jordan, Jody Powell, Jerry Rafshoon, and John Sears. On the other hand, the Carter, Reagan, Bush, and Kennedy campaigns were well represented and John Anderson and Bill Brock added insights from their own unique perspectives.

The book moves chronologically, beginning with an assessment of each candidate's position in 1979 and proceeding briskly through the primaries, conventions, and general election. Because of the number of participants, there is, especially in the first chapters, a tendency to ask a question and go around the table. This often leads to superficial responses and, more seriously, limited opportunity for follow-up questions and interaction.

The discussions are enormously wide ranging, touching on problems of perception, personality, organization, and substance. Clearly, the pressure to do well early is overwhelming. John Connally's representative, for example, stated that his candidate had lost by the end of 1979—before a single delegate was chosen. In addition, Howard Baker's failure to live up to expectations in the Maine straw vote in November 1979 effectively ended his effort while at the same time gave George Bush credibility crucial to his breakthrough in Iowa and emergence as the alternative among Republicans to Ronald Reagan.

Concern associated with raising and spending money was a recurring theme. Connally's decision to forego federal matching funds, the plight of the Kennedy (after Iowa) and Anderson campaigns, and huge spending differentials as candidates targeted or conceded particular states (Bush spent $800,000 in Pennsylvania; Reagan $30,000), and the impact of the Republican National Committee war chest, are among the most salient examples.

The book explores virtually all the major (and many minor) issues, events, and decisions: the Republican debate in Nashua, New Hampshire, the flurry over a Reagan-Ford ticket at the Detroit convention, Kennedy's decision to stay in the race after Carter had mathematically clinched the nomination, the Republican emphasis on the economy, and the Democratic attempt to shift the focus to Ronald Reagan and war/peace. It graphically describes the uphill battle the Carter campaign faced. As Pat Caddell put it, "the American people simply did not want Jimmy Carter as their president if they could possibly avoid it." Given this reality, it is difficult to argue with the assertion of Reagan-Bush campaign manager, Bill Casey, that "it would have been hard to lose that election."

The Campaign for President is an important contribution to what will certainly be a growing literature on the 1980 election. I believe that scheduling the conference so soon after the election is an advantage, though both expert and general readers will want to temper its views and conclusions with offerings of more depth. It contains some surprises, not the least of which is the implied influence of the respective pollsters, Caddell for Carter and Richard Wirthlin for Reagan, as revealed in the extent to which they naturally and consistently assume principal roles as spokesmen for their campaigns. Moreover, it is both easy and enjoyable to read and should revive old memories and provide fuel for many discussions of what was and might have been. I recommend it highly.

JOSEPH ANTHONY IMLER

Arlington
Virginia

RICHARD MORAN. *Knowing Right from Wrong: The Insanity Defense of Daniel McNaughtan.* Pp. xiii, 234. New York: Free Press, 1981, $15.95.

Every first year law student knows about the McNaughtan case and the rules by that name that evolved concerning insanity as a defense to criminal prosecution. Briefly stated the proposition is that a defendant is not guilty by reason of insanity if at the time he committed the act he "was laboring under such a defect of reason, from disease of the mind, as not to know the nature and quality of the act he was doing." For the American and English courts that applied this principle for the century and more after the 1843 verdict, the question was succinctly whether the defendant knew right from wrong.

Although the legal reasoning on questions of insanity as a defense have matured to some extent since the McNaughtan case, the issues that it raises remain quite difficult and have by no means been settled today. In fact the uncertainty and confusion that still exist in this area of the law are likely to be increased by Moran's revealing new book on the McNaughtan trial, *Knowing Right from Wrong: The Insanity Defense of Daniel McNaughtan.*

The first point that Moran makes is how little even lawyers know about the actual facts in the famous McNaughtan case. The basics seem to be that McNaughtan, a mildly radical member of various labor organizations, shot and killed Edward Drummond, private secretary to Britain's Prime Minister Sir Robert Peel, believing him to be the Prime Minister. Since McNaughtan was immediately caught and there were numerous witnesses, there was never any question that he performed the act. The only question was whether the defendant would be found not guilty because of insanity. After a very brief trial and even briefer jury deliberation, McNaughtan was found not guilty by reason of insanity and was remanded to Bedlam Prison for criminal lunatics. He died in prison 22 years later of diabetes.

Moran's theory is that this was not a case involving insanity at all, but rather one whose primary ingredient was politics. His argument is that McNaughtan, as a strong supporter of the Chartists, sought to assassinate Peel and that, although the court's judgment was phrased in humanitarian terms, the verdict was one designed to resolve an accute political problem. A guilty verdict, given the temper of the times, might have created a political martyr. By declaring McNaughtan not guilty by reason of insanity and subsequently incarcerating him indefinitely, the government was able both to eliminate him from the scene and destroy his credibility.

This book is as much a social and political history of England in the mid-1800s as it is an account of the insanity defense. Indeed the author does almost nothing to show how more recent developments in the law have impinged on the viability of the McNaughtan rules. By focusing on the context in which the crime was committed rather than on what the verdict has come to stand for, Moran radically changes our perception of both individuals and events in this case. As much as anything else Moran's book demonstrates the ease with which intimations of psychiatric disorder can discredit political offenders.

Although Moran's analysis of the underlying facts and motivations in the McNaughtan case are imminently sensible and believable, he tries to stretch the materials of the case to fashion an argument in favor of a political act defense to criminality. Moran is correct in noting that our legal system is generally unable to deal with statutory violence that raises issues of political and social justice, but he fails to make a convincing case for the alternative. To say that a political act may be legally wrong and morally right, while in many senses possibly true, is not sufficient to build into our legal framework the notion that assassination for political purposes should ever be given even limited legitimacy. There may be rare cases—Hitler is the example Moran uses—in which the defense would be publicly plausible, but such examples are extremely rare and never unmuddied.

JAMES R. SILKENAT
Member of the District of
   Columbia Bar
Washington, D.C.

PREBLE STOLZ. *Judging Judges: The Investigation of Rose Bird and the California Supreme Court.* Foreword by Anthony Lewis. Pp. xxv, 453. New York: Free Press, 1981. $19.95.

In November 1978, on the day of a bitterly contested statewide election, the Los Angeles *Times* reported that the California Supreme Court delayed issuing a controversial law and order decision until after the election. On the ballot, seeking popular confirmation of her appointment as Chief Justice of that court, was Rose Bird. This charge and the ensuing controversy led to an extraordinary investigation of the highest court of the nation's largest state. Preble Stolz, a law professor at Boalt Hall, Berkeley, and a former colleague of Rose Bird as well as a confidant of both Governor Jerry Brown and former governor Pat Brown, used this investigation to offer a rare glimpse into the workings of this court. Stolz shows the dedication, pettiness, personality conflicts, and idiosyncrasies of an institution which, absent this investigation, would certainly never have washed its linen, dirty or otherwise, in public.

Not simply a narrative of the investigation—which was suddenly cut short when one of the justices successfully sued to enjoin the public hearings—*Judging Judges* analyzes the judicial opinions that fueled the controversy and the role of politics, the press, and the bar. Although geared to the general public, Stolz's case analysis would be equally appropriate in a law review essay.

Given the controversy that triggered the investigation, it is hardly surprising that Stolz's account is similarly controversial. Much of this is due to the other name on the cover, Anthony Lewis, New York *Times* columnist, author of *Gideon's Trumpet*, and lecturer on the constitution and the press at Harvard Law School. In his foreword to *Judging Judges*, Lewis takes issue with Stolz, saving his most pointed criticism for Stolz's negative treatment of Rose Bird and his kid-glove treatment of Bird's two hostile colleagues and the Los Angeles *Times*. Lewis "review," since it is a foreword, gets in the first word with readers, and his comments remain in focus throughout the book.

Judging Judges, despite its faults—and Lewis has pinpointed them fairly succinctly—takes important strides in demystifying the judiciary. Unlike Woodward and Armstrong's *The Brethren, Judging Judges* relies not on leaks and innuendo, but rather on public record. Accordingly, it is often as dry as the investigation apparently was. As between Lewis and Stolz, readers will have to reach their own verdict.

MICHAEL STEPHEN HINDUS

San Francisco
California

GRAHAM K. WILSON. *Interest Groups in the United States.* Pp. ix, 161. New York: Oxford University Press, 1981. $29.95; Paperbound, $9.95.

For those who believe that interest groups dominate American politics, that they have all-powerful lobbies, that they influence legislators unduly, and that they largely control the agenda of public debate on crucial questions of the day, this book will come as a consciousness-raising surprise. But for those who are aware of the limited power of interest groups, this book will merely confirm their awareness. Graham Wilson's book treats the whole variety of interest groups in the United States: business, labor, agricultural, and voluntary (public interest). His overarching message is that interest groups have no secret or special numerical or persuasive powers whereby they are able to control the political process in America. That is good news.

What I found most interesting in Wilson's book is his discussion of the rise of public interest groups as opposed to single-issue or special interest groups. Why have so many blossomed since 1960? What changes in American life account for their proliferation? Most readers will find the explanations intrinsically interesting. Repeating and amplifying MacFarland's account, Wilson gives the following reasons for the growth of public interest groups. First, an electorate with a "greater awareness of political issues" exhibited a weakened "loyalty to political parties." Second, affluent America was ready to raise a lot of questions not previously aired by people preoccupied with primary goods like housing, food, and employment, hence the rise of environmental groups like the Sierra Club, Audubon, Zero Population Growth, and the like. Third, middle-class participation in politics has increased. Fourth, "technological change has aided public interest groups" with WATS telephone lines and computerized mailing lists as technological aids to the organizer. Fifth, strong political entrepreneurs like Ralph Nader and John Gardner have made groups like Common Cause and Ralph Nader Public Citizen viable. Sixth, public "scepticism about all major institutions," which swept the country during the 1960s and 1970s, added impetus to the formation of public interest groups—interest groups interested in pursuing broader social goals.

What is surprising is that even Common Cause, the largest of the public interest groups, numbers only about 325,000—about one-half the size of a Congressional district. With a $15 membership fee, this means that even the most powerful of the public interest groups controls very few financial resources compared to the total available to influence the political process.

It is also interesting to note that, although public interest groups like Common Cause have influenced the political process, as when it filed a lawsuit forcing the Nixon Committee to Re-Elect the President to "disclose all its contributors, a major step in unravelling Watergate," there are cases where their powers have been sharply circumscribed. Here is what Graham cites as evidence for the limited power of interest groups:

When in March 1979, Judge John Sirica, the hero of the Watergate cases, ruled that he would not recognize the Nader organizations in his court as spokesmen for the public interest on the grounds that they had no machinery by which Nader might be removed from the leadership by members and hence were undemocratic, his ruling was greeted with much amusement and little criticism.

What if we suddenly decided that because no public interest group was democratically elected, then none could testify as an amicus in court proceedings, appear at Congressional hearings, file suits at law, and so on? Would public interest groups lose their force? Would American political life suffer? Graham Wilson's book raises this question, and while it is not the preoccupation of the book, one cannot avoid feeling that it is important and that the Wilson book has helped us begin to answer this question.

STEPHEN W. WHITE

East Tennessee State University
Johnson City

WILLIAM K. WYANT. *Westward in Eden: The Public Lands and the Conservation Movement.* Pp. xiii, 536. Berkeley, Los Angeles, and London: University of California Press, 1982. $24.50.

This comprehensive overview of American conservation policy illustrates the changing role of government in dealing with the nation's natural resources. Originally the government's role was merely to dispense with land, oil, minerals, and forests via sales and grants to private citizens, states, and corporate interests for their exploitation and use. More recently, the government has involved itself in conservation, resource management, and ecological impact.

The first warning for change came in 1952 with the Paley Commission report *Resources for Freedom*, which alerted the nation that it was consuming its resources faster than any other nation on earth. The final warning came in 1973 when the National Commission on Materials Policy cautioned policy makers that there must be limits to population and industrial growth if the human species expected to survive permanently.

The author called the past wealth of American's land resources an "incomparable Garden of Eden." The government at one time controlled four-fifths of the land and transferred it by sales and grants to the public through the authority of the Northwest Ordinances (1787), the Land Act of 1803, and the Homestead Act of 1862. Altogether 1.1 billion acres were disposed of through the General Land Office. Since the government's only interest in farm, timber, and mineral lands was revenue, this office was located in the Treasury Department.

Beginning with Theodore Roosevelt in 1901, the nation began its commitment to conservation. The Progressive Movement created the Forest Service and the Newlands Reclamation Act. The New Deal of FDR made further commitments to conservation to counter drought and the Dust Bowl. By 1946 the Interior

Department established the Bureau of Land Management, and in 1956 the Fish and Wildlife Service.

The ecological movement of the 1960s and 1970s resulted in an ever-increasing role of governmental participation in resource management. President Nixon established the Council on Environmental Quality to coordinate and supervise from the Executive Branch this new and larger role of government.

Despite this new policy approach, President Carter issued the rather pessimistic report: *The Global Report to the President Entering the Twenty-First Century.* It predicts that unless even more effort is put forth, "the world in 2000 will be more crowded, more polluted, less stable ecologically, and more vulnerable to disruption than the world we live in now." The author believes the necessary governmental machinery has been created to protect the environment if public opinion supports and sustains its endeavors.

FREDERICK H. SCHAPSMEIER
University of Wisconsin
Oshkosh

SOCIOLOGY

EMMETT H. BUELL, Jr. *School Desegregation and Defended Neighborhoods.* Pp. xiv, 202. Lexington, MA: D. C. Heath, 1982. $22.95.

There are a number of human events that illustrate the long and bitter struggle for equal rights in contemporary America. Some of these events are local, like open housing ordinances or a demonstration at the court house; others transcend their local environments and specific time periods to become symbolic, like the Selma marches. Among the latter symbolic battles of the equal rights war stands the antibusing violence of South Boston during the 1970s. This book examines the dramatic and visceral opposition by whites to school desegregation and busing in Boston. It seeks to answer the question, "Why Boston?"

Emmett Buell repeats the reasons most often given for opposition to desegregation: racism, social class differences, or resistance to governmental regulation. He recognizes these as competing rationales, but does not dwell on them. Rather, Buell analyzes the Boston desegregation battles from a policy studies perspective, using the concept of "defended neighborhood" as a basis for explaining South Boston's abominable behavior.

A defended neighborhood, according to Buell, is an enclave like an urban village where community traditions are exceedingly important and where residents have a safe and intimate contact within the neighborhood. He draws on Gerald Suttles's *The Social Construct of Communities* (1972) to identify the features of a defended neighborhood as

—acute awareness of commonly understood territorial boundaries,
—shared view of a common plight,
—concept of community and personal safety within it,
—residents linked through mutual aid and other networks,
—willingness to employ violence against unwanted social change.

Buell examines theories of judicial implementation in policy studies literature and notes the difficulties inherent in obtaining compliance with judicial rulings even under favorable conditions. Under conditions of a defended neighborhood, as Buell describes South Boston, and the growing regional and national resistance to busing, the court-ordered desegregation of Boston schools created an explosion. Buell seems to blame Judge Garrity, who issued the order and the follow-up amendments, more than any others for these events.

Buell, and Richard A. Briskin, interviewed key participants and antibusing activists to discern their view of what had transpired. Antibusing respondents tended to stereotype black students and to argue that violence was inevitable because South Boston youth could not ignore the challenge of an alien culture. Further, antibusing respondents believed that busing had been responsible for white flight, resegregation and worse racial imbalance, ruin of educational quality in Boston schools, and the city's financial crisis and immense property tax increases. Buell examines each of these positions and reports that there was some substance to them, but that direct causality could not be shown.

A final chapter proposes policy recommendations for implementing judicial policy in defended neighborhoods. These include the need to take neighborhood identities seriously, to establish that educational quality does not decline as a result of desegregation, provide better justification for busing, and enlist community groups in the effort. These seem more commonsensical than theory based.

This book is an interesting examination of a volatile situation. However, the theoretic framework used does two disservices to the Boston busing violence: it sanitizes it, losing the moral basis against which the incidents must be judged; and it provides an explanation, defended neighborhoods, which would apparently justify any reprehensible actions.

JACK L. NELSON
Rutgers University
New Brunswick
New Jersey

ELLIOT J. FELDMAN and JEROME MILCH. *Technocracy versus Democracy: The Comparative Politics of International Airports.* Pp. xxix, 299. Boston: Auburn, 1981. $21.95.

Airport development, whether it involves expansion of existing facilities or construction of totally new complexes, has generated substantial controversy in numerous cities around the world. By comparing case histories of such conflicts in five Western advanced industrial countries, the authors attempt to identify and examine the role of social, cultural, and political factors in resolving a particular technological issue.

The major thesis of this important work is that the technocratic mission of airport development organizations is in frequent and seemingly inevitable conflict with the democratic tenets of Western societies. Questions of land use, noise, and surface transport access are considered by elite aviation groups with little regard for the legitimate concerns of common citizens. Mechanisms for citizen participation in decision making are often limited by law or tradition.

The authors examine the decision-making process regarding airport development in Canada, the United States, Britain, France, and Italy, the role of airport development experts, the nature of citizen participation, and the bureaucratic response to public protest. Their research methodology is sound and thorough, and their writing is fluid and comprehensible to both social scientists and transportation specialists. The foreword by Theodore Lowi is also commendable.

Precisely because this book has so much to offer, one wishes that the authors were less self-righteous, less elitist in their views toward the business community in general and air transport consultants in particular. Not all of the latter automatically echo the biases of their sponsors; some even have refused contracts from potential employers whose conditions preclude an honest appraisal of the situation at issue. One further objects to such sweeping statements as "the vigorous selling of airport development to the Third World is no more than a further colonial exploitation." If the sellers are guilty as exploiters for offering the technology, the purchasers are guilty as unwise consumers for demanding that elaborate complexes be built when simpler facilities would be more appropriate. Many of the authors' condemned consultants have advised Third World countries against massive airport development—as well as large-scale airline fleet acquisition and route expansion—only to see their clients proceed with such programs for reasons of prestige vis-à-vis neighboring states or potential individual profit in the context of local corruption.

The reader may also be annoyed by the authors' frequent references to their own previously published works and their self-serving, gratuitous comments in the first appendix about the substantial amounts of labor and money required for their research. That their study necessitated both is self-evident.

One hopes that the moralizing in this volume against the business sector and aviation community does not deter individuals so employed from reading it. It is a valuable book on the collision between modern technology and Western democracy, and should be of interest to those in the air transport/ airport industry as well as those in the social science field.

BETSY GIDWITZ
Massachusetts Institute of
    Technology
Cambridge

LOREN R. GRAHAM. *Between Science and Values*. Pp. x, 449. New York: Columbia University Press, 1981. $19.95.

Between Science and Values is so titled because it attempts, with considerable success, to transcend the false dichotomy of fact versus value implicit in much of modern thinking about science. The "expansionists" and the "restrictionists" are the designations Loren Graham, who is Professor of the History of Science at MIT, uses for those at the extremes of the debate over whether science explains all or none of our values. Graham does accept the philosophical distinction between is and ought and agrees with those who say that confusing the two can only be called the "naturalistic fallacy." But the history, as opposed to the philosophy, of modern science reveals a great deal of interaction between statements of fact and those concerning values. Graham thus tries, via close analysis of the interactions of factual and normative statements in the twentieth-century revolutions in physics and biology, to illustrate what has actually happened in relations between the realms of *Naturwissenschaft* and *Geisteswissenschaft* during these transformations. This external history of science, he hopes, can lead us away from the too-rigid dichotomization produced by more traditional internal histories of science.

Graham's examples of science-value interactions certainly illustrate the widely varying interpretations of the meaning of the relativity revolution in physics. The unique feature is his inclusion of not only the great scientists (Einstein as a restrictionist except for the value of objectivity, Bohr as an expansionist) but also of the great popularizers like Eddington and Heisenberg. The public role of physics, which is to say the influence of science on sociopolitical values in the early part of this century, is thereby shown to have arisen from an interaction of the new facts with normative statements introduced at some point in the ideological debates of the time. Eddington the restrictionist thus used relativity to reintroduce the English-speaking world's freedom and religious values into the Newtonian world-machine, whereas Fock the expansionist in the Soviet Union drew universalist and materialist political conleusions from the same facts of general relativity. Heisenberg's popular writings showed him wrestling with the same conflicts of relativism versus absolutism and idealism versus materialism, according to Graham, and the restrictionist-expansionist theme surfaced in France in Bergson and Monod, respectively.

Graham likewise shows that the biologicization of ethics predicted again and again as a result of evolution, eugenics, sociobiology, and behaviorism demonstrates the failure of facts to set values and vice versa. His treatment of the rise and fall of Social Darwinism and of eugenics mainly recapitulates the well-known record, although his decision to focus on eugenic debates preceding the polarization into Nazism and Lysenkoism enhances our understanding considerably. By way of contrast, his critique of the expansionist claims of Francis Crick, E.O. Wilson, and B.F. Skinner, among others, brings the value implications of the new biology and of behaviorism into sharper outline than I can recall seeing anywhere else. The heart of the matter is Graham's claim that, while the newer studies of the human organism raise more subtle issues of science-value interaction, they in no way justify an expansionism that derives consciousness from body chemistry, at least not yet.

Philosophers of science will probably find fault with *Between Science and Values* because empiricists want to make science safe from ideological opinion and phenomenologists want to make room for values in the face of scientistic arrogance. Graham, on the other hand, presents a historical account of actual happenings in fact-value interactions. His conclusions in the section on "What Kind of Expansionism Do We Want?" are operational, not philosophical, and very tentative. Hence the striking chapter called "Attempts at Historical Understanding" specifies ways science and values interpenetrate each other—through value-laden scientific terms like charm and normal and even force, through application of scientific methods to normative questions, and so on. The chapter on "Attempts to Provide a Philosophical Overview" rejects the too-simple approaches of scientific reductionists (Crick), religious natural philosophers (Teilhard), and holistic materialists (Marxists). And the chapter on the social control of science, which earlier appeared as one of the high points of Gerald Holton's edited study *Limits of Scientific Inquiry* (1979), draws some vital distinctions between which parts of science are subject to public accountability and which are answerable only to peer review. In brief, Graham is using a functional rather than a structural model.

The model suggests that the historical arena where scientific facts and social values meet is influenced as much by the communications process as by the facts and the values themselves. The way Galileo and the Catholic Church framed the debate over heliocentrism, says Graham, had as much influence as the ideas of Copernicus and Ptolemy. What this model amounts to is an assertion that science (or values, for that matter) cannot stand above the historical fray. Heidegger's followers, or Whitehead's would no doubt contend that Graham has not adequately defended values from the aggressive expansionism of the scientific mode of thinking. Yet Graham's neglect of such thinkers does not derive from his stance as an expansionist of sorts. It arises because Graham is an empiricist, not a rationalist, and therefore not impressed by efforts at tracking down alleged epistemological abuses such as the genetic fallacy or the fallacy of misplaced concreteness. *Between Science and Values* should therefore be compared with Kuhn's *The Structure of Scientific Revolutions* and Baier and Rescher's *Values and the Future*, or even with the works of Harvey Brooks and Daniel Greenberg, because it is really concerned with the politics of science. Graham has once again shown the mastery in this area which earned his *Science and Philosophy in the Soviet Union* (1972) a National Book Award nomination.

THOMAS J. KNIGHT

Pennsylvania State University
University Park

JAMES W. GREEN *Cultural Awareness in the Human Services*. Pp. xiii, 257. Englewood Cliffs, NJ: Prentice-Hall, 1982. $14.95.

For more than a decade hundreds of thousands of documented and undocumented refugees and immigrants have entered the United States. They have come from poor and embattled countries of the Caribbean, Latin America, Southeast Asia, Eastern

Europe, the Soviet Union, and the Middle East. Almost all of these individuals require or receive services from public or voluntary social service agencies. In light of this situation Green believes that there is a real need for providers of social services to become more aware and knowledgable of the cultural norms and values of their clients. Second, they indicate that colleges and universities who provide training for human service professionals must establish an educational curriculum that sensitizes students to cultural differences. Thus the primary emphasis of this text is to make the reader more cognizant of many significant factors that the service provider must understand when serving culturally diverse population groups. This book represents a collaborative effort of the Center for Social Welfare Research and the Multi-Ethnic Training project at the University of Washington. The authorship of this text combines the experience and expertise of both cultural anthropologists and social workers. The text is divided into two parts. The first four chapters are devoted to a detailed discussion of the significance of cultural traits and attributes that must be understood by the helping profession in order to provide clients with needed services. The author presents a theoretical model for understanding what is defined as a transcultural interaction process between service provider and client. It is "a way of thinking about social services from the perspective of the client and the *client's culture.*"

The remainder of the book is devoted to a discussion of the cultural dynamics of working with specific population groups including Blacks, Asians and Pacific Americans, urban Indians, and Chicanos. Each chapter in this section provides an instructive and revealing analysis of those factors that must be understood by the practitioner to provide adequate service to each of these groups.

Because this book is intended for training service providers, the author has included a useful appendix that provides instructive material for training students. It includes materials that can be used within the context of a classroom setting or for inservice training for professionals. The objective of this section is to provide an instructive method for sensitizing individuals to the salient cultural differences that persons of various ethnic, racial, and linguistic groups exhibit.

Although this text is an important contribution to social work education, there are several weaknesses inherent in the author's presentation of materials included in this book. Professor Green's discussion and analysis of the role of cultural awareness in the provision of services to ethnically defined groups assumes that the reader has a background in cultural anthropology and ethnology. Second, the author fails to provide sufficient illustrative case studies to support his thesis. These editorial deficiencies do not negate contributions this text provides. It is a book that should be used as a reference and a textbook for students of social work and for service providers.

STUART W. ZISOOK
Roosevelt University
Chicago
Illinois

DAVID LEBEDOFF. *The New Elite: The Death of Democracy.* Pp. 194. New York: Franklin Watts, 1981. $11.95.

AMOS PERLMUTTER. *Modern Authoritarianism: A Comparative Institutional Analysis.* Pp. xiv, 194. New Haven, CT: Yale University Press, 1981. $17.50.

The New Elite: The Death of Democracy is a spirited attack on the American intelligentsia of the 1970s and 1980s, the teachers, commentators, planners, officials, and other salaried professionals who in Lebedoff's view manage our society—an "emergent class of those who believe themselves to be measurably brighter than everyone else." Once romantically and pragmatically attached to the common people and in good part of working-class origin themselves, the intelligentsia have beome snobbish, antiparty, antimajoritarian, power hungry, and, he argues, a serious threat to democracy. Anyone who reads this book is certain to be the target of at least a few score of Lebedoff's pot shots.

The book is imaginative, fun, and flawed, and best read as a list of extravagant hypotheses, many of which would prove untrue if tested. There is no testing here. It is a lawyerly brief by a Minnesota lawyer and political activist, entirely one-sided, all points scored against the accused, without leniency. There are highly questionable arguments about IQ, inbreeding, and inheritance, and analyses of taste reminiscent of Russell Lynes's *Highbrow, Lowbrow, Middlebrow* but far less evenhanded. It is truly the intelligensia alone who are snobbish, manipulative, and distrustful of majorities? Is a preference for European cars sillier than an attraction to large American cars? If New Elitist George McGovern manipulated the nominating procedures of the Democratic Party for the benefit of his own kind, was he really, as Lebedoff implies, the first to do so? Are the New Elite the only ones who freely claim to speak for others in the political process? The New Elite may not be as novel, or as deadly, as Lebedoff would have us believe.

Amos Perlmutter's short book on modern authoritarianism is a formal analysis of Bolshevik, Nazi, fascist, corporatist, and praetorian regimes. It argues for the similarity of authoritarianism of the right and the left and for the importance of examining the political structures of authoritarianism: state; party; military; institutions paralleling traditional legislative, executive, administrative, and judicial bodies; and auxiliary structures (political police, praetorian guards, and militant subelite groups). Each of the major forms of authoritarianism has a characteristic array of structures and locus of power.

Perlmutter's prime objection to existing theory is the stress laid on ideology:

Although ideology can provide the initial momentum for a revolutionary movement and enhance a regime's efficiency in mobilizing human resources, it is neither a fundamental nor a permanent requirement for the development of authoritarianism. In fact, in the Soviet Union today, authoritarian legitimacy is enhanced more by creating stable authoritarian structures than by attending to ideology.

Indeed, authoritarianism is seen to have become more efficient and stable in the Soviet Union, China, and Nazi Germany as ideology waned.

Modern Authoritarianism is a book for specialists who might be interested in a reworking of the literature rather than for the ordinary reader who wishes to learn about specific regimes.

ROBERT J. SICKELS
University of New Mexico
Albuquerque

AUSTIN T. TURK. *Political Criminality: The Defiance and Defense of Authority.* Pp. 232. Beverly Hills, CA: Sage, 1982. $22.50; Paperbound $12.95.

What are called political crimes are not only problems to those in control; they also often provide opportunities to justify the tightening of instruments of domination. Turk believes that the "key to understanding the process of political organization at the societal level is to analyze the relationship between political criminality and political policing." His current book is an effort to do so on the basis of considering a broad survey of literature on dissent, violence, and political controls.

The definition of political criminality is not easy. "In some cases it may even be hard to decide whether the individual is 'really' engaged in political crime or in political policing." Thus, there is "nothing empirically distinctive about *all* political 'criminals' other than the fact that they happen to have been labeled as current or potential political threats."

The definition of political policing is easier in the sense that all policing is political, but to sketch the significance and effectiveness and especially the consequences of policing presents many problems. Police are not neutral. They are "designed for use in behalf of the politics of social order and continuity," but their typical methods do not always serve those aims; sometimes they are self-defeating. Turk points to the "internal contradictions in the process of political policing." These "not only preclude eliminating all resistance but even help to create it." Reference is to contradictions between the use of explicit force and of persuasion, and between covert surveillance and manipulation on the one hand and open repression on the other. He points especially to the incompatibility of political policing with conflict resolution and management.

Conflicts between authorities and resisters, as Turk sees them, involve "the fundamental struggle . . . between (a) those who see human freedom as a better risk than regimentation, and (b) those whose fear of freedom motivates attempts to limit and regulate it." He thinks both sides can furnish considerable evidence to support their contentions. He would thus like to see a liberal polity in which neither could destroy the other. Economically, he claims this would mean genuine socialism.

Turk provides a rich theoretical discussion of a highly significant subject. His cogent relativism is refreshing.

ALFRED McCLUNG LEE
Drew University
Madison, New Jersey
City University of New York

ECONOMICS

HENRY J. AARON, ed. The Value-Added Tax: Lessons from Europe. Pp. xi, 107. Washington, DC: Brookings Institution, 1981. $10.95; Paperbound $4.95.

This informative book presents six abridged papers from an October 1980

Brookings Institution conference on the use of value-added taxation in Western Europe. However, even though the frame of reference is Western Europe, the orientation of the book is toward the possible adoption of a federal government value-added tax in the United States in light of the European experience. Separate chapters describe and evaluate use of the tax in France, Italy, the Netherlands, Sweden, the United Kingdom, and Germany, respectively. In addition, the editor provides an introductory chapter that summarizes the major points to follow in the six national chapters. Fortunately, the potential inherent in any book of readings for discontinuity in coverage is avoided in this book which carries a consistent theme and format of analysis.

Several performance criteria are used to evaluate Western European use of the tax. In general, these relate to the distributional equity, allocational neutrality or efficiency, saving and investment, balance of payments, and inflation effects of a value-added tax. Moreover, the effectiveness of administrative and enforcement procedures is considered. Widespread agreement exists among the contributors on several important issues. For example, it is agreed that (1) a consumption-type value-added tax, which would be regressive to income if the tax applies a uniform rate with few exemptions for necessity goods, can be converted to a proportional or mildly progressive value-added tax via a system of differential rates and/or exemptions; (2) a significant efficiency tradeoff cost is incurred as this equity gain is achieved in the six nations through rate and base differentiation; and (3) similar equity improvements could be attained without such efficiency costs if alternative fiscal instruments such as income taxes and direct transfers are appropriately used.

Several important differences between conditions now present in the United States and those present in the European nations when they adopted the tax are noted. The most significant of these differential circumstances may well be the fact the European nations were not using broad-based sales taxes at the subnational government level when their national governments imposed the value-added tax. This clearly is not the situation in the United States where the general retail sales tax is the primary revenue source for states and, in addition, is an important revenue source for local governments. The intergovernmental fiscal implications of this difference are apparent. Moreover, even though the value-added tax was introduced in all six nations as a replacement for existing broadbased sales taxes, the ultimate result in five of the six was an increase in overall tax revenues relative to gross domestic product. Indeed, the Western European experience with value-added taxation provides a useful frame of reference for American consideration of the tax.

BERNARD P. HERBER
University of Arizona
Tucson

WILLIAM H. BECKER. *The Dynamics of Business-Government Relations. Industry and Exports, 1893-1921.* Pp. xvi, 240. Chicago: University of Chicago Press, 1982. $22.00.

The starting date of this study was precisely a hundred years after Alexander Hamilton proposed to make the federal government the patron of industry, agriculture, and commerce. He could not guess the developments that would ensue in the century here subtended. Professor Becker confronts official departments prodigiously expanded and others, the Department of Commerce particularly, which did not exist at the outset. A complement of American business corporations surpassed the bureaucracies in ingenuity and resources. Now and again the author glances beyond his stated period to remind of fluctuations in the comparative roles of public and private economic agencies.

The reader must be prepared for much inescapable detail in recital of legislative history and shifts of strategy of business associations. Fortunately in a final chapter these complexities are summarized. Generally in the period here viewed large producers depended not so much on the Departments of State and Commerce as did their lesser counterparts. The major firms, particularly in foreign trade, relied on Congress for tariff adjustment, exemption from antitrust restriction, and expansion of the merchant marine. Often the departments were as eager to be served by big business—rallying support for congressional appropriations—as the other way around. Giant industries, requiring a flow of exports to sustain mass production, maintained sales organizations abroad far exceeding promotional efforts of government agencies. Indeed private industrial expansion at times was in conflict with Washington intentions, as in the establishment of plants on foreign soil held to deprive workers at home.

In contrast, small exporters and those who looked to foreign markets only when American demand fell off valued consular services for information, translation, and any approaches to a sales staff. The small producers, though well organized in trade associations in this country, applied to government departments rather than to Congress. In the course of these contacts there was rivalry, not to say conflict, between bureaucracies.

Professor Becker portrays the reaction of American exporters up to the aftermath of World War I. Frequently the obligation to assist the industrial rebuilding of Europe and to buy from foreigners to whom we wanted to sell was reluctantly accepted. Of course the enormous American overseas grants for economic and military aid are beyond the limits of this volume.

The author has consulted appropriate manuscript materials as well as extensive printed sources as revealed in his notes and bibliography. His Appendix B, taken from A.D.H. Kaplan's *Big Enterprise in a Competitive System* (1964) contains surprises; it compares the ranking of the hundred largest industrial corporations by assets in 1909 and 1919.

BROADUS MITCHELL
Rutgers University
New Brunswick
New Jersey

LEON GRUNBERG. *Failed Multinational Ventures: The Political Economy of International Divestments.* Pp. xi, 176. Lexington, MA: D. C. Heath, 1981. $23.95.

ALLEN M. RUGMAN. *Inside the Multinationals: The Economics of Internal Markets.* Pp. 179. New York: Columbia University Press, 1981. $25.00.

Here are two scholars explicitly researching multinational enterprises (MNEs), and implicitly the nature of the world economy, who would benefit from reading the other's work. Their analyses contain considerable substance and insight, but, as might be expected, each has only a partial view of the situation. Their works partly complement, partly contradict—and to a limited degree support—the contrasting view of multinationals.

Rugman as a free-market economist stresses in a world of effective market competition the efficiency-achieving characteristic of profit-maximizing MNEs. When government intervenes with various and sundry protectionist programs, matters go from not-so-bad to worse. Efficiency is the prime goal for proper public policy in Rugman's judgment, with justice receiving but passing attention in his discussion. This is a typical free-market normative stance, but is a limited one given the pressure for equity both in nations and in the world economy.

Demonstrating that the subject matter of MNEs is complex, dynamic, and ambiguous, Grunberg, a sociologist with considerable background in matters economic, sees MNEs as political-economic organizations with considerable discretionary power that insulates them at least in the short and medium term from the workings of competition. The visible hand of MNE management exists as does the unseen hand of market coordination of managerial decision making. Government is viewed as possessing positive power to redress and alter MNE efforts to shape the world economy to corporate benefit.

Both writers recognize that market forces are internalized into corporate organization as a means of avoiding the bounded rationality, self-interest with guile, and informational asymmetries of real world transactions. They extrapolate to MNEs as from Oliver Williamson's work that portrays vertical integration and conglomeration as efforts to avoid what Rugman calls "natural market imperfections." These researchers see the MNE as an institutional innovation to reduce risk and uncertainties that flow from intrinsic market characteristics and from government protectionist policies. Rugman, in particular, draws attention to direct foreign investment as a defensive response by MNEs to wrong-headed government policy.

While both use the internalization hypothesis, with Rugman's study having it as the core paradigm, they come to opposite conclusions about the consequences of MNEs. Rugman recognizes that markets are absorbed into MNEs, but certainly implies that market forces in the long-run remain strong enough to police and direct the pursuit of monopoly advantage to global consumer welfare. Oligopolistic competition between giants can be expected to benefit consumers. Grunberg, on the other hand, suggests that with corporations of world economy size, complex hierarchy is a fundamental reality. Ken Boulding, perhaps only partly tongue-in-cheek, pointed to the same phenomenon some decades ago with the definition of General Motors as "a communist state about the size of Yugoslavia."

Grunberg emphasizes that strategic planning and centralized direction by MNEs prompt a reallocation of resources between industries and/or nations with such intensity of purpose that a Soviet planner might express professional appreciation. He describes in fascinating detail the efforts with Leyland Innocenti, Chrysler UK, and Litton Imperial Typewriters to withdraw from failed ventures. Rugman would point to these episodes as demonstration of market forces constraining even giant MNEs. Grunberg, however, develops the argument along Cyert-March behavioral theory of the firm lines that internal political-economic processes and forces led to failure with these ventures as much as exogenous market realities. By his perspective large corporations are not simple, internal markets, or rational profit-maximizing institutions, but are complex hierarchical political institutions that paradoxically are instruments of centralized power as they are also coalitions of interest groups of both conflict and cooperation in turbulent settings.

It is perhaps an exaggeration to emphasize the differences between these most informative volumes. Both are case study focused: Rugman emphasizing the Canadian experience, while Grunberg builds his theories on three failed multinational ventures. Neither conclusively via a crucial experiment demonstrates the validity of his arguments. Both recognize the pressures of market competition and of continuing efforts by interest groups to seek equity in the functioning of an evolving world economy. Rugman closes with counsel to MNE managers that they be increasingly sensitive as a matter of prudence to the crucial social/political environment in which MNEs function. There is joint recognition that the mixed economy is here to stay, with the hard task of social scientists to analyze in a second-best, case-by-case fashion the impact of MNEs in the world economy. As a personal note, ideologies of left and right must be set aside for the more pedestrian but useful assignment of sorting out the implications of economic change in a world of ambiguous sociopolitical-economic realities. Both of these books make worthy contributions toward such clarification.

HAROLD L. JOHNSON

Emory University
Atlanta
Georgia

CHARLES F. MANSKI and DANIEL McFADDEN, eds., *Structural Analysis of Discrete Data with Econometric Applications*. Pp. xxv, 477. Cambridge, MA: MIT Press, 1981. $29.95. $29.95.

This important and difficult book is a sustained discussion of a problem of great interest to all social scientists. A series of examples illustrates the wide field of application. An individual decides whether or not to migrate, and to where (demography/history); chooses a transport mode for a journey to work (transportation economics/planning); selects a residential location (regional science); decides how to vote in an election (political science/political economy). An appellate judge must decide whether to affirm or reverse a lower-court decision (law); a bureaucracy must come to a decision on a public endeavor (political science); individuals decide on contraceptive technique (demography/sociology); select a college and decide on a major (education). The common features of these examples are, first, that they concern the analysis of decisions at the micro (often individual) level; and second, that the choice set available to the decision maker is finite and discrete (qualitative) in the sense that precisely one element must be chosen. In these circumstances it is natural to conduct the analysis in terms of a causal relation between the observed and unobserved attributes of the alternatives and the decision maker on the one hand, and the *probability* of making a given choice on the other. Specification of a particular probability model up to a vector of unknown parameters gives rise to a structural model of the discrete data.

An immediate question concerns the estimation of the unknown parameters from a sample of observed choices and attributes, and in particular on estimates with desirable properties. It turns out to be critically important to know the underlying design of the observed sample. In two papers McFadden and Manski, and S. C. Cosslett provide a general theory of single-equation maximum-likelihood estimation in the face of different designs. Consistency of a number of estimators is proved, and, in a notable paper Cosslett provides estimators that are also asymptotically efficient. The discussion is given an empirical flavor in papers by M. Ben-Akiva and T. Watanatada, who extend the logit model to consider location choice, where one is beset by too many alternatives, and by J. A. Hausman and D. A. Wise, in the context of the Gary Income Maintenance Experiment. These papers limit themselves to samples taken at a single point in time (although the last contains a hint of a temporal generalization). In two excellent papers J. J. Heckman considers the problem of formulating and estimating dynamic models of discrete choice using panel data, that is, data in which the choices of the same individual are observed over time. A particularly rich set of structural models results from the imposition of particular stochastic processes on Heckman's general model, and clearly they will be a source of much valuable analysis.

A somewhat different set of issues arises if one considers individual choosers as deciding on the basis of utility maximization, that is, as being *homines economici*. This is not as strong as assumption as it often seems, for if individuals have preferences satisfying certain weak conditions, there exists a (utility) function which represents those preferences in the sense that one alternative is preferred to another if and only if the function's value is greater for the preferred alternative. The question then arises as to which structural models are consistent with the utility-maximization assumption, that is,

which could have been generated by utility-maximizing deciders. A comprehensive discussion of probabilistic choice by McFadden is particularly notable, first, for the way in which alternative decision sequences (decision trees) are explicitly recognized and analyzed; and second for his answer to the question of when, in a situation of discrete choice, a traditional technique of postulating a representative consumer with fractional consumption rates is valid.

The earliest research on qualitative choice exploited an assumption of population independence among the unobserved (random) determinants of choice. It has by now been recognized that this assumption can lead to unacceptable results. Consequently a good deal of effort has been expended on models which do not restrict the choice probabilities in this way; and among those models, extended probit specifications have received the most attention. In this volume G. W. Fischer and D. Nagar discuss the relative merits of probit models with and without independence; and in the context of a particular binary choice experiment conclude that it is models without independence that are to be preferred. The further extension to situations of more than two objects of choice is made extremely difficult by the fact that the multivariate probit probabilities cannot be obtained in closed form. One must therefore have recourse to approximation. S. R. Lerman and Manski discuss a widely implemented procedure due to Clark and conclude that its accuracy appears acceptable.

A final set of considerations arises from the observation that qualitative choices are but one aspect of many interdependent choices. This leads naturally to the specification of simultaneous-equations models, where the dependent variables may be continuous or qualitative in various ways. Theoretical issues involved here for binary discrete choice are discussed in papers by L.-F. Lee, allowing for all kinds of choices, and by P. Schmidt in the context of probit or tobit models.

Empirical applications are given by D. J. Poirier, in a discussion of physician behavior (specifically, whether a physician practices under the Ontario Health Insurance Plan or not) and by R. B. Avery in the context of a market-equilibrium model of consumer credit.

I have said that this book is important: I know of no other source offering so sophisticated an analysis of so wide a variety of concerns in qualitative choice. But it is also difficult. For all the undoubted lucidity of the papers, the book makes few concessions to the uninitiated. It may therefore be valuable to suggest two useful sources of more elementary material, both, as it happens, by the editors of this book. First, Manski's essay in the 1981 *Sociological Methodology* (Jossey-Bass, 1981) can be read almost as an introduction to this book. Second, *Urban Travel Demand* by T. Domencich and McFadden (Elsevier North-Holland, 1975) remains an exceptionally accessible treatment. It concerns a particular applied problem, of course, and does not consider many of the subtleties discussed in the book here reviewed, but the interested researcher will easily make the necessary adjustments. And once having mastered the elementary material, *Structural Analysis of Discrete Data* is the book to have.

PHILIP A. VITON
Department of Regional Science
University of Pennsylvania
Philadelphia

ANDREW SCHOTTER *The Economic Theory of Social Institutions.* Pp. 240. New York: Cambridge University Press, 1981. $29.50.

The influence of Professor Schotter's highly original and rigorous melding of game theory and public choice with the rather more subjective turn-of-the-century theories of social organization will be felt for a long time. By opening up a new dimension—that of time or iteration—he paves the way toward a more realistic understanding of social institutions as representing the equilibrium set of behavior patterns for their constituent interests to follow responsive to certain types of problems that have to be dealt with over and over again.

Schotter limits the scope of his work quite clearly (but perhaps more narrowly than is really necessary) in two crucial aspects. First, he views social institutions not in terms of structure, rules, and procedures, but as constituting a regularity in social behavior that (1) is agreed to by all members of the society, (2) specifies behavior in specific recurrent situations, and (3) is either self-policed or policed by some external authority. Further, he specifically excludes deliberately created institutions. Recognizing the obvious fact that all social institutions are to some degree human-made, he follows Menger in defining organically created institutions as those which came into being in the absence of a common will directed toward their establishment.

Accordingly, the work deals almost exclusively with social institutions that "grow like Topsy" in response to recurrent problems of two types: coordination and "prisoner's dilemmas." Several key terms are defined quite explicitly as the basis for developing the author's concepts. Most importantly, he defines

economics as the study of how individual economic agents who are pursuing their own selfish ends evolve institutions to satisfy them; and

welfare economics as the study of the optimal rules of the game for economic and social situations to further societal welfare while preserving individual sovereignty.

Whereas conventional economic theory has rather single-mindedly concentrated upon market-like institutions and one-shot decision making, Schotter's emerging theory takes into account that, because the problems under their ken continually recur, social institutions live for a long time, consequently the persons involved accumulate experience both in dealing with such problems and in dealing with the strategies of their fellow-players. He also recognizes the transferability of experience and strategy to newcomers or successors. This leads to small n-player games and from there, by virtue of iteration and evolution, to supergames. These tend to be cooperative because their information content, though not infinite, is naturally incomparably greater than that of conventional noncooperative games with only two or a few affected interests. Apparently such supergames as well as simple games may be of either the zero-sum or positive-sum type.

The mathematical expression by Simeon M. Berman of the theory, though comprehensive, is not particularly abstruse and is developed rigorously and clearly—even elegantly.

Taken as a whole the argument is both stimulating and satisfying. Accordingly, one can only agree with his prefatory statement that the time has come to begin the task of concrete application of the work. The overriding question is, "Where to begin?" The numbers and kinds of Topsy-like social institutions are so nearly infinite that Schotter's thesis, if it is to be fruitful, should not be applied in random fashion. A subdivision of institutions that comes naturally to mind is the class of government (externally-policed) as distinguished from spontaneous (self-policed) ones. The latter is not an empty or trivial class because in it are found those institutions by which almost all financial and commercial behavior is governed. Generally accepted accounting practices, for example, are formally and concretely established through the mechanism of the Financial Accounting Standards Board. More ubiquitous and more varied are the standards for identity and character-istics of producers' goods as well as consumers' goods. In fact, because the latter category entails both societal values and economic benefits, it may provide wider scope for the application of welfare economic considerations such as these. Nearly 500 organizations currently exist for the purpose of providing material and product standards; probably none was created by a common will directed toward establishing an equilibrium social institution. It would be of more than passing interest to determine which if any of these fall within the equilibrium set of economic behavior patterns that Schotter's approach would predict.

WALTER V. CROPPER

Philadelphia
Pennsylvania

THEODORE W. SCHULTZ. *Investing in People: The Economics of Population Quality.* Pp. xii, 173. Berkeley, CA: University of California Press, 1981. $12.95.

For fifty years T. W. Schultz has directed his research to aspects of one large question: we observe in the United States an historically unprecedented increase in the productivity of labor, especially in agriculture. In 1817 the weekly wage of an unskilled worker purchased 2.1 bushels of wheat; in 1977 it purchased 110 bushels of wheat. From 1900 to 1975 the purchasing power of labor increased over five-fold. Why has this occurred and what are the lessons of this experience for the poor countries of the world?

Investing in People is a short, clear, nontechnical summary of Schultz's answer. The book will be of interest to the professional economist, but is written primarily, I think, for the well-educated layman who may be in need of an antidote for a great many popular misconceptions about economic development. Schultz's main proposi-tion is implicit in the title. In underdeveloped countries as in the United States, the source of economic growth is to be found in the quality of the people.

But quality is to be understood in a very special sense. It has nothing whatsoever to do with intrinsic differences among people. Quite the reverse, Schultz's major premise is that "poor people are no less concerned about improving their lot and that of their children than those of us who have incomparably greater advantages. Nor are they less competent in obtaining the maximum benefit from their limited resources." Quality in this book is really a synonym for knowledge accumulated through education and research. Quality has been accumulated in the United States and other advanced countries, and may equally well be accumulated anywhere in the world. The emphasis is on the quality of people as opposed to the availability of land or capital.

Much of the book is about what governments can do and what they should avoid. Though Schultz is concerned about the harm done by government interference with the market—instituted because peasants need to be organized by their betters, as a means of taxing farmers for the benefit of their cousins in the city, or in the interests of social justice—he is by no means antigovernment in the manner of many recent conservatives. For Schultz, the primary and indispersible economic role of government is to build population quality, that is, to supply the research and education that the private sector would not otherwise provide for itself. This assessment extends to foreign aid which can be usefully directed to increasing population quality in poor countries, though it is frequently mischievous in practice due to the antimarket bias of granting agencies. Though he does not say this in so many words, one has the feeling that Schultz's heroes are the American land grant colleges that educated many generations of American farmers and whose research in developing new varieties of crops constituted the matrix from which the green revolution ultimately emerged.

DAN USHER

Queen's University
Kingston
Canada

LEWIS C. SOLMON, LAURA KENT, NANCY L. OCHSNER, and MARGO-LEA HURWICZ. *Underemployed Ph.D.'s*. Pp. xvii, 350. Lexington, MA: D. C. Heath, 1981. $32.95.

This book is a comprehensive, readable compilation of studies conducted by the Higher Education Research Institute (HERI) concerning the job market for doctorate holders in the humanities, the sciences, and engineering. Supplementing *Alternative Careers for Humanities Ph.D.'s: Perspectives of Students and Graduates* (Solmon, Ochsner, and Hurwicz 1979), the manuscript is divided into two sections: Part I concerns the employment of doctorate holders in the humanities in relation to federal, state, and local government employment; Part II addresses issues facing science and engineering Ph.D.s who pursue nonacademic employment. This arrangement seems well-suited for two so diverse educational groups, and the policy formulations that flesh out the statistical analyses are thus more easily understood.

In Chapter 1 the authors examine the crucial indicia of the next generation of potential Ph.D.s: the size and quality of undergraduate enrollments. The available data correspond with the maturation of the post-World War II baby boom children who have moved en mass into the labor market, and the authors reason, this movement portends a serious challenge to the graduate school industry to adapt to the change in demographics. The authors are not reticent about their assessment of current data indicating that student quality has declined both in the sciences and the humanities.

In subsequent chapters the authors provide some well-considered solutions to the problems facing Ph.D.s in the humanities (an amorphous term which itself defies adequate definition); the need for financing new academic positions; methods to stimulate demand for humanities education; and ultimately, the reorganization of academe.

The most promising solutions to the Ph.D. glut (Chapter 4), according to the authors, involve expanding the nonacademic job market to encompass humanists; though this section smacks of wishful thinking, it is beyond cavil that establishing a nexus between humanists and the nonacademic world would be beneficial to many.

Public sector employment opportunities, according to HERI study results, are overlooked for a variety of reasons. Nevertheless, the authors observe, Ph.D.s have found employment at all levels of government, though not all doctorate holders' primary work activity is in their discipline. Chapters 6 and 7 provide a valuable glimpse into job hunting in nontraditional, nonacademic employment arenas.

Issues concerning the female Ph.D. in the public sector are discussed in Chapter 8; and a realistic appraisal of the practical value of graduate training in the humanities vis-à-vis public sector employment can be found in Chapter 9.

The second part of the book, concerning science and engineering Ph.D.s, is much more positive, since these doctorate holders are increasingly induced into leaving the academic world for the greater profits that the public and private sectors are both willing to pay. The book sets down clear guidelines for identifying the nonacademic career options (Chapter 10); illustrates where the jobs are, who is filling them, and with what degrees (Chapter 11); and elaborates upon the breadth and variety of elements that make up the various physical and social science positions available in the nonacademic world.

Chapter 13 concerns overall job satisfaction, as well as that term can be defined and quantified; Chapter 14 presents an overview of the dynamics of job change, or job mobility. Subsumed within this issue is the dilemma (or option) of career change. An excellent summary of the salient points of preceding chapters is provided in Chapter 15; the bleak forecast concerning a potential shortage of highly trained manpower, cited by the authors, is made all the more severe and imminent in view of recent government proposals to cut federal student loan programs, starting of course, with graduate students.

The final chapter in the book illuminates the possibilities of a new crisis, though some say that it is already upon us: a prospective shortage of scientists and engineers. The problem, based essentially if not entirely on economics, stems from the fact that graduate and post-doctorate level scientists and engineers earn more outside of the academic world than within. Therefore, the authors argue, a decreasing number of professors, less talented than their colleagues who have opted for nonacademic employment, will be left in colleges and universities to teach the next generation of scientists and engineers. Letting free market forces work has become a popular philosophy, the authors observe, but there are those who believe that intervention in natural market-adjustment at crucial points is a superior approach. The authors correctly acknowledge that "blind reliance on market forces could be a serious abdication of national responsibility."

The book ends on a note of guarded optimism, declaring that a prosperous nation based on high technology and productivity is possible once a tripartite interdependence between academe, industry, and government is forged. Perhaps a guarded optimism is needed to forge this interdependence; if so, the authors can draw some satisfaction from knowing that their book represents a positive step in the right direction.

JOSEPH KALET

The Bureau of National Affairs, Inc.
Washington, D.C.

PETER R. STOPHER, ARNIM H. MEYBURG, and WERNER BRÖG, eds. *New Horizons in Travel Behavior Research*. Pp. xxxviii, 744. Lexington, MA: D. C. Heath, 1981. $39.95.

The 1970s witnessed an explosion of research into the determinants of individual travel demand. This was stimulated largely by the development of a theory of qualitative choice consistent with microeconomic behavioral postulates, and the concurrent observation that this theory yielded, under certain circumstances, relatively straightforward econometrically estimable functional forms. For once, theory and data appeared to coalesce neatly.

The success of qualitative-choice models within economics has not unnaturally lead to attempts to extend the scope of the theory. And the study of travel behavior, a topic of interest to a large number of researchers from many disciplines, is a natural field for extension. This book, a record of the Fourth International Conference on Behavioral Travel Modeling held in Tananda, Australia in 1979, largely reflects these attempts. The book may be divided in its interests into seven broad topics. Parts I and II contain valuable general surveys of the principal formal and conceptual issues. This is followed, in Parts III-VI, by considerations of psychometrics and the activity context of travel behavior, and in Part VII by a discussion of nonlinearities (such as threshold or lexicographic preference structures) that may arise in choice contexts. Parts VIII, IX, X, and XIV are devoted to several important policy-relevant issues including, importantly, the question of whether models estimated on data from one locale are transferable to other areas. Parts XI, XII, and XIII are concerned generally with questions of uncertainty, and with reasons for mispredictions in modeling. Nontransportation topics get the attention of a single paper; and the volume concludes with a general summary by the editors.

This is not the place for a detailed evaluation of the 41 chapters; some remarks, however, are appropriate. In general, when the papers are concerned with summarizing the travel demand literature or with discussing relatively straightforward extensions or new results of the theory, the quality is high, though one might wish that more attention had been given to the currently important topic of models lacking independent and identically distributed disturbances. The discussion of psychometrics and activity analysis strikes me as less satisfactory. Because the concepts themselves do not seem well explicated, the authors are forced into broad, almost philosophical discussions. The result is that meta-research—how one might go about doing something rather than actually attempting the research—receives the lion's share of the discussions. In my opinion the value of these extensions, in the applied context of understanding empirical travel behavior, remains to be firmly established.

The book's usefulness, moreover, is substantially marred by its editing. It contains no index, when especially in a conference report an index can be a most valuable tool for picking up cross-references. It suffers too from an incredibly inept system of citations. In a field characterized by a large number of sources referred to by virtually all writers, the advantages of keying citations to a single bibliography should surely have been obvious. Even within individual papers tracking down prior references is hardly facilitated by habits of citing to abbreviated titles (in some cases, a single word) with no indication of the footnote in which the full source is to be found. From an editing standpoint, this is a frustrating and sloppy volume.

As it is, the book remains the record of an interesting conference on a topic of wide interest. It contains useful reviews of the state of travel behavior research, and some indications of the way in which the field might move. But it could have been much more.

PHILIP A. VITON
Department of Regional Science
University of Pennsylvania
Philadelphia

DAN USHER. *The Economic Prerequisite to Democracy.* Pp. 224. New York: Columbia University Press, 1981. $17.50.

The central thrust of *The Economic Prerequisite to Democracy* might be characterized as "Making Democracy Safe for Democracy." Usher tells us that government by majority rule on important issues—democracy—is "necessary but deeply flawed." Assuming unalterable, self-interested man and the inevitability of a society with significant differences in power, prestige, and wealth, Usher uses the insights of game theory to conclude that the assignment of income and advantage in a society cannot be accomplished by democratic means. The issue of assignment is not susceptible either to an enduring communal consensus about ends (matters of general concern) or to a transitive ordering of preferences (single-peaked issues). Rather, assignment issues (factional issues) prompt an endless succession of unstable coalitions.

People solve the meta-game of liberal democratic society by designing two distinct, though not unrelated, games: politics and economics. The capitalistic economic game (a system of equity) uniquely has the capacity to determine and regulate these assignments acceptably—with sufficient satisfaction for the bottom 50 percent that they prefer this arrangement to the disorganization of democratic assignment. Only conscious regard for the equitable implications of policies will limit democracy to the realm of social decisions it is capable of resolving.

This book is written clearly and without unnecessary jargon. Usher candidly recognizes certain problems of capitalistic political economy: inequality, monopoly and technological development, corporate welfare, and freedom. Yet this analysis might be most productive as a first position paper in an interdisciplinary, scholarly seminar. Usher's candor, clarity and conciseness lapse into brevity, which is a mixed blessing—provocative annoyance. His interesting sketches of application of the equity criterion to policy choice invite further analysis but do not suffice as mid-range theory. Usher casually accepts critical assumptions that may be settled for some economic analysis but cannot be for political economy without predetermining conclusions. Where is there to go when the author supposes, "as economists are accustomed to do, that all men are greedy" and when he resigns himself in the opening sentence of the preface to the fact that "every society must decide who is to be rich and who is to be poor, who is to command and who is to be commanded"?

Though one must be careful criticizing a book for the questions it did not address, several concerns implicit in the analysis never receive explicit attention. Usher admits that his model depends upon indefinite economic progress without considering the limits to growth. Usher cites *Federalist 10* on factions without exploring Madison's dependence upon representation to moderate factional strife. And one reflecting upon the gaming perspective must wonder how people too greedy and short-sighted to create stable assignments of income can be far-sighted and communal enough to create a prenuptial agreement to commit their incomes to a process wherein their control is not only speculative but also cumulative from inequitable first positions. Analyses of legislative process, symbolic politics, issue formation and agenda building, and participation—especially citizen apathy and alienation—ought to have been considered.

Some ancient and modern philosophers posit a political community in which man grows toward humanity through a life of citizenship with all its risks and responsibilities. Perhaps this explains Aristotle's preference for polity over democracy; perhaps a democracy that fulfills Usher's criteria is not worth saving—or even worth calling democratic.

JAMES E. LENNERTZ
Lafayette College
Easton
Pennsylvania

OTHER BOOKS

AGNEW, NEIL McK., and SANDRA W. PYKE. *The Science Game: An Introduction to Research in the Behavioral Sciences.* Pp. xiv, 285. Englewood Cliffs, NJ: Prentice-Hall, 1982. $11.95. Paperbound.

ANTHONY, HARRY ANTONIADES. *Human Settlement 3. The Challenge of Squatter Settlements: With Special Reference to the Cities of Latin America.* Pp. 76. Vancouver, Canada: University of British Columbia Press, 1978. No price.

BARRETT, RICHARD N., ed. *International Dimensions of the Environmental Crisis.* Pp. xviii, 198. Boulder, CO: Westview Press, 1982. $20.00. Paperbound.

BARRY, BRIAN and RUSSELL HARDIN, eds. *Rational Man and Irrational Society?* Pp. 432. Beverly Hills, CA: Sage Publications, 1982. $30.00. Paperbound, $14.95.

BERTSCH, GARY. *Power and Policy in Communist Systems.* 2nd ed. Pp. x, 192. Somerset, NJ: John Wiley & Sons, 1982. $10.95. Paperbound.

BLAUSTEIN, ARTHUR I., ed. *The American Promise: Equal Justice and Economic Opportunity.* Pp. xxxi, 127. New Brunswick, NJ: Transaction Books, 1982. $9.95. Paperbound.

BLOOM, MARTIN and JOEL FISCHER. *Evaluating Practice: Guidelines for the Accountable Professional.* Pp. xi, 512. Englewood Cliffs, NJ: Prentice-Hall, 1982. $24.95.

BREAK, GEORGE F. *Financing Government in a Federal System.* Pp. xi, 276. Washington, DC: Brookings Institution, 1980. $17.95. Paperbound, $6.95.

BRESNICK, DAVID. *Public Organizations and Policy: An Experimental Approach to Public Policy and Its Execution.* Pp. vi, 250. Glenview, IL: Scott, Foresman and Company, 1982. $10.95. Paperbound.

BRUCHEY, STUART W., ed. *Small Business in American Life.* Pp. viii, 391. New York: Columbia University Press, 1980. $25.00.

CABANIS, PIERRE-JEAN-GEORGES. *On the Relations between the Physical and Moral Natures of Man.* Vols. I & II. Pp. 796. Baltimore, MD: Johns Hopkins University Press, 1982. $28.50.

CHANDLER, RALPH C. and JACK C. PLANO. *The Public Administration Dictionary.* Pp. ix, 406. Somerset, NJ: John Wiley & Sons, 1982. No price.

CLARK, ROBERT. *Power and Policy in the Third World.* 2nd ed. Pp. viii, 168. Somerset, NJ: John Wiley & Sons, 1982. $10.95. Paperbound.

FEDOSEYEV, P. N., et al. *What is Democratic Socialism?* Pp. 143. Chicago, IL: Imported Publications, 1980. $3.50. Paperbound.

GERTLER, LEN. *Human Settlement Issues I. Habitat and Land.* Pp. 42. Vancouver, Canada: University of British Columbia Press, 1978. No price.

GOODE, WILLIAM J. *The Family.* 2nd ed. Englewood Cliffs, NJ: Prentice-Hall, 1982. $13.95. Paperbound, $8.95.

HANF, THEODOR, HERIBERT WEILAND, and GERDA VIERDAG. *South Africa: The Prospects of Peaceful Change.* Pp. xviii, 492. Bloomington, IN: Indiana University Press, 1981. $35.00.

HOLSWORTH, ROBERT D. and J. HARRY WRAY. *American Politics and Everyday Life.* Pp. xv, 204. Somerset, NJ: John Wiley, 1982. $8.95. Paperbound.

JOHNSON, DONALD BRUCE, compiler. *National Party Platforms of 1980.* Pp. 233. Champaign, IL: University of Illinois Press, 1982. $14.95. Paperbound.

KEMP, ROGER L. *Coping with Proposition 13.* Pp. xv, 222. Lexington, MA: Lexington Books, 1980. No price.

KHARIN, YURI A. *Fundamentals of Dialectics.* Pp. 256. Chicago, IL: Imported Publications, 1981. $6.40.

KOZAK, DAVID C. and JOHN D. MACARTNEY. *Congress and Public Policy: A Source Book of Documents and Readings.* Pp. xviii, 522. Homewood, IL: Dorsey Press, 1982. $14.95. Paperbound.

LEVY, MICHAEL B. *Political Thought in America: An Anthology*. Pp. xvi, 474. Homewood, IL: Dorsey Press, 1982. $15.95. Paperbound.

LICHFIELD, NATHANIEL. *Human Settlement Issues 4. Settlement Planning and Development: A Strategy for Land Policy*. Pp. 52. Vancouver, Canada: University of British Columbia, 1980. No price.

LONG, SAMUEL, ed. *Political Science Abstracts 1980: Annual Supplement*. Vols. 1, 2, & 3. Pp. 2041. New York: Plenum, 1982. $350.00.

LOW, PETER W., JOHN CALVIN JEFFRIES, Jr. and RICHARD J. BONNIE. *Criminal Law: Cases and Materials*. Pp. xlix, 984. Mineola, NY: Foundation Press, 1982. No price.

LUM, DOMAN, ed. *Social Work and Health Care Policy*. Pp. xvi, 224. Totowa, NJ: Allanheld Osmun, 1982. $24.95. Paperbound, $11.95.

MARIEN, MICHAEL. *Future Survey Annual 1980-81*. Pp. 290. Bethesda, MD: World Future Society, 1982. $25.00. Paperbound.

MILLER, RANDALL M., ed. *"A Warm & Zealous Spirit": John J. Zubly and the American Revolution, A Selection of His Writings*. Pp. xii, 211. Macon, GA: Mercer University Press, 1982. $14.95.

MONTAPERTO, RONALD N. and JAY HENDERSON, eds. *China's Schools in Flux*. Pp. 200. White Plains, NY: M. E. Sharpe, 1980. $18.50.

MOSHER, FREDERICK C. *Democracy and the Public Service*. 2nd ed. Pp. xvi, 251. New York: Oxford University Press, 1982. $6.95. Paperbound.

OIZERMAN, T. I. *The Making of the Marxist Philosophy*. Pp. 496. Chicago, IL: Imported Publications, 1981. $9.60.

PAGE, STANLEY W. *The Geopolitics of Leninism*. Pp. 238. New York: Columbia University Press, 1982. $20.00.

PLANTEY, ALAIN. *The International Civil Service: Law and Management*.

Pp. xiii, 456. New York: Masson Publishing, 1981. No price.

POTASH, ROBERT A. *The Army & Politics in Argentina 1945-1962: Peron to Frondizi*. Pp. ix, 418. Stanford, CA: Stanford University Press, 1980. $25.00

PYE, LUCIAN. *The Dynamics of Chinese Politics*. Pp. xxv, 307. Cambridge, MA: Oelgeschlager, Gunn & Hain, 1981. $22.50. Paperbound, $9.95.

RENIER, GUSTAAF. *History: Its Purpose and Method*. Pp. 272. Macon, GA: Mercer University Press, 1982. $14.95.

SANDERS, DAVID. *Patterns of Political Instability*. Pp. xvii, 244. New York: St. Martin's Press, 1981. $27.50.

SCOTT, HARRIET FAST and WILLIAM F. SCOTT, eds. *The Soviet Art of War: Doctrine, Strategy, and Tactics*. Pp. x, 323. Boulder, CO: Westview Press, 1982. $26.50. Paperbound, $13.00.

SEIDLER, HARRY. *Human Settlement Issues 2. Planning and Building Down Under*. Pp. 38. Vancouver, Canada: University of British Columbia Press, 1978. No Price.

SHARP, GENE. *Social Power and Political Freedom*. Pp. xv, 440. Boston, MA: Porter Sargent, 1980. $15.95. Paperbound, $8.95.

STARLING, GROVER, *Understanding American Politics*. Pp. xii, 538. Homewood, IL: Dorsey Press, 1982. $21.00.

TIMOFEYEV, TIMUR. *Workers in Society: Polemical Essays*. Pp. 320. Chicago, IL: Imported Publications, 1981. $8.00.

ULYANOVSKY, ROSTISLAV. *Present-Day Problems in Asia and Africa: Theory, Politics, Personalities*. Pp. 240. Chicago, IL: Imported Publications, 1980. $7.20.

VYGODOSKY, VITALY. *The Economic Substantiation of the Theory of Socialism*. Pp. 278. Chicago, IL: Imported Publications, 1981. $8.00.

WALLER, DEREK J. *The Government and Politics of the People's Republic of China*. 3rd ed. Pp. 228. New York:

New York University Press, 1982. $22.50. Paperbound, $9.00.

WILLIAMS, ROBERT BRUCE. *John Dewey: Recollections.* Pp. 208. Lanham, MD: University Press of America, 1982. $20.75. Paperbound, $10.25.

WINDMULLER, J. P. *The International Trade Union Movement.* Pp. 174. Hingham, MA: Kluwer Law and Taxation Publishers, 1980. No price.

WOLFGANG, MARVIN E. and FRANCO FERRACUTI. *The Subculture of Violence.* Pp. xxiii, 387. Beverly Hills, CA: Sage Publications, 1982. $27.50. Paperbound, $12.95.

ZITOMERSKY, JOSEPH, ed. *On Making Use of History: Research and Reflections from Lund.* Pp. 206. Solna, Sweden: Esselte Stadium AB, 1982. No price. Paperbound.

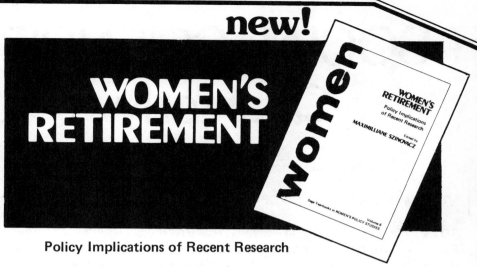

SOCIAL SCIENCE
Quarterly

Announcing Another Double-Length Topical Issue:

THE MEXICAN ORIGIN POPULATION: EXPERIENCE OF A DECADE

SSQ's most successful single issue was its 1973 special issue on *The Chicano Experience in the United States.* Its 22 articles by 35 authors represented a thorough treatment of a previously neglected topic. Response to the issue was intense. Although the press run was the largest ever scheduled for *SSQ*, all extra copies were sold within six months of publication. Most articles in the issue have been reprinted in anthologies and all have been widely cited in the social science literature. Since that time, *SSQ* has published more articles on the Mexican origin population than any other general social science journal.

Another double-length issue on this topic is scheduled for late 1983. We are especially interested in manuscripts dealing in any way with the Mexican origin population. Our preference is for articles of short to medium length (14 to 25 pages including tables, references and notes) and no longer than 30 typewritten pages. For style and format, see recent issues or write for our style sheet.

Issue co-editors for *The Mexican Origin Population: Experience of a Decade* are Rodolfo Alvarez, Frank D. Bean, Rodolfo de la Garza and Ricardo Romo. Issue co-sponsor will be the Center for Mexican American Studies at the University of Texas at Austin. Manuscripts will be considered for this issue until summer, 1983, and should be sent directly to:

> SOCIAL SCIENCE QUARTERLY
> Will C. Hogg Building
> The University of Texas at Austin
> Austin, Texas 78712

Your cooperation in bringing this forthcoming issue to the attention of interested colleagues would be greatly appreciated.

SAGE PUBLICATIONS
The Publishers of Professional Social Science
Beverly Hills / London / New Delhi

SINGLES
Myths and Realities
by LEONARD CARGAN and MATTHEW MELKO

Published in cooperation with **National Council on Family Relations**

This timely volume dispels many traditional stereotypes about the singles scene in America, and provides the first in-depth study of single lifestyles. Demonstrates distinctions between single subgroups—the divorced, the widowed, and the never-married.
New Perspectives on Family Series
1982 / 288 pages / $25.00 (h) / $12.50 (p)

JOB STRESS AND BURNOUT
Research, Theory, and Intervention Perspectives
edited by WHITON STEWART PAINE
Offers incisive perspectives on the state of the art and future prospects of job stress prevention and management. Key issues such as the causes of job stress, their relationship to important social trends, and their increasing economic and legal costs are discussed.
Sage Focus Editions, Volume 54
1982 (Sept.) / 296 pages / $25.00 (h) / $12.50 (p)

LIVES IN STRESS
Women and Depression
edited by DEBORAH BELLE
Reports on one of the first in-depth field studies of the causes and consequences of depression in women. Focusing on low income mothers with children, the authors use extensive interviews to explore the relationship between a woman's life situation and her emotional well-being.
Sage Focus Editions, Volume 45
1982 / 248 pages / $22.00 (h) / $10.95 (p)

HELPING WOMEN COPE WITH GRIEF
by PHYLLIS R. SILVERMAN
A practical guide that focuses on the plight of widows, women who have given up their children, and battered women during the difficult transition from grief to the creation of new lives and relationships. Using quotes from personal interviews to illustrate her analysis, the author develops a clear framework for helping all bereaved persons who must reshape their lives following the severance of important relationships.
Sage Human Services Guides, Volume 25
1981 / 112 pages / $6.50 (p)

AGE OR NEED?
Public Policies for Older People
edited by BERNICE L. NEUGARTEN
Focuses on such significant—and controversial—policy questions as: Do older persons absorb funds needed by disadvantaged persons of all ages? Would a new emphasis on need, rather than age, undo recent improvements in the general well-being of older people?
Sage Focus Editions, Volume 59
1982 (Fall) / 256 pages (tent.) / $25.00 (h) (tent.) / $12.50 (p) (tent.)

CHRONIC PAIN
Its Social Dimensions
by JOSEPH A. KOTARBA
Illuminates the world of people who suffer from continuous pain, and describes how pain affects self-images, careers, and personal relationships. Examines the quest for relief from both traditional and nontraditional sources, including chiropractors, acupuncturists, and faith healers.
Social Observations, Volume 13
1982 (Fall) / 224 pages (tent.) / $25.00 (h) (tent.) / $12.50 (p) (tent.)

WORLDS OF FRIENDSHIP
by ROBERT R. BELL
Synthesizing contemporary research in a variety of fields, noted sociologist Robert Bell explores the nature of friendship, gender-related variations in friendships, and changes in friendship over the course of the life cycle.
Sociological Observations, Volume 12
1981 / 216 pages / $22.00 (h) / $10.95 (p)

SOCIAL NETWORKS AND SOCIAL SUPPORT
by BENJAMIN H. GOTTLIEB
Original essays examine how human attachments—the natural helping network—serve to support people. They show that these support systems, which may take the form of mutual help groups, neighborhood voluntary associations, or family ties, can play an important role in helping individuals to cope with stressful life events.
Sage Studies in Community Mental Health, Volume 4
1981 / 304 pages / $22.00 (h) / $10.95 (p)

SAGE PUBLICATIONS
The Publishers of Professional Social Science
275 South Beverly Drive Beverly Hills, California 90212